THE TAOIST CLASSICS

The Collected Translations of
Thomas Cleary

THE TAOIST CLASSICS

VOLUME ONE

Tao Te Ching
Chuang-tzu
Wen-tzu
The Book of Leadership and Strategy
Sex, Health, and Long Life

VOLUME TWO

Understanding Reality
The Inner Teachings of Taoism
The Book of Balance and Harmony
Practical Taoism

VOLUME THREE

Vitality, Energy, Spirit
The Secret of the Golden Flower
Immortal Sisters
Awakening to the Tao

VOLUME FOUR

The Taoist I Ching
I Ching Mandalas

The Taoist Classics

VOLUME TWO

Understanding Reality
The Inner Teachings of Taoism
The Book of Balance and Harmony
Practical Taoism

SHAMBHALA
Boston
1999

SHAMBHALA PUBLICATIONS, INC.
Horticultural Hall
300 Massachusetts Avenue
Boston, MA 02115
http://www.shambhala.com

© 1986, 1987, 1989, 1996 by Thomas Cleary
Understanding Reality: A Taoist Alchemical Classic was first published by The University of Hawai'i Press, 1987.
The Book of Balance and Harmony is reprinted by arrangement with Farrar, Straus & Giroux.

All rights reserved. No part of this book may be reproduced in any form or by any means, electronic or mechanical, including photocopying, recording, or by any information storage and retrieval system, without permission in writing from the publisher.

9 8 7 6 5 4 3 2 1

FIRST EDITION
Printed in the United States of America

♾ This edition is printed on acid-free paper that meets the American National Standards Institute z39.48 Standard. Distributed in the United States by Random House, Inc., and in Canada by Random House of Canada Ltd

LIBRARY OF CONGRESS CATALOGING-IN-PUBLICATION DATA

The Taoist classics: the collected translations of Thomas Cleary.
    p. cm.
    ISBN 1-57062-485-2 (v. 1).—ISBN 1-57062-486-0 (v. 2).—ISBN 1-57062-487-9 (v. 3).—ISBN 1-57062-488-7 (v. 4)
    1. Taoism. I. Cleary, Thomas, 1949– .
    BL1920.T33. 1999   99-27951
    299'.51482—dc21   CIP

CONTENTS

UNDERSTANDING REALITY

Acknowledgments	3
Foreword	5
Introduction	9
Understanding Reality: A Direct Explanation	33
I. Sixteen verses, representing "eight ounces" of yin and "eight ounces" of yang, forming "one pound" of elixir	35
II. Sixty-four verses modeled on the number of signs in the *I Ching*	66
III. One verse representing the Great One engulfing true energy	131
IV. Twelve verses on the moon over the West River, representing the twelve months	133
V. Five verses, representing the five elements: metal, wood, water, fire, earth	153
The Outer Collection	159
I. Four four-line verses	161
II. Verses on various themes	164
The moon on the West River—twelve verses	180
Glossary	189
Readings	207

THE INNER TEACHINGS OF TAOISM

Introduction	211
Part One: The Inner Teachings	223
Part Two: Solving Symbolic Language	263
Part Three: Related Texts	313

The Book of Balance and Harmony

Introduction	329
1. The Source Message of the Mystic School	353
2. Statements	356
3. Secret Meanings	359
4. Secrets of the Gold Pill	368
5. Explanation of the Three Fives	373
6. The Opening of the Mysterious Pass	375
7. The Gold-Testing Stone	376
8. Nine Grades of Practices: Sidetracks and Auxiliary Methods	378
9. Three Vehicles of Gradual Method	382
10. The Highest Vehicle	384
11. Dialogues: The Underlying Unity of Taoism, Confucianism, and Buddhism	385
12. Questions and Answers	397
13. Some Questions on Alchemy	404
14. Live Teachings on Complete Reality	411
15. Spoken Teachings	416
16. Discourses	418
17. Explanatory Talks	423
18. Songs	430
19. Poems	461
20. Veiled Words	481

Practical Taoism

Translator's Preface	491
Introduction	493
Essential Sayings to Assist Potential	507
The Way of Eternal Life through Perception of Vital Spirit	511
Alchemy Takes Its Rules from Creation	512
Foundations of Alchemy	512
A Point Falls into the Yellow Court	513
Alchemical Ingredients	513
Basic Vitality	514
Basic Vitality Is Sexual Vitality	514
Basic Energy Produces Basic Vitality	515

Detachment from Emotional Consciousness to Nurture Basic Harmony	515
Alchemy Requires Interruption of Craving	516
Basic Spirit Using Medicine	517
The Basic Spirit Is the Thinking Spirit	518
The Opening of the Mysterious Pass	518
The Handle of Alchemy	519
Alchemical Operations	520
The Bellows	521
Sixty Hexagrams Symbolizing the Alchemical Firing Process	522
Symbolizing the Firing Process by the Year, Month, and Day, Humanity and Duty, Joy and Anger, Reward and Punishment	522
Intent As the Go-Between	523
The Way of Seeing Vital Spirit and Perpetuating Life	524
The River Source Where Medicine Is Produced	527
The Receptive Is the Abode of the Way	528
Yang Disburses, Yin Receives	528
Congealing Spirit in the Energy Aperture	529
Turning the Light Around to Illumine Inwardly	530
Beginning Work on Turning the Light Around to Illumine Inwardly	531
The Womb Breath	536
The Primal	538
The Arising of Positive Energy	538
Culling	539
Keeping the Attention on Heaven	540
The Central Path	542
The Firing Process	543
Incubation	544
Punishment and Reward	545
Refining the Spirit	546
Crystallizing the Elixir	547
Release from the Matrix	548
Returning to the Origin	550
Twin Cultivation of Essence and Life	550

PUBLISHER'S NOTE

The works contained in The Collected Translations of Thomas Cleary were published over a period of more than twenty years and originate from several publishing houses. As a result, the capitalization and romanization of Chinese words vary occasionally from one text to another within the volumes, due to changes in stylistic preferences from year to year and from house to house. Thus the reader will find both *I Ching* and *I-ching*; both *Huai-nan-tzu*, rendered according to the Wade-Giles system of romanization, and *Huainanzi*, by the Pinyin system. In all cases the terms are rendered consistently within each text.

UNDERSTANDING REALITY

A Taoist Alchemical Classic

by CHANG PO-TUAN
With a Concise Commentary by
LIU I-MING

ACKNOWLEDGMENTS

Thanks are due to a number of people for their invaluable assistance in this project: to Wang Po-hsueh, for unparalleled inspiration in Taoist studies; to Wong Leok Yee and Liu Shih-i, for their help in the study and interpretation of Taoist teachings on spirit and energy; and to Sha-ch'uan Ho-tzu, the most remarkably ordinary person I have ever met, for unique demonstrations of the art of integrating being and nonbeing.

T.C.

FOREWORD

Taoism, in many forms, has long had an important role in the development of Chinese civilization, particularly in the fields of natural science, medical arts, and psychology. An extremely complex phenomenon, Taoism has used many media of expression and influenced many realms of thought and action through its long history. Among its modes of projection and spheres of influence may be counted philosophy, politics, religion, folklore and mythology, satire and other forms of humor, visual art and design, poetry, music and song, drama and fiction, herbal and psychosomatic medicine, physical education, martial arts, military strategy, and alchemy, both material and spiritual.

In view of this remarkable profusion of forms, any attempt to establish historical links joining every one of the forms of activity that have been labeled Taoist meets with formidable problems. Perhaps the single most widely accepted Taoist text is the famous *Tao Te Ching*, but since the meanings of this often cryptic work cannot be definitely established by ordinary literary methods, and interpretations vary enormously at certain points, the notion of affiliation through association with the teachings of the *Tao Te Ching* is of dubious value. Moreover, Taoist literature has noted for over two thousand years the existence of degenerations and aberrations under the rubric of the Tao; thus an assumed link between different forms of Taoism may well be one that has in fact lapsed, or one that was from the beginning fabricated by false analogy.

Nevertheless, if one were to hypothesize an inner link among quite different forms of Taoism (without presuming to encompass everything called Taoistic in this hypothesis), a key to the rationale behind the enormous variety of frameworks through which Taoist teachings and practices have been presented might be found in the opening lines of the *Tao Te Ching* itself: "A path that can be verbalized is not a permanent path; terminology that can be designated is not a constant terminology." The first part of this opening statement might also be read, "A path which can be taken as a path is not a permanent path," and understood to refer to the distinction between means and end. From this point of view, it might be said that like Buddhism, a parallel teaching which emphasizes ongoing reformation of doctrine and praxis to meet contemporary needs, Taoism has appeared in many guises throughout the ages, corresponding to changing conditions in its host society.

While it is beyond the scope of the present study to enter very far into the maze of Taoist history, it is of some interest to glance at a few outstanding manifestations of Taoism while pursuing this theme of adaptation to the times. For example, one of the oldest texts of Taoism, presented in the form of a divination manual, was composed in a time when divination was formally considered a branch of government. Later, in an era when all serious thinkers wrote in the subject of political and social science, another classic appears in a form that can be read as a treatise on political and social theory. During a period marked by the accelerated rise of hegemonism and tyranny, yet another text appears libertarian, even libertine and anarchic. Under similar conditions, with the rise of militarism, a classic manual of military strategy advocates a policy of minimal expenditures of lives, energy, and material. Satire and fantastic poetry appear during a time of social upheaval and decay of an old order along with its world view; grass roots political organization emerges under the same conditions. Religious texts come to the fore during the growth of Chinese Buddhist churches, and collections of sayings of Taoist adepts parallel similar developments in Ch'an Buddhist literature. Martial arts are refined in an era marked by the overthrow of an alien dynasty as well as by repeated popular uprisings. Colloquial drama and fiction transmitting Taoist ideas appear during a time of growth of vernacular literature. Most recently, secularized Taoistic teachings are published as therapeutic arts after an anti-religious communist revolution.

This is, of course, a very simplistic picture of Taoism, somewhat in the spirit of Taoist imagery itself, designed to evoke a certain point of view and not to define historical fact. The historical origins of Taoism, like nearly everything else about it, are extremely obscure, veiled in allegory and myth; it may be that much of the material relating to the question of origins consists of, or is interlarded with, initiatory lore, the understanding and application of which would vary according to circumstances. Sometimes Taoism is called the Huang-Lao teaching, after two important figureheads of the teaching alleged to have lived thousands of years ago; but even these people are presented in tradition as transmitters rather than originators of Taoistic teachings. Certain cultural prototypes often associated with Taoism are said to have gained their knowledge through systematic observation, contemplation, and experiment; other teachings are attributed to spiritual revelations. A Taoist encyclopedia says that "Taoism" antedating all formulations is found in a recondite realm of mind where the customary divisions of thought do not exist.

In short, it may well be that the origins or derivations of Taoism cannot be positively ascertained by conventional methods; this situation is due not only to the variety and nature of the data in Taoistic literature, but also to the paucity of associated data which would pin the origins of Taoism to specific times, people, or places. What seems to be a common theme is the idea that Taoism transcends history—vertically, so to speak, in the sense that it claims contact with another dimension of experience beyond the terrestrial, and horizontally in that it claims to reach back before history. Taoist tradition generally associates its early articulation on the terrestrial plane with the very beginnings of proto-Chinese civilization, but also claims ongoing or periodically renewed contact with a higher source. It is not, of course, at all necessary to give literal credence to any of the fantastic tales of Taoist history in order to appreciate them as representations of the common contention that the structure of the universe as perceived by the conventionally socialized mind, within its framework of time and space, is not absolute, and that there exists within humanity the potential for extradimensional perception.

In a sense, it might be possible to interpret the presence of so many marvels and wonders in Taoist lore as an indication of interest in human possibilities. It has often been observed, moreover, that much the same descriptions of extraordinary powers alleged to be available through esoteric knowledge are to be found all over the world. What is perhaps more significant than such possibilities is their effect on the world, and some esoteric traditions stress the issue of the use and function of supernormal knowledge and power more than the mere fact of their possibility. Within Taoism, the question of the actual individual and collective benefit or harm deriving from the exercise of knowledge and power led some practitioners to subordinate everything in their path to the quest for permanent stabilization of consciousness.

Among these practitioners were the Taoists of the schools which came to be known by the name of Complete Reality. Complete Reality Taoism, which arose as a distinct movement between the eleventh and thirteenth centuries, was concerned with the totality of experience and with furthering human progress in the realms of both conventional and ultimate truth. This concern manifested itself accordingly in both social and mystical practices, as the followers of Complete Reality strove to encompass what they considered to be the essence of Buddhism and Confucianism as well as Taoism.

The impact of Complete Reality Taoism was very powerful, and in some areas it superseded the aged and failing schools of Ch'an Buddhism, which had for centuries exerted enormous influence on Chinese civilization. To be sure, Complete Reality Taoism had much in common with Ch'an Buddhism, notably including concentrated meditation exercises and the practice of introducing fresh views of traditional teachings. Among the literary formats used in the projection of Complete Reality Taoism was the vocabulary and imagery of alchemy, one of the most ancient and widespread realms of interest in China, now adopted by these new Taoists as an allegory for a process of inner transformation and sublimation. The present text, *Understanding Reality*, is one of the classics of this spiritual alchemy, and is still considered a basic document of Taoist mental science.

INTRODUCTION

Understanding Reality (Chinese *Wu Chen P'ien*) is one of the basic classics of Taoist spiritual alchemy as practiced in the Complete Reality (Ch'uan-chen) school of Taoism. Writing in the year 1841, the Taoist Chu Chung-t'ang described its status within the tradition in these terms: "Wei Po-yang of the Eastern Han dynasty (23–220 C.E.) first revealed the celestial mechanism and expounded its esoteric truths, composing the *Ts'an T'ung Ch'i*. . . . In the Sung dynasty (960–1279) Chang Tzu-yang composed the *Wu Chen P'ien*. Both texts are perennial guides to the study of the Tao."[1]

Chang Po-tuan, styled Tzu-yang, lived from approximately 983 to 1082. He is considered the founder of the so-called southern school of Complete Reality Taoism. As he lived before the widespread public recognition and institutionalization of Complete Reality Taoism that took place under the successors and descendants of Wang Che (1113–1171), founder of the northern school, little is known about his life. Indeed, apart from his retrospective recognition as the first patriarch of the southern school of Complete Reality Taoism, Chang is mainly known simply as the author of *Understanding Reality*, considered a basic text by practitioners of both northern and southern schools.

Chang Po-tuan originally studied Confucianism but eventually turned to esoteric studies after repeated failure to pass civil service examinations. He also read widely in secular subjects, including law, mathematics, medicine, military science, astronomy, and geography. According to one source, he experienced an awakening while studying Buddhist literature, but as his attainment of "the Tao of unification with the fundamental" was still incomplete, he continued to travel in search of enlightenment.[2]

Chang's search ended when he met the Taoist master Liu Ts'ao in western China in the year 1069. Liu is supposed to have learned the secrets of Taoism from Chung-li Ch'uan and Lu Tung-pin, who are also said to have later been the teachers of the Wang Che in the middle of the twelfth century.³ In any case, Chang is believed to have learned the esoteric lore of alchemy from Liu Ts'ao and to have subsequently completed the process successfully. Finally he became a teacher in his own right, though there is no trace of his ever having founded any sort of organization;⁴ near the end of his life he composed *Understanding Reality* and entrusted it to a patron, requesting him to circulate it: "All I have learned in my life is herein," he is reported to have said on this occasion. "Circulate it, and someday there will be those who arrive at the way through this book."⁵

According to Chang's own preface to his *Understanding Reality*, he composed this text because he thought alchemical literature and its exegesis in his time obscure and confused. He also wished to emphasize the confluence of Buddhism, Confucianism, and Taoism, even adding an appendix devoted to Buddhist subjects.

The present translation of *Understanding Reality* is based on, and includes, the commentary of Liu I-ming, a Ch'ing dynasty Taoist who like Chang Po-tuan was deeply versed in Buddhism and Confucianism as well as Taoism, and expressly dedicated his works to removing obscurities surrounding technical terminology in alchemical literature. Liu felt that alchemical terminology, originally a protective device, had become a field for imagination, resulting in all sorts of aberrated cults; his commentaries on Taoist classics are thus marked by great simplicity, directness, and unequivocal repudiation of practices he regarded as ineffective or harmful.

As with Chang Po-tuan, there is no evidence of Liu I-ming's membership in any formal organization, and the details of his life are rather obscure. According to his own writings, which date from the end of the eighteenth century through the first quarter of the nineteenth century, he left home at the age of eighteen in search of truth, and followed teachings which he eventually rejected as degenerate after meeting a teacher who instilled in him a sense of the essential importance of balance. Thirteen years later he met another teacher whose guidance enabled him to resolve all his doubts. For twenty years he practiced concealment in the world while working on himself, and in places as widely separated as Ninghsia and Fukien, he assumed the various guises of traveling merchant, Confucian scholar, manual laborer, and recluse. Sometimes he appeared as a mystic, sometimes he worked as a teacher, or else engaged in construction and repair of public facilities such as roads and bridges. Eventually he rebuilt an abandoned Taoist cloister and lived there for another twenty years. During this period he seems to have attracted a circle of disciples and composed commentaries on classics such as the *I Ching*, the *Ts'an T'ung Ch'i*, and *Understanding Reality*, along with a considerable number of original poems and essays.[6]

The comparative study of Chinese alchemical lore is an immense task, full of inconsistencies. A modern Taoist says, "Chinese alchemical texts are not unified into a system; without extensive study and thorough investigation, it is hard to understand them. Why is it that no one with profound learning in Taoism has come forth to organize them?"[7] That there is a certain irony underlying this question becomes apparent when one reflects again on the opening statement of the *Tao Te Ching*. In any case, by way of introduction to the present work, I will simply focus on the main points of the teaching of *Understanding Reality* as Liu explains it,[8] and append a glossary-index to deal with special terms not touched upon in the introduction. The basic concepts which seem to stand out for emphasis here are yin and yang, the five elements, and essence and life; in addition, the use of *I Ching* signs and the question of praxis will be briefly considered.

Yin and Yang

The concept of yin and yang forms one of the basic and pervasive themes of Taoist thought, used to describe all manner of oppositions and complementarities in the physical and metaphysical worlds. In the teachings of Complete Reality Taoism as we find them in the present work, yin and yang have a number of associations which represent various qualities and procedures involved in Taoist methods of human development.

Generally speaking, three aspects or phases of Taoist practice are expressed in terms of yin and yang. These are referred to as fostering yang while repelling yin, blending yin and yang, and transcending yin and yang. In interpreting these phases, the associations of yin and yang differ according to the specific process being described.

In Taoism one of the basic equivalents of yin and yang is the pair of terms "heaven and earth." At one level of interpretation, heaven refers to a world-transcending higher consciousness, beyond the bounds of ordinary thought and emotion; earth refers to the experience of the everyday world. The complete or "real" human being is considered a balanced combination of these two levels of experience; this is expressed in the Taoist slogan "being beyond the world while living in the world." Thus to maintain contact with the higher, vaster dimension of "celestial" consciousness while at the same time living effectively in the "earthly" domain is one meaning of blending or uniting yin and yang.

However, since the effort to achieve a harmonious union of these two "poles" of human potential is usually undertaken after temporal conditioning has already become ingrained, so that the "mundane" prevails over the "celestial," there is the work of "repelling yin" and "fostering yang." The aim of this practice is to bring about a balance in which celestial consciousness guides earthly consciousness. In religious terms, this is described in Liu I-ming's commentary as "unconsciously following the laws of God." In secular terms, it is sometimes described as the body obeying the mind, or desire conforming to reason.

A practical procedure for repelling yin and fostering yang often presented in Taoist texts basically consists of standing aloof from the dominant mundane aspect of the mind—that is, acquired habits of thought and feeling—in order to increase awareness of the recessive celestial mind, which is considered the original, primordial mind.

Complete Reality Taoism finds an indication of this practice in the famous lines of the ancient classic *Tao Te Ching*: "Effect emptiness to the extreme, guard stillness carefully; as myriad things act in concert, I thereby watch the return" (XVI). According to the Complete Reality interpretation, emptiness and stillness refer to quieting the mental talk which sustains the acquired world view and habitual involvement therein. "As things act in concert, I thereby watch the return" is taken to mean that during this practice one leaves things to themselves, not becoming involved with external objects but instead, by means of emptiness and stillness, "watching" for the "return" of yang, the original mind which has been obscured by acquired mental habits and entanglement in things of the world. So according to the Complete Reality school's understanding of this practice, stillness is not an end but a means, and the practice of emptiness and stillness is supposed to have a definite climax and outcome.

The process of repelling yin is often called the "yin convergence," and Complete Reality texts speak of operating the yin convergence as well as repelling the yin convergence. Thus it has two meanings:

excluding mundane conditioning to the extent that it will not interfere with or imprison higher potential; yet including mundane conditioning to the extent that it is necessary or useful for life in the world.

A convenient illustration of the balance of exclusion and inclusion may be found in the habit of language. Language is a form of conditioning which is both potentially useful and potentially debilitating. The usefulness of language is a matter of common experience and so needs no further comment. If one is so conditioned by language, on the other hand, that one's whole experience is molded by fixed labels and categories, compelled by the associations and structures afforded by a particular language, or by language in general, then this habit has become restrictive, like a prison of the mind. Modern psychologists recognize that automatic associations or reactions to labels, be they emotive or intellectual, effectively block absorption of information, to say nothing of understanding; this is a basic point of Taoist learning theory.

The same point is made in the opening lines of the *Tao Te Ching*—"A path that can be verbalized is not a permanent path, terminology that can be designated is not constant terminology." This might be paraphrased by saying that there is always more than what can be encompassed by any formulation, whether that formulation be a word, a language, a system of thought, or a whole culture. This does not deny the relative validity or usefulness of any such tools; rather it affirms the existence of greater potential, the possibility of progress and freedom.

Therefore Complete Reality Taoist teaching does not say that mundanity or conditioning is evil, only that it should be a servant rather than a master. From this standpoint, mundane conditioning is not bad per se, it is the source of what is bad—the suffocation of the organic living potential of the individual and community. One advantage of being able to stand aside from the mundane and recover the awareness of the unconditioned primordial mind is that it allows a more objective assessment of the value or otherwise of particular habits or patterns of behavior; and it allows leeway within which to modify behavior.

What the Complete Reality Taoist strives for is to attain autonomy, the freedom to be or not to be, to do or not do, according to the needs of the situation at hand. In this sense the adept is said to transcend yin and yang, reaching an undefinable state in which one "does nothing, yet does anything." This is alluded to in the present text in expressions such as "neither being nor nonbeing, neither material nor void." The accomplished Taoist in this sense is neither a worldling nor an otherworldly anchorite, but uses both involvement and withdrawal as necessary means to an ultimate balance and completeness.

Another pair of important terms analogous to heaven and earth is "the mind of Tao and the human mind." According to the *Chung Ho Chi*, the mind of Tao is the "shining mind," while the human mind is the "wandering mind." What the Taoist tries to do, in these terms, is to still the wandering and sustain the shining, effecting thereby a stabilization of lucid awareness.

This practice is also suggested by another famous line of the *Tao Te Ching*, "Empty the mind, fill the belly" (III), which is interpreted to mean clearing the human mind of its ramblings and preoccupations, and filling the center of the being—representing the focus of life—with the direct awareness of reality.

The mind of Tao and the human mind are also associated with "real knowledge" and "conscious knowledge." Real knowledge is held to be nondiscursive, immediate knowing, originally inherent in the human being and not the product of learning. Conscious knowledge is the everyday awareness of ordinary life, formed by training and experience. The Taoist aim is to open consciousness and thereby allow greater access to reality, bypassing mental habit, stabilizing conscious knowing by real knowledge so that it is not subject to distorting influences. This is also expressed in terms of making real knowledge conscious and conscious knowledge real.

Real knowledge and conscious knowledge are in turn associated with "sense and essence." Essence is the essence or fundamental nature of consciousness itself; sense is its function. In the conditioned state, essence is frozen into personality and temperament, while sense wanders into feelings. The effort here is to join sense and essence; this may be described as developing a sense of the real essence of mind, and sensing reality directly from the essence of consciousness rather than through the acquired psychological configurations of temperament. This is said to involve keeping consciousness open and fluid while clearing sense of subjective feelings; this means transcendence of restrictive mental fixations through the greater perspective afforded by the mind of Tao.

Yin and yang are also commonly defined as flexibility and firmness, and these terms are then applied to other yin/yang associations. For example, the essence of conscious knowledge in the human mind is said to be flexible, because it has not definite form originally; the sense of real knowledge in the mind of Tao is said to be firm, because it is objective and unequivocal. The joining of these two means that the flexible consciousness, instead of conforming to the arbitrary influences of history and environment, is stabilized by the firmness of real knowledge. Without conscious knowing, it is said, there is no point of access to real knowing; without real knowing, on the other hand, there is no stable objectivity of consciousness.

The qualities of flexibility and firmness, or softness and hardness, have numerous other points of reference besides their application to the essence of conscious knowledge and the sense of real knowledge. In his *Shen Shih Pa Fa*, Liu I-ming describes firmness as strength, sturdiness, decisiveness, keenness, incorruptibility, and indomitability; he also associates it with detachment, independence, serenity, will, consistency, dedication, and objectivity. As for flexibility, Liu defines this in terms of self-control, humility, consideration of others, simplicity, sincerity, and modesty; he also refers to flexibility as tolerance, courtesy, self-examination, freedom from compulsive habit, contentment, and absence of random thought and imagination. All of these qualities and practices may thus be suggested by the simple terms yin and yang; in respect of these associations, it is the blending of yin and yang that is the aim, and these forms of yin and yang are sometimes given the special name of true yin and true yang.

Speaking in general terms about the need to balance flexibility and firmness, Liu I-ming in his *Wu Tao Lu* says that if one is always "hard," one will be impetuous, aggressive, and impatient; on the other hand, if one is always "soft," one will vacillate and be ineffective. Balance, he concludes, calls for firmness of will with flexibility in action, neither rushing ahead nor lagging behind. The correct balance of yin and yang, in terms of these qualities and applications of firmness and flexibility, is considered important both for social life as well as for spiritual life.

In the context of spiritual practice, yin and yang also correspond to stillness and movement, both of which are used in Complete Reality Taoist training. Stillness may mean actual physical stillness, commonly used as an aid to achieving inner stillness; it is also used to mean the stilling of certain undesirable qualities such as vindictiveness and greed, and it is used to refer to a state of inward tranquility in the midst of action.

Movement has a number of meanings in Complete Reality Taoist praxis; it may mean travel, physical exercise, psychosomatic exercise, or ordinary activity in the world. Charitable activities in particular are often given special emphasis as being an important part of the overall process of human development, encompassing inner benefit to oneself within outward benefit to others.

A somewhat more subtle meaning of stillness and movement is essence and function of awareness. This association appears in the context of a specific exercise described as silencing the mind to revert from function to essence, until quiescence reaches a climax followed by spontaneous activation of the conscious potential formerly stifled by mental routine. One of the finer points of Taoist practice here is to discern the exact quality of the movement following stillness, to determine whether it is in fact movement of the primordial mind of Tao, or whether it is mixed with the acquired human mentality.

As in Ch'an Buddhism, Complete Reality Taoist teaching asserts that stillness produced by concentration alone is not necessarily sufficient to break through the boundaries of psychological conditioning, and may only hold it in temporary abeyance. Altered states thus produced are called "phantom elixir," because they vanish in time. According to the Taoist theory of blending and transcending yin and yang, in the final analysis there is supposed to be no fixed duality between stillness and movement; in Liu I-ming's commentary on *Understanding Reality*, this balanced integration is referred to by means of an expression from the *I Ching*, "Tranquil and unperturbed, yet sensitive and effective," and by a common Taoist phrase, "Always calm yet always responsive, always responsive yet always calm." This is considered to be a basic aspect of the uniting of heaven and earth within humanity, a primary aim of Taoist practice.

The Five Elements

The concept of the "five elements," like that of yin and yang, is one of the basic descriptive frameworks found in the Complete Reality school of Taoism. So well established was the notion of five elements composing the universe in ancient Chinese thinking that it became routine to classify things in terms of fives—five notes in music, five viscera in physiology, five constants and five virtues in sociology, five senses and five emotions in psychology. It was no doubt convenient for Taoists as well to use this time-honored scheme to structure some of their teachings.

In the Complete Reality school's projection of Taoism, one of the most common constructs for referring to the unification or reconstruction of the human being is called "assembling the five elements." The five elements are represented by the physical elements of fire, water, metal, wood, and earth; these in turn stand for conscious knowledge, real knowledge, sense, essence, and intent. Thus, substituting these equivalents, the assembling of the five elements represents the same blending of yin and yang that has been discussed above: the essence of conscious knowledge and sense of real knowledge are united, with this unification being accomplished through the medium of intent, or will, the concentrated attention used to bridge the acquired gap between the conscious and the unconscious.

Another construct based on the five elements is the contrast between "going along" and "reversal." The form of this construct derives from the ancient idea that the five elements in one order overcome one another, while in another order give rise to one another: Taoist "reversal" inverts both orders. To interpret this scheme, it is necessary to introduce the idea of the conditioned versus the primordial five elements. In Taoist terminology, the conditioned five elements are antagonistic or harmful to one another whereas the primordial five elements cooperate with and foster one another; the conditioned five elements are fragmented whereas the primordial five elements are unified.

The classic order of production of the five elements is wood-fire-earth-metal-water-wood-, and so on. In the conditioned state, "wood" stands for temperament, "fire" for volatility, "earth" for arbitrary intentions, "metal" for feelings, "water" for desire. In these terms, temperament produces volatility, volatility produces arbitrary intentions, intentions produce feelings, feelings produce desires, desires produce temperament. This represents a circle of conditioning, somewhat reminiscent of the Buddhist idea of the twelvefold circle of conditioning.

In the primordial state, wood stands for essence, fire for open consciousness, earth for true intent, metal for true sense, and water for real knowledge. Hence, reversing the order of wood-fire-earth-metal-water-wood-, essence produces real knowledge, real knowledge produces true sense, true sense produces true intent, true intent produces open consciousness, open consciousness produces essence.

The classic order of the mutual overcoming of the five elements is wood-earth-water-fire-metal-wood-. The conditioned equivalents produce the circle of temperament overcoming will so that the latter degenerates into arbitrary intentions; arbitrary intentions overcome real knowledge so that it degenerates into desire; desires overcome consciousness so that it becomes volatile and unstable; volatility overcomes sense so that it fragments into feelings; feelings overcome essence so that it is molded into temperament. This is another way of describing the circle of conditioning.

Reversing the mutual-overcoming cycle, essence overcomes feelings so they return to true sense; true sense overcomes volatility so that it returns to clear consciousness; clear consciousness overcomes desire so that it returns to real knowledge; real knowledge overcomes willfulness so that it returns to true intent; true intent overcomes temperament so that it returns to essence.

In dealing with Taoist teachings, it is useful to remember that virtually every didactic device employed in Taoism, even within a particular school of Taoism, can be defined in different ways, with the result that there is no one standard scheme that is universally applied. The importance of this provision in dealing with Taoist literature may be guessed from the fact that it derives from the opening statement of the *Tao Te Ching*. One and the same author may even use different explanations at different times.

This variety of interpretative methods is certainly much in evidence when it comes to a pervasive framework such as the five elements. In his *Shuo P'o Hsiang Yen*, for example, Liu I-ming gives another treatment of the reversal of the five elements that could profitably be applied to the present text. According to this interpretation, fire produces wood in the sense that the essence of a human being is refined in the "furnace" of creation—that is, through experience—to become stabilized; water produces metal in the sense of true sense passing through desire to become undefiled. The reversal of earth then means the reversal of intention and orientation—using the world for self-refinement rather than for self-indulgence.

Another important set of associations of the five elements is the so-called five bases. In the present text, the five bases, or fundamental elements of a human being, are referred to as basic essence, basic sense, basic vitality, basic spirit, and basic energy. The first two, essence and sense, have already been discussed as the essence of consciousness and the sense of real knowledge; the remaining three form the so-called three jewels or three treasures, an important trinity in Complete Reality Taoist thought.

Vitality, energy, and spirit might be defined as the fundamental productive, kinetic, and conscious forces of life. In Taoism they are said to be originally one, yet spoken of as threefold because of their temporal specialization into the energies of sexuality, metabolism, and thought. There are practices which involve the temporal conditioned forms of the three treasures—sexual exercises, breathing exercises, and controlled imagination; but these are said (by numerous authors, including Chang Po-tuan, author of *Understanding Reality*) to be limited in that they do not produce permanent results. In addition, there are said to be mental and physical dangers associated with such practices. Many texts therefore make a point of dismissing them or relegating them to a secondary place.

The metaphysical practice based on the three treasures is generally seen as a progressive refinement: refining vitality into energy, refining energy into spirit, refining spirit into space, and finally breaking through space to merge with the reality of the Tao. This is sometimes described as a progressive detachment and shifting from awareness of the body to awareness of breath, from awareness of breath to awareness of mind, from awareness of mind to awareness of space, from awareness of space to awareness of the Tao, or objective reality.

In certain systems generally classified as belonging to a "lesser vehicle" of Taoism, the vitality, energy, and spirit are associated with specific physical locations. The vitality is associated with the genital or umbilical region, the energy with the area of the solar plexus, and the spirit with the head. These areas are then successively made the focus of concentration, according to the stage of practice; some practitioners, however, concentrate only on one point. In either case, it is commonly noted that this type of practice has the advantage of ease, but also has the disadvantages of being incapable of producing final realization and also having undesirable and potentially dangerous side effects. Such are the dangers of this sort of practice, in fact, that some teachers (such as Liu I-ming) appear to reject it entirely. Modern

Taoist literature abounds with warnings in this connection, particularly in reference to concentration on points in the head.

In a different dimension of interpretation, the "upward" progression of vitality-energy-spirit-space-Tao may be used to illustrate an important contention of Complete Reality Taoism. The degeneration of humankind from its original "celestial" state, it is held, is characterized by a "downward" regression of thought into aggression and greed—mundane manifestations of spirit, energy, and vitality. Complete Reality praxis attempts to reverse this regression, channeling vitality and energy "upward" to boost consciousness. This boosting is enhanced by clarification and purification of consciousness so as to make it "spacelike" and therefore receptive to objective reality. Complete Reality Taoist literature using Buddhist terminology also equates vitality, energy, and spirit with the realms of desire, form, and formlessness, similarly indicating a progressive refinement.

In the present text, Liu I-ming's commentary on *Understanding Reality*, the "five bases" represent the energies of the five elements in the primordial, unconditioned state; in the temporal conditioned state, they degenerate into five "things" which are referred to as the wandering higher soul, the ghostlike lower soul, the earthly vitality, the discriminating mind, and the errant intent.

This concept of higher and lower souls derives from an ancient Chinese idea of multiple souls which separate from the individual at death; one group rises up, while one group sinks down. Traditionally, both higher and lower souls are multiple, but in Complete Reality Taoist usage this factor is ordinarily irrelevant, and it is convenient to use the singular form when translating this particular text. The higher and lower souls tend to be ill defined, or undefined, but in some literature, including the present text, the association of the higher soul with imagination and the lower soul with emotion may suggest itself to the modern reader. This interpretation accords, at any rate, with the association made here of the conditioned form of the essence or nature of consciousness with the higher soul, and of conditioned sense or feeling with the lower soul. Those familiar with Western psychoanalytic terminology might also be tempted to see the ego or superego and id in the higher and lower souls.

The earthly vitality, here called the conditioned form of the basic vitality, generally refers to sexuality. In Complete Reality Taoism, sexuality has no moral associations, and its operation and employment are treated as a practical issue. The basic premise in this regard is that sexual activity can either boost or deplete energy; the fundamental aim of Complete Reality praxis seems to be to control and consciously direct sexuality—neither celibacy nor indulgence, according to Chang Po-tuan, author of *Understanding Reality*, will take one to the goal. In Chang's southern school of Complete Reality Taoism, sexual intercourse (both physical and mental) was used to cultivate energy, bliss, and health, especially in the case of practitioners of advanced age. As with breathing exercises and psychosomatic concentration practices, sexual techniques are considered hazardous if improperly performed. Taoist literature abounds with warnings about the misuse of sexuality, both technically and generally; as with other aspects of life in the world, the matter is presented as a question of whether one is controlled by one's energies or in control of them.

The discriminating mind refers to conceptualization. This is regarded as a characteristic of the human mind, conditioned by personal and collective history; it is useful for everyday affairs but ultimately limited and limiting. One feature of the discriminating mind is that it cognizes multiplicity; without the balancing factor of direct perception of organic unity, it is prone to fragmentary awareness and bias. Furthermore, as the patterns according to which the discriminating mind organizes and rationalizes its activities are associated with and influenced by social and cultural identity, they tend to become intimately bound up with emotion, which then increases the tendency to narrowness and prejudice.

As is the case when speaking of the human mentality in general, Complete Reality Taoist teachings often appear extremely negative in their attitudes toward the discriminating mind; it is explained that this is because such teachings are addressed to those in whom the discriminating mind has through long use developed into a jealous tyrant which seeks to exclude or discount knowledge not within its range. It is interesting to note in this connection that attainment of enlightenment in Complete Reality Taoism is said to be easier for women and children than for adult males; one reason for this could be that women and children in post-tribal society have traditionally had less of a stake in, and hence less compulsive need to uphold and defend, the conceptual rationale of a given system. According to Liu I-ming, for example, flexibility is the beginning of the practice of the

Tao and as this quality is conventionally demanded of women and children to a greater extent than it is of men, it might be said that women and children have a head start in Taoist practice in this respect.

The errant intent is considered a degeneration or deviation of the "true intent." True intent is autonomous will or concentration, associated with truthfulness, sincerity, and reliability, which acts as the focal point of Taoist practice, and of life as a whole, in what is called a "real" or "free" human being. Errant intent, on the other hand, is more willfulness than will, and it is influenced by external pressures and subjective desires. In contrast to the sober, deliberate focus of "true intent," the activity of "errant intent" is unstable and fickle.

The five bases and five things are further said to contain, respectively, five virtues and five thieves. The five virtues represent qualities which are held to simultaneously promote social health and personal development. The five thieves are emotions and cravings, called thieves or bandits because their indulgence robs the individual of energy, reason, and inner autonomy. This drainage is held to be the cause of physical and mental decline. Thus the aim of Complete Reality Taoism is to govern the five things by the five bases, and subordinate the five thieves to the five virtues.

The ancient idea of the five virtues seems to have taken final shape in the work of the second century B.C. Confucian scholar Tung Chung-shu, who is said to have introduced the old scheme of the five elements into Confucianism. Prior to this, the great Confucian thinker Mencius (372–289 B.C.) had spoken of four virtues: benevolence, justice, courtesy, and knowledge. He considered benevolence an outgrowth of sympathy, justice an outgrowth of shame at doing evil, courtesy an outgrowth of deference, and knowledge or wisdom an outgrowth of judgment or a sense of right and wrong. Mencius considered the bases of these virtues to be inherent in all people.

The names of the five virtues are variously translated in English, illustrating different aspects or implications of the qualities they represent. Benevolence is associated with humanity, kindness, and compassion. Justice is associated with righteousness and duty. Courtesy is associated with decorum and social grace. Knowledge or wisdom is associated with investigation of things and understanding of principles. In general, these virtues are not rigidly defined, being applied in different ways by different interpreters according to context. In Taoist texts, mention is also made of relevant attitudes and actions such as loving people, promoting social welfare, deferring to others, and pursuing theoretical and practical studies.

The fifth virtue, truthfulness, is perhaps the quality most precisely defined in Complete Reality Taoism. The word can be translated as faith or trust, but in this school of Taoist practice it is specifically associated with sincerity and truth, and regarded as the central quality which gives all the other virtues authenticity. It thus is seen as constituting the core of the individual.

Essence and Life

The inner and outer integration of the human being is called the science of essence and life (*hsing-ming hsueh*), and this term is commonly used to indicate the general subject matter of Complete Reality Taoist study. This expression is particularly significant in that it illustrates the contention of the Complete Reality school that both mundane and transcendental development are important for the realization of human completeness.

In Confucian tradition, where the term seems to originate, *hsing-ming* generally means human nature and destiny; in Complete Reality Taoist usage, it means essence and life, defined as mind and body, or spirit and energy. These are said to be one in the primordial state, then divided by temporal conditioning; in this sense the science of essence and life is aimed at restoration of the primal organic unity of mind and body, spirit and energy.

As in the expression "essence and sense," in this case essence also means the basic nature of consciousness, so it may be called mind or spirit. The special study of the science of essence deals with realization of this basic nature. In terms of Plato's metaphor of the cave, the study of essence is commonly practiced by turning the attention from the shadows on the wall to the source of the light itself. Done not by discursive thought but by a direct inner sense, this is what is known in Ch'an Buddhism as "seeing essence" (*chien-hsing*), and Complete Reality Taoist texts often use the Ch'an expression "turning the attention around to look inward" to describe a basic practice used in both schools for this purpose.

The science of life, dealing with the energy of being, includes physical exercise, massage, psychosomatic exercise, energy conservation, and conduct in general. While some manifestations of the study may thus be primarily physical, nevertheless even physical exercises are generally accompanied by certain mental postures or attitudes. The special emphasis of this part of Taoist study is health and well-being. The practices involved in the science of life may be complex, and it is generally in this area that most differences among individual teachers and sects within Complete Reality Taoism are found.

Among the various types of physical exercise, the two systems best known in the Complete Reality tradition are the *pa tuan chin*, "eight step brocade," and the *t'ai chi ch'uan*, "absolute boxing." The former is said to have been transmitted by Chung-li, ancestor of Complete Reality Taoism; the invention of the latter is attributed to the extraordinary Ming dynasty adept Chang San-feng, whose work is often cited in Complete Reality literature. Eight step brocade is quite simple while absolute boxing is fairly intricate; both systems have numerous variations, and both are still in popular use.

There are also various systems of massage, generally included under the rubric of *tao-yin*, "induction," which may combine stretching and bending with massage. Induction practices are noted for their effects on circulation, and are recommended for maintaining health. Like eight step brocade and absolute boxing, induction practices seem to have taken on a life of their own in the course of time, and may be presented simply as exercises for health, without necessarily including the total context of Complete Reality theory and practice.

The main psychosomatic exercise seen in Complete Reality Taoism is what is known as the "waterwheel" (*ho-ch'e*). This involves generation of inner heat by concentration or sexual arousal, then circulating this heat through the psychic channels called the active and passive (*tu* and *jen*) channels, up the spine, through the head, and down the center line of the front of the torso. An abbreviated version of this exercise, using the active channel up the spine to the brain, is called "returning the vitality to repair the brain" (*huan ching pu nao*). This is often, though not necessarily, practiced in conjunction with sexual intercourse; in the male, ejaculation is suppressed, either by muscular contraction or external pressure, creating an extremely intense and prolonged orgasm, the heat of which is then conducted by concentration up the spine into the brain, where it "burns" away mundane thoughts and feelings by bliss.

Some Taoists do not use the waterwheel or brain-repairing exercises, instead emphasizing the practice of energy conservation as a means of preserving health and extending life. Energy conservation involves minimizing the use of the mind and senses: this includes both exercises of extreme withdrawal and quiescence as well as general reduction of unnecessary expenditures of energy. It is a rather common Taoist contention that excitation of thought and emotion drains people of energy, and thus hastens deterioration of the organism. Disconnection of emotion, thought, and even sense from objects is a three-level restorative exercise believed to aid in recovery of depleted energy and thus in maintenance of physical health. As previously mentioned, in Complete Reality Taoism withdrawal and quietude are not general life patterns or goals of Taoist practice, but specific techniques to be applied only at appropriate times.

The general practice of avoiding frivolous waste of energy involves not only relinquishment of compulsive mental and physical activity in pursuit of stimulation, but also the harmonization of the individual with the social milieu. In this sense, social ethics, insofar as they promote interpersonal harmony, are considered an integral part of the "science of life," helpful in reducing both psychic and physical wear and tear on all concerned. In his introduction to *Understanding Reality*, Chang Po-tuan mentions the overt teachings of Confucius as being mainly concerned with "life," citing the five virtues and "four no's"—no willfulness, no fixation, no insistence, no egotism. These attitudes are thus considered beneficial both in the context of life in the ordinary world and in the context of higher psychological development, by fostering the accumulation of the energy needed to sustain enhanced consciousness.

In sum, the pursuit of the "science of essence and life" calls for the inner and outer integration of the total human being. This means the inward unification of the psychological and physical energies and their faculties of expression, combined with outward unification of the individual with the environment. Both inner and outer harmonizations are viewed as essential in forming a channel through which proceeds a continuous flow of energy between "heaven and earth."

The Use of I Ching *Signs*

In common with other Taoist alchemical literature, *Understanding Reality* uses certain signs from the ancient classic *I Ching* in presenting its teachings. The most common of these are the four signs called *heaven, earth, fire,* and *water.*

The signs *heaven* ☰ and *earth* ☷ are the "parent signs" representing pure yang and pure yin, respectively. These two signs thus may be used to indicate qualities or modes of being or praxis, such as movement and stillness, associated with yin and yang. As in the case of the terms yin and yang, the associations of the signs and their components differ according to the context of usage.

The sign *fire* ☲ is generally used to refer to awareness, particularly the consciousness in the human mind. *Fire* is treated as a modification of heaven, indicating that awareness is originally "celestial." The yin ⚋ component in the middle of *fire* ☲ is understood in two ways, according to the specific sense of yin applied. In one sense, yin stands for flexibility, adaptability, and receptivity; in this sense, in the middle of *fire* ☲ it represents the quality of openness or flexibility that is originally a characteristic of consciousness. Hence *fire* can be "open consciousness." In another sense, yin stands for mundanity, conditioning, susceptibility; in this case *fire* ☲ symbolizes fundamentally celestial awareness having been invaded by mundane influences, producing the human mentality, which is centered on and susceptible to the things of the world.

In contrast to the conscious knowledge of the human mind represented by *fire* ☲, the sign *water* ☵ is used to refer to the real knowledge of the mind of Tao. The yang ⚊ component in the middle stands for the originally integrated real knowledge that has become buried by mundane conditioning, here represented by the two yin ⚋ components surrounding it. Thus a basic operation of Taoist alchemy is described as taking the solid yang ⚊ out of *water* ☵ and using it to replace the broken yin ⚋ inside *fire* ☲ so as to produce whole *heaven* ☰. This means, in other words, to retrieve real knowledge from the overlay of artificial conditioning, and use that to replace the mundanity infecting conscious knowledge, thereby restoring the basic completeness of the primordial celestial mind. Associated nuances of this operation are explained in the commentary to the text.

Another way in which this combination is expressed is in terms of "inversion of *fire* and *water.*" In the ordinary worldly human being, it is said, fire is above water: just as fire rises, consciousness is volatile and given to imagination and wandering thought; and just as water flows downward, real knowledge tends to become submerged in the unconscious, to sink away into oblivion. Thus when fire is above and water is below, consciousness and real knowledge go their separate ways and do not combine. Therefore Taoist alchemy speaks of inverting fire and water so that they interact—water "cools" fire, in the sense that real knowledge stabilizes consciousness and removes volatility, while fire "warms" water, in the sense of consciousness bringing real knowledge into action in life.

The eight basic signs of the *I Ching* are also used to represent fundamental elements involved in human development; hence the alchemical expression "the crucible of the eight trigrams." In this scheme, *heaven* ☰ is firmness, *earth* ☷ is flexibility, *fire* ☲ is awareness, *water* ☵ is danger, *thunder* ☳ is action, *mountain* ☶ is stillness, *lake* ☱ is joy, and *wind* ☴ is obedience.

As we have already seen, however, the usage of the signs in Taoist texts may vary just like that of any other symbol or expression. One of the signs often used more or less in isolation from others is *thunder* ☳, representing one yang appearing under two yins, symbolizing the appearance of the primordial mind after profound quiescence: ☷ turning to ☳ stands for the resurgence of the celestial after the climax of the stilling of the mundane; here the "action" of thunder means activation of the innate potential of the original mind. In another context, however, *thunder* ☳ represents essence, paired with *lake* ☱ representing sense: *thunder* as "action" here refers to the excitable nature of temperament, which is the conditioned form of essence; and *lake* as "joy" refers to emotional feelings, the conditional form of sense.

A number of six-line signs of the *I Ching* are also used in alchemical texts to represent phases of practice. Among the most commonly encountered are *difficulty* ䷂ and *darkness* ䷃, as in the standard expression "difficulty in the morning, darkness at night." This maxim is generally used to allude to the so-called "martial" and "cultural" phases of the alchemical work, involving active struggle and passive nurturance. These complementary aspects of practice are also known as doing and nondoing, striving and nonstriving.

Also mentioned in *Understanding Reality* are the pairs *obstruction* and *tranquility*, *settled* and *unsettled*. Obstruction ䷋ represents failure of yin and yang to interact and combine, thus obstructing human progress; *tranquility* ䷊ stands for the interaction of yin and yang, which is the basis of growth. Similarly, *settled* ☷☲ symbolizes the interaction of *fire* and *water*, conscious knowledge and real knowledge, thus producing balance; while *unsettled* ☵☲ indicates the isolation of *fire* and *water* from one another, resulting in bias.

Finally, *Understanding Reality* also alludes to what are known as the six yang signs and six yin signs. The six yang signs are *return* ☷☳, *overseeing* ☷☱, *tranquility* ☷☰, *great power* ☳☰, *parting* ☱☰, and *heaven* ☰☰. Conversely, the six yin signs are *meeting* ☰☴, *withdrawal* ☰☶, *obstruction* ☰☷, *observing* ☴☷, *stripping away* ☶☷, and *earth* ☷☷. These signs are not used in this case according to their individual values as outlined in the *I Ching*, but simply as representations of the gradual growth of yang followed by merging with yin: hence they symbolize the "yang fire" and "yin convergence," the two predominant operations of the alchemical process.

Praxis

One of the interesting features of *Understanding Reality* is that it does not give details of any concrete form of practice through which the alchemical transformation is to be accomplished. This can be easily appreciated on the principle that practices can have their intended effect only when performed according to proper measure, which depends on individual needs and timing. What the text does indicate is what is to be achieved through the alchemical work; the specific method, tailored to the individual case, is to be learned in person from an adept.

It is sometimes said that there are three thousand six hundred practices in Taoism; some writers repudiate all formal practices as "sidetracks," hinting at the metaphysical nature of the Tao and confirming the contention that truth is formless. In his preface to *Understanding Reality*, Chang Po-tuan mentions some common exercises such as star-gazing, visualization, breathing exercises, massage, incantation, celibacy, fasting, fixation of attention, and sexual yoga, and says that the effects of such practices are all impermanent, at best leading to physical health and well-being.

Generally speaking, the most pervasive practical concern in Complete Reality Taoism appears to be the purification and deautomization of the mind so as to make it sensitive to reality; and it is well known that practitioners commonly practiced quiet sitting as an aid in accomplishing this. Nonetheless, Liu I-ming, who generally presents an interpretation of *Understanding Reality* characteristic of the "pure serenity" approach of the northern school of Complete Reality Taoism, which emphasized quiet sitting, still makes a point of repudiating even this as a magic key to enlightenment. There are indisputable indications that Liu did himself practice abstract trance in quiet sitting, but he did not preach it as a mechanical cure-all; rather, he emphasized more the use of everything in life as a means of self-refinement, with abstract trance a means of finding the "medicines" of unconditioned spirit and energy, which subsequently have to be refined in the "furnace" of everyday life. There is no indication that he, or Chang Po-tuan for that matter, ever set up any sort of fixed program for students to follow.

Perhaps the most provocative issue in Complete Reality practice is the difference in the approaches of the so-called northern and southern schools. As noted in the beginning of this introduction, both schools are believed to derive from the teachings of Chung-li Ch'uan and Lu Tung-pin, and to have the same goal; nevertheless there are methodological differences. One modern Taoist puts it this way: "Whatever the school, all practitioners gather the unique unconditioned energy; the way of getting it and the provenance are not the same, but the accomplishment is one."[9]

The main difference in the methods of the northern and southern schools apparently lies in the use or otherwise of sexual yoga and the waterwheel exercise. This is suggested by the epithets given to the schools based on their practices: the northern school is commonly called the sect of "pure serenity," referring to silent meditation, while the southern school is often called the sect of "grafting" or "twin cultivation of yin and yang," in reference to the use of sexual exercises.

One modern Taoist gives an interesting explanation of the reason for this difference: "The northern school emphasizes purity and stillness, as transmitted by Ch'iu Ch'ang-ch'un (a disciple of Wang Che); the southern school emphasizes grafting, as transmitted by Chang Po-tuan. Ch'ang-ch'un's lineage involved people who practiced the Tao in youth or middle age, none of whom were over sixty years old. Chang Po-tuan's lineage mostly included elderly people over eighty, whose temporal vitality and energy were insufficient and had to be replenished by grafting; therefore it is also called the method of mutual supplementation of yin and yang. However, after replenishment, they also had to practice in the same way as the school of pure serenity."[10]

As usual, however, the situation does not seem to have been quite as clear-cut as generalizations make it appear. Although differences in method and emphasis apparently came to be exaggerated by some groups as a basis for sectarianism, nevertheless those Taoists who continued to emphasize the unity of the goal insist that the documents of the northern and southern schools can be interpreted coherently in each other's terms. For example, a modern Taoist says, "The books of the southern school may be interpreted perfectly well in terms of the practice of pure serenity."[11] Another says, "The southern and northern schools are extremely difficult to differentiate. Chang Po-tuan's *Understanding Reality* is, to be sure, a specialist book of the southern school, but it can also be viewed as an alchemical classic of the northern school. What one sees in it depends on the person."[12]

A further complication arises when we consider the southern school to be marked by the use of "grafting," sexual yoga for energy boosting, since Chang Po-tuan himself deemphasizes sexual practices in his own preface to *Understanding Reality*, and so does Tao-kuang, third patriarch of the southern school, in his commentary on this text. These apparent denials may, of course, be protective camouflage, not only to guard against outside interference by scandalized Confucian authorities, but also to guard against abuse of such practices by ignorant imitators, because sexual yoga is held to be potentially hazardous, as a modern Taoist explains: "The interaction of yin and yang (here meaning female and male) is inconceivable; if the practice of the southern school is not done properly, it can easily cause illness."[13]

According to other modern Taoists who speak of the differences and similarities of the two schools, the grafting practice of the southern school must be combined, as previously noted, with the pure serenity practice of the northern school: "If one wants to practice the yin-yang twin cultivation of the southern school, unless one has sufficient grounding in the practice of pure serenity one will be unable to be unminding in face of objects; many have failed in the eleventh hour because of this."[14] "In the practice of the southern school, even if one can obtain elixir from one's partner, one must then resume the practice of pure serenity, embrace the fundamental, preserve unity, return to emptiness and go back to nothingness; only thus can one achieve final settlement. Otherwise, hopes of attaining reality will in the end vanish."[15]

In sum, the aim of Complete Reality Taoism is to be a "real human being" rather than a willy-nilly product of socio-cultural accident, to be fully awake, autonomous, capable of exercising free will and of perceiving reality directly without artificial constructs. It is not necessary to believe in the possibility of attaining this goal to draw the lesson from religious history that arbitrary adoption of formal practices because of tradition or attraction can simply automatize people in another way, just "adding chains to fetters," in the Ch'an phrase. The value of texts like *Understanding Reality* is not in providing an A to Z manual of Taoist enlightenment, but in providing a theoretical basis for understanding the elements of a praxis in the context of a comprehensive framework, in relation to specific possibilities. This removes the charisma from externals and focuses attention on effect, so that a system can be assessed in terms of what it does rather than what it looks like.

Notes

1. *Ting P'i Shang-yang-tzu Yuan Chu Ts'an T'ung Ch'i* (Hsin Wen Feng Publishing Co., Taiwan, 1978), p. 4.
2. See *Hsuan Men Pi Tu* (Tzu Yu Publishing Co., Taiwan, 1965), and *Li Tai Shen Hsien Shih* (Hsin Wen Feng Publishing Co., Taiwan, 1978).
3. There are obvious chronological problems involved in trying to trace Complete Reality Taoism back beyond Chang Po-tuan and Wang Che. Liu Ts'ao is said to have lived in the tenth century, a hundred years before Chang Po-tuan met him. Lu Tung-pin, to whom a vast body of apocrypha is attributed, is said to have lived in the eighth century. Chung-li is generally said to have been a man of the T'ang dynasty, but his teacher was supposedly born in the middle of the second century C.E. Taoists, of course, have long claimed that a sort of hibernation or suspended animation can be achieved by practice; interestingly enough, amid contemporary fears for the planet, scientists in the West have recently begun to seriously examine the question of whether human hibernation is possible, quite apart from any interest in Taoism. If the works of Chang Po-tuan and Wang Che are studied on the basis of the Ch'an Buddhist maxim, "Refer everything to yourself," historical con-

cerns subside to the relatively superficial plane of terminology and organizational patterns.
4. In general, the formation of large organizations in Taoist history relates more to economic and political conditions than to intrinsic qualities of Taoism. Taoist circles such as that represented by Chuang Tzu were apparently esoteric in the sense that they had no readily identifiable social presence. Stories of the encounters of Chung-li Ch'uan, Lu Tung-pin, and Liu Ts'ao are centered on individual, personal recognition and interaction. Indications of the situation in the times of Chang Po-tuan and Wang Che seem to point to individuals or small groups of associates; the organizational boom of Complete Reality Taoism took place after Wang's time and was connected with social factors such as alienation of the gentry from politics under foreign rule, disturbed conditions in northern China due to military action, and the recognition and entitlement of Wang's successor Ch'iu Ch'ang-ch'un by the Mongol hegemon Jenghiz Khan.
5. *Li Tai Shen Hsien Shih*, scroll 4.
6. Other classics commented on by Liu include the *Yin Fu Ching*, attributed to Huang Ti; *Huang Ting Ching*, attributed to Tung Hua; *Ch'iao Yao Ke*, attributed to Lu Tung-pin; *Wu Ken Shu*, by Chang San-feng; and *Chin Tan Ssu Pai Tzu*, by Chang Po-tuan. For Liu's explanation of the *I Ching*, see my *The Taoist I Ching* (Shambhala, Boston, 1986); for his explanation of *Chin Tan Ssu Pai Tzu*, see my *The Inner Teachings of Taoism* (Shambhala, Boston, 1986).
7. Li Lo-ch'iu, *Fang Tao Yu Lu* (Chen Shan Mei Publishing Co., Taiwan, 1965), p. 2.
8. Again, in the spirit of the *Tao Te Ching*, it must be remembered that no claims of unique validity can be made for this or any other interpretation. For broader studies in alchemical lore, see Joseph Needham's *Science and Civilization in China*, 5 vols. (Cambridge University Press). For some indication of the variety of interpretative frameworks applied to alchemical terms, see *Chung Ho Chi* in volume 17 of *Tao Tsang Chi Yao* (Hsin Wen Feng Publishing Co., Taiwan, 1976). For Liu I-ming's critical examination of metaphysical and physical interpretations of Taoist symbolism, see my *The Inner Teachings of Taoism*.
9. Li Lo-ch'iu, *Fang Tao Yu Lu*, p. 321.
10. Ibid., p. 251.
11. Ibid., p. 330.
12. Ibid., p. 349.
13. Ibid., p. 119.
14. Ibid., p. 332.
15. Ibid., pp. 327–328.

Understanding Reality
A DIRECT EXPLANATION

I. *Sixteen Verses, Representing "Eight Ounces" of Yin and "Eight Ounces" of Yang, Forming "One Pound" of Elixir*

[1]

If you do not seek the great way to leave the path of delusion, even if you are intelligent and talented you are not great. A hundred years is like a spark, a lifetime is like a bubble. If you only crave material gain and prominence, without considering the deterioration of your body, I ask you, even if you accumulate a mountain of gold can you buy off impermanence?

The realm of dust is the world of sound and form, the land of name and gain where misery is taken for pleasure, where the artificial is taken to be real. Diminishing the vitality, wearing out the energy, destroying essence and life, in it there is death only. Those who realize this and can go beyond it are the people of attainment; those who are unaware of it and fall into it are people astray. Therefore since ancient times the immortals and real people who achieved the Tao took care of their family and social duties when they were young, thereby fulfilling human ethics; when they reached the age of forty they practiced the Tao of not stirring the mind, whereby they preserved their essence and life. After all, a hundred years is only a brief interval; a lifetime of glory and disgrace is a blink of an eye. If you do not know how to return to the fundamental and go back to the origin, to return to the root and go back to life, when the limit of your time here comes, even if you have a pile of gold you'll leave empty-handed. Our author says, "Even if you accumulate a mountain of gold, can you buy off impermanence?" Truly this is a golden bell, a drum of truth, to wake everyone up.

[2]

Though human life has a limit of a hundred years, the length of life, and whether it will be difficult or smooth, cannot be known beforehand. Yesterday riding a horse through town, today a sleeping corpse in a coffin: family and wealth cast off, they are not your own possessions; with evil deeds coming on, you cannot fool yourself. If you come upon the great elixir without even looking for it, having come upon it, you are a fool if you do not refine it.

Worldly people compete and struggle for fame and profit, not resting day or night. They assume their lives will never end, and they will be able to go on forever enjoying happiness. How can they realize that no one can know beforehand how long they will live, whether their lives will be difficult or easy, or whether their lives will be filled with gain or loss. Do not say people rarely live to be a hundred years old—even if they do, they still cannot escape the grave. We frequently see people who do not take life or death seriously; but after all there are countless numbers of people who die horrible and violent deaths even as they walk along the road, as they talk and laugh. While your eyes are open, your family and goods are yours, but when your eyes close forever everything is one void. You do not take anything at all along with you when you go; only the demons of your misdeeds come back to you for a thousand years. It is better to see through worldly affairs as soon as possible, and hasten to call on enlightened teachers, whereby to seek the great elixir. If your potential and circumstances are meet, and you do find the great elixir, this is very fortunate, a great basis; set right about refining it with the best of your power, and you can leave death and enter life, thereby comprehending impermanence. If you do not willingly and straightforwardly cultivate it, you are ruining yourself and throwing yourself away; such fools are on a par with those who cannot see through worldly things—after all they will die; then what is the value of knowledge?

[3]

If you are going to study immortality, you should study celestial immortality; only the gold elixir is worthwhile. When the two things join, sense and essence merge; when the five elements are complete, the tiger and dragon intertwine. Starting with heaven-earth and earth-earth as go-betweens, finally they have husband and wife conjoin happily. Just wait for the achievement to be completed to pay court to the north palace gate; in the light of ninefold mist you ride a flying phoenix.

The first two sections told people to see through things of the world and hasten to seek the great elixir whereby to shed birth and death. The way to shed birth and death is the way of learning immortality. But there are numerous classes of immortals. Those who comprehend essence and project the yin soul are ghost immortals. Those who understand life and keep their bodies in the world are earthly immortals. Those who understand both essence and life, who have bodies outside their bodies, who are both physically and mentally sublimated and who join the Tao and merge with reality, are celestial immortals. Though the spirit of ghosts is the yin soul and can exit and enter at will, still since the abode is not permanent they still have the affliction of abandoning one body and entering another. Though earthly immortals keep their bodies in the world, still they cannot free the spiritual body and still have the burden of the illusory body relying on things. Of these two, one falls into having death, one falls into having birth—both are equally unable to completely shed birth and death. Only celestial immortals shed the illusory body and achieve the spiritual body; they go beyond creation, and have no birth or death. Able to shed birth and death, their life span is equal to heaven, never decaying.

If students want to shed birth and death, they should learn celestial immortality; if they want to learn celestial immortality, they cannot do so but by the great science of gold elixir. Gold is something incorruptible; elixir is a symbol for blending without hindrance. Incorruptible, freely blending, the undifferentiated one energy is like the measureless empty sphere of heaven, enclosing everything, invulnerable to anything. Therefore after the way is accomplished, one is called a celestial immortal; because of being forever incorruptible, this is also called a gold immortal; because of appearing and disappearing unfathomably, this is also called a spirit immortal. In reality, gold immortals and spirit immortals are all celestial immortals. If you want to learn celestial immortality, there is no method of doing so save the science of the gold elixir.

This gold elixir is the innate knowledge and innate capacity received by humans from heaven—it is completely good, with nothing bad in it; the completely perfect spiritual faculty, it is formed of a coagulation of primordial positive energy. Therein are included yin and yang, therein are stored the five elements: that is, there is the energy but not the substance—it cannot be compared to the conditioned corporeal polluted matter of an individual body. If it is passed through yin convergence and yang fire and refined to perfection, it becomes eternally incorruptible—this is called the great restored elixir of gold liquid through sevenfold reversion and ninefold restoration.

Gold elixir is another name for the unfragmented original essence; there is no gold elixir besides the original essence. This elixir is inherent in everyone, not more in sages or less in ordinary people. It is the seed of immortals and enlightened ones, the root of saints and sages. It is only that as long as it has not been put through fire and refined, when the positive culminates it must turn to negative, when waxing culminates it must wane, and it falls into the temporal: intellectual knowledge develops and private desires get mixed in; temperament emerges and the natural good dims, innate knowledge and innate capacity both lose their innocence, and there is no more body of pristine purity.

Therefore ancient sages set up the method of reversion and restoration of gold elixir, just to have people return home and recognize their ancestor, to revert to what is fundamentally inherent. Why is it called reversion and restoration? Reversion means the self comes back after it has gone; restoration means the self is regained after it has been lost.

When the spiritual root of the fundamental essence is obscured, it is because yin and yang are not in harmony and the five elements harm each other. If yin and yang are united and the five elements are assembled, the former completeness is regained.

As for the "two things" mentioned in the text, one is hard, one soft, one firm, one submissive, one real knowledge, one conscious knowledge, one true sense, one conscious essence. Real knowledge is included in the mind of Tao, and controls hardness and firmness; it emerges as true sense. Conscious knowledge hides in the human mind, and controls softness and submission; it is receptive as conscious essence. When real knowledge and conscious knowledge separate, one is firm when one shouldn't be firm, and submits to what one shouldn't submit to: hardness and softness lose their proper measure, and true sense and conscious essence turn into false feeling and false nature. When real knowledge and conscious knowledge are conjoined one is firm where one should be firm and submits to what one should submit to; hardness and softness are properly timed, and false feeling and false nature turn into true sense and true essence. Is it not clear when the author here says, "When the two things join, sense and essence merge"?

As for the "five elements," they are the five energies of metal, wood, water, fire, and earth. In the primordial state, these five energies constitute the five bases—basic essence, basic sense, basic vitality, basic spirit, and basic energy. In the conditioned state, they constitute five things—the wandering higher soul, the ghostlike lower soul, the earthly vitality, the discriminating mind, and the errant intent. The five bases contain the five virtues of benevolence, justice, courtesy, knowledge, and truthfulness; the five things contain the five thieves, which are joy, anger, sadness, happiness, and lust. When the five elements are complete, the primordial and the temporal are conjoined, and the five bases control the five things. The "dragon" is yang; it commands the life-impulse. It belongs to the sphere of "wood" in the eastern direction. In humans, it is the essence. The "tiger" is yin; it commands the death-impulse. It belongs to the sphere of metal, in the western direction. In humans it is sense. When the five elements are not in harmony, their natures become isolated; the five bases turn into the five things, and the five virtues change into the five thieves; the dragon remains in the east and the tiger in the west, essence is disturbed and sense is awry, thus becoming temperament and errant feeling, so that the energy of death saps the energy of life.

When the five elements are complete and whole, they all return to one nature; the five things turn into the five bases, the five thieves change into the five virtues. The dragon coils, the tiger sits, essence is stabilized and feelings are forgotten, thus constituting true sense and real essence; so the energy of death becomes the energy of life.

The path of spiritual alchemy is no more than harmonizing hard and soft, causing firmness and submissiveness to balance each other and essence and sense to unite with each other. When essence and sense unite, yin and yang join and the five elements are complete;

this is the primordial noumenon of heaven. It is wholly good, with no evil, the basic phenomena of innate knowledge and capacity—hence the gold elixir is restored.

But after the primordial original basis is lost and scattered, essence goes east while feeling goes west, and hard and soft do not interact. If there is no harmonizing substance to convey communication, they will be cut off from each other and not know each other at all. The harmonizing substances are the two earths, the heaven-earth and the earth-earth.

The heaven-earth is in charge of movement, and is in the domain of yang; the earth-earth is in charge of stillness, and is in the province of yin. That which is quiescent and unmoving is earth-earth; that which is sensitive and effective is heaven-earth. Among the five virtues, the two earths are real truthfulness. When real truthfulness is in the center, essence is stable; when the function of true stability is externalized, sense is harmonious. When essence is stable and sense harmonious, essence and sense return to the root, like husband and wife in blissful embrace. Benevolence, justice, courtesy, and knowledge return to one truthfulness; essence and sense, vitality and spirit, join in one energy. Heaven, earth, and humanity meet, the five energies go back to the basis, return to the origin and revert to the fundamental, and the gold elixir congeals. One name for this is the spiritual embryo.

Then go on to advanced cultivation, entering from doing into nondoing, nurturing it warmly for ten months, making it solid and complete, firmly sealed. Take out the excess of firm sense, augment the insufficiency of submissive essence. Using the natural true fire, beginning in the morning, flowing on unceasingly at night, burn away the conditioned mundane energy. Producing substance from no substance, going from subtle to apparent, when the energy is full and the spirit complete, with a peal of thunder you shed the shell, and have a body outside the body. Then the accomplishment is achieved, and you go to the celestial court, the "North Palace," riding on a phoenix, flying aloft in broad daylight, becoming a pure celestial immortal. Wouldn't that be pleasant? The original true essence is called the gold elixir; with the physical elements as the furnace, it is forged into a ball. Those who realize this ascend to the ranks of sages right away; those who do not know it are sunk for myriad eons. How can those with will not work on this?

[4]

This method is the sublime and real of the real. It all depends on oneself alone, apart from others. One knows inversion oneself, starting from fire and water. Who discerns floating and sinking, establishes host and guest? In the gold crucible, if you want to keep the mercury within cinnabar, in the jade pond first send down the silver within water. The spiritual work operating the firing does not take a whole day before it brings out the orb of the sun in the deep pool.

The foregoing section said that cultivating the gold elixir requires that essence and sense be joined into one, and the five elements all be complete; only then can it be accomplished. However, while the medicinal substances are easy to know, the firing process is most difficult.

The firing process is the process of the method of cultivation and refinement. Master Lu said that those of superior virtue make their bodies complete by means of the Tao, this being because their pure yang is not yet broken, while those of lesser virtue extend their lives by means of techniques, because water and fire have already formed. In general, those of lesser virtue need artificial methods.

Method means technique: without method, without technique, one cannot return to the basis and revert to the origin; when the life-foundation is unstable, the great Tao is difficult to achieve. Therefore the author says here, "This method is the sublime and real of the real. It all depends on oneself alone, apart from others." The method called the real and sublime is an utterly real and utterly sublime method. As the method leads to the real, one can appropriate yin and yang and take over creation, turning enlivening and killing around, reverse the working of energy. As the method leads to the sublime, even spirits and ghosts cannot fathom it, divination cannot read it. In the primordial state, nature does not differ from it; in the temporal state, it obeys the times of nature. So it is the way to become a sage; it is impenetrable by the minor methods of all auxiliary techniques.

Wherein lies the marvel of the real method of refinement? The marvel is in inversion alone. Inversion means inversion of yin and yang and reversal of creation. As for fire and water, *fire* ☰ is male outside and female inside; the female inside is true yin, which in people is conscious knowledge concealed within the human mind. When the human mind stirs, conscious knowledge flies, like the rising of flames of fire. *Water* ☵ is dark outside and light inside; the light inside is true yang, which in people is real knowledge, inherent in the mind of Tao. When the mind of Tao is obscured, real knowledge is obscured, like water flowing downward.

By inverting these, we produce the mind of Tao and stabilize the human mind. When the mind of Tao emerges, real knowledge is strong and firm, and the pure and whole water rises. When the human mind is stabilized, conscious knowledge is flexible and adaptive, and the rising, drying fire descends. When water rises and fire descends, they equalize each other.

Conscious knowledge is essence; essence is in the province of wood: the essence of wood is soft, and it easily floats up. Real knowledge is sense; sense is in the province of metal: the sense of metal is hard, and it easily sinks down. Conscious knowledge floating up and acting in affairs is the "host"; there is artificiality within the real. Real knowledge sinking and not being manifest is the "guest"; the artificial overcomes its reality. This is the usual course. To "establish host and guest" is to make the sense of real knowledge the host, causing that which sinks to float up, and to make the essence of conscious knowledge the guest, causing that which floats up to sink down. With host and guest inverted, metal and wood join.

When fire and water mix, and metal and wood join, the mind of Tao is strong, and the human mind submits to it. Real knowledge and conscious knowledge are joined into one, essence and sense commingle. How could the gold elixir then not crystallize?

However, this real, sublime method is not material and not void; it is done unbeknownst to others, where only one can know oneself. That is why the text says, "One knows oneself," and it also says "Who discerns?" People do not discern it—you know it yourself. That snatching of potential is invisible and unknowable to anyone.

In this path, there is before and after, there is intensity and relaxation; if you do not know the subtle function of before and after, intensity and relaxation, even if you can recognize the medicinal substances inversion will be impossible to effect and host and guest will not be determined. Therefore the text follows right up with "In the gold crucible, if you want to keep the mercury within cinnabar, in the jade pond firs send down the silver within water." Here, "gold" is something hard, "jade" is something soft; the "crucible" is something for refining the elixir, the "pond" is something for nourishing the fire. The gold crucible and jade pond symbolize the path of cultivation of reality; hardness and softness is its body.

The human mind belongs to *fire* ☲, which is based on the body of *heaven* ☰. This is the gold crucible, containing the fire of *earth* in the second place (— —) as conscious knowledge; this is that in which the softness and adaptability of *earth* ☷ is balanced in the center—that is, the original innate capacity. The human mind is originally empty and clear, its immaterial spirit unclouded: because it is mixed with conditioned discriminating consciousness, awareness is used to produce illusion; perceiving objects, it arouses dust, raising waves along with the wind, without a moment's rest, like the mercury within cinnabar, which flies when it meets fire and is most difficult to keep. This is what the *Ts'an T'ung Ch'i* refers to when it says, "The bead flowing in the sun always tries to leave the person."

The mind of Tao belongs to *water* ☵, which is based on the body of *earth* ☷. This is the jade pond, containing the water of celestial unity (———) as real knowledge; this is that in which the hardness and firmness of *heaven* ☰ is balanced in the center—that is, the original innate knowledge. Because of falling into the temporal state, working with conditioned energy, the true energy recedes, yang falls into yin, the real is covered by the artificial, one sinks in the ocean of desire, and innate knowledge is obscured, like silver in water, virtually nonexistent, barely existent. Silver is metal; silver in water is the metal concealed in water. This metal primordially is the innate knowledge of the original essence; in the temporal state it is the real knowledge of the mind of Tao. By that real knowledge one reaches strength and health, so it is represented metaphorically as true lead. By that real knowledge one becomes immortal and attains the Tao, so it is represented metaphorically as true seed.

Sages since antiquity have all comprehended essence and life by gathering these same medicines. Though the conscious knowledge of the human mind is easily moved, if you get the real knowledge of the mind of Tao to control it, the consciousness will return to reality and will not fly off. Instability is due to the unsettledness of the consciousness of the human mind, which in turn is due to lack of the mind of Tao. If you want to retain the conscious knowledge of the human mind, you must first set down this real knowledge of the mind of Tao. Where there is the true seed of real knowledge, there is inner autonomy which is unmoved by contaminated energies; then the conscious knowledge of the human mind naturally stabilizes and does not fragment.

The mind of Tao is used to control the human mind, the human mind is made to follow the mind of Tao; real knowledge governs conscious knowledge, conscious knowledge nurtures real knowledge. Hard and soft balance each other, firm and submissive become as one, essence and sense conjoin; within a short time they crystallize into a single round, luminous jewel, its spiritual light shining brightly, invulnerable to any aberrant energies. Therefore the treatise says, "The spiritual work operating the firing does not take a whole day before it brings out the orb of the sun in the deep pool." The spiritual work is the silent operation of the light of the spirit being careful when alone; the fire is the harmonious energy of real knowledge and conscious knowledge, hard and soft, merging into one. Operating the firing means being careful and wary about the unperceived, operating this real knowledge and conscious knowledge so the hard and soft unite, not letting any garbage stay in the mind. This fire of spiritual work is like setting up a pole and seeing its shadow, shouting into a valley conveying one's voice; if you do it straightforwardly without reservations, it won't take all day before you can restore the positive from within the negative, like the sun emerging in a deep pond, negative energy receding of itself.

The essential point in this section is the words "if you want to keep" and "first send down." Therein is the meaning of "first developing control over the person, duty not extending to a guest"—if you get the meaning of this, then inverting yin and yang and uniting the four forms is as easy as turning your hand over. This is the form of the method of the outer elixir. "Outer elixir" is another name for the restored elixir. Because it is gone and comes back, is lost and restored, it is called the outer elixir and also called the restored elixir. After the elixir has been restored, it then is the inner elixir; this is the distinction between the inner and outer elixir.

[5]

The tiger leaps, the dragon soars, the wind and waves are rough; in the correct position in the center is produced the mysterious jewel.

Fruit grows on the branches, ripe at the end of the season; how can the child in the belly be any different? The source of north and south overturns the trigram signs; the firing process of morning and evening joins the pivot of heaven. You should know the great hermit is concealed in the city; what is the necessity of keeping to tranquil solitude deep in the mountains?

The preceding section spoke of the matter of restored elixir; this one speaks of the way of the great elixir. The way of the great elixir is the work of one time. This one time joins the qualities of heaven and earth, joins the light of sun and moon, joins the order of the four seasons. It is hard to find and easy to mistake. If there is any carelessness, the energy of primordial true unity is lost. The primordial truly unified energy is the restored elixir; it is formed by the combination of hard and soft energies based on the restored elixir, so it is called the truly unified energy. It is not that there is a truly unified energy apart from the restored elixir.

When the restored elixir is obtained, the mind of Tao is firm and strong, and the human mind is soft and docile; real knowledge and conscious knowledge merge into one, round and bright. This is the innate knowledge and innate ability, tranquil and unperturbed, sensitive and effective, the property of the original self. This property is called the true lead because of its essential firmness; it is also called the male tiger because of the robustness of its energy. The true lead, or male tiger, is one single flowing energy, all good, with no evil; it is simply preservation of the natural reality of the innate knowledge and capacity. Once you have managed to recover this natural reality, you need to return this natural reality to where the five elements do not reach, before your parents gave birth to you; only then can it be an everlasting incorruptible natural reality.

So when natural reality has been recovered, nurture it, guarding it carefully and storing it securely. Become utterly empty, quiet, and sincerely intent; when filled with positive energy, from ultimate stillness you again go into motion, and the spiritual sprouts emerge.

At this time, the positive light emerges from its lair, like the robustness of the tiger, its momentum unstoppable: quickly meet it with the point of fire of clear consciousness in the true essence. The fire of clear consciousness is called the female dragon. "The tiger leaps, the dragon soars" is a representation of the gathering of yin and yang. As for "wind and waves are rough," when the tiger emerges from its cave wind rises, and when the dragon emerges from its pool waves arise. This means the contact of yin and yang: dragon and tiger mate, essence and sense merge, joining into one, entering the center.

The primordial energy comes from nothingness and congeals into a bead of jewel: "The spiritual embryo assumes form." The spiritual embryo is the "valley spirit," the valley spirit is the spirit of mystery and femaleness merging into one. The mystery of yang is the tiger, sense; the femaleness of yin is the dragon, essence. When essence and sense join, the spiritual embryo forms; when the mysterious female stands, the valley spirit is born. When you get to this state, doing is ended and nondoing appears; it is no longer necessary to strive—leave it to nature. It is like fruit growing on the branches—eventually they will ripen; the child in the belly will one day be born.

But though the consolidation of the spiritual embryo calls for nondoing, there is still the work of preventing danger and being wary of peril, which one must know.

As for "The source of north and south overturns the trigram signs," south is fire, and north is water: with the spiritual embryo consolidated, a harmonious energy permeates; water and fire return to the source, naturally heating and boiling together. Let it proceed naturally; one must successfully avoid both inattentiveness and forcing the issue.

As for "the firing process morning and evening joins the pivot of heaven," morning is the beginning of a day, when the yang energy works; evening is the beginning of a night, when the yin energy works: the pivot of heaven is the incipience of energy, yin and yang. When yang is appropriate, use yang; when yin is appropriate, use yin: the waxing and waning of the firing accords with the potentials of morning and evening. This is the accomplishment of work by day and cautious by night.

Do not be inattentive, yet do not force; working by day and cautious at night, nurture it warmly for ten months, exchange the temporal trigrams, free the primordial spiritual body. Your life depends on yourself, not on heaven. This is the Tao. It is cultivated among humanity, done in the marketplace. The great function of great potential, the realistic work of true action, is not the study of vacant, inactive quiescence; that is why it says, "You should know the great hermit is concealed in the city; what is the necessity of keeping to tranquil solitude deep in the mountains?"

[6]

Everyone originally has the herb of long life: It's just that they don't understand it, and throw it away in vain. When the sweet dew descends, heaven and earth join; where the yellow sprouts grow, water and fire mix. A frog in a well would say there is no dragon's den; how could a quail in a cage know there is a phoenix nest? When the elixir is fully developed, naturally gold fills the room; what is the need to look for herbs and practice burning reeds?

The preceding three sections explain the restored elixir, the great elixir, the medicinal substances, and the firing process. However, it may happen that students may get the false idea that the gold elixir is made by burning and forging ordinary substances; therefore this section follows up quickly with a warning about this.

The gold elixir is the fundamental essence of innate knowledge and innate capacity inherent in people. This essence is intrinsically complete in everyone; it is not more in sages or less in ordinary people. It is not obtained from another, it is inherent in oneself. If you accord with it, you ascend directly into the realm of sages; essence is stabilized, life is solidified, never to disintegrate. This fundamental essence of innate knowledge and innate capacity is the great elixir of long life.

Those who are deluded do not investigate the true principles of sages, do not consider the basis of essence and life; they abandon what is near and seek afar, reject the true and accept the false. Thus they waste their lives, growing old without fulfillment, foolishly throwing themselves away. Is this not to be pitied and lamented?

The firm quality of innate knowledge inherent in people is received from heaven—this is "heaven." The original adaptable quality of innate capacity is received from earth—this is "earth." The original spirit of open awareness without obscurity is the spiritual essence, which is a product of the energy of earth—this is "fire." The original pure, unadulterated vitality is true sense, which is a product of the energy of heaven—this is "water." If people can be both firm and adaptable at once, then the heaven and earth within themselves join. This is like sweet dew descending and washing the heart; vexations are shed all at once. If people can avoid dissipating their vitality and spirit, then the water and fire in themselves will mix, and the original energy will be restored.

The descent of sweet dew is purity of heart; the growth of the yellow sprouts is tranquility of mind. The unique spiritual true essence of innate knowledge and innate capacity hangs in space, silent, unstirring; sensing, it accomplishes effects. Ever responsive, it is ever tranquil: creation cannot move it, things cannot cramp it. One's destiny depends on oneself, not on heaven; the path of long life is herein.

How can a frog in a well know of the existence of this dragon cave? How can a quail in a cage know of the existence of this phoenix nest? Those who hear tell of medicinal substances and firing and imagine it refers to some chemical process do all kinds of strange things—they still do not know that when the cultivation of the great elixir is complete, gold and jade fill the room, preserving life, making the body sound, riches beyond compare. How can any material things be worthy of attachment?

[7]

If you want to know the location of the river source which produces the herb, it is just in the southwest, its original homeland. When lead meets the arising of the younger water, you should gather quickly; when metal comes to the passing of the middle of the lunar month, it won't do to taste. Send it back to the earthen pot and seal it tightly; next put in flowing pearl, to combine with it. For the weight of the medicine to be one pound requires two times eight; adjust the firing process harmoniously, relying on yin and yang.

The preceding section says everyone has the herb or medicine of immortality, but it still doesn't say where and when this herb grows; therefore this section reveals the facts about the growth of the herb, to enable students to work on it according to the time, and be careful with the firing process.

The southwest is the direction of *earth* ☷; it is the realm where the new moon returns, where yin at its extreme gives birth to yang. In people, this is the time of beginning movement when stillness has reached its extreme. This movement from the extreme of stillness is precisely when the great medicine appears. However, this movement is not the stirring of emotions at external influences, and it is not the stirring of thoughts in the mind. It is the movement of the innate knowledge of the natural mind, the movement of the real knowledge of the mind of Tao.

This innate knowledge of the natural mind and real knowledge of the mind of Tao are represented as medicinal substances because they are able to transcend the ordinary and enter into the spiritual, to rise from death and return to life. Because at the time of extreme stillness, when all entanglements have ceased, the innate knowledge of the natural mind and the real knowledge of the mind of Tao have a point of brilliance which reveals a glimpse of them, this is represented as the place where the medicine or "herb" is produced. Because the innate knowledge of the natural mind and real knowledge of the mind of Tao are white within black, coming from within empty nothingness, movement born from stillness, like a river having its source in a spring, this is represented as the river source where the herb is produced.

This herb, in the primordial state, is the innate knowledge of the natural mind; in the temporal state, it is the real knowledge of the mind of Tao. The mind of Tao is a reflection of the natural mind, real knowledge is a reflection of innate knowledge. Because the natural mind falls into the temporal state, it cannot abide forever; sometimes it appears, and is called by another name, the mind of Tao. Because innate knowledge sinks into the sea of desire, its radiant energy is obscured; on the occasions when it is not obscured, it is called by another name, real knowledge. After you have reached the point of reversion and restoration, the mind of Tao is as before the natural mind, and real knowledge is as before innate knowledge.

Sometimes appearing and sometimes not being obscured is the homeland of the mind of Tao and its real knowledge. That is to say, in this place of sometimes appearing and sometimes not being obscured there is a point of primordial, real, unified living potential subsisting there. If you use this point of living potential and cultivate it in opposition to the usual course of conditioning and deterioration, it shouldn't be hard to return to the natural mind and its innate knowledge by way of the mind of Tao and its real knowledge.

But for the return not to be difficult, it is necessary to know clearly where the source of the river is, movement coming from the extreme of stillness. Lao Tzu said, "Effect emptiness to the extreme, guard stillness carefully; as myriad things act in concert, I thereby watch the return." The *I Ching* says, "Repeating the path, coming back in seven days." Both of these point to this river source where the mind of Tao and its real knowledge arise.

Once you know the river source where the medicine is produced, you need to understand the timing for practical application. The subtle application of cultivation of the elixir is just a matter of taking the uniform taste of the mind of Tao as the matrix of the elixir. Because the mind of Tao is firm and strong, containing within it the sense of real knowledge, it is represented as true lead. Within lead there is silver; it is black outside, white inside: within the mind of Tao there is real knowledge, which is dark outside and light inside. So the immortals and real people have all likened the mind of Tao and real knowledge to elixir and lead; they were unwilling to speak explicitly, being cautious lest the wrong people misappropriate it.

When the real knowledge of the mind of Tao is covered and buried by emotion and desire and has sunken deeply, it cannot get itself out; once you know the river source, you can gradually collect it and restore it. The method of restoration is to be sought while in the midst of emotion and desire. Real knowledge is the product of heaven, pure clear yang "water," which is the "elder water." Emotional desire is the product of earth, polluted yin "water," which is the "younger water." The elder water is hidden within the younger water; but for the rising of younger water, the elder water would not appear, and the true lead would not be manifest. "When lead meets the arising of the younger water" is the mixing of the two energies, yin and yang, when the younger water has just arisen but is not yet used, the elder water has not yet dispersed and real knowledge is not yet obscured: you must gather it quickly and return it to the "crucible," which is like a womb in suspension—then emotional desire will not be activated and will disappear of itself.

As for "When metal comes to the passing of the middle of the lunar month," once you have gotten real knowledge to come back, you use this point of true sense of real knowledge, increase and expand it, progressing to the correct balance of firm strength, the pure unadulterated vitality. This is light refining white metal out of lead, its color fully bright and clear. When you reach this stage, innate knowledge and innate capacity are clear and unobscured, able to deal with things, whether indirectly or directly, acting or not acting, at will, going along freely, everywhere being the Tao. This is like the bright moon in the sky, lighting up the world to view, penetrating the darkness. One can then cease to employ effort involving increase and decrease, give up doing and enter nondoing.

If you do not know the firing process, before fulfillment of the preparations is complete fullness will wane, light will return to darkness, like after the middle of the lunar month, when yin arises within yang. Real knowledge will be damaged, the true will go into obscurity and the false will come. What will be there is the pollution of temporal conditioning—it is not worth tasting. Therefore, when real knowledge has returned to completeness, you must quickly send it into the "earth pot" in the center and seal it up tightly, not letting even a little of it leak out. Then you take the flowing pearl of open awareness in the fundamental essence and mix it in, using yin to balance yang, using emptiness to nourish substantiality. Guarding against danger, wary of perils, aim for attaining unity of firmness and flexibility, balance of yin and yang, with twice eight ("eight ounces each"), no excess or lack, progressing until the slag is removed and the gold is pure, after there is not so much as a speck of temperament any more.

However, if you want a full measure of the two eights, it all depends on adjusting the firing process harmoniously, understanding maturity and immaturity, knowing to be content with sufficiency, distinguishing what bodes well and what bodes ill, discerning when to hurry and when to relax. When it is time to advance yang, then advance yang; when it is time to operate yin, then operate yin. Then great and small are unharmed, both countries are sound. The primordial real whole energy will naturally come forth from nothingness, will crystallize and not disperse, and the spiritual embryo will take on form.

Adjusting the firing is properly harmonized by firmness and flexibility not becoming stationary. When "the weight of the medicine is one pound," firmness and flexibility both wind up in correct balance, the two eights balance each other; there is yang in yin, there is yin in yang—yin and yang merge, firmness and flexibility sublimate. Tranquil, unstirring, yet sensitive and effective; sensitive and effective, yet tranquil and unstirring—it is something eternally imperishable.

The moon waxing to fullness is a secret passed on by word of mouth; the subtlety of the time reaching midnight is transmitted by mind. The medicinal substances are hard to know, and the firing process is not easy to understand. Students should hasten to find a genuine teacher.

This section includes within it the medicinal substances, the firing process, the subtle application of the restored elixir; it is the most critical of the sixteen sections in the first part, and should be studied carefully, without passing over a single word lightly. If you actually have some understanding, go to a genuine teacher for affirmation; you know myriad things by way of a single statement.

[8]

Refining the three yellows and four spirits, if you look for herbs, it is not real anymore. Yin and yang, finding their counterparts, return to intercourse; when the two eights match, they naturally join closely. The sun in the pool is scarlet, shades vanish; the moon on the mountain white, the herb sprouts are new. If people of the time want to know the true lead and mercury, it is not ordinary cinnabar and quicksilver.

The preceding section says that the gold elixir can only be produced by the combination of two medicines, true lead and true mercury; however, people might get the wrong idea that the gold elixir is a material substance made by refinement with fire, so this section follows up quickly with the saying, "Refining the three yellows and four spirits, if you seek herbs, it is not real anymore." The three yellows are sulfur and sulfur compounds; the four spirits are cinnabar, quicksilver, lead, and saltpeter. The three yellows and four spirits are not of a kind with us, so how can they extend our lives? How can they enable us to understand our essence? If they do not function to extend life and understand essence, they are useless, not the real path.

The *Triple Analogue* says, "It is easy to work with what is of the same kind, hard to work with what is not of the same kind." People are born as receivers of the twin energies of yin and yang of heaven and earth, so they have the yin and yang energies in their bodies. As for the qualities of yin and yang, yang is firm and yin is yielding; the quality of firmness governs life, the quality of yielding governs essence. This firmness of yang and yielding of yin is the wellspring of essence and life.

As for the "counterparts" mentioned in this section, yang has yin as its counterpart, yin has yang as its counterpart; so firmness and yielding respond to each other, like a husband and wife suddenly meeting after a long separation, never failing to have intercourse.

As for "two eights," yang within yin is true yang, sound strength in correct balance; yin within yang is true yin, flexible adaptability in correct balance: firmness and flexibility both return to correct balance, yin and yang match each other, without partiality. Naturally they join intimately and merge into one energy, solidifying so that it does not dissolve.

When yin and yang have their counterparts in each other and balance each other, the primordial is restored within the temporal. The mind of Tao is firm, strong and sound, the human mind is yielding, flexible and adaptable. Real knowledge and conscious knowledge combine, and the original spiritual root of innate knowledge and innate capacity appear from within nothingness, like the scarlet sun at the bottom of a pool rising up, shades naturally disappearing, like the crescent moon over the mountain hanging on high, the medicinal sprouts fresh and new. This is because the sane energy arises and aberrant energy naturally recedes, the real returns and the false dissolves.

The scarlet of the sun in the pond and the white of the moon over the mountain both depict the emergence of true yang and the reappearance of the natural mind. Then knowledge and capacity are both innocent—this is called the gold elixir. This gold elixir is the true yin and true yang inherent in oneself, formed by the combination of the firm and the flexible. This is the true treasure which completes and perfects essence and life—it is not made by firing cinnabar and quicksilver.

[9]

The substance of the yin-vitality within yang is not firm; if you only cultivate one thing, it will result in increasing weakness. Belaboring the body and concern with reflections is not the path; swallowing air and ingesting fog is crazy. Everyone idly seeks the conquering of lead and mercury; when will they get to see the dragon and tiger come down? I urge you to find out the place where your body was born; going back to the basis, returning to the origin, this is the production of the medicine.

The preceding section says that the medicinal substances of the gold elixir are not external chemicals or herbs, that those who cultivate the Tao must do it in their own bodies. What they still don't know is that after the primordial true yang has slipped away, what people have in their bodies is only the yin vitality within yang. The yin vitality is not only sexual fluid; all bodily fluids and also air are yin vitality. Their substance is not firm; they are there as long as the body subsists, they disappear when the body dies. Their existence or nonexistence depends on the phantasmic body: if you cultivate this one thing, the yin vitality within yang, and want to preserve the body thereby, you will feel increasingly weak, and will ultimately not succeed. Those in the world who belabor their bodies, concerned with reflections, swallow air and ingest fog, and do all sorts of other such practices, either cultivate yin vitality or replenish the yin vitality, are off the right track; the more they work, the further off they will become. How can they conquer the true lead and true mercury and return them to one energy, how can they chase the true dragon and true tiger and join them into one?

The path of the gold elixir is the path of giving life to the body; the path of giving life to the body is the path of uniting yin and yang. When yin and yang unite, there is living potential therein. The way of giving life to humans uses the ordinary father and mother to give birth to the phantasmic body; the way of giving life to immortals uses the spiritual father and mother to give birth to the real body. The spiritual father is the sound strong real knowledge; the spiritual mother is the flexible adaptable conscious knowledge. Giving birth to humans and giving birth to immortals both are in the realm of yin and yang, but there is a distinction between the spiritual and the mundane, between going in reverse and going along with the usual course. If people thoroughly investigate the principle of giving birth to the body, and achieve great understanding and great penetration, and know clearly how the father and mother can meet, how they can mate, how conception takes place, how gestation takes place, how the development of the fetus takes place, how birth is accomplished, how nursing is done, how action is accomplished, and how growth and maturation are accomplished, then the whole process of practice of the Tao will be clear, and one can go straight ahead, return to the origin, arise from death and restore life, preserve life and make the body complete, becoming master of the great medicine. After all, the great way of cultivating reality is just this principle of giving birth to the body; there is nothing else to it. How can those who take the side doors, cultivating only one thing, yin alone or yang alone, sticking to emptiness or clinging to forms, know this exists?

[10]

Take a good hold on the true lead, and seek attentively; do not let yourself pass the time taking it easy. Just use the earthly soul to capture the red mercury; naturally there will be the heavenly soul to govern the water metal. It could be said that when the path is lofty the dragon and tiger submit; one might say that when the virtue is great ghosts and sprites are respectful. Once you know life is eternal, equal to heaven and earth, vexations have no way to rise in the mind anymore.

The preceding section teaches people to find out where the body is born and return to the origin. But to go back to the root and return to the origin requires knowledge of the uniform flavored great medicine of true lead. When you know the true lead, you know the one, and myriad tasks are finished—everything else is easy.

The true lead is nothing else but the aforementioned real knowledge of the mind of Tao. Real knowledge is also called the true seed. If you do not know the true seed, there is no basis for practicing the Tao, and whatever you do will be a waste of effort. That is why it says, "Take a good hold on the true lead and seek attentively."

The words "Seek attentively" contain the directed work of investigating principles, examining things to bring about knowledge. If students want to practice the great Tao, nothing is better than to first investigate true principles. The approach to practice follows naturally. If you do not investigate and penetrate, you beg in vain for the celestial jewel—this has no reality or truth to it, and is only wasting time.

The "earthly soul" and the "water metal" are yang within yin, both symbols of real knowledge. The "heavenly soul" and "red mercury" are yin within yang, both symbols of conscious knowledge. "Just use the earthly soul to capture the red mercury" means to control conscious knowledge by real knowledge. "Naturally there will be the heavenly soul to govern the water metal" means to nurture real knowledge by conscious knowledge.

Real knowledge is "firm," in the province of yang, and is the "husband." Conscious knowledge is "flexible," in the province of yin, and is the "wife." The husband governs the wife, the wife obeys the husband; the wife obeys the husband, the husband loves the wife. When husband and wife have each other, the living potential always exists. Real knowledge and conscious knowledge unite, firmness and flexibility return to the center, changing into innate knowledge and innate capacity, tranquil and unstirring, yet sensitive and effective. The spiritual embryo then takes on form; when you reach this stage, the path is lofty and dragon and tiger submit; the virtue is great and ghosts and sprites are respectful. Then life is eternal, equal to heaven and earth; how can vexations arise in the mind anymore?

[11]

The yellow sprouts and white clouds are not hard to seek; those who arrive must rely on depth of virtuous practice. The four forms and five elements all depend on earth; the three bases and eight trigrams are not apart from elder water. Refined into spiritual substance, they are inscrutable to men; having dissolved all that is negative and harmful, one is invulnerable to ghosts. I wish to leave the secret among humankind, but I have not yet met a single perceptive person.

The preceding section says that when the path is lofty and virtue great, the dragon and tiger, ghosts and sprites, all become docile and obedient; that is, where there is the Tao there must be virtue, and where there is virtue there must be the Tao. The ultimate Tao is not complicated, the fire and medicine are not remote; the white clouds are right before your eyes, the yellow sprouts grow in your own home. If you are straightforward, you can obtain them at will; that's why it says they are "not hard to seek."

However, this path is to transcend the ordinary and enter sagehood, to rise from death and return to life, something rare in the world. Even though it is not hard to seek, it can only be known by those of great virtue and great practice. Therefore it says, "Those who arrive must rely on depth of virtuous practice." In effect, it is for the superior person of virtuous practice that it is not hard to seek.

The "four forms" are the four energies of metal, wood, water, and fire; add earth, and they make the five elements. The "three bases" are the basis of heaven, the basis of earth, and the basis of humankind. Also the upper basis, middle basis, and lower basis constitute three bases too. The "eight trigrams" are the yin and yang of the four forms and five elements: *heaven* ☰ is yang metal, *lake* ☱ is yin metal; *water* ☵ is yang water, *mountain* ☶ is yin water; *thunder* ☳ is yang wood, *wind* ☴ is yin wood; *fire* ☲ is yang fire, *earth* ☷ is yin fire. Although the eight trigrams are distributed among the yin and yang of the four forms, *earth* ☷ and *mountain* ☶ also contain the two earths, heaven-earth and earth-earth. *Earth* ☷ is yin earth, *mountain* ☶ is yang earth. The energies of the five elements are also therein.

In humankind, the five elements are the five bases—essence, sense, vitality, spirit, and energy; in action, they are the five virtues—benevolence, justice, courtesy, wisdom, and truthfulness. In humans, the three bases are the basic vitality, the basic energy, and the basic spirit. In humans, the eight trigrams are the firm and flexible essences of the five bases and five virtues. The four forms, three bases, and eight trigrams are all transformations of the five elements, and do not exist separately. When it says, "the four forms and five elements all depend on earth," it means that benevolence, justice, courtesy, and wisdom develop based on truthfulness. When it says "the three bases and eight trigrams are not apart from elder water," it means essence, sense, spirit, and energy are not apart from vital unity.

The "yellow sprouts" are the living potential of earth; truthfulness is in the center. The "white clouds" are the light clarity of water, vitality arriving at unity. When benevolence, justice, courtesy, and wisdom return to truthfulness, and preserve the mean, the yellow sprouts gradually grow. When essence, sense, spirit, and energy return to one, being vitality, being unified, the white clouds fly in the sky, unity of vitality keeps in the center.

Cultivate and refine this, growing in strength the longer you persevere, and the mind of Tao will always be active while the human mind will always be tranquil. Real knowledge and conscious knowledge unite, and a round and bright pearl hangs in space. Ever responsive yet ever tranquil, untrammeled by form or emptiness, you appear and disappear according to the times, unopposed by nature in the primordial state, serving the seasons of nature in the temporal state.

Unopposed even by nature, how much less by people, or by ghosts or sprites; people cannot know you, ghosts cannot attack you. This is not idle talk. This path is most simple and easy; it is quintessential, uncomplicated. Those who know it rise at once to the rank of sages, without awaiting twelve years of training. However, there are few people in the world who practice virtue, there are no real true people. Most consider the Tao far away when in fact it is near at hand. The author says, "I want to leave the secret among humankind, but I haven't met a single perceptive person yet." Is it not a pity?

[12]

Yin and yang are also equal in plants and trees; if one is lacking they do not flower. When the green leaves first unfold, yang is acting first; with the subsequent blooming of scarlet flowers, yin follows along. The ordinary course is in daily action; the true source reverses this, but who is there who knows? I inform those of you who study the Tao: If you do not know yin and yang, do not act at random.

The preceding section said virtue must be cultivated; this one says the Tao must be understood. The *I Ching* says, "One yin and one yang is called the Tao." It also says, "Heaven and earth incubate, myriad things develop; male and female join their vitality, myriad beings evolve." The path of the gold elixir operates entirely through the strength of yang and the adaptivity of yin: when yin and yang unite, they produce the elixir and prolong life; when yin and yang are at odds, they turn away from each other, causing loss of life. Take a look at things like plants and trees: "When the green leaves first unfold, yang is acting first; with the subsequent blooming of scarlet flowers, yin follows along." Yin and yang are not apart from each other; extending the analogy, we find the ordinary course of all sentient beings does not take place outside of yin and yang.

But while the ordinary course follows along, the path of immortals goes in reverse. Following along means going along with yin and yang in the ordinary course; reversing means reverse operation of yin and yang. People of the world only know the way to go along, and do not know the way of reverse operation. Therefore they pursue artificial objects and stray from the true source; when yang culminates, they shift to yin, and when yin culminates they die.

For students, the first move is to get to know both yin and yang. When you know yin and yang, you know the true source. The true source is the door of the "mysterious female." The birth of yin is herein, the birth of yang is herein too; following is herein, and reversing is herein too. When you know the eternal and return to the root, you ascend at once to the realm of the sages.

However, there is not only one kind of yin and yang. There is primordial yin and yang, and there is conditioned yin and yang. There is yin and yang within life, and there is yin and yang within essence. There is real yin and yang, and there is artificial yin and yang. There is external yin and yang, and there is internal yin and yang. It is necessary to study all these kinds of yin and yang and understand them clearly before starting the alchemical work. If you do not know the real yin and real yang, and act at random, you will turn away from the real and enter the artificial, forgetting your own essence and life.

[13]

If you do not know the inversion within the mystery, how can you know to plant a lotus in fire? Leading the white tiger, go back home and nurture it; you will produce a bright pearl round as the moon. Stay relaxed beside the alchemical furnace and watch the firing process; just settle your spirit and breath, and leave it up to nature. When all mundanity has been stripped away, the elixir is complete; leaping out of the cage of the ordinary, life is myriad years.

The preceding section tells people to recognize yin and yang; this section tells people to find out about the work. The work is the method of inverting yin and yang. If you don't know the method of inversion of yin and yang, how can you know the subtlety of planting a lotus in fire?

What is inverted? The white tiger is associated with metal, which is the sound strong energy in the middle of the palace of *heaven* ☰. This is called the mind of Tao; in action it is the sense of real knowledge. Because of mixture with temporal conditioning, doing things with the human mentality, the mind of Tao is not manifest, true sense is obscured, and deluded feelings arise. This is like the white tiger leaving one's own home and going out, running to another house and injuring people. Inversion means while in the midst of deluded feelings to restore true sense, and combine it with true essence. This is like leading the white tiger from another's house back to your own home and taking care of it.

Once true sense is restored, true essence becomes manifest; essence and sense cleave to one another, and the primordial true one energy comes from nothingness and forms a pearl like the full moon, its light shining bright throughout the world, as if in the palm of one's hand. This is what the *Ts'an T'ung Ch'i* means when it says, "When metal first comes back to essence, it can be called restored elixir." Once the restored elixir is crystallized, innate knowledge and innate capacity are nonstriving when still, spontaneous when in action, equanimous and serene on the path of balance.

The medicine is the fire, the fire is the medicine; the work of gathering is effortless. Just settle the spirit and breath, letting them be natural. Using the energy of the harmony of yin and yang in the furnace of creation, the true fire burns away the mundanity of conditioning, producing pure celestial energy. This is called the completion of the elixir; ingesting this, you become liberated and transformed, leap out of the cage of the ordinary, and live as long as heaven, never to die.

[14]

Three, five, one: It is all three words; those who understand are rare in all times. Three in the east, two in the south, together makes five; one in the north and four in the west are the same. Earth in its own abode has the production number five. When the three meet, they form an infant. The infant is one, containing true energy; in ten months the fetus is complete, and enters the spiritual foundation.

The preceding section talks about the principle of reversing yin and yang; this section talks about the work of assembling the five elements. In the beginning of human life, the natures of the inherent five elements are originally one energy which is undifferentiated. Their natures become individuated because of mixture with conditioning: metal and wood are unjoined, water and fire are unmixed, true earth is buried, false earth grows wildly, essence goes awry and life is shaken, positive energy runs out and negative energy becomes total, so it is impossible not to die.

The author here brings up the three words "three," "five," and "one" to teach people to assemble the five elements and return them to one house, restoring innate knowledge and innate capacity, the whole natural self. However, the three words "three," "five," and "one" have confused untold numbers of intrepid people, past and present. Those who have understood are few enough to count.

This "three" and "five" are the production numbers of the five elements according to the River Diagram. To the east is the third element, wood; south is two, fire: fire produces wood, so fire and wood are one, together making one five. To the west is the fourth element, metal; north is the first, water: water produces metal, so water and metal are one, together making one five. Earth in the center constitutes one five by itself.

If practitioners of the Tao can understand these three fives, and cultivate them in reverse, combining the four forms and aggregating the five elements, then essence, sense, vitality, energy, and spirit congeal; benevolence, justice, courtesy, wisdom, and truthfulness are the same energy. This is called "the three meet." In Confucianism, this is called the Great Ultimate, or the principle of heaven, or ultimate good, or perfect sincerity. In Taoism this is called the infant, or the primordial one energy, or the spiritual embryo, or the restored elixir. In Buddhism this is called complete awakening, or true emptiness, or the reality body, or the sacred relic, or the wish-fulfilling gem. There are various such names, all referring to the naturally good original essence. The path restores the innate knowledge and innate capacity of the original essence, going back to the fundamental, returning to the root: incubating and nurturing it for ten months, the energy is replete, the spirit is whole; one escapes from the ocean of misery, has a body outside the body, and enters the unborn and unperishing spiritual foundation.

[15]

If you do not know the true source, real lead, whatever you do will be in vain: Celibacy will idly cause yin and yang to be separated, fasting will futilely make your stomach empty; plants and wood, gold and silver, are all trash, clouds and mist, sun and moon, are vacuous; even breathing exercises and meditation have no resemblance to the matter of the gold elixir.

The preceding section said you only enter the spiritual foundation when you have gathered the five elements and returned them to one energy. But to aggregate the five elements requires knowledge of the primordial truly unified energy; only then can you begin. The one yang in *water* ☵ is the centrally balanced sound strong energy of *heaven* ☰, the real knowledge of the mind of Tao, represented as real lead. This is a product of celestial unity, and contains the primordial truly unified energy, which is the generative energy that produces beings. Attainment of sagehood is therein, attainment of buddhahood and immortality is therein; it is the root of sages, the seed of immortals and Buddhas, the true source of the gold elixir. This is what is referred to by the saying, "If you know that one, myriad tasks are done." If you do not know the real true lead, you have no source, no basis of cultivating the gold elixir. Then whatever practices you do—celibacy, fasting, burning plants and wood to refine gold and silver, drinking in clouds and mist, sun and moonlight, breathing exercises, meditation and visualization—either sticking to emptiness or clinging to forms, is all a waste of effort and has no connection with the matter of the gold elixir.

[16]

The words of the myriad books on immortality are all the same— the gold elixir alone is the root source. The substance is produced on the ground of the position of earth, *planted in the chamber of intercourse in the house of* heaven. *Do not think it strange that the celestial working has been leaked—it is because students are confused and ignorant.*

Because the foregoing fifteen sections have at times spoken of going along, at times of going in reverse, sometimes explain separately, sometimes explain together, sometimes indicate the medicines, sometimes indicate the firing process, distinguish true and false and set forth right and wrong, with subtle gradations, scattered without as yet being put into order, this section sums up the intent of the preceding fifteen sections, indicating to people the path of utter simplicity and ease, lest they get confused by the complexity of the matter and find it difficult to progress.

Since ancient times the immortals and real people, the alchemical texts and Taoist books, have used a thousand similes, a hundred metaphors, setting up symbols and terms, exerting their powers of description to bring to light the marrow of the Tao. Although their terminology is different, the principles are the same—all of them explain the root source of the gold elixir. This is not like the situation in later eras when the more books there were the more people got confused, each clinging to his own views, pursuing them into sidetracks. They did not know the root source of the gold elixir is only a matter of taking from *water* ☵ to fill in *fire* ☲, returning *earth* ☷ to *heaven* ☰.

"The substance is produced on the ground of *earth*" is the one yang in the center of *water* ☵. "The chamber of intercourse in the house of *heaven*" is the one yin in the center of *fire* ☲. *Water* ☵ is based on the body of *earth* ☷, therefore it is called the position of *earth*. *Fire* ☲ is based on the body of *heaven* ☰, so it is called the house of *heaven*. By *heaven* it is easy to know, by *earth* it is easy to do. *Heaven* is firm and strong, *earth* is flexible and obedient. Because of this firm strength, it is easy to know, without getting into difficulty; because of this flexible obedience, it is simple to do, without forcing. In people, easy knowing and simple doing are the original nature of the innate knowledge and capacity.

In the beginning of human life, strength and obedience are as one, firmness and flexibility are merged. Without being consciously cognizant of it, they follow the laws of God; round, luminous, clean, naked, there is only the single fundamental nature of innate knowledge and innate capacity, without any pollution. Reaching the age of sixteen, the celestial culminates, giving rise to the mundane; people become conditioned and do things with mundane energy. Reason and desire get mixed up, strength and obedience do not balance each other, firmness and flexibility lose their proper measure.

At this point the celestial is overcome by the mundane, and natural reality is obscured. This is like *heaven* mixing with *earth*; the yang in the middle of *heaven* ☰ enters the palace of *earth* ☷, so that the trigram of *earth* is filled in and becomes *water* ☵. The mundane taking the position of the celestial, intellectual knowledge gradually developing, is like *earth* mixing with *heaven*: the yin in the middle of *earth* goes into the palace of *heaven*, so the trigram of *heaven* is emptied and becomes *fire* ☲.

When natural reality is obscured, the mind of Tao is concealed and is faint. When intellectual knowledge develops, the human mentality grows and is insecure. Being faint means being virtually nonexistent, barely surviving; the celestial does not predominate over the mundane. Being insecure means producing feelings in regard to objects; the mundane predominates over the celestial.

However, though the mind of Tao is faint and the human mentality is perilous, the mind of Tao is still not entirely obliterated, and the human mentality is still not entirely prevalent. The mind of Tao is not entirely obliterated in that sometimes it may produce clarity in the midst of obscurity; this is called real knowledge. Nevertheless, it is inconsistent, now here, now gone. The human mind is not entirely predominant in that it can adapt to situations; this is called conscious knowledge. However, it uses consciousness to produce illusions.

The practice of alchemy is to restore the celestial in the midst of the mundane, to extract the real knowledge of the mind of Tao, to transmute the conscious knowledge of the human mind so that conscious knowledge returns to reality: then real knowledge is consummately conscious, the mind of Tao is sound and strong, the human mind is flexible and submissive, yin and yang commingle, hard and soft correspond, strength and obedience are balanced. When reality and consciousness do not separate, we return to the innate knowledge and innate capacity of before, the state of the creative foundation. This is called taking from *water* to fill in *fire*, and also called planting *heaven* by *earth*.

Actually, "the substance is produced on the ground of the position of *earth*, planted in the chamber of intercourse in *heaven*" means taking from *water* ☵ and filling in *fire* ☲. Taking from *water* means the yang fallen in the center of *water* comes out, and *water* ☵ becomes *earth* ☷; filling in *fire* means the yin mixed in the center of *fire* changes, and *fire* ☲ becomes *heaven* ☰.

When the bodies of *heaven* and *earth* are formed, the mysterious female is established, and the valley spirit exists; the gold elixir crystallizes, and essence and life come into our hands, not constrained by conditioning.

This is the celestial mechanism transmitted once in ten thousand eons. The immortals and real people of antiquity were unwilling to make it explicit, but our author is so kind and compassionate that in sixteen poems he reveals what the ancients did not reveal. At the end he points directly to the root source of the gold elixir; the celestial mechanism has been revealed too much. If people understand the subtle meaning herein, they will ascend directly to the realm of sages.

II. Sixty-four Verses Modeled on the Number of Signs in the I Ching

[1]

ON THE CRUCIBLE AND FURNACE (2 VERSES)

First take Heaven *and* Earth *for the crucible, next take the medicines of raven and rabbit and cook them. Once you have chased the two things back into the yellow path, how could the gold elixir not be produced?*

Heaven is strong, taking its symbol from the sky; *earth* is submissive, taking its symbol from the ground. In humans, these are the natures of firmness and flexibility. In the sun there is a raven, which is the yin within yang; among the trigrams, this is *fire* ☲. *Fire* ☲ is yang outside and yin inside; the one yin inside is true yin, which in humans is the conscious knowledge latent in the human mind. In the moon is a rabbit, which is yang within yin; among the trigrams, this is *water* ☵. *Water* is yin outside and yang inside; the one yang inside is true yang, which in humans is the real knowledge inherent in the mind of Tao.

"First take *heaven* and *earth* for the crucible" means you use firmness and flexibility for the substance of production of the elixir. "Next take the medicines of raven and rabbit and cook them" means you use real knowledge and conscious knowledge for the function of the production of the elixir. Cooking and refining real knowledge, nothing in it is not real; so firmness winds up in correct balance. Cooking and refining conscious knowledge, there is no obscurity in it; so flexibility winds up in correct balance. When firmness and flexibility have both returned to correct balance, the mind of Tao is strong and the human mind submits to it; real knowledge and conscious knowledge, though two, are unified. This is likened to chasing raven and rabbit back into the yellow path; the "yellow path" is the middle way, which is the path traveled by the sun.

The sun traverses the middle path, the moon traverses nine paths. There are two each of blue, red, white, and black paths, which are apart from the yellow path: inside and outside, together they make eight paths. When sun and moon meet, sun and moon travel in concert; adding this, altogether there are nine paths. When sun and moon converge is referred to as the two things returning to the yellow path.

When people are first born, they only have the single essence of real consciousness with innate knowledge and innate capacity; they do not have either the human mentality or the mind of Tao. It is only after mixing with the conditioned state that there is a division between the human mind and the mind of Tao, a distinction between real knowledge and conscious knowledge. The mind of Tao is that which is unconfused in all situations: not being confused is real knowledge.

The human mind is only capable of conscious knowledge, not of real knowledge; its nature is weak, so it is called yin. Since the mind of Tao has real knowledge, it is also capable of conscious knowledge; its energy is strong, so it is called yang. Even sages have the human mind, and even ordinary people have the mind of Tao. Sages have the human mind in that they cannot annihilate perception; ordinary people have the mind of Tao in that they have moments of lucidity. The reason sages are different from ordinary people is simply that in them reality and consciousness are unified, they have knowledge and perception, and they are capable of permanent lucidity. The reason ordinary people are different from sages is that for them reality and consciousness are separated, and though they have knowledge and perception they are incapable of permanent lucidity.

The human mind has discriminatory awareness in it, which uses consciousness to create illusions: seeing objects, it gives rise to feelings, reverberating with whatever influences it. So consciousness takes refuge in the false, and the human mind is insecure. With the human mind insecure, perverse energies are rampant and sane energy weakens; the mind of Tao does not come to the fore, and becomes faint.

Practice of Tao refines the firmness of the real knowledge of the mind of Tao, restoring it to proper balance, and refines the flexibility of the conscious knowledge of the human mind, restoring it to proper balance. This is the joining of firmness and flexibility, the matching of strength and submission: precisely unified, one maintains true balance; innate knowledge and innate capacity are merged in the celestial design, and unified energy flows. How could the gold elixir not be produced?

The gold elixir is produced by the solidification of two energies, strong and yielding; true knowledge and conscious knowledge return to proper balance, and heaven and humanity merge, a precious pearl hangs in space, illumining everywhere. The gold elixir forms, at first subtle, becoming manifest, at first raw, becoming ripe. How could anyone not be emancipated?

[2]

Setting up the furnace and crucible is patterned on Heaven *and* Earth; *refining the sunlight and moonlight stabilizes the yang and yin souls. Congealing and dissolving, the incubating warmth produces transmutation; presumptuously do I idly discuss the mysterious and marvelous.*

The furnace is that whereby the fire is operated, the crucible is that whereby the medicines are refined. The science of the gold elixir patterns the furnace on the flexible submissiveness of *earth*, gradually progressing in an orderly way: it models the crucible on the firm strength of *heaven* cooking fiercely and forging quickly. Capable of being firm, capable of being flexible, capable of being strong, capable of being submissive, with a firm will, getting stronger as time goes on, the crucible and furnace steady, not shaking, not moving, one can thereby cull the medicine and operate the fire.

The conscious knowledge of the human mind is yang outside, yin inside; it is like sunlight, which radiates outward. The real knowledge of the mind of Tao is like moonlight, stored within. The external yang of conscious knowledge belongs to the yang soul; the external yin of real knowledge belongs to the yin soul. The sunlight yang soul of conscious knowledge is what is called the spirit which is spirit; the moonlight yin soul of real knowledge is called the spirit which is not spirit.

"Spirit which is spirit" means there is artificiality within the real;

"spirit which is not spirit" refers to containing reality within the artificial. "Refining sunlight and moonlight" means melting away the artificiality within reality of the conscious knowledge of the human mind, and refining out the reality within artificiality of the mind of Tao. When false consciousness is removed, real consciousness is steady; then the yang soul doesn't fly off, but is stabilized. When real knowledge is revealed, false knowledge vanishes; then the yin soul doesn't dissolve, but is stabilized.

Once the yang soul and yin soul are stabilized, then real knowledge and conscious knowledge, sense and essence, merge into each other and solidify into one energy, warm and gentle, transmuting by collecting and dispersing, tranquil and unstirring yet sensitive and effective. Every step is the celestial mechanism; the spiritual subtlety herein cannot be described in words.

[3]

ON THE CRESCENT MOON FURNACE (2 VERSES)

Stop wasting effort at an alchemical oven; to refine the elixir you must seek the crescent moon furnace. It has of itself the natural true firing—you do not need purple coal or bellows.

The crescent moon refers to the moon of the third day of the lunar month, appearing as a hook of light in the direction of *earth* (southwest). That light curves upward, that is why it is called the crescent moon. What this crescent moon symbolizes in humans is a point of yang light shining through in the middle of extreme quiet. Among the trigrams, it is *thunder* ☳. This is what is referred to by the lines, "On the third day *thunder* appears in the west; on the curving riverbank the moonlight gleams." This point of yang light is nothing but the light of the mind of Tao. In alchemy, what is hard to get is the mind of Tao; once the mind of Tao appears, the principles of nature are clearly evident, and strong energy gradually becomes active; then the whole world is spiritual medicine, which you may take freely—everywhere is the Tao. The medicine is the fire, the fire is the medicine; there is of itself the furnace of natural evolution, the fire of truth—what is the need for an alchemical oven, working with coal and bellows?

[4]

In the crescent moon furnace, jade flowers grow; in the cinnabar crucible, quicksilver is level. Only after harmonization by means of great strength can you plant the yellow sprout, which gradually develops.

The crescent moon furnace is, as mentioned before, the mind of Tao. As for the jade flowers, jade means something warm and soft, in the province of yin, while flowers mean something luminous, in the province of yang; so the jade flowers are yang within yin, representing the real knowledge in the mind of Tao.

The cinnabar crucible is the human mind. Quicksilver is something fluid and unfixed. This is in the province of yin, and is the yin within yang, representing the conscious knowledge of the human mind. When the mind of Tao is always manifest and real knowledge is not obscured, the conscious knowledge of the human mind is naturally level and calm, and cannot fly off.

Then you use effort to harmonize, using the true fire inherent in the mind of Tao to burn away the false consciousness in the human mind, and return it to completely receptive consciousness, so that heaven and humanity work together, real knowledge and conscious knowledge become unified.

When knowledge arrives, the intent is sincere; this is called the yellow sprout. The yellow sprout is planted by real consciousness. When real consciousness has earth, it develops, like a plant in the ground; when sprouting, it is yellow (central), so it is called the yellow sprout. After real knowledge and conscious knowledge are harmonized by the strength of the fire, they return to balance in the proper place. Once they are in the central earth pot, then you apply true intent to nurture them. After ten months, the energy is sufficient, and they naturally mature and become free, transmuted.

[5]

ON THE TRUE LEAD (4 VERSES)

Swallowing saliva and doing breathing exercises are human actions; only when you have the elixir can evolution occur. If there is no true seed in the crucible, that is like taking water and fire and boiling an empty pot.

The real knowledge of the mind of Tao has in it the primordial true unified energy, which is symbolized by lead. This is the true seed of enlightenment. If you want to cultivate the great elixir, there is no substitute for this true seed. Ignorant and confused people of the world vainly cultivate the body in a physical sense, swallowing saliva and doing breathing exercises, thinking they are thus practicing the Tao. They still do not realize that what the body produces is all conditioned and polluted: how can that produce the primordial elixir of highest consciousness? This means that if you don't have the true seed in the crucible, it is like taking water and fire and boiling an empty pot.

[6]

Harmonization of lead and mercury is needed to produce the elixir; without injury to great or small, both countries are safe. If you wonder what the true lead is, moonlight shines on the west river all day.

The gold elixir is made by the true lead of real knowledge of the mind of Tao plus the true mercury of the conscious knowledge of the human mind. If you want to cultivate the gold elixir, first harmonize lead and mercury. The firmness of the mind of Tao belongs to yang; this is "great." The flexibility of the human mind belongs to yin; this is "small." If the human mind lacks the mind of Tao, it can defeat the Tao by using consciousness to produce illusion. If you govern it by the mind of Tao, the conscious light is clear and can thereby help the Tao. So the mind of Tao is not to be diminished, and yet the human mind is not to be annihilated—just don't let the human mind misuse its consciousness. When the ancients told people to kill the human mind, what they meant was to kill the false consciousness of the human mind, not to kill the true consciousness of the human mind.

If you do not distinguish true and false, and kill them both, you become indifferent and nihilistic; hurting the small, you injure the great. Yin and yang become isolated, and the breath of the living mechanism has not the means to produce the gold elixir. That is why the text says, "Without injury to great or small, both countries are safe." "Both countries are safe" means the conscious knowledge of the human mind and the real knowledge of the mind of Tao are unified, with real knowledge governing conscious knowledge, and conscious knowledge conforming to real knowledge. When reality and consciousness do not separate, innate knowledge and innate capacity integrate with the principles of nature, and the gold elixir of the round and luminous fundamental essence is attained.

After all, real knowledge and conscious knowledge are extensions of innate knowledge and innate capacity; in the primordial state they are called innate knowledge and innate capacity, in the temporal state they are called real knowledge and conscious knowledge. When the primordial is restored within the temporal, real knowledge is innate knowledge, conscious knowledge is innate capacity. Originally they are one, without duality, but because of mixture with the conditioned, the natural reality of innate knowledge is lost outside and becomes the property of another, and the consciousness of the innate capacity remaining within oneself is also adulterated and becomes unstable.

If you want to go back to the fundamental and return to the original, it is necessary to seek out reality from the midst of artificial knowledge, and recover it; only then can conscious knowledge be lucid. This real knowledge is something most firm and strong, so it is represented as true lead. As real knowledge contains the primordial truly unified energy, it is also represented as metal in water, and also represented as light in the moon. Metal in water and light in the moon both mean the presence of yang within yin.

However, as long as this real knowledge has not been recovered and restored, it still is in another's domain and is not one's own. Hence the saying, "Moonlight shines on the west river all day." Moonlight represents real knowledge being dark outside and light inside. Shining all day on the west river and not shining on the east means the shining of the light is elsewhere, in another. A later verse says, "The metal man is originally a child of the eastern house, sent to grow up in the western neighborhood." This is exactly what "moonlight shines on the west river all day" means. If people can know that moonlight shines on the west river all day, this is truly knowing where real knowledge rests, and they can thereby use it to shine on the east and meet with conscious knowledge.

Alas, going along to death, coming back to life, again and again having you seek, without finding—do you think real knowledge is easy to know?

[7]

Don't go into the mountains before you have refined the restored elixir; in the mountains, inside and out, is not lead. This supreme treasure is in everyone's house; it's just that ignorant people do not fully recognize it.

Retirement from the world and going into the mountains to cultivate tranquility is something that is properly done only after the restoration of the elixir. People who don't know this go into the mountains to cultivate tranquility and think they can thereby live forever. But the way of eternal life requires that one acquire pure true lead; only then can effect be obtained.

However, the true lead must be sought out in the midst of the social world; if you go into the mountains to cultivate the Tao, in the mountains, inside and outside is all yin energy—how can there be true lead, which is pure yang? The true lead is the primordial root of consciousness; it is also called the root of heaven, or the true unified vitality, or the true unified energy, or lead from the homeland of water, or metal within water, or black within white, or the yang soul within the yin soul, or the black tiger, or the metal man, or the method of immortality of that house: the ancients represented it symbolically in many ways, but when we get back to the important point, they are all just depicting the mind of Tao.

This mind of Tao, when active, is the subtle being of real knowledge; when latent, it is the true openness of total concentration. It is inherently complete in everyone, not more in sages or less in ordinary people. Everyone has it, but they do not possess it themselves; after all, when you view it you cannot use it, and when you use it you cannot view it. Because everyone has it but they do not possess it themselves, ignorant people do not recognize it when they encounter it, and stumble past it even though it is right before their eyes.

At the end of the Ming dynasty, P'eng Hao-ku, who didn't understand this principle, took the phrase "is in everybody's house" to refer to woman as the alchemical crucible, and in recent times I don't know how many people have explained it as referring to sexual practice. Nothing is more blameworthy than such ignoramuses misleading students.

[8]

When bamboo breaks, you should use bamboo to repair it; to hatch a chicken you need an egg. It's a waste of effort if you're dealing with different species; it's better to join the spiritual potential with true lead.

Broken bamboo is repaired with bamboo, chickens are hatched from eggs—you seek to accomplish something by what is homogeneous with it. The *Triple Analogue* says, "With the same species, it's easy to work; it's hard to work with different kinds. What is not of the same species is not the true seed; whatever you do with it is a waste of effort." What this all means is that the great science of the gold elixir is the business of sages; if you want to learn sagehood, you must seek the seed of sagehood. The seed of sagehood is the real knowledge which is referred to as true lead. If you use real knowledge to practice and maintain the great Tao, you will surely accord with the potential of sagehood. The potential of sagehood is simply the integral principle of nature. With real knowledge there is nothing you do not know, nothing that is not real. You can thereby return to the principle of nature; so the text speaks of joining the spiritual potential. Once you accord with the spiritual potential, you become a sage—why are students recalcitrant?

[9]

ON USING LEAD

"Empty the mind, fill the belly"—the meanings are both profound. It is precisely in order to empty the mind that it is necessary to know the mind. It is best when refining the lead to first fill the belly, and cause the gathering in of the gold that fills the room.

Alchemy involves two tasks, to empty the mind and fill the belly. Emptying the mind means to empty the human mind; this is the task of cultivating essence. To fill the belly means to fulfill the mind of Tao; this is the task of cultivating life. The two matters of emptying the mind and filling the belly, dealing with essence and life, are both of profound meaning.

If you want to empty the mind, it is necessary to know the mind. In the mind there is the human mind and there is the mind of Tao. The human mind should be empty, not full, and the mind of Tao should be full, not empty. If you do not distinguish true and false, right and wrong, in the mind, and empty both, not only can you not comprehend life, you cannot even comprehend essence.

If you know the mind, you do not need to empty the human mind; first you should refine the mind of Tao, the true lead, to fill the belly. When the belly is full, sane energy arises through accumulation of right action, and the energy of conditioning dissolves of itself. The human mind will spontaneously become empty, the four forms will be in harmony, the five elements will aggregate, gold and jade will fill the room, the jewel of life will be in your hands. With this you can empty the human mind and nurture the mind of Tao, understand the essential source, and return to the homeland of nothingness.

[10]

On not using lead

In using lead, you must not use ordinary lead. Even true lead is abandoned after its use is finished. This is the true secret of using lead. Using lead and not using it—these are veracious words.

In cultivating the elixir, it is essential to gather true lead. There is also a difference in lead—there is ordinary lead, and there is true lead. Ordinary lead is extracted from mines, and is a gross material substance, and a pollutant. It has no sympathy with ourselves. True lead is produced in one's own home; it is the formless mind of Tao, and is of a kind with ourselves. The immortals since antiquity who have been able to transcend the ordinary and enter into sagehood have all relied on the work of the true lead, the mind of Tao. So the text says not to use ordinary lead.

However, though the mind of Tao is the primordial jewel of reality, it is produced from within the temporal; there is a time to use it, and a time not to use it. Before you have crystallized the elixir, you need to use the real knowledge of the mind of Tao to govern the conscious knowledge of the human mind. When the human mind has been stabilized, conscious knowledge is lucid; the mind of Tao and the human mind are as one in action and stillness, real knowledge and conscious knowledge correspond in openness and fulfillment.

When the spiritual embryo has formed, you should hasten to extract the hardness of the mind of Tao, and incubate the embryonic breath. The use of the mind of Tao is to govern the human mind; after the human mind is quiet, and discriminatory awareness is extinguished, innate knowledge and innate capacity are tranquil and unstirring yet sensitive and effective. Real consciousness exists independently, bright and lucid, the mind of Tao then has no function; it is thus possible to not set up either being or nonbeing, so things and self all return to emptiness. One alchemist said, "The rule of using lead is that it is like a trap to catch game, the game being caught by means of the trap; once you've caught the game, the trap has no further use." Herein lies the real secret of using the lead. If you don't know the secret of using the lead, when the elixir has crystallized, yet you still are concerned about the mind of Tao, you will not avoid using the mind of Tao to reactivate the human mind. Real consciousness will again scatter, and the gold elixir, once gained, will be lost again. Therefore the text says, "After its use is finished, the true lead too is abandoned." The secret of using the lead and not using it can be known from this.

[11]

On lead and mercury

In a dream I visited the sublime energy and reached the nine heavens; a real person gave me a book pointing to the origin. The book is simple, without many words; it just teaches people to refine mercury and lead.

The science of the gold elixir is most simple, without much talk—it is not more than refining the real knowledge in the mind of Tao and the conscious knowledge in the human mind. When the firm strength of the mind of Tao is centrally balanced, the mind of Tao is always present, governing conscious knowledge by real knowledge. When the flexible receptivity of the human mind is centrally balanced, the human mind is always calm, with conscious knowledge cleaving to real knowledge. When firmness and flexibility match each other, and reality and consciousness are united, this is called lead and mercury mixing and the gold elixir crystallizing. The method is very simple and uncomplicated; even ordinary people can rise directly to sagehood if they accomplish it.

However, most people are lacking in character, so they cannot attain it easily. If people are rich in virtue and get to meet real people who will show them the method of simple spiritual sublimation, it is like waking up from a dream, finally to realize the great medicine is in oneself, not gotten from another, and may be taken and used at will.

There is certainly a deep meaning in the author's saying that he visited the sublime energy in a dream and received a transmission. This is not made up. The sublime energy is where the true gold is produced, representing the radiance of pure light of true gold. The "nine heavens" is the realm of pure yang with no yin.

True gold is a representation of real knowledge: in the midst of yin darkness, suddenly the yang light of real knowledge appears; take this real knowledge and bring it home, mix it with conscious knowledge, cook it with fire, until there is pure yang with no yin—this is called the great elixir of gold liquid, reverted seven times and restored nine times. Is it a dream, after all?

[12]

ON THE ONE ENERGY OF NOTHINGNESS

The Tao produces one energy from nothingness, then from one energy gives birth to yin and yang. Yin and yang then combine to form three bodies; the three bodies reproduce, and myriad things grow.

The Tao of essence and life is the Tao of creative evolution; the Tao of creative evolution is the Tao which produces and reproduces unceasingly. When we investigate the source of the Tao, we find it produces one energy from nothingness, and from the one energy produces heaven, produces earth, gives birth to yin and yang. Yin and yang recombine therein, and while containing the one energy produce three bodies. Once the three bodies are formed, the one energy goes into motion, from yin to yang, yang to yin; thus myriad things and beings are born.

So this is like the growth of plants and trees: first one sprout grows from the earth—this is one energy born from nothingness. Once the sprout has emerged from the ground, it opens into two leaves—this is producing yin and yang from one energy. Then a stem grows up from between the two leaves—this is yin and yang combining to form three bodies. From this branches and leaves grow—this is the three bodies reproducing so that myriad things grow.

Everything in the world, sentient or insentient, grows out of this one single energy of nothingness; but then all follow the course of creation. If practitioners of the Tao know about following the course of creation, they practice it in reverse, returning the myriad to three, returning the three to two, returning the two to one, returning the one to nothingness. Then that which is beyond the senses is reached.

[13]

On water and fire

Water lightning boils and thunders in the region of metal water; fire arises in the k'un-lun, yin and yang. If the two things are restored and mixed together, naturally the elixir develops, fragrant throughout the body.

Water lightning represents producing fire in water, a metaphor for the real knowledge of the mind of Tao appearing in utter darkness. When it appears is the "living midnight" in our bodies. "Boiling and thundering" represents the vacillation of rapture.

As for the "region of metal water," the real knowledge of the mind of Tao is the true sense of total concentration, which contains the two energies of "metal" and "water."

The K'un-lun mountains are in the west, and are the mountain range from which myriad mountains stem, the place where true metal is produced.

When the real knowledge of the mind of Tao appears in the midst of utter darkness, it is like flashing lightning; all of a sudden it is light, then at once it is dark. The rapture vacillates; it is hard to get and easy to lose. Quickly use the fire of open awareness to meet it; then real knowledge and conscious knowledge, essence and sense, will cleave to one another, yin and yang will join. Therein is produced the primordial spiritual elixir: then activate the natural real fire and burn away conditioned polluted energy. When the slag is gone, the gold is pure, and the gold elixir is perfected. Ingest this, and you are released from what encloses you and you become transformed, revealing the pure spiritual body. Then a fragrant breeze fills the world—not only is the body filled with fragrance.

[14]

ON HEAVEN-EARTH AND EARTH-EARTH

If fire and water are returned without heaven-earth and earth-earth, though they contain the four forms, they will not make elixir. It is only through these latter two, embracing true earth, that the gold elixir can be restored.

Water in humans is the original vitality, which manifests as knowledge. Within water is hidden metal; in humans it is true sense, which manifests as justice. Fire in humans is the original spirit, which manifests as courtesy. Fire produces wood; in humans this is the original essence, which manifests as benevolence. The mind of Tao has the form of *water*, the human mind has the form of *fire*; so the mind of Tao and the human mind contain the four natures of metal, wood, water, and fire.

But the four natures are separate; if you want one energy to produce them, this depends wholly on the work of heaven-earth and earth-earth. Heaven-earth is yang earth; it is the original energy, which manifests as truthfulness. Earth-earth is yin earth; it is intention, which manifests as desire. *Water* takes in heaven-earth; in the mind of Tao this is truthfulness. *Fire* takes in earth-earth; in the human mind, this is intent. If you want to rectify your mind, first make intent sincere. Once intent is sincere, earth-earth is stabilized and the human mind is calm. If you want to traverse the Tao, first establish truthfulness. Once truthfulness is established, heaven-earth appears and the mind of Tao manifests.

If the mind of Tao is without truthfulness and the human mind is insincere, even if one has benevolence, justice, courtesy, and knowledge, they do not relate to each other. How then could it be possible to crystallize the spiritual elixir of consummate awareness and wisdom?

Therefore those who practice the Tao must consider sincerity of intent and truthfulness to be the main concern. With sincerity and truthfulness, the mind of Tao is manifest and the human mind is correctly oriented. When these two are joined harmoniously, yin and yang correspond, and the primordial energy emerges from nothingness and crystallizes into a black pearl; that which was scattered is reassembled, that which had gone is restored. That is why the text says it is only through these two things, embracing true earth, that the gold elixir can be restored. So the work of heaven-earth and earth-earth is very great indeed.

[15]

On inverting water and fire

The sun, in the position of fire, turns into a woman; water, in the moon palace, turns out to be a man. If you do not know the meaning of inversion herein, stop engaging in lofty discussion with your restricted views.

Conscious knowledge is originally yang; but it is light outside yet dark inside, and always draws external influences. This is like the sun being in the position of *fire* ☲, yang outside, yin inside, yet turning into a female. Real knowledge is originally yin; but it is dark outside yet light inside, and contains true energy. This is like *water* ☵ being in the palace of the moon, yin outside, yang inside, yet after all being male.

The conditioned human mentality uses consciousness to create illusions, so the natural reality of the mind of Tao is buried away. This is also like a woman taking over the home, whereat the man retreats from his position. The path of alchemy is to govern the human mind of conscious knowledge by means of the mind of Tao with real knowledge, to follow the mind of Tao of real knowledge with the human mind of conscious knowledge. When the man (real knowledge) is firm and the woman (conscious knowledge) is flexible, the man taking charge of things and the woman obeying directions, there is no great work that cannot succeed.

"If you don't know the meaning of inversion herein" refers to not perceiving the real knowledge of the mind of Tao and not recognizing the conscious knowledge of the human mind, resulting in confusion, in both cases taking the false for the true; "stop engaging in lofty discussion with your narrow views," or you'll fool yourself and deceive others.

[16]

Take the solid in the heart of the position of water, *and change the yin in the innards of the palace of* fire: *from this transformation comes the sound body of* heaven—*to lie hidden or to fly and leap is all up to the mind.*

The solid in the heart of the position of *water* ☵ is the real knowledge in the mind of Tao; the yin in the innards of the palace of *fire* ☲ is the conscious knowledge of the human mind. Take out the reality-knowing mind of Tao that has fallen into water and with it replace the consciously knowing mind in the palace of fire. In a short time the yin energy will dissolve and the yang energy will return, and you will again see the original face of *heaven* ☰, recovering your original nature of innate knowledge and innate capacity, tranquil and unperturbed yet sensitive and effective, sensitive and effective yet tranquil and undisturbed. Therefore it says, "From this transformation comes the sound body of heaven—to lie hidden or to fly and leap is all up to the mind."

This "body" is not the material substance of the ephemeral mortal body; it is the real body of the spiritual being. The spiritual being, or spiritual body, is the original essence. At the start of human life, the original essence of real consciousness is round and bright and lucid; firm strength is balanced, and it is unadulterated, pure, without a trace of pollution: this is like the three whole lines of the trigram *heaven* ☰, the image of pure yang without yin.

Subsequently, upon mixture with acquired conditioning, natural goodness is obscured, and there is artificiality in conscious energy. This is like the center of the *heaven* trigram becoming hollowed, forming *fire* ☲, the center of the *earth* ☷ becoming solid, forming *water* ☵. The hollow in the center means the real has left *fire*; the solid in the center means the real has fallen into *water:* taking from *water* to fill in *fire* means restoring natural reality, recovering the original nature of real consciousness. This is likened to the *fire* trigram again changing into the *heaven* trigram.

Once real consciousness is restored, it is at your command, always responsive yet always calm, able to adapt appropriately to any situation. Whether to lie hidden or fly and leap—whether to act or not—is all up to the mind.

People of later times have thought taking from *water* to fill in *fire* means taking the energy in the genitals and mixing it with the heart. There are also those who take the genital energy, make it rise up the spine, then draw it down the front of the body into the solar plexus. Indeed, there is something else, wonder of wonders. The heart and genitals are actually not *fire* and *water*; those who consider *fire* and *water* the heart and genitals are very foolish.

[17]

ON THE FIVE ELEMENTS

The thunder *dragon mercury comes from the land of* fire; *the* lake tiger *lead is born in the region of* water. *The two things both are based on the child giving birth to the mother; the whole essence of the five elements enters the middle.*

Thunder ☳ is a dragon, and is mercury associated with wood. *Lake* ☱ is a tiger, and is lead associated with metal. "Dragon mercury comes from the land of *fire*" is producing wood in fire. "Tiger lead is born in the region of water" is producing metal in water. The wood produced in fire is wood that never rots; the metal produced in water is metal that never rusts.

Wood originally produces fire, yet fire paradoxically produces wood; metal originally produces water, yet water paradoxically produces metal—this is called the child giving birth to the mother. This is what an old classic means when it says, "When the five elements do not go in the usual order, the dragon emerges from the fire; when the five elements go in reverse, the tiger is born in water."

The temperament of humans is easily stirred, and is likened to the natural buoyancy of wood and mercury; if you use the fire of the original spirit to burn away pollutants, the temperament is converted and the true nature becomes manifest, as a nature which is permanently stable.

The arbitrary feelings of humans are very heavy, like the density of metal, lead; if you use the water of total concentration to wash away the dust and dirt, then arbitrary feelings will vanish and true sense will solidify, becoming permanent unemotional sense.

Furthermore, when the temperament is transmuted, there is no fire in one's nature; the spirit of discrimination dies out and the original spirit lives permanently. When emotional desires vanish, there are no thoughts of lust; polluted vitality is sublimated and the original vitality does not leak out.

When true nature is manifest, true sense is solidified, the original spirit is alive, and the original vitality is stable, then essence, sense, vitality, and spirit return to one energy; benevolence, justice, courtesy, and knowledge return to one truthfulness. This is called the wholeness of the five elements. Once the five elements are whole, they merge in the center of unity; this is called the five elements entering the center.

When the five elements enter the center, without imbalance, and yin and yang join, this is called the crystallization of the gold elixir. If you look for medicinal ingredients other than these elements to form the elixir, it will be impossible. The most important part of this section is the line "the whole essence of the five elements enters the middle." If the five elements are not in the center, they will separate, and the gold elixir will not form. If the five elements go into the center, then they are one energy, and the elixir naturally crystallizes. So students should first understand the five elements.

[18]

ON THE TWO POLES

As soon as the half moon is bright on the horizon, already there is the sound of the dragon's howl and the tiger's roar. Then one should apply effort to cultivate the two eights; within an hour see the elixir form.

The gold elixir is produced by the mixture of the energy of the two poles of the dragon-essence and the tiger-sense. First take "eight ounces" of the "metal" of the upper pole, for the matrix of the elixir; then take "half a pound" of the "wood" of the lower pole, to form the spiritual embryo.

What are the poles? From the third day of the lunar month the first yang is born; by the eighth, there is half yang within yin, so that the edge of the moon is flat as a stretched rope, and the moon looks like a strung bow. Because the yang light is above, this is called the upper pole. On the fifteenth, the moon is full; on the sixteenth, the first yin is latent, and on the eighteenth the first yin appears. On the twenty-third, there is half yin within yang, so that the edge of the moon is flat as a stretched rope, and the moon looks like a strung bow. Because the yang light is below, this is called the lower pole.

The yang light of the moon gives birth to the tiger from the west, in the province of metal, which is in the west; therefore the moon on the eighth day of the lunar month is called the polar energy of the tiger. The yin body of the moon produces the dragon from the east, in the province of wood, which is in the east; therefore the moon on the twenty-third day of the lunar month is called the polar energy of the dragon.

The sense of real knowledge is firm; represented as a tiger, it is like the yang light of the moon. The essence of conscious knowledge is flexible; represented as a dragon, it is like the yin body of the moon. The firm sense of real knowledge progressing to correct balance is like the yang light produced by the upper pole of the moon. This is "eight ounces of metal." The flexible essence of conscious knowledge withdrawing to correct balance is like the yin body of the waning moon at the lower pole. This is "eight ounces of wood."

"As soon as the half moon is bright on the horizon" is when the firm sense of real knowledge advances to correct balance. When real knowledge advances to correct balance, there is firmness within flexibility; conscious knowledge is governed by real knowledge and cannot become flighty. Yang controls yin, and yin follows yang; so there is the effect of the dragon's howl and the tiger's roar responding to each other with the same energy.

At this point, one should apply effort in cultivation, using yang to equalize yin, causing the flexible essence of conscious knowledge also to revert to correct balance. When conscious knowledge reverts to correct balance, there is firmness within flexibility. When real knowledge and conscious knowledge are both restored to correct balance, the "two eights," the twin polar energies, are present in sufficient quantity; yin and yang balance each other, firmness and flexibility are united—in an hour's time you can see the elixir form.

However, if you do not reach sufficiency of the two eights, and have too much yang with too little yin, or too little yang with too much yin, neither can form the elixir. It is only when yin and yang are matched, evenly balanced, that you can see the elixir form in an hour. Do you think the work of that hour is easy to do? If you do not put in decades of dedicated effort, you cannot all at once reach this realm.

[19]

ON HARMONIZATION (2 VERSES)

On the top of Flower Crag Mountain, the male tiger roars; at the bottom of sacred tree ocean, the female dragon howls. The yellow female naturally knows how to get them together, so they become man and wife and share the same mind.

The "flower crag" is in the west, the "sacred tree" is in the east; the tiger is metal, sense, the dragon is wood, essence. In the beginning of life, essence and sense are combined, metal and wood are together; after mixture with acquired conditioning, the artificial comes and the real is obscured—essence and sense separate, like the dragon going east and the tiger west.

The tiger is called male because "metal" sense is firm; the dragon is called female because "wood" essence is flexible. Even though true sense is blocked by artificial feelings, and true essence is covered by artificial nature, true sense and true essence always want to meet. The male tiger roaring on the mountain and the female dragon howling in the ocean represents subtle communication of separated yin and yang.

Since there is subtle communication through the barrier separating them, it is possible for them to meet; it is just because there is no harmonizing agent between them that they cannot meet. "The yellow female" or "yellow woman" is also called true earth, true intent, true sincerity. Once true sincerity appears, the intent is truthful, and the mind is right; the false leaves and the real comes, sense returns to essence. In a short time essence and sense join, like an engagement joining two families, sending them to become man and wife and share the same mind.

[20]

The red dragon and black tiger take to the west and east; the four forms mix with the two earths in the center. Restoration and beauty henceforth go into operation; who says the gold elixir will not be achieved?

Wood can produce fire; fire and wood are in the same house, so they are called the red dragon. Metal can produce water; metal and water are in the same house, so they are called the black tiger. Metal, wood, water, and fire are the four forms: earth can combine the four forms, and when earth is added to the four forms they make the five elements.

When the five elements proceed in order, the universe is a pit of fire; when the five elements are reversed, the world is made of jewels. The only question is how this operates in people. When the sense of real knowledge in the mind of Tao is active, this is called restoration; one should properly advance the yang fire to make the elixir. When the essence of conscious knowledge in the human mind is still, this is called beauty; one should retreat into yin convergence to incubate.

Using yang when yang should be used, using yin when yin should be used, yang is strong and yin receptive; use of yang and use of yin each according to the time, real knowledge and conscious knowledge unite and go into the center. The five elements aggregate, and the golden elixir is formed, as a natural process.

[21]

ON THE DRAGON AND TIGER

Just when the white tiger on the west mountain goes wild, the blue dragon in the east sea cannot handle it. Catching them both, have them fight to the death, and they will turn into a mass of violet gold frost.

Although the sense of real knowledge and the essence of conscious knowledge are primordial things, yet when they fall into temporal conditioning, reason and desire get mixed up together, and reality and artificiality get confused. When reality and consciousness have been separated for a long time, they cannot be immediately reconciled; this is why the text says "Just when the white tiger on the west mountain goes wild, the blue dragon in the east sea cannot handle it."

But in spiritual alchemy there is a method of using the artificial to cultivate the real, using the real to convert the artificial. The method is to go along with what one desires, gradually guiding desires, making dedicated effort on one level to lead from disharmony to harmony, so that after a long process of gradually increasing one's strength, arbitrary feelings will spontaneously vanish and true sense will spontaneously arise, temperament will dissolve and true essence will be exposed, the false will die out and the true will remain.

Only unemotional sense is true sense, only impersonal essence is true essence. When true sense and true essence unite, the mind dies while the spirit lives; unconsciously following the laws of God, they change into a mass of violet gold frost. Gold is something stable and incorruptible: when gold reaches violet, coming from smelting in a great furnace, it is considered gold in full hue. Violet gold becoming frost represents the psycho-physiological being melting into one unified energy, transcending beyond yin and yang.

[22]

ON CULTIVATING THE SELF (3 VERSES)

First observe heaven and understand the five bandits; then examine earth, to pacify the people. When the people are settled and the country rich, you should seek war; when the war is over, then alone can you see the sage.

Observing heaven means observing our own celestial essence. Understanding the five bandits means understanding how the five elements of metal, wood, water, fire, and earth overcome one another. Examining earth means examining the ground of our mind. Pacifying the people means settling vitality, spirit, yang-soul, yin-soul, and intent, each in its own place.

In the path of spiritual alchemy, nothing takes precedence over cultivation of the self, refinement of the self. The essential point of refining the self is first to observe the celestial essence. When the celestial essence is not obscured, the five bandits cannot fool you. Next one should examine the mind ground; when the mind ground is clear and clean, the five things are all settled. When the five things are settled, the vitality is firm, the yang soul is stable, the yin soul is calm, the intent is sincere. This is called the richness of the country.

At this point one should battle the five bandits and repel all negativities; when negative energy turns into positive energy, the killing potential transmutes into the enlivening potential, and one can thereby see the sage.

The sage is the original aspect of innate knowledge and innate capacity. It is also called the spiritual embryo. When the five bandits are overcome, they change into the five bases, which in action become the five virtues. Tranquil and unstirring, yet sensitive and effective, unconsciously obeying the laws of God, is this not the spiritual embryo?

The word "war" in the text has a profound meaning. The five bandits are in the mind, and they go into action in heaven; if you do not have the great spiritual power to be a match for heaven, you cannot conquer them. Doing battle with them is precisely how to activate great function and bring forth great potential, progressing vigorously, growing stronger as time goes on, not letting yourself give up halfway along. An ancient immortal said, "As long as there is even the slightest positive energy left, you do not die; as long as there is even the slightest negative energy left, you do not become immortal." In refining oneself it is necessary to refine oneself until there is no more negative energy, so that the five elements fuse and transmute, the slag is gone and the gold is pure.

[23]

In employing generals, you should divide left and right armies; let the other be the host and you be the guest. Bringing the ruler to the battle line, do not take the adversary lightly; you may lose the priceless treasure of your own house.

In refining oneself, one cannot achieve success immediately; it is necessary to concede to desires, gradually guiding them in the right direction. In most people, the opening of real consciousness has been locked up tight for a long time; their accumulated habits are deep-seated, and the five bandits have been causing afflictions for a long time, so they are most difficult to exterminate.

"In employing generals, you should divide right and left armies; let the other be the host, and you be the guest" means when you want to get you must first give. "Bringing the rule to the battle line, do not take the adversary lightly; you may lose the priceless treasure of your own house" means that you do not lose yourself in desiring to get from the other. By inwardly forestalling danger, wary of perils, and outwardly working on refinement, the false can be removed and the real can be preserved; why worry that the great Tao will not be achieved?

[24]

Fire arising in wood inherently contains danger; if you do not know how to investigate, do not force the issue. The occurrence of calamity is all due to the harm of this; it is necessary to control it and seek the metal man.

When people act from acquired conditioning and the spirit of discrimination rules, the afflictive perceptions borne all along by the energies of the conditioned five elements in the body, as well as the pollution of present habits, are active all at once; if you haven't great spiritual power and great method, how can you overcome them? If you do not know how to investigate true principle, and start out impetuously to control mind by mind, attacking them too fiercely, sometimes the fire of the ruler and the fire of the minister flare up at once, and not only are you unable to attack the bandits, you are even attacked by the bandits. It is not only not beneficial, it is even harmful. It is like fire arising in wood; when the calamity arises, it will overcome—the wood is burnt by the fire, destroying its life.

The *Ts'an T'ung Ch'i* says, "The flowing pearl of the sun always wants to leave people; finally finding the golden flower, they change and stay by each other." The golden flower is the mind of Tao. The mind of Tao is mind which is not mind; it originally emerges from the body of natural reality and is imbued with the sense of real knowledge. It has indestructible true energy, and nothing can deceive it. Once the light of the mind of Tao appears, all falsehood retreats. Its efficacy and firm resolution are like sharp metal, so the mind of Tao is called the metal man. Investigating true principle is simply investigating the true principle of using metal to control wood.

Over all, the "metal man" is the master of spiritual alchemy: if you want to refine yourself without the metal man, you will merely bring on calamity. Therefore Chang San-feng said, "When refining the self, you must use true lead." True lead and the metal man are both names for the mind of Tao.

[25]

ON THE METAL MAN

The metal man is originally the son of the family to the east, living instead at the neighbors' to the west. Recognized, he is called back home to grow up, and espoused to a beautiful girl, becoming intimate.

The metal man is the real knowledge of the mind of Tao, as mentioned before. Real knowledge constitutes true sense. In human life originally essence and sense are one and not separate: in terms of substance, it is called essence; in terms of function, it is called sense—sense is essence, essence is sense; they have the same origin but different names, yet they are not two.

Mixing with acquired conditioning, sense and essence change; true sense becomes obscured and arbitrary feelings arise. The indestructible true energy is covered by external influences, and is no longer at one's command. This is likened to the son of the family to the east living at the neighbors' to the west. But though he be living at the neighbors' to the west, it is not that we never meet—yet when we see him we don't recognize him.

If one is determined and investigates truth penetratingly, when one recognizes real truth it comes when called, like an empty valley transmitting a voice, without using up any energy at all. Then one can nurture it in a closed room, always protecting and sustaining it. Wedding it to the "beautiful girl" of true essence, yin and yang are one energy, joining in intimacy. As before it is of the eastern house.

The beautiful girl is the essence of conscious knowledge. The reason why essence is called a girl even though it is originally yang is that essence commands flexibility. It is represented by wood. The reason sense is called male even though it is originally yin is that sense commands firmness. It is represented by metal. The metal man having been out for a long time, when one day he returns home and meets the beautiful girl, they become extraordinarily intimate, and unfailingly produce the elixir. Therefore the *Ts'an T'ung Ch'i* says, "When metal first comes back to essence, it can be called restored elixir." Metal and wood joining—sense and essence merging—is the restored elixir. There is no other restored elixir.

[26]

ON THE BEAUTIFUL GIRL

The beautiful girl traveling has her own direction; the first trip should be short, the next trip long. Coming back, she goes into the yellow woman's house, marries the metal man and makes him her old man.

The beautiful woman is the essence of conscious knowledge, as explained in the preceding section. When it goes into temporal conditioning, there is the spirit of discrimination of the human mind which dwells there, so there is artificiality with the real. Producing illusion by consciousness, seeing fire it flies and wanders unsettled; this is what is called going out and in irregularly, not knowing where home is. If you want to practice spiritual alchemy, you must first cause this conscious essence to travel in the direction it should go, opening the awareness up and not obscuring that consciousness, so that it returns to real consciousness.

"The first trip should be short" refers to seeking sense through essence; "the next trip should be long" refers to nurturing reality through consciousness. Seeking sense through essence is the subtlety of the momentary congealing of the elixir, so it is said to be short. Nurturing reality through consciousness is the work of the ten months of incubation, so it is said to be long. Short when short is appropriate, long when long is appropriate—this is referred to by the line "she has her own direction." If you go in the right direction, the alchemy can succeed.

But you must first dismiss intellectualism and turn your attention inward: take this point of conscious essence and place it in the center. This is called "coming back and going into the yellow woman's house." The yellow woman's house is the abode of balance, without bias or inclination. When the conscious essence is correctly balanced, the mind is straightforward and the intent is sincere. When the intent is sincere, truthfulness is real; when truthfulness is real, it does not meander outside. Thereby one seeks sense through essence; when sense returns to essence, essence and sense become attached to each other and join into one energy. This is referred to here as "marrying the metal man and making him her old man."

"Making him her old man" is not an ordinary expression—it has a deep meaning. Generally speaking, spiritual alchemy begins with summoning true sense through conscious essence. When true sense returns, the conscious essence is no more disturbed or agitated, and it also returns to reality. Once the conscious essence is linked to true sense, it is necessary to nurture true sense in the realm of pure yang with no yin. This is likened to husband and wife growing old together, not letting there be any rift between them along the way. This is in fact the meaning of "the latter trip should be long." Students should study this deeply.

[27]

On the firing process (2 verses)

Even if you know the red cinnabar and black lead, it is useless if you do not know the firing process. The whole thing depends on the power of practice; if you deviate even slightly, you will not form the elixir.

The science of the elixir of restoration is simply to take the two medicinal materials, red cinnabar and black lead, and forge them into a jewel, with which to extend the life of the essence. The cinnabar is the energy of open consciousness within *fire* ☲; this is conscious knowledge, which is the realm of the human mind. The lead is the energy of firm rectitude within *water* ☵; this is real knowledge, which is in the province of the mind of Tao. Because the conscious knowledge of the human mind is light outside and dark inside, and light belongs to fire, which is red, it is symbolized by red cinnabar. Because the real knowledge of the mind of Tao is dark outside and light inside, and darkness belongs to water, which is dark, it is symbolized by black lead. These are immaterial formless cinnabar and lead, not the material cinnabar and lead of the world.

Once you know the cinnabar and lead of real knowledge and conscious knowledge, you can freely gather them without difficulty.

However, when you gather them you must refine them, and if you know the medicines but not the method of refining them, it is the same as if you didn't know them. Therefore the text says, "Even if you know the red cinnabar and black lead, it is useless if you don't know the firing process." The formation of the gold elixir totally depends on the practice of the firing process. The "fire" is the power of effort in practice, the "process" is the order of procedure of practice.

In gathering the medicines, one must know their levels of gravity and energy; in refining the medicines, one must know the proper timing. There is a firing process of "cultural" cooking, and a firing process of "martial" refining; there is a firing process of getting started, and a firing process of stopping. There is a firing process of advancing yang, and a firing process of withdrawing yin; there is a firing process of increasing and decreasing, and a firing process of incubation. There are many processes of firing, which must be thoroughly understood from beginning to end before it is possible to succeed in the work. A slight deviation produces a great loss, making it impossible to form elixir.

[28]

Treatises, classics, and songs expound ultimate reality, but do not express the firing process clearly in writing. If you want to know the orally transmitted teachings and penetrate the arcana, this requires careful discussion with the spiritual immortals.

Since ancient times the writings of the immortals and real people have meticulously discussed the medicinal substances and firing process of cultivating reality. What they have said is true and not false, but though they discuss it, discussion cannot reach it; though they speak of it, speech cannot exhaust it. It is not that they haven't written about the firing process, but the meanings of the writings are deep and mysterious. Some say essence, some say life, some say medicine, some say fire; some speak of the firing process of cultivating life, some speak of the firing process of cultivating essence, some speak of an external firing process, some speak of an internal firing process.

So it is not that they haven't spoken of the firing process, but what they say is not organized. If you do not meet an illumined teacher, who will indicate the order for you, you will not be able to know it. That is why the text says they haven't expressed the firing process clearly in words, and it also says it is necessary to discuss it carefully with spiritual immortals. This is telling people to study the writings and also seek illumined teachers for certainty. One should not just seek a teacher without reading texts, and one should not take the writings as one's own understanding and fail to seek a teacher.

If there were no firing process in the writings—the treatises, classics, and songs—why would it say the writings expound ultimate reality? Generally speaking, students should both read the alchemical writings and seek enlightened teachers too. By reading the texts they can distinguish false and true, genuine and bogus, and can extend their knowledge and perspective; calling on enlightened teachers, they can ascertain the verity of the principles they have discerned. Study on one's own and finding a teacher are both necessary.

[29]

ON THE FIRING PROCESS OF GATHERING
THE MEDICINE

On the fifteenth day of the eighth month, enjoying the moonlight, this is precisely when the gold essence is in its prime. When you reach the point where one yang begins to move, then you should advance the fire, without delay.

When the moon comes to mid-autumn, the gold essence is in its prime; when the path comes to proper balance of firm strength, the original nature is completely illumined, the achievement of complete illumination rests completely in the mind of Tao. The point where one yang begins to move is when the yang light of real knowledge of the mind of Tao stirs but is not yet very active; only then is a glimpse of the root of heaven revealed. At this time you should quickly set about increasing the fire, gathering the yang and putting it into the furnace of evolution, gradually gathering, gradually refining, from vagueness to clarity, from one yang to complete purity of six yangs. This is also like the mid-autumn moon, exceptionally bright, shining through the universe.

The words "without delay" express urgency; because the light of real knowledge of the mind of Tao is hard to find and easy to lose, if you hesitate and delay, the energy of the light will again dissipate, and you will miss it even though it is near at hand.

[30]
ON THE FIRING PROCESS OF EXTRACTION AND ADDITION

When one yang stirs, making the gold elixir, the lead crucible, warm, shines dazzlingly. The beginning of reception of energy is easily gotten; in the operation of extraction and addition, it is urgent to prevent danger.

This section follows up urgently on the preceding one. When one yang stirs, you gather it back into the crucible: the mind is peaceful, the energy harmonious; "brightness arises in the empty room," its radiance collecting inside, producing light from within darkness, shining dazzlingly.

Master Ts'ui said, "Receiving energy is auspicious; prevent it from becoming unfortunate." The return of one yang is easy; but pure completeness is most difficult. It is necessary to forestall danger, aware of perils, using the technique of extraction and addition, increase and reduction, in order to accomplish the work. Extraction means reduction of excess of the conscious knowledge of the human mind; addition means increasing real knowledge of the mind of Tao where it is lacking.

Extracting and extracting, adding and adding, until you reach the point where there can be no more extraction or addition, then the human mind does not arise, while the mind of Tao is always present; real knowledge and conscious knowledge conjoin, and inside and outside are illumined. Only then will you not be afflicted by "wind and thunder at midnight."

In particular, because when the mind of Tao first returns the yang energy is weak while yin energy is strong, if you do not work on extraction and addition, as soon as you slack off you lose what you have gained. Therefore the work of extraction and addition is important. This work of extraction and addition is the work of preventing danger. There is no preventing danger without this extraction and addition, and extraction and addition is not beyond preventing danger. Preventing danger is extraction and addition—the two are one thing. Students should pay attention to this.

[31]

ON THE FIRING PROCESS OF INCUBATION

The mystic pearl takes on form, born following yang; when yang peaks, yin grows, gradually stripping away grossness. In ten months the frost flies, and the elixir is now developed; at this time even spirits and ghosts will be surprised.

The mystic pearl is the pearl of complete yang, something round and bright and unclouded; it is a different name for the gold elixir, and is the fundamental essence of innate knowledge and innate capacity which human beings originally have. This fundamental essence is silent and calm, yet sensitive and effective; it is represented as a mystic pearl. This pearl is the stable, strong real knowledge of the mind of Tao, which takes on form through correct concentration. When it grows and grows until its bountiful energy is all-pervasive and its shining light waxes full, this is the peak of yang.

When yang peaks, you should receive it with yin; yin growing and stripping away grossness is using yin to nurture yang, getting rid of the hot energy of the adamancy of yang. Gradual stripping away requires ten months of work: after ten months of incubation, the dross is gone and the gold is pure, transmuting into spiritual frost, really empty yet including subtle existence, wondrously existent yet containing true emptiness, unconsciously following the laws of God. Being like frost flying in the sky is a representation of not falling into being or nonbeing—now the elixir is developed. At this stage, creation cannot constrain you, myriad things cannot move you; your work is done in the human world, your name is recorded in heaven. How could the spirits and ghosts not be startled?

[32]

ON THE FIRING PROCESS OF FORMING THE EMBRYO

After the prior pole, before the latter pole, the taste of the herb is even, the form of the energy is complete. Gathering it, return it to the furnace and refine it; when it is refined, keep it warm, and it will cook by itself.

The prior pole is yang within yin, real knowledge reverting to correct balance. The latter pole is yin within yang, conscious knowledge returning to correct balance. When real knowledge and conscious knowledge both return to correct balance, firmness and flexibility match each other. Where they match is called "after the prior pole, before the latter pole." At this time, real knowledge and conscious knowledge, the great and the small, are free from defect—"both countries are whole." Therein is produced a primordial spiritual sprout; the taste of the herb is even—yin and yang are merged: quickly gather it and put it in the furnace of evolution, refining it into reality, consolidating it into the spiritual embryo. At this stage, the medicine is the fire, the fire is the medicine. Applying the work of ten months of incubation, there will spontaneously be natural true fire cooking, from vague to clear, producing form from no form.

[33]

ON YIN AND YANG RETURNING TO THE CENTER

Just as the eldest son drinks the wine of the west, the youngest daughter first opens the flower of the north. After the meeting with the green beauty, lock them up at once in the yellow house.

The eldest son is *thunder* ☳. The wine of the west is metal-water. On the third of the lunar month, the moon appears in the west; under yin, one yang arises—this is represented by the trigram *thunder*. Therefore it says, "Just as the eldest son drinks the wine of the west." The youngest daughter is *lake* ☱. The flower of the north means producing the flower of metal within water. The development of the moonlight goes to *lake* from *earth* ☷; within yin, yang appears. Therefore it says, "The youngest daughter first opens the flower of the north." The two lines both symbolize the arising of one yang. "Just as he drinks" means he has not drunk before, and now suddenly drinks. "First opens" means he has not drunk before, and now suddenly drinks. "First opens" means not having previously opened, only now opened. Both describe the sense of the real knowledge of the mind of Tao being easy to lose and hard to find. The mind of Tao having been long buried away, real knowledge is obscure; when suddenly, in the midst of utter quietude, it happens to become manifest, this is like just drinking wine, or first getting a flower to bloom. This is the opportunity for restoration, a fortunate encounter on a good night, not to be missed. You should take advantage of the opportunity to gather it, mating it with conscious knowledge, shutting them in the room of the central yellow court; husband and wife meet and naturally give birth to the elixir.

Conscious knowledge is essence, yin within yang. It is in the province of wood; because the color of wood is green, conscious knowledge is symbolized as a "green beauty." When real knowledge and conscious knowledge meet, with the same mind, one energy, they naturally return to the center. When they return they return, but if you do not know how to lock up, they may again separate after joining. Having shut the door, lock it: with the door locked tight, if they haven't joined they will join, and when they have joined they will stay together always. This is what Chang San-feng meant when he said, "The woman of the eastern house and the man of the western house mate as husband and wife and enter the empty room. The yellow woman urges them to drink wine of the finest flavor, and they revel in intoxication."

The words "lock up" convey the work of forestalling danger. When yin and yang first meet, essence and feeling are not yet pure and simple. It is essential not to forget, yet not to force. Only if you guard strictly can you avoid leakage. The gold elixir crystallizes from within nothingness. This is the celestial mechanism, which cannot be known without a teacher.

[34]

ON BATHING

When the moon in the east and west reaches its season, punishment and reward are at hand; the medicine is patterned on this. At this point the gold elixir should be bathed; if instead you increase the fire, that is dangerous.

The moon in the east is the spring equinox, when yang energy rises between heaven and earth. The moon in the west is the autumn equinox, when yin energy rises between heaven and earth. The spring equinox, in the sphere of wood, is the enlivening energy, which is "reward." The autumn equinox, in the sphere of metal, is the killing energy, which is "punishment." Reward is that whereby to enliven people, punishment is that whereby to mature people. Without punishment, reward is not perfect; without reward, punishment is not complete. When there is both punishment and reward, the evolution of heaven and earth can circulate unceasingly by the flow of one energy.

In practitioners of the Tao, the return of the firmness of real knowledge to proper balance is like the autumn solstice; the return of the flexibility of conscious knowledge to proper balance is like the spring solstice. The reversion of both real knowledge and conscious knowledge to proper balance is like the reward of spring and the punishment of autumn. The firm strength of real knowledge is that whereby to control the deviant energy of the human mind; the flexible receptivity of conscious knowledge is that whereby to nurture the right energy of the mind of Tao.

Being firm when it is appropriate to be firm, being flexible when it is appropriate to be flexible, not missing the time, firmness and flexibility then are balanced, like the spring and autumn equinoxes each coming in their time. Therefore the text says the moon in the east and west reaches its season. When there is flexibility in firmness, and firmness in flexibility, firmness and flexibility are as one; then reality and consciousness are not disparate. It is like spring reward and autumn punishment alternating in course; therefore the text says punishment and reward are at hand, the medicine being patterned on this.

When the path reaches correct balance of firmness and flexibility, the mind of Tao is always present, and the human mind is utterly quiet; real knowledge is completely conscious, and conscious knowledge is completely real. When reality and knowledge are united, and innate knowledge and capacity take form in the gold elixir, one should bathe it and keep it warm, taking the firewood out from below the furnace. Otherwise, if one does not know when enough is enough, and still adds fire, then firmness is excessive and flexibility insufficient; so firmness and flexibility are not balanced, the medicine dries out and the elixir is damaged—how can danger be avoided?

[35]

ON CULTURAL COOKING AND MARTIAL REFINING

The sun and moon meet once in thirty days; exchanging hours for days is the pattern of the spiritual work. Guarding the castle, bat-

tling in the field, knowing bad and good, you increase the spiritual cinnabar, filling the crucible, red.

The moon originally has no light; its light depends on the sun. In one year it meets the sun twelve times. In one month, thirty days, they meet once between the beginning and end of the month. People's real knowledge is hidden away, pure yin without yang, like the moon's having no light; it needs conscious knowledge before it can produce light. When real knowledge and conscious knowledge meet, it is like the sun and moon meeting in thirty days.

Developed people, emulating the image of sun and moon meeting, place thirty days within one day, and also place one day within one hour: in one hour activating strong energy, they use the human mind to produce the mind of Tao, use the mind of Tao to govern the human mind, produce real knowledge by conscious knowledge, and purge conscious knowledge by real knowledge; they gather the undifferentiated primal energy for the mother of the elixir, and follow the spiritual mechanism of the transformations of yin and yang as the firing process.

This path has cultural cooking and martial refining. "Guarding the castle" is cultural cooking; "battling in the field" is martial refining. To apply the cultural when it is appropriate and the martial when it is appropriate is good; to apply the martial when the cultural is appropriate or the cultural when the martial is appropriate is bad. The cultural fire is turning the attention within, dismissing intellection, nurturing the true energy single-mindedly, like guarding a castle. The martial fire is controlling anger and desire, getting rid of falsehood and maintaining truth, forcefully removing acquired energies, like battling in the field.

Knowing the cultural and the martial clearly, understanding good and bad clearly, when there is some matter, use the martial fire, and when there is no matter use the cultural fire. Culturally cooking and martially refining, yin energy is exhausted and yang energy is purified; real knowledge and conscious knowledge join, and turn into innate knowledge and innate capacity—the original nature of ineffable awareness is round and bright, clean and naked, tranquil and unstirring yet sensitive and effective, sensitive and effective yet tranquil and unstirring. Integrating with the celestial design, there is no human desire. This is like "spiritual cinnabar filling the crucible red."

When the cinnabar is spiritualized, the substance of energy changes; being neither material nor immaterial, neither existent nor nonexistent, it is wholly the energy of pure yang. By ingesting this one can get rid of illness and extend life, nullify calamity and avoid problems. Restoring one's original nature, open awareness without obscurity, truly empty yet subtly existing, creation cannot limit one, yin and yang cannot constrain one, myriad things cannot hurt one. And yet, there are also people in the world who know good and bad but still will not do the spiritual work.

[36]

ON THE MEANINGS OF HEXAGRAMS (2 VERSES)

When obstruction and tranquility mix, myriad things are full; the two hexagrams difficulty and darkness receive life and growth. Getting the meaning herein, stop seeking symbols; if you study the lines, you use the mind in vain.

With *heaven* ≡ above and *earth* ≡≡ below, the celestial energy descends from above, while the terrestrial energy ascends from below; yin and yang do not mix, so this is *obstruction*. With *earth* above and *heaven* below, the terrestrial energy descends from above, while the celestial energy rises from below; yin and yang mix, so this is *tranquility*. When obstruction ends, tranquility comes; as soon as yin and yang mix, myriad things are born, filling the universe.

Difficulty has *water* ≡≡ above and *thunder* ≡≡ below; within water there is thunder—yang arises within yin, thereby dissolving yin and giving birth to things. *Darkness* has *mountain* ≡≡ above and *water* ≡≡ below; under the mountain is water—yang falls into yin, thereby nurturing yang and developing things.

Obstruction and *tranquility* refer to the flow or blockage of myriad things; *difficulty* and *darkness* refer to the birth and development, are all operated by the coming and going of yin and yang. The coming and going of yin and yang, the flow and blockage, birth and development of myriad things, all come about naturally and are not forced.

In the path of cultivation of reality, when firmness and flexibility are not yet joined, this is *obstruction;* when firmness and flexibility join, this is *tranquility*. When firmness is appropriate, to promote firmness to cultivate reality is *difficulty;* when flexibility is appropriate, to use flexibility to nurture reality is *darkness*. When firmness and flexibility are used according to the appropriate timing, their variations produce the sixty-four hexagrams; this is within our own mind.

Generally speaking, the way the hexagram symbols produce meanings, we can forget the symbol when we have grasped the meaning. If one does not know the intent of the hexagram and just clings to the form of the hexagram, one will want one yang, two yangs, three yangs to effect *tranquility,* and will want one yin, two yins, three yins to prevent *obstruction*. To produce three yangs to effect *tranquility* is somewhat close to the principle, but when it comes to producing three yins to prevent *obstruction,* that would be impossible. Furthermore, one might take the midnight hour as yang energy stirring within *water,* focusing the mind on the genital region at midnight, and considering this *"difficulty* in the morning," then take the noon hour as yang energy having a limit and stopping, focusing the mind on the heart at noon, and considering this *"darkness* in the evening." If you take these to be *tranquility, obstruction, difficulty,* and *darkness,* how can you align all the lines of the sixty-four hexagrams in practice? If you study all the lines and try to align them all, would that not be a vain use of mind?

An ancient immortal said, "It is not necessary to seek midnight and noon in the sky; in the body one yang naturally arises." This can be a clear testimony for those who work on the lines of the hexagrams—students should think it over carefully.

[37]

Setting up symbols in the hexagrams is based on descriptions of the modes; understanding the symbol, forget the words—the idea is clear of itself. The whole world is astray, only clinging to symbols, acting out the energies of the hexagrams, hoping to fly aloft.

The sixty-four hexagrams of the *I Ching,* with three hundred and eighty-four lines, only elucidate the modes of yin and yang, and the representations of balance and imbalance. If you understand the meaning of balance and imbalance of yin and yang, you can harmonize yin and yang, spontaneously fitting in with the symbols of the hexagrams.

Nevertheless, the deluded who do not investigate this meaning instead cling to the symbols; they intend to act out the energies of the hexagrams by practicing *difficulty* in the morning and practicing *darkness* at night, beginning with *difficulty* and *darkness* and ending with *settled* and *unsettled,* hoping thereby to attain the Tao and fly aloft. They do not know that when the adepts have spoken of *"difficulty* in the morning, *darkness* at night," this is to teach people that the arising of yang is difficult and the falling of yang is darkness.

The rising of yang is like the morning of the day, the falling of yang is like the evening of the night. To advance the yang fire to gather yang when yang arises is called *"difficulty* in the morning." To operate the yin convergence to nurture yang when yang falls is called *"darkness* at night." *Settled* and *unsettled* teach people that when yin and yang are joined, that is being settled, and when yin and yang have not yet joined, that is being unsettled. Once yin and yang are joined, the gold elixir crystallizes, and the work of the yang fire is finished. Once settled, it is necessary to prevent unsettling, for which the work of yin convergence is required. If yin and yang have not joined, and the gold elixir is not crystallized, yin convergence is no use—what is unsettled should speedily be settled, and for this the work of the yang fire must be used.

The meanings concealed in these hexagrams are the meanings of these four hexagrams; considered in this light, the other sixty hexagrams are all permutations of yin and yang. That is why the text says, "Understanding the symbol, forget the words—the idea is clear of itself." If you understand the meaning of the hexagram symbols, the pivot of heaven is in your hand, the axis of earth depends on your mind. Wherever you go, everywhere is the Tao—there is no need to cling to the hexagram symbols, for you spontaneously accord with them.

[38]

ON THE BEGINNING OF YANG AND CULMINATION OF YIN

The filling and emptying of heaven and earth have their own times: if you are discerning and capable of dissolving and generating, then you will know the mechanism. Based on the beginning of yang and culmination of yin making plain the order, killing off the three vermin, there is hope of attaining the Tao.

The Tao of heaven and earth is the Tao of filling and emptying. When filling culminates, then there is emptying; when emptying culminates, then there is filling—each has its time. If practitioners of the Tao can clearly discern the true principle of fullness and emptiness, and also can dissolve their yin and generate their yang, only then can they be said to know the mechanism of filling and emptying, dissolving and generating.

Overcoming and dissolving the yin is the mechanism of emptying, generating and expanding the yang is the mechanism of filling. But dissolving and generating are not apart from the sense of real knowledge and the essence of conscious knowledge. The sense of real knowledge is firm, and is in the realm of the beginning of yang, associated with metal. The essence of conscious knowledge is flexible, and is in the realm of the culmination of yin, associated with wood. Using firmness to govern the external, overcoming acquired energies from outside influences, using flexibility to deal with the internal, quietly nurturing natural reality, firmness and flexibility are both employed, the inner and outer are both cultivated—this is called "the beginning of yang and culmination of yin making plain the order."

When the order is clear, firmness and flexibility are in their proper places, dissolving and generating accord with the time; the true energy prevails and false energy is transformed. Inwardly thoughts do not emerge, while external things do not get in. There are no accretions defiling the sense faculties; one is naked and clean. This is called "killing off the three vermin." Once the three vermin are killed off, all negative elements are transmuted, and there is hope of attaining the great Tao.

The important point of this section is in the line "If you are discerning and capable of dissolving and generating, then you will know the mechanism." Discernment involves thorough consideration, penetrating every subtlety. Only after profound work over a long period of time can one see reality. When one can see reality, only after attaining correspondence of understanding and action is one able to dissolve and generate. When one can dissolve and generate, only then is this knowing the mechanism. If one cannot dissolve and generate, one still cannot be said to know the mechanism; this means one has not thoroughly discerned the principles—how can one then make the order plain and kill the three vermin? Therefore the study of correcting the mind and making the intent sincere is all a matter of investigating things and attaining knowledge.

[39]

ON THE MYSTERIOUS FEMALE (2 VERSES)

If you want to attain the eternal immortality of the valley spirit, you must set the foundation on the mysterious female. Once the true vitality has returned to the room of yellow gold, the globe of spiritual light never parts.

The valley spirit is the unique energy of primordial nothingness; this is what is called the spiritual embryo. This energy is not matter or emptiness, yet is both material and empty at the same time. It is in the darkness of profound abstraction—when you look for it you cannot see it, when you listen for it you cannot hear it, when you try to grasp it you cannot find it. It is the border of the mind of Tao and the human mind, the root of real knowledge and conscious knowledge, the basis of firm sense and flexible essence. It gives birth to heaven, gives birth to earth, gives birth to humanity: Confucians call it the Great Ultimate, or ultimate good, or ultimate truth; Buddhists call it complete awareness, or the body of reality, or the relic of Buddha; Taoists call it the gold elixir, or the spiritual embryo, or the valley spirit. In reality it is the innate knowledge and innate capacity fundamental to human life, the spirit of open consciousness like an empty valley.

When this valley spirit falls into temporal conditioning, yin and yang separate; the artificial acts while the real recedes, and the valley spirit is buried away, as though dead. If you want to cultivate the gold elixir, it is necessary to revive this valley spirit; if you want to enliven the valley spirit, it is first necessary to harmonize yin and yang. If yin and yang are not in harmony, the gold elixir will not crystallize.

The "mystery" is yang, which is firm strong sense. The "female" is yin, which is flexible receptive essence. When there is both firmness and flexibility, the valley spirit lives forever, and the foundation of immortality is established. The valley spirit consists of the combination of polar energies, with firmness and flexibility in proper balance. When the poles combine, in the darkness of transic abstraction there is something which is called the vitality of the real unity. The vitality of the real unity is another term for the valley spirit. Before cultivation and refinement, it appears and disappears—then it is called true vitality; after cultivation and refinement it solidifies and does not dissolve—then it is called the valley spirit.

Once true vitality has been returned to the room of yellow gold, mental focus is restored to central balance, and the valley spirit stabilizes. When the valley spirit is stable, the mind of Tao is always there, and the human mind obeys it docilely: real knowledge and conscious knowledge unite, and innate knowledge and capacity integrate completely with the celestial design, tranquil and unperturbed yet sensitive and effective, sensitive and effective yet tranquil and unperturbed. Always responsive, yet always calm, the globe of spiritual light never parts. When the spiritual light never parts, this is the immortality of the valley spirit. This is what the author is referring to in the statement, "When you have ingested a grain of the gold elixir, then you will know your destiny doesn't depend on heaven." The valley spirit, true vitality, and the spiritual light are one thing: the only difference is whether or not one has developed it in oneself. Students should be aware that they are not three different things.

[40]

Rare are those in the world who know the opening of the mysterious female; stop fooling around with mouth and nose. Even if you do breathing exercises for many years, how can you get the golden raven to catch the rabbit?

Lao-tzu said, "The valley spirit doesn't die; this is called the mysterious female. The opening of the mysterious female is called the root of heaven and earth." The "mystery" is *heaven*, yang, the quality of firm strength; the "female" is *earth*, yin, the quality of flexible receptivity. Yang rules movement, yin rules stillness; the movement and stillness of the valley spirit is the opening of the mysterious female.

This opening gives birth to heaven, earth, humans and other beings; it is ultimately nonexistent yet contains ultimate existence, it is ultimately empty yet contains ultimate fulfillment. In the human body it is the place where the physical elements do not adhere; right in the middle of heaven and earth, one hole hangs in space, opening and closing at particular times, moving and resting spontaneously. Fundamentally it has no fixed position, and no form or shape; it is also called the aperture of the mysterious pass. The mysterious pass is utterly empty and utterly inconceivable; being and nonbeing have no place there. It is also called the door of all marvels. "All marvels" means that it includes all principles and contains all virtues.

If you take the mouth and nose to be the mysterious female and do breathing exercises with polluted air, how can you chase the golden raven and jade rabbit back into the yellow path and solidify them into the elixir of supreme consciousness? The golden raven is a symbol for the sun; within yang there is yin, in humans the quality of correct balance of flexible receptivity, which is the spiritual essence of conscious knowledge. The jade rabbit is a symbol for the moon; within yin there is yang, in humans the quality of correct balance of firm strength, which is the true sense of real knowledge.

The quality of correct balance of conscious knowledge and real knowledge is the energy of the twin poles of the yang mystery and the yin female; the valley spirit is formed by the consolidation of the energies of the two poles. If you do not know the mysterious female, how can you know the raven and rabbit? If you do not know the raven and rabbit, how can you be capable of the immortality of the valley spirit? What opening is this? If you go along, you die; if you come back, you live. Time and again it has had you seek without finding—how could the mysterious female be easy to know?

[41]

ON ESSENCE AND SENSE

Few people know these are different names from the same source; both of them, mysterious, are the essential key. Preserving life, making the physical being whole, clarifying enhancement and reduction, the purple gold elixir is most marvelous.

Spiritual alchemy is accomplished by two medicinal ingredients, one firm, one flexible—nothing else. Firmness belongs to the sense of real knowledge; flexibility belongs to the essence of conscious knowledge. Though essence and sense have different names, really they both come from the primordial energy of true unity in nonbeing. This is what is called the mysterious female in the preceding verse. Mystery and femaleness, mystery upon mystery, are the essential key of the undying valley spirit.

In the primordial spontaneous Tao, the valley spirit gives birth to the mysterious female; in the temporal restorative Tao, the mysterious female becomes the valley spirit. If mystery and receptivity do not combine, openness and consciousness do not join: the reason the mysterious female is the essential key is simply that it is that whereby to form the valley spirit. When the mysterious female is established, the valley spirit forms; thereby can life be preserved and the physical being made whole, and also enhancement by advancing yang and reduction by repelling yin is clarified.

When yang is increased until it cannot be increased any further, and yin is reduced until it cannot be reduced any further, when yin is exhausted and yang is pure, the valley spirit lives forever, merged into one energy, without any polluting substance, round and bright, clean, naked, free, unconstrained by creation, unharmed by myriad things. It is like the firing process forging purple gold elixir, restoring life from death, most marvelous.

[42]

ON DOING

Starting with doing, people can hardly see; then when nondoing is reached, everyone knows. If you only see nondoing as the essential marvel, how can you know that doing is the foundation?

The real people of ancient times said that essence and life should both be cultivated; so the work requires two stages. One of the paths of spiritual alchemy is cultivating life, one is cultivating essence. The path of cultivating life is the path of doing; the path of cultivating essence is the path of nondoing. The path of doing is prolonging life by certain arts; the path of nondoing is making the being whole by the Tao.

"Starting with doing" means the path of doing is used to build life. The science of building life is carried out entirely according to rules, the essential path of snatching the primal energy before the differentiation of chaos, gripping the mainspring of evolution, turning back the process of time. Heaven and earth cannot know it, ghosts and spirits cannot fathom it, divination cannot figure it out; since even heaven and earth, ghosts and spirits, and divination cannot know it, how can people know?

Ending up in nondoing means the path of nondoing is used to cultivate essence. The path of cultivating essence is embracing the fundamental, keeping to unity, all things empty, like a hen incubating an egg, like an oyster embracing a pearl. When this work reaches its consummation, one becomes ultimately truthful and has prescience; the mind of wisdom opens up, and one develops instantaneous comprehension. One has prior understanding of good and bad consequences, so everyone knows.

However, if people only know the path of nondoing is the essential marvel and do not know the path of doing is the foundation, not knowing doing, only nondoing, they are not only unable to cultivate life, they are also unable to cultivate essence. Even if they have some cultivation, this is only cultivation of the acquired nature—how can they cultivate the primordial fundamental essence?

The fundamental essence is the essence of the life bestowed by heaven; originally essence and life are one, with no duality. Due to mixture with temporal conditioning, yin and yang separate, and one becomes two—essence and life differentiate. When essence and life are separate, then essence cannot attend to life and life cannot attend to essence: life is usurped by things and cannot be autonomous; essence too is disturbed by this. When essence is disturbed and life shaken, false and true are lumped together, reason and desire get mixed up; the artificial handles affairs while the real recedes from its position. Day by day, year by year, negative energy strips away the positive until it is exhausted, so essence and life inevitably break down and perish.

Therefore spiritual alchemy must start with doing, restoring the primordial while in the midst of the temporal, recovering one's original jewel of life. When the jewel of life is in the hand, its control depends on oneself, and it is not moved by creation. At that point one embraces the fundamental and preserves unity, traveling the path of nondoing, thereby realizing the original essence of real emptiness, directly transcending to the marvelous path of the supreme one vehicle. What can be done for all the quietists who only know nondoing and do not know doing?

[43]

ON FEMALE AND MALE

Within black there is white, which is the matrix of the elixir; within the male is enclosed the female, which is the spiritual embryo. When the absolute one is in the furnace, it should be carefully watched; gathered jewels in the three fields correspond to the three treasures.

"Within black there is white" is the real knowledge awakened by the mind of Tao; it is the path of correct balance of firm strength, so it is called the matrix of the elixir. "Within the male is enclosed the female" refers to the original conscious knowledge of the human mind; it is the quality of correct balance of flexible receptivity, so it is called the spiritual embryo. When strength and receptivity are joined in one, and firmness and flexibility are one energy, the human mind changes into the mind of Tao, and conscious knowledge returns to real knowledge. This is called the absolute one, containing true energy.

The absolute one is pure unified spirit in which yin and yang are merged together; it is a different name for the gold elixir. Putting this true energy of absolute unity into the furnace of evolution, incubating and nurturing it, carefully keeping it securely sealed, watching over it and not losing it, will result in wholeness of vitality, wholeness of energy, and wholeness of spirit. These jewels gathered in the three fields are like the "three terraces," the three stars that surround the star representing the lord of the heavens. Then evolution is in your hands.

These three fields do not refer to the perineum, center of the torso, or center of the brain, nor to the umbilical region, solar plexus, or center of the brow, or to the coccyx, center of the spine, or back of the brain; they are the places where the three great medicines—primordial vitality, primordial energy, and primordial spirit are produced. They are formless and have no location, but because they are where the vitality, energy, and spirit are produced, they are called fields, and because vitality, energy, and spirit are spoken of separately they are called three fields.

In reality, the three fields are all one field, and the three jewels are all one jewel. Because there are three levels of work—refining vitality into energy, refining energy into spirit, and refining spirit into space—three fields are spoken of separately; but when you reach refinement of spirit into space, there is only one space, and vitality, energy, and spirit too return to tracklessness—how can there be any more talk of three fields?

[44]

ON BEING AND NONBEING

Seeking within abstraction for the impression of being, looking within trance for the true vitality, from this being and nonbeing interpenetrate—without having seen it, how can you imagine it?

Abstraction is an indefinable impression which is neither formal nor void; trance is an invisible realm which is utterly silent and tranquil. The impression of being within ecstasy is conscious knowledge; the true vitality in trance is real knowledge. Conscious knowledge is light outside and dark inside—this is nonbeing within being. Real knowledge is dark outside and light inside—this is being within nonbeing. If practitioners of the Tao want to make the gold elixir, they must seek conscious knowledge in abstraction and seek real knowledge in trance. If they can actually attain intellectual understanding and spiritual realization, and find the real truth, this is called having seen. Once one has seen clearly, one controls conscious knowledge by real knowledge, and nurtures real knowledge by conscious knowledge. Then being and nonbeing are henceforth wed, interpenetrating and communing. The gold elixir is thereupon formed. Otherwise, if you don't know the impression within abstraction or the vitality within trance, you have not seen what the medicinal ingredients of the gold elixir are; if you try to form the elixir according to arbitrary ideas, how can you even imagine it?

[45]

ON INGESTION OF THE ELIXIR (2 VERSES)

When the four forms meet, the mystic body is made; where the five elements are complete, the violet gold is bright. Freeing it from the matrix and ingesting it, the body reaches sagehood; limitless dragons and spirits all become lost in amazement.

The path of spiritual alchemy lies entirely in aggregating the five elements and combining the four forms. If the four forms are joined, then essence, sense, vitality, and spirit unite; thus the mystic body is made. If one can then go on to truly keep balance, and use the fire of natural reality to refine it, this is called the completeness of the five elements.

Once the five elements are complete, benevolence, justice, courtesy, and wisdom all return to one truthfulness; essence and sense, vitality and spirit all transmute into one energy. Strength and receptivity combine, firmness and flexibility are traceless; real knowledge and conscious knowledge also turn into innate knowledge and innate capacity, ultimately good without evil, integrated with the celestial design, all-pervasive, unobstructed. Open awareness unobscured, it includes all principles and responds to myriad things. This is like yellow gold refined into violet gold, its light radiant. When you ingest this, it dissolves acquired mundanity and exposes the primordial spiritual body. Entering into the foundation of sages, one's fate depends on oneself and not on heaven. How can dragons and spirits not be amazed?

The meaning of ingestion is sudden enlightenment; it does not mean swallowing something. When the primordial energy has been refined to perfection, there is an abrupt shift from a gradual process to a sudden realization, from clarification to truth. This is like myriad diseases vanishing when medicinal elixir is ingested. Therefore the body can reach sagehood. Students should clearly understand the intent which is outside the words: if you look upon "ingesting" as swallowing, think carefully about the primordial energy—it has no substance, no form; what would one swallow? This should clarify the matter.

[46]

When the party is ended at the flower pond, the moon shines clear; astride a golden dragon, one visits the star of the lord of heaven. Henceforth, after the meeting of the immortals, let the oceans, hills and vales, move as they may.

"The party ended at the flower pond" refers to taking the true yang within *water* ☵ and putting it in the furnace of evolution; the mind of Tao peacefully settles and "fills the belly." "The moon shines clear" means the mind of Tao is always present, the light of real knowledge shines clearly, without concealment or deception. As for "astride a golden dragon," *heaven* ☰ is represented by gold and by a dragon: taking the mind of Tao within *water* ☵, the one yang of real knowledge, filling in the human mind within *fire* ☲, the one yin of conscious knowledge, conscious knowledge then also transmutes into real knowledge, and *fire* ☲ again becomes *heaven* ☰. The original self becomes completely manifest, wholly integrated with the celestial design, round and bright, pure yang with no yin.

As for "visiting the star of the lord of heaven," the lord of heaven is the lord of creation; when practice of reality reaches the point of restoration of the body of heaven, the lord is in oneself, the key of heaven is in the hand, the axis of earth depends on the mind. Then creation cannot constrain you, myriad things cannot move you; you visit the lord of heaven and become a companion of heaven. Your work is accomplished in the human world, your fame is proclaimed in heaven above. Henceforth you meet with the immortals; even if the oceans should overturn and the hills and valleys shift, the spiritual body is permanently indestructible.

[47]

ON THE ELIXIR CRYSTALLIZING FROM WITHIN

If you want to know the method of recovering elixir of gold liquid, you must cultivate your own garden. It does not require huffing and puffing or application of force; spontaneously the elixir matures and is released from the matrix of reality.

In the method of recovering elixir of gold liquid, the great medicine is extremely close at hand, not far away; the work is simple, not complicated. Your garden naturally has the herbs; you can cultivate it any time. You don't need an external furnace and crucible, or effort to operate the fire, huffing and puffing, the elixir naturally develops to maturity and comes out.

The "elixir" is the energy of true unity, of primordial nothingness; in connection with the root of consciousness when chaos first becomes differentiated, it acts as the generative energy which produces beings. Latent, it is true emptiness; apparent, it is ineffable existence.

Functioning, it is the mind of Tao; nurturing, it is the valley spirit. It is ultimate nonbeing, yet contains ultimate being; it is utterly empty, yet contains complete fulfillment. In it are the energies of the five elements, but not the substances of the five elements. It is immanent in the five elements, but not trapped in the five elements. Becoming sage, becoming wise, becoming enlightened, becoming immortal—all are based on this.

This is nothing else but our original, inherent endowment, which is neither material nor void. It is just because of involvement with acquired conditioning, working with the spirit of discrimination, that it is buried and not apparent. If you meet a genuine teacher who points it out to you, for the first time you realize it is already in your own garden, and is not obtained from another. The seed is then settled, and gradually grows, naturally developing to maturity. The author says, "You should cultivate your own garden"—maybe this will wake up those on deviated paths who seek outside themselves and change their minds.

[48]

On medicine coming from without

Stop applying clever artifice at work, and recognize the other's method of not dying. Add life-extending wine to the pot; gather soul-restoring broth in the crucible.

The preceding section said to cultivate your own garden; lest people cling to the individual body in practice, this section immediately follows up by saying, "Stop applying clever artifice at work, and recognize the other's method of not dying." The statement "cultivate your own garden" refers to the fate that the medicinal substance of the gold elixir is not more in sages or less in ordinary people but complete in everyone, not needing to be sought from another but inherent in oneself. The expression "the other's method of not dying" refers to the fact that the primal energy mixes with temporal conditioning, so that the spirit of discrimination does things and yang is trapped by yin, like something of one's own becoming the possession of another.

If you want to return to the basis and restore the fundamental, it is necessary to use the method of pursuit and incorporation, so that the primordial true yang which is gone can come back: when it returns, it is as before one's own. Before it has come back, it belongs to other; once it has come back, it belongs to self. There is a distinction between other and self because there are times when it has not come back and when it has come back. Therefore in the future it is necessary to tread on the ground of reality, gradually gathering, gradually refining, adding more and more, collecting more and more, thereby carrying out work in which there is striving. But though we say there is striving, in reality there is no striving. To say there is striving is in reference to appropriating yin and yang and taking over evolution; it does not refer to all the other clever artifices. It is all natural function.

"Adding life-extending wine" means adding the real knowledge of the mind of Tao, so as to stabilize life. "Gathering soul-restoring broth" means emptying the conscious knowledge of the human mind, so as to nurture essence. The life-extending wine is metal juice; the soul-restoring broth is wood liquid. Adding the metal, gathering the wood, metal and wood join—sense and essence unite—and real knowledge and conscious knowledge solidify, and the basis of the elixir takes form.

The words "adding" and "gathering" have a most deep meaning. As yin and yang have been long fragmented, without adding and gathering, progressively advancing, metal and wood cannot join, sense and essence cannot unite. Adding and gathering, working hard by day and being careful by night, neither forgetting nor forcing, the accomplishment deepening as time goes on, metal and wood naturally join, sense and essence naturally combine; only then can one extend life, restore the soul, and enter the realm of immortality.

[49]

ON THE TWO ELIXIRS, INNER AND OUTER

The fine ghee of the snowy mountains, of one flavor, pours into the eastern sun's furnace of evolution. If he crosses the K'un-lun, going northwest, Chang Chien will finally get to see Ma Ku.

The snowy mountains (Himalayas) are in the west; they stand for metal, representing basic sense. Ghee stands for water, representing basic vitality. The eastern sun stands for wood, representing basic essence. The furnace of evolution stands for fire, representing basic spirit. Taking the metal and water of basic sense and basic vitality and pouring them into the wood and fire of basic essence and basic spirit, use the wood and fire to refine the metal and water, use the metal and water to control the wood and fire. Using discipline to perfect award, using award to complete discipline, when discipline and award are both employed, metal and wood join, water and fire balance each other; the four elements are harmoniously combined, and the elixir is recovered. This is the model of the outer elixir.

The K'un-lun mountains are in the northwest; as the mountain range from which myriad mountains extend, it is compared to the energy of the primordial true unity, which is the generative energy that gives birth to beings. Northwest is the province of *heaven* ☰, the highest place on earth. Height stands for yang. Chang Chien, the famous traveler, is yang; Ma Ku, a female immortal, is yin. When the restored elixir has crystallized and transmuted into the true unitive energy, going from vagueness to clarity, yang energy is replete and the great medicine arises; wholly integrated with the celestial design, firm strength balanced correctly, it frees a grain of elixir of pure positive energy. With this elixir one sublimates the body's acquired force of mundanity, like a cat catching a mouse; false yin vanished and true yin appears. Yin and yang merge and coalesce into the spiritual embryo. Therefore the text says that if he crosses the K'un-lun, going northwest, Chang Chien will finally get to see Ma Ku.

The words "will finally get to see" contain the stages of the work. Before this restored elixir reaches the peak of yang, "Chang Chien" cannot yet see "Ma Ku." Only when it is developed to the peak of yang will "Chang Chien" get to see "Ma Ku." When true yin and true yang meet, the mind of Tao and the human mind both transform into the original mind; real knowledge and conscious knowledge transform into the original mind; real knowledge and conscious knowledge transform into innate knowledge. A tiny black pearl hangs in the middle of nothingness, neither material nor immaterial, illumining the universe to view, with no obstruction whatsoever. This is the model of the inner elixir.

The outer elixir is a matter of regaining what has been lost, returned inside from outside. This is the "restored" or "recovered" elixir. The inner elixir is a matter of refining away the force of mundanity from the elixir once it has been recovered, manifesting the true light from within. This is the "great" elixir. When the outer elixir is complete and the inner elixir perfected, one roams in the land of nothing-whatsoever.

[50]

ON POSITIVE VITALITY

Without knowing the positive vitality, as well as host and guest, who knows which is near, which far? Vainly shutting the coccyx opening in the bedroom has thoroughly deluded so many people on earth.

Yuan-tu-tzu said, "A point of positive vitality is hidden in the physical body: it is not in the heart or genitals, but in the aperture of the mysterious pass." Positive vitality is so called because it is completely positive and pure, without a trace of mundane polluted energy. This is the original pure vitality, firm, strong, balanced correctly: latent, it is true emptiness; active it is ineffable existence. This is what is called the innate good mind; it is also called the mind of Tao. It cannot be compared with the conditioned mundane polluted vitality.

In the human body, the positive vitality governs creation and gets rid of aberrations. Ancients called it the vitality of true unity, the water of true unity, and the energy of true unity. In reality, these are all one thing, the positive vitality of the mind of Tao.

The positive vitality is primordial, and is the "host." The mundane vitality is acquired, and is the "guest." The host is close to the self, the guest is far from the self. If you mistake the mundane vitality for the positive vitality, practice the art of sexual yoga, shut your coccyx and control the sexual fluid, imagining you will thereby form the elixir, how can you accomplish it?

Though the positive energy is obtained in a "room," this does not mean an actual bedroom, but rather the "room" of the body. Similar expressions, like "house" and "garden," are also used with the same meaning—how can you take it to mean an actual room? If students want to know the positive vitality, first seek the mysterious pass. When you know the mysterious pass, the positive vitality is herein.

[51]

ON RETURNING TO THE ROOT

Myriad beings, in all their multiplicity, each return to the root; returning to the root, restoring life, they then exist forever. People can hardly understand knowing eternity and returning to the root; again and again we hear of false practices bringing on misfortune.

Myriad beings are born in spring, grow in summer, are gathered in autumn, and stored in winter: this is the constant Tao. Having produced and fostered them, then to gather and store them, is called returning to the root. Returning them to the root is called restoring life. Restoring life means restoring the living energy of the natural order. Once the living energy is restored, it again emerges from the root and therefore can exist forever without dying. If people can know the natural mechanism of eternal existence of all beings, and can return to the root and restore life, then they also can exist forever and be immortals.

However, the principle of the path of knowledge of eternity and returning to the root is very profound, and its practice is very subtle. There is the matter of the density and energy level of the medicines, and the matter of the degrees of intensity of the firing process. There are inner medicine and outer medicine, inner firing and outer firing. There is gentle firing and intense firing, there is a process of crystallizing the elixir, there is a process of freeing the elixir, there is a process of cultivating life, there is a process of cultivating essence.

These steps each must be transmitted by a genuine teacher before they can be put into practice. Otherwise, if you don't know to seek and inquire from others, you rely on your own intelligence and perception, making your own personal assessments and taking your private guesswork to be understanding, impetuously setting about the task, still unaware that the slightest deviation produces tremendous error. It is inevitable that false practice, arbitrary action, will bring on disaster.

[52]

ON THE SWORD OF WISDOM

Ou-yeh personally transmitted a method for casting a sword; Mo-yeh, with metal and water, alloyed flexibility and strength. When the forging is complete, it can read people's minds, a flash of lightning slaying demons for ten thousand miles.

A sword is something to protect the body; here it means the tool of wisdom to become enlightened and immortal, the means to become a sage. This is what is called the restored elixir; there is no "sword" other than the restored elixir. The "restored elixir" means restoration of the original innate knowledge and innate capacity, the true consciousness in which strength and flexibility are combined. "Casting the sword" means casting this tool of wisdom of innate knowledge and capacity in which strength and flexibility are united. In terms of substance, it is called elixir; in terms of function is called a sword. In reality the sword and elixir are one.

In ancient times there was a smith named Ou-yeh: as he was casting a sword, it repeatedly failed to turn out; his wife, Mo-yeh, jumped into the forge, and the work was accomplished in one firing. People called it the precious sword of Mo-yeh; it was incomparably sharp. In practicing the Tao, casting the sword is first: taking energy with a proper balance of strength and flexibility, using water and fire to forge it into a masterpiece, it is called the sword of wisdom. Wearing it at one's side, using it at will, in a flash of lightning it cuts through demons for ten thousand miles.

The author uses Ou-yeh and Mo-yeh to symbolize the combination of strength and flexibility—indeed there is a subtle meaning in this. Practitioners of the Tao need to know strength and flexibility must both be properly balanced before it is possible to transmute the mundanity of acquired conditioning. If one yields when it is appropriate to be firm, or is adamant when it is appropriate to be flexible, or is strong but too aggressive, or flexible but too weak, this is not correct balance, and so the casting of the sword will not succeed. If the casting of the sword is unsuccessful, inwardly one has no mastery, and will get bogged down every step of the way—how can one complete the great Path then?

But the method of casting the sword is not easy to know; the combination of strength and flexibility is most difficult to understand. If you do not meet a genuine teacher and get personal instruction, you will just be indulging in vain guesswork.

[53]

ON HARMONIOUS COMBINATION
OF ESSENCE AND SENSE

Drum on bamboo to call the tortoise to swallow the jade mushroom; strum a lute to summon the phoenix to drink from the al-

chemical crucible. Shortly a golden light pervading the body will appear; do not speak of this rule to ordinary people.

Bamboo is something empty inside; it sounds when you drum on it. A lute is something musical; tune it and it is harmonious. A tortoise is a being that nurtures breath energy. A phoenix is a concretization of civilization. A jade mushroom is something soft and tender with a long life. An alchemical crucible is something pure and unadulterated. The tortoise and crucible belong to yang, the phoenix and jade mushroom belong to yin.

Spiritual alchemy involves two things, "emptying the mind" and "filling the belly." There is nothing else besides this. When the human mind is emptied, the mind of Tao arises and fills the belly; this is like drumming bamboo to call the tortoise. Once the belly is full, the flexibility of the human mind is governed by the firmness of the mind of Tao; this is like the tortoise swallowing the jade mushroom. When real knowledge becomes manifest, conscious knowledge is quiet and the mind is clear; this is like strumming the lute and summoning the phoenix. Once the mind is clear, the essence of conscious knowledge is used to nurture the sense of real knowledge; this is like the phoenix drinking from the alchemical crucible.

When the emptiness and fullness of the real knowledge of the Tao mind and the conscious knowledge of the human mind correspond, firmness and flexibility are united; always responsive yet always calm, round and bright, clean and naked, bare and untrammeled, the whole being is crystal clear, inside and out illumined, and one enters the sages' realm of equanimous serenity on the middle way. This is a matter of the path of appropriating yin and yang, taking over evolution, revolving heaven and earth, controlling potential and energy, primordial and unopposed by nature; how could it be discussed with ordinary people?

[54]

On gradual and sudden

When the medicines meet in energy and kind, only then do they take on form; the Tao is in imperceptible subtlety, merging with nature. When one grain of spiritual elixir is swallowed into the belly, for the first time you know one's destiny does not depend on heaven.

The medicines which are of the same energy and same kind are the true yang of real knowledge and the true yin of conscious knowledge. Only when they conjoin is it possible to crystallize form from formlessness. What cannot be seen or heard is called imperceptibly subtle; unseen and unheard, the Tao returns to emptiness, one energy undifferentiated, lively and active, without thought, without contrivance, silent and unstirring, yet sensitive and effective, not depending on forced effort for any reason in the world, merging with nature, for the first time yin and yang congeal.

Once yin and yang merge, a grain of spiritual elixir hangs in space, illumining the whole world. If you ingest this, light arises within, dissolving aggregated conditioning, changing acquired characteristics. Then for the first time you know one's destiny depends on oneself, not on heaven.

The first two lines speak of ending up at naturalness by way of effort; the third phrase speaks of ending up at sudden enlightenment by way of naturalness. The spiritual elixir entering the belly means sudden enlightenment. When practice of Tao reaches sudden enlightenment, neither being nor nonbeing stand, and the universe returns to emptiness. Leaping beyond yin and yang, not constrained by yin and yang, one's destiny depends on oneself, not on heaven. Before you have reached sudden enlightenment, when you are still within yin and yang, destiny still depends on nature; this can be known by considering the words of the text, "for the first time."

[55]

ON THE SUPREME EASE OF CRYSTALLIZING
THE ELIXIR

Shining bright, the gold elixir is made in one day; what the ancient immortals said is truly worth listening to. Those who speak of nine years and three years are all delaying and wasting time.

The great medicine of the gold elixir is inherent in everyone: if you can thoroughly investigate the true principle, call on enlightened teachers, know the two medicines of real knowledge and conscious knowledge, find the opening of the mysterious pass, and actually plunge in without reservation to climb directly up onto the other shore, in one day of work you can make the shining elixir of pure yang—what's the necessity of three years and nine years?

This saying of ancient immortals is true indeed, but while the crystallization of the elixir is done at once, incubation to develop it requires ten months. Without incubation, the gold elixir is not stabilized, and will surely be lost again after having been obtained. The statement that it is completed in one day only refers to the blending of yin and yang, not to the complete maturation of the gold elixir.

Complete maturation requires the work of yin convergence and yang fire, withdrawing and adding, increasing and decreasing. Increasing and increasing, decreasing and decreasing, until no more increase or decrease is possible, only then do you get a complete elixir of brilliant pure yang. If it is really completely developed elixir, how could it be completed in a day? A previous section of the text said, "Even if you know the cinnabar and lead, if you do not know the firing process, it's of no use: it all depends on the power of practice—the slightest deviation, and you will fail to crystallize the elixir." Later on it says, "If you want to cultivate the nine transmutations, first you must refine yourself and control the mind." Here we can see the meaning of the gold elixir being made in one day.

[56]

On difficulty and ease

There is difficulty and ease in cultivating the great medicine; and it is known to depend on oneself as well as on heaven. If you do not cultivate action to accumulate hidden virtue, there are apt to be demons to cause obstruction.

The preceding section said the elixir is made in one day; this is not difficult. But this section teaches virtuous action, lest students take the great Tao lightly and improperly desire the path of immortality without cultivating virtuous action. What heaven enjoins on people is virtue; and virtue is also that whereby people requite heaven. If you have virtue, heaven is glad; then carrying out this mandate is very easy, and depends on oneself. If you have no virtue, heaven is angry; then practicing this path is very difficult, and depends on heaven. Why is this? Without virtue and application, one will not be countenanced by the spirits, and there are apt to be demons which cause obstruction; suffering difficulty and sickness, one will inevitably give up along the way. Therefore, those who practice the Tao must make it a priority to cultivate virtue. When one studies and practices the Tao rich in virtue, the Tao is easy to learn and practice, particularly because heaven is glad and the obstacles of demons spontaneously vanish.

[57]
ON THE MECHANISM OF TAKEOVER

The three components take each other over when the time comes; the spiritual immortals conceal this mechanism. When myriad transformations rest, all thoughts cease; the whole body is in order, and nonstriving is realized.

"The three components take each other over" means heaven and earth take over myriad things, myriad things take over people, and people take over myriad things. As for "when the time comes," myriad things flourish by taking the energy of heaven and earth; through the flourishing of myriad things, heaven and earth absorb them when the time comes—so heaven and earth take over myriad things. People see things and give rise to greed and folly; through people's greed and folly, when the time comes things steal people's vital spirit—so things take over people. Things come to fruition through people's care and cultivation; when the time comes, as things are developed, people take and use them—so people also take over things.

"Takeover in time" has the meaning of taking before and after. Over the ages, spiritual immortals have hidden and not come out in the open; their hiding is because of the mechanism of timely takeover—appropriating yin and yang, taking over evolution, turning over enlivening and killing, controlling the workings of energy, they dissolve acquired influences and foster sane energy. Therefore myriad transformations rest, all thoughts cease, the whole body is in order, and they realize the Tao of nonstriving spontaneity.

The important point in this section is "when the time comes." If you take it when the time is right, the energy of heaven, earth, and myriad things becomes your own; if you try taking at the wrong time, your energy will be snatched away by heaven, earth, and myriad things. When the time comes, it is a takeover; when the time is not right, it's not a takeover. The word "time" is very subtle.

[58]
ON THOROUGH INVESTIGATION OF PRINCIPLE

The precious words of the yin convergence exceed three hundred, the spiritual words of the power of Tao are fully five thousand: the superior immortals of past and present have all arrived at the true explanation herein.

The two books *Yin Convergence* and *Power of Tao* are basic books for practice of Tao: they divulge the mechanism of creation and evolution of the universe, and reveal the opening of yin and yang, enlivening and killing. From ancient times to the present, the adepts have all investigated the true principles in these two classics and arrived at the real explanation, whereby they have comprehended essence and life. This book, *Understanding Reality*, is also composed based on the *Yin Convergence* and *Power of Tao*; if students can understand this book, they will also be able to understand the meanings of the *Yin Convergence* and the *Power of Tao*.

[59]
ON SEEKING A TEACHER

Even if you are intellectually bright, if you have not met a real teacher, do not indulge in guesswork. As long as you do not have personal instruction in the gold elixir, where can you learn to form the spiritual embryo?

The preceding section mentioned the *Yin Convergence* and *Power of Tao* classics as precious and spiritual writings, which students should thoroughly examine. However, lest students cling to the alchemical classics, consider these enough and not seek realized persons, this section tells people to call on true teachers without delay.

The alchemical classics and books of the adepts tell about the medicines and the firing processes, with many metaphors, all enabling people to understand these principles and know this path. However, the science of essence and life is occult and profound; it is not easy to discern the reality. Whatever you may perceive or understand, you should seek a teacher for verification. If you do not seek a teacher but rely on your intelligence to guess and make your own interpretations, aren't you taking on the burden of essence and life? Therefore the text says, "Even if you are intellectually bright, if you haven't met a real teacher, don't indulge in guesswork."

The quintessence of the science of essence and life is to gather primal energy. But primal energy is formless, imperceptible, ungraspable—how can it be cultivated, how can it be recovered? The alchemical classics and works of the adepts all speak of this energy, all speak of cultivation, all speak of recovery; but no matter how much they say, words cannot describe it. It is necessary to rely on the personal instruction and mental transmission of a true teacher to be able to recognize the medicines, understand the firing process, and go straight forward without impediment.

Otherwise, if you don't seek the personal instruction of a true teacher, and only rely on the words of the alchemical classics, thinking you're enlightened as soon as you distinguish some minor points, and immediately act on your ideas, either clinging to emptiness or sticking to forms, where will you form the spiritual embryo? The personal instruction of a real teacher should be sought without delay.

[60]

On stopping machination

Thoroughly understanding the mind-monkey, the machinations in the heart, by three thousand achievements one becomes a peer of heaven. There naturally is a crucible to cook the dragon and tiger; why is it necessary to support a household and be attached to spouse and children?

Students' failure to understand the Tao and attain the Tao is all due to instability of mind and insubstantiality of approach. If you succeed in emptying all objects, being aloof of everything, reducing and reducing until you reach nondoing and your heart is clear and calm, then the inner work is done. When you then go on to build up virtue and cultivate action, taking hardship on yourself for the benefit of others, doing what is necessary in each situation, unaffected by wealth, poverty, authority, or power, walking the earth unattached, passing the days according to conditions, all psychological afflictions gone, then the outer work is done.

When the inner work is done and the outer work is done, "three thousand achievements are fulfilled," and one's virtue is on a par with heaven. Then it is possible for the life span to be equal to heaven. As it is said, those with great virtue will attain corresponding longevity.

Not a mote of dust is to be allowed into the human mind; as soon as there is any defilement, essence and sense do not join, the dragon and tiger are out of harmony, and various ills occur. If you succeed in getting rid of the machinations of mind so that it is open and clear, it is not necessary to seek a crucible besides this—this itself is the crucible. Once the crucible is set up, action and stillness unconsciously accord with the laws of God, essence and sense join into one, and harmonious energy pervades you. This itself is the cooking of the dragon and tiger—it is not necessary to ask further about cooking the dragon and tiger.

This is that path: the medicinal substances are at hand, the crucible is there of itself; if those who know this practice it diligently, even be they ordinary ignorant people, they can ascend to the ranks of sages. But worldly people do not see through things of the world; accepting unreal nature and life, they are attached to their spouses and children and do not sever the bonds that entangle them. Expending all their mental potential, when the oil is exhausted the lamp goes out, when the marrow dries up the person dies. What a pity!

[61]

On stopping at sufficiency

If you have not yet refined and restored the elixir, then quickly refine it; when you have refined it, then you should know to stop at sufficiency. If you keep the mind going at full blast, you will not escape danger and degradation one day.

Restoring the elixir means restoring innate knowledge and capacity, in which strength and flexibility are unified, the fundamental essence of true consciousness. After yang culminates in people, giving birth to yin, the primordial enters into the acquired, innate knowledge turns into artificial knowledge, innate capacity turns into artificial capacity, strength and flexibility do not match, and true consciousness is obscured. It is as if something of one's own were lost outside.

Restoring means recovering what was originally there, like regaining something that was lost, returning something that had gone.

Generally speaking, the method of restoring the elixir involves a process of advance and withdrawal, intensification and relaxation, cultivation and cessation: it is necessary to operate it with correct timing, regulating it properly depending on events. It will not do to go too far, it will not do to fail to go far enough. So before the elixir is restored, one proceeds energetically, gradually culling and refining, urgently seeking its recovery. Once the elixir has been restored, it is as before innate knowledge and capacity, with strength and flexibility joined into one true consciousness without obscurity; the labor is done, the medicinal energy is replete, striving is finished, and nonstriving comes to the fore. At this point one should quickly stop the fire, take the fuel out from under the stove, and apply incubation, gentle nurturing, guarding against danger, preserving this bit of true consciousness; in the furnace of evolution the natural fire of reality will spontaneously cook and simmer it, dissipating all mundanities, extracting something indestructible; only then is there complete success.

Otherwise, if you do not know to stop at sufficiency once the elixir has been restored, and keep going at full blast, continuing to pour on the fire, the yang energy will dry up and the medicine will go stale; the real will leave and the false will arise—what was gained will be lost. One day danger and degradation will be unavoidable. There are cases of ancient adepts failing in their early efforts because of this.

Generally speaking, "cultural cooking" and "martial firing" each has its proper time; the yang fire and yin convergence each has a subtle function. Even a slight deviation will result in a great loss, so practitioners of the Tao must be careful.

[62]

On life and death (2 verses)

Take the door of death for the door of life; do not take the gate of life as the gate of death. If you comprehend the killing mechanism and understand reversal, then you will know that blessing is born within injury.

The gate of life and the door of death are basically one; that is, the gate and door of the aperture of the mysterious pass. In this gate and door, if you go along with the energies of the five elements in the internal organs, then the five elements destroy each other, so each one is isolated, and the five virtues turn into the five thieves; then the door of life is the door of death, the gate of life is the gate of death. If you reverse this, the five elements give rise to each other, all return to the same one energy, and the five thieves become the five virtues. Then the door of death is the door of life, the gate of death is the gate of life. The mechanism of life and death is simply in going along or reversing this.

If you understand how to seek the mechanism of life in the killing mechanism, using it in reverse, then blessing is born within injury; the gate of death and the door of death can become the gate of life and the door of life. This is eternal life. "Door" is odd-numbered, "gate" is even-numbered: the door of death turning into the door of life is false yang leaving and true yang arising; the gate of death turning into the gate of life is false yin retreating and true yin arising. When true yin and true yang arise, both joining into one, this is the original self which is completely good without evil, fully integrated into the celestial design, flowing without cease, the mechanism of life subsisting eternally—how could it not extend one's life?

[63]

The origins of calamity and fortune depend on and inhere in each other, just as shadows and echoes follow forms and sounds. If you can reverse this mechanism of enlivening and killing, calamity will turn to fortune in the time it takes to turn over your hand.

The way of reaction in the world is that calamity comes when fortune goes, fortune comes when calamity goes; calamity and fortune are interdependent, much as shadows go along with forms and echoes follow sounds. If practitioners of Tao know calamity and fortune depend on and inhere in each other, then they can know that the enlivening and killing of their own bodies are dependent on and inherent in each other. If you can reverse this mechanism of enlivening and killing of their own bodies are dependent on and inherent in each other. If you can reverse this mechanism of enlivening and killing, seeking enlivening within killing, then in the time it takes to turn over your hand calamity will turn to fortune, without expending any energy.

The mechanism of enlivening and killing is the energies of the five elements in the body. If you go along with the energies of the five elements, there is punishment within reward, and it is the killing mechanism; if you reverse this, there is reward within punishment, and it becomes the enlivening mechanism. With the enlivening mechanism one subsists; with the killing mechanism one perishes. A classic says, "When the five elements go along in order, the universe is a pit of fire; when the five elements are reversed, the world is made of jewels." The difference between going along and reversing is a matter of life and death; so there is great power in "reversal."

This reversal is only possible for those who share the virtues of heaven and earth, who share the illumination of sun and moon, who share the order of the four seasons, who share the fortune and misfortune of ghosts and spirits, who are aloof of everything and see all as void, who take the Tao as their own responsibility. It is not difficult to know this; what is difficult is to carry it out. The mechanism of enlivening and killing is not easy to reverse.

[64]

ON MIXING WITH ORDINARY SOCIETY AND INTEGRATING ILLUMINATION

Cultivating spiritual practice involves mixing with ordinary society and integrating illumination, adapting to fit situations. Now appearing, now concealed, now opposing, now conforming, incomprehensible to others—how could people be able to perceive how one acts or remains hidden?

The light of spiritual alchemy, the great path of the gold elixir, is truly magnificent; it is practiced in the world, within society, and is not a small path of solitary quietism in which one avoids the world and leaves society. It is necessary to mix with ordinary society and integrate illumination before one can adapt perfectly to the world, now appearing, now concealed, now opposing, now conforming, now active, now hidden, now passive, now effective, being unpredictable. Only this is great activity, great work.

As for occultists, who sit in meditation halls, contemplate emptiness and fix the mind, or circulate energy and practice visualizations, or manipulate vitality, or get involved in other extraneous practices like material alchemy and sexual alchemy, how can they dare do what they do out in the open? If you dare not do it out in the open, it is destructive practice, not spiritual practice—how could you be able to comprehend essence and life thereby?

In ancient times, Bodhidharma observed that China had the atmosphere for the Great Vehicle, came to China, and thus completed the great task. Once Hui-neng had gotten the transmission of the fifth patriarch of Ch'an, he disappeared among hunters in Ssu-hui, thus perfecting true realization. Once Tzu-hsien had gotten Hsing-lin's transmission, he went to the city and was supported by a powerful family, and thus perfected essence and life. These three sages all mixed with the ordinary world and integrated illumination; therefore they were able to become Buddhas and immortals.

If you reject the world, there is no Tao, and if there is no Tao, what can be practiced to return to the fundamental and revert to the origin, to preserve life and make the being complete? The celestial mechanism of mixing with the ordinary world and integrating illumination can be spoken of to those who know, but it is hard to tell those who do not know.

III. *One Verse Representing the Great One Engulfing True Energy*

The woman puts on a green robe, the man dons plain silk. What you see is not to be used; what is used cannot be seen. Meeting in ecstasy, there is conjuration within trance. In a moment flames fly, and the true person spontaneously emerges.

Conscious knowledge is yin without yang. It contains the essence of flexibility; essence governs lifegiving, and is associated with wood, which is green, so the verse says "The woman puts on a green robe." Real knowledge is yang within yin. It contains the sense of firmness; sense governs killing, and is associated with metal, which is white, so the verse says "The man dons plain silk."

However, essence and sense are divided into primordial and acquired. That which is acquired is temperament and emotion, which are the nature and feelings of the psycho-physical constitution. These have form and appearance, and are visible; these are not to be used. The primordial is fundamental essence and fundamental sense, which are the essence and sense of true emptiness. Having no form or appearance, that which is to be used is invisible.

Being invisible, that which is to be used exists in ecstasy and trance, in profound abstraction. Ecstasy and trance means there is energy but no materiality; it is imperceptible, ungraspable. How then is it possible to crystallize the elixir? Even though imperceptible and ungraspable, the essence of conscious knowledge and the sense of real knowledge are sometimes encountered in ecstasy, conjured up in trance. At this time of encounter and conjuration, spiritual illumination silently operates, bringing them into the furnace of creative evolution, refining them with fire; in a while the primal energy comes from nothingness and crystallizes into form, whereat the true person in a dark room emerges. This representation of the method of restoring the elixir is referred to in the saying, "In an hour, watch the elixir form." This appearance of the true person is the appearance of the living potential when true yin and true yang merge within; it is what is called the "spiritual embryo," and is not the appearance of the "body outside the body," which emerges after ten months when the embryo is fully developed. As for the emergence of the "body outside the body," how could the release and transmutation resulting in the body outside the body be accomplished in a short time?

This poem represents the Great One engulfing true energy: if someone asks me the meaning of the appearance of the true person, I would say it is precisely the Great One engulfing true energy.

IV. Twelve Verses on the Moon Over the West River, Representing the Twelve Months

The author, Tzu-yang, says,
"The west is the direction of metal,
the river is a body of water;
the moon is the function of the elixir."

[1]

The inner medicine is after all the same as the outer medicine; when the inner is mastered, the outer should be mastered too. In the compounding of the elixir, the ingredients are of the same type; the incubation involves two kinds of operation. Inside there is natural real fire, bright in the furnace, ever crimson. The adjustment of the outer furnace requires diligent work. Nothing is more sublime than the true seed.

The inner medicine is the spiritual essence of conscious knowledge; the outer medicine is the true sense of real knowledge. Because that conscious knowledge is hidden in the human mind, and the human mentality takes charge of affairs, using consciousness to create illusion, therefore it is called inner medicine. Because real knowledge is inherent in the mind of Tao, and as the mind of Tao recedes real knowledge is not manifest, therefore it is called outer medicine. Real knowledge and conscious knowledge are originally of one family—they come from the same source but have different names. Therefore the verse says, "The inner medicine is after all the same as the outer medicine."

The inner medicine is that whereby one cultivates essence, so of course it should be understood; the outer medicine is that whereby one cultivates life, so it too should be understood. An ancient classic says, "To cultivate life without cultivating essence is the number one disease of practice; if you cultivate essence without cultivating life, the yin spirit will never enter sagehood." Therefore the text says, "When the inner is mastered, the outer should be mastered too."

Essence is yin, life is yang: the great elixir of gold syrup is made by taking the polar energies of true yin and true yang, which are of the same type, and blending them together. If you cultivate life and not essence, or cultivate essence and not life, this is solitary yin or isolated yang, and the great elixir will not form. This is what is meant by the saying that essence and life must be cultivated together.

However, for essence there is the operation of essence, and for life there is the operation of life. Essence is a matter of the spiritual body, while life is a matter of the ephemeral body. The two kinds of operation of incubation are quite different. That is to say, the work must be of two kinds. The path of cultivating essence is the path of nonstriving, or nondoing. Nonstriving is based on stillness, and doesn't involve any action; "keeping to the middle, embracing oneness," the "inner furnace" has of itself a real "fire" which ever glows crimson. This is using the "cultural fire" for "incubation."

As for the path of cultivating life, this is the path of striving, doing. Striving is based on action, and requires adjustment of the "outer furnace," diligent effort at refinement. This is using the "martial fire" for "cooking." Adjustment means increasing and decreasing: increasing means increasing real knowledge where it is insufficient, picking out the good and cleaving to it; decreasing means decreasing the excess of conscious knowledge, getting rid of intellectualism.

When increase reaches the point where there can be no more increase, and decrease reaches the point where there can be no more decrease, essence is stabilized, life is solidified, and the "true seed" is obtained. Only this is to be considered sublime. When these two kinds of operation, of essence and life, and the outer elixir, are completed, when brought into the "crucible," this is the inner elixir. That is, before it has come it is called outer, once it has come it is called inner. This is what is meant by the saying that when metal first comes back to essence, then it can be called restored elixir.

[2]

This path is most spiritual and wise; but I fear your endowment is meager and you will have trouble digesting it. Blending lead and mercury does not take all day; you soon see the form of the original jewel appear. If determined people can practice cultivation, what does it matter if they live in the city? The work is easy, the medicine is not far off—if I told all, people would surely laugh.

The preceding verse brought up understanding both the inner and outer medicines; this one speaks of the application of the outer elixir. The path of the gold elixir is most spiritual and wise; those who practice are guided by its standards and climb straight up to the ranks of sages. However, it may be that people's endowments are shallow and slight, so they are hardly able to digest and absorb the teaching.

What is difficult to obtain for the gold elixir is the true lead of real knowledge and the true mercury of conscious knowledge. If you discern real knowledge and conscious knowledge and blend them, then strength and flexibility balance each other, essence and sense are as one; the form of innate knowledge and innate capacity will soon appear, without taking all day. This is also like the original jewel producing light in the dark.

Because the spiritual root of innate knowledge and innate capacity has been buried for a long time, it cannot emerge of itself: now with real knowledge and conscious knowledge uniting, though the spiritual root of innate knowledge and innate capacity cannot become pure and complete immediately, yet its point of living potential has already taken on form in abstract trance. Once there is the point of living potential, from vagueness it becomes clear, and gradually can be restored to pure completeness. The "appearance of the form" is the foretaste of pure completeness.

If there are people of determination who can diligently practice this, it is not necessary for them to leave society—there is no harm in living in the city. This is especially so since in the path of the gold elixir the medicine is at hand and the work is simple. It needn't be sought outside, being in the individual. If it were all told, it would make people laugh. The laugh is that ordinary people and sages are on the same road, there is one principle for heaven and earth—the only difference is in going along or going in reverse.

[3]

The start of the course of the white tiger is most precious; the spiritual water of the flower pond is real gold. Higher good is beneficial as the wellspring is deep; it is not comparable to ordinary medicines. If you want to accomplish the nine transmutations, first you should refine yourself and control the mind. Extracting at the right time, stabilizing floating and sinking, as you advance the fire you should forestall danger.

The previous verse said when you blend lead and mercury you can form the elixir. But if you want to blend lead and mercury, first you must perceive the homogeneous great medicine of real knowledge which is the true lead; only then can you start work. Real knowledge is true sense; in the symbols of this science it is called the start of the path of the white tiger, and also called the spiritual water of the flower pond.

True sense is hidden by random feelings; since sense is associated with metal, it is called the white tiger. But though true sense is hidden by random feelings, sometimes it appears, and the mind of heaven and earth is again manifest, the living potential sprouts. Therefore it is called the start of the path. The start is the beginning, and the course is the eternal path. The start of the path is producing being within nonbeing, embracing yang within yin, as the mother of all things. This is the living potential. This bit of living potential is the root of attainment of sagehood and wisdom, the basis for realization of immortality and enlightenment; therefore it is called precious.

This living potential is also called the spiritual water of the flower pond. The flower pond is the opening of the mysterious pass, the door of all wonders. Because it stores the living potential, it is called the flower pond; because that living potential orders the physical constitution and washes the internal organs, it is called spiritual water. Because that living potential also goes through refinement by fire and crystallizes so that it does not disperse but remains stable, it is also called real gold.

The start of the course, the spiritual water, the true gold, are all one thing, the living potential; this is also called the essence of higher good. Higher good is ultimately good. Being ultimately good, without evil, embodying all truths and dealing with all events, it is like water having a source. When the wellspring is deep, the flow is long, benefiting all beings without exhaustion. This is the most real medicine, which preserves life and completes the body; it is not comparable to ordinary mineral or vegetable medicines.

However, this medicine is hidden by acquired conditioning, only appearing occasionally; time and again it is lost as it is found, and cannot be kept for long. If you wish to accomplish the nine transmutations to stabilize it permanently, you must first refine yourself and control your mind, erasing acquired influences and feelings about objects, culling the medicine at the right time, thus stabilizing its floating and sinking.

Conscious knowledge is stored in the human mind; when the human mind stirs, conscious knowledge flies—it easily floats. Real knowledge is inherent in the mind of Tao; when the mind of Tao is obscured, real knowledge is concealed—it easily sinks. To refine the self and control the mind means to refine away the conscious knowledge of the human mind, making that which is floating sink. Culling at the right time means culling the real knowledge of the mind of Tao, making that which is sunken float.

Floating and sinking reversed, controlling the human mind by the mind of Tao, the human mind obeying the mind of Tao, governing conscious knowledge by real knowledge, nurturing real knowledge by conscious knowledge, the human mind is quiet and the mind of Tao is present; real knowledge and conscious knowledge are continuous branches of the same energy, and the gold elixir is within view.

However, the medicine may be easy to know, but the firing process is difficult. In working to advance the fire, it is necessary to know the level of gravity and energy of the medicinal substances, and when it is beneficial or harmful to hurry or relax. If you go to work impetuously, not only will there be no benefit, it will even cause harm. Therefore the text says, "When advancing the fire you should forestall danger."

[4]

If you want the true lead to stabilize the mercury, keep near the center and do not leave the servant. When wood and metal are separated, they have no means of meeting; it all depends on the inducement of a go-between. Wood, the essence, loves the righteousness of metal; metal, sense, loves the benevolence of wood. When they embrace and nurture each other in mutual intimacy, then you realize the man has conceived.

The preceding verse said that culling the medicine depends on self-refinement; self-refinement aims at the meeting of vitality, energy, and spirit. Spiritual alchemy is just a matter of firmness and flexibility: balance and correct orientation of firmness is real knowledge, symbolized by true lead; balance and correct orientation of flexibility is conscious knowledge, symbolized by true mercury. Taking these two things and blending them makes the elixir.

However, when real knowledge is not manifest, conscious knowledge tends to be flighty, so real knowledge is what regulates conscious knowledge. And while real knowledge can regulate and stabilize conscious knowledge, conscious knowledge can also nurture real knowledge; so conscious knowledge is the servant of real knowledge. If you do not settle conscious knowledge first, real knowledge will not appear; therefore it says, "If you want the true lead to stabilize the mercury, keep near the center and do not leave the servant."

"Keeping near" means the combining of real knowledge and conscious knowledge, the firm and the flexible. Real knowledge is the master, conscious knowledge is the servant: if the servant is disobedient, the master has trouble acting. The difference between real knowledge and conscious knowledge is a fine line: if conscious knowledge is complete, real knowledge is manifest; if real knowledge is present, conscious knowledge is receptive. When real knowledge is present, one is firm and strong; when conscious knowledge is calm, one is flexible and receptive. Firm and strong, flexible and receptive, essence and sense join; therefore spiritual alchemy takes only two medicinal ingredients, true lead and true mercury.

The "lead" of real knowledge, sense, is associated with metal; the "mercury" of conscious knowledge, essence, is associated with wood. When you do things on the basis of acquired conditioning, sense and essence are disparate; this is likened to metal and wood being separated, each keeping to itself, unable to meet. Unless sense and essence commune, true sense and true essence do not manifest, and real knowledge and conscious knowledge do not combine.

Genuine truthfulness is called true intent; it is also called true earth. Once true earth appears, metal and wood spontaneously join; once genuine truthfulness comes through, essence and sense spontaneously unite. So genuine truthfulness is the go-between of true sense and true essence.

True essence is "wood," and it governs receptivity and benevolence; true sense is "metal," and it governs firmness and righteousness. With truthfulness, essence and sense are blended in the center; then "wood," the essence, loves "metal," sense, and accords with right; "metal," sense, loves the benevolence of "wood," the essence. When essence and sense unite, and firmness and flexibility correspond, benevolence and righteousness are both complete: real knowledge and conscious knowledge are the same energy, they embrace and nurture each other; the essence is stabilized, feelings are forgotten, and the primordial energy comes from nothingness and crystallizes into a black bead, the spiritual embryo takes on form—this is what is called "the man having conceived."

[5]

Whose daughters are two and eight? Where are the men three and nine from? They call themselves wood liquid and metal vitality; meeting earth, they make three clans. Going on to use Mr. Fire for refining, husband and wife begin their connubial bliss. The waterwheel dare not be stopped for a moment, conveying to the summit of the K'un-lun mountains.

The preceding verse spoke of the meeting of vitality, energy, and spirit, which forms the spiritual embryo. However, the spiritual embryo will not form by the meeting of vitality, energy, and spirit without refinement by the true fire. Two is the number of yin fire, eight is the number of yin wood; therefore they are called women. Nine is the number of yang metal, three is the number of yang wood; therefore they are called men. The "liquid" of wood is fire; wood producing fire is one clan. The "vitality" of metal is water; metal producing water is one clan. Earth in the center makes one clan itself. These five elements are divided into three clans; when the three clans meet, they combine into one clan—this is called the completion of the five elements.

This is a metaphor for practicing the Tao: original essence and original spirit are the clan of wood and fire, original sense and original vitality are the clan of metal and water, and the original energy is the earth clan. These are the inner three clans. Benevolence and courtesy form a clan associated with wood and fire, justice and wisdom form a clan associated with metal and water, and truthfulness makes a clan associated with earth. These are called the outer three clans. Practitioners of the Tao govern the outer three clans by the inner three clans, and complete the inner three clans by the outer three clans. The final outcome is to make the three clans into one clan.

However, these three clans require vigorous practice and intense work before they can become one clan. The "refinement of Mr. Fire" is this vigorous practice. By vigorous practice, those who are not benevolent will reach benevolence, the unjust will reach justice, the uncourteous will reach courtesy, the unwise will reach wisdom, the untruthful will reach truthfulness. Benevolence, justice, courtesy, and wisdom all wind up in one truthfulness, and essence, sense, vitality, and spirit all transmute into one energy. The three clans merge, strength and flexibility correspond, essence and sense unite, and "husband and wife begin their connubial bliss."

Once husband and wife are joined in bliss, the firing work continues steadily, the longer the stronger, one energy accomplishing the work, until you arrive at pure yang, beyond the realm of the senses. Therefore the text says, "The waterwheel dare not stop for a moment, conveying to the summit of the K'un-lun mountains." The "waterwheel" is the true energy, associated with the north: it does not refer to the yogic practice of conveying the genital energy into the spine and up to the top of the head. It means that the one energy accomplishes its work, dousing fire with water, water and fire steaming without interruption. It is like a waterwheel in a river, carrying water up and sending it down, revolving day and night without stopping. The K'un-lun mountains are the source of myriad mountains: "conveying to the summit of the K'un-lun" is the state of "the three flowers gathered on the peak," "the five energies returning to the origin," entering into true emptiness and ineffable existence, unconsciously obeying the laws of God.

[6]

The seven-reverted cinnabar reverts to the origin, the nine-restored gold liquid returns to reality: stop counting from three to nine and one to nine—it only requires the five elements to be in order. The basis is pure mercury, flowing throughout the times: When the number of yin and yang is complete, it naturally communes with the spirit; going in and out, it does not leave the mysterious female.

The preceding verse said that the work can be accomplished when the five elements are aggregated and the fire is operated to refine them; but the refinement requires knowledge of the true principle of seven-reversion and nine-restoration. Seven is the yang number of fire, nine is the yang number of metal. The essence of conscious knowledge is flexible, inside it harbors a false fire; when the false fire is extinguished, the true fire arises. This is like the mercury of consciousness solidifying into cinnabar, losing its volatility forever; fire reverts to the origin. The sense of real knowledge is firm, it has in it dry gold; when the dry gold melts, real gold is pure. This is like contaminated gold being liquified, permanently becoming most pure and bright gold; gold returns to reality. This is the meaning of seven-reversion and nine-restoration in the alchemical classics.

In aberrated schools, they count the zodiac signs from the first to the ninth as "nine restorations," and count from the third to the ninth as "seven reversions"—they do not know the meaning of seven-reversion and nine-restoration. If you do not know the meaning of seven-reversion and nine-restoration, how can you know the order of the five elements? As for the ordering of the five elements, when fire reverts to the origin, wood is produced in fire, and the spirit is aware; when the spirit is aware, conscious knowledge is not obscured. When metal returns to reality, metal is produced in water and the vitality is unified; when vitality is unified, real knowledge is ever present. Real knowledge being conscious knowledge, conscious knowledge being real knowledge, the four forms—metal, wood, water, and fire—are blended and return to the center; the five elements being one energy, perfectly balanced, wholly integrated with the celestial design, the five elements are in order.

However, the accomplishment of ordering the five elements is all carried out by the great medicine of metal in water. "Mercury" is "metal in water," which is the point of true sense of real knowledge. Real knowledge contains within it the primordial real unified energy, which is the root of the five elements, the basis of the four forms. In motion it produces yang, in stillness it produces yin, and flows throughout the times of the four forms and five elements. The path of restoration is to advance the yang fire when it is time for yang, thereby gathering this real knowledge, and to operate the yin convergence when it is time for yin, thereby nurturing this real knowledge. When the number of yin and yang is complete, the five elements merge, innate knowledge and innate capacity are tranquil and unstirring yet sensitive and effective, spontaneously communing with the spirit. The spirit refers to something that cannot be assessed in terms of yin and yang.

Unfathomable by yin and yang, the spiritual embryo coalesces; this is called "the valley spirit not dying." The valley spirit not dying is called the mysterious female. The opening of the mysterious female is called the root of heaven and earth. When the number of yin and yang is complete, this mysterious female has been established; when the mysterious female is established, the valley spirit goes in and out of the opening of the mysterious female, living forever, not dying. Then the path of reversion and restoration is complete. This is what is meant when it is said, "If you want to attain the immortality of the valley spirit, you must set up the basis on the mysterious female."

[7]

Containing female substance within the male, bearing yin yet embracing yang, when the two are combined the medicine is then produced, changing the slightness in the yin spirit and the predominance in the yang spirit. Truly it is said of a grain of the gold elixir that a snake that swallows it is immediately transformed into a dragon and a chicken that eats it is then changed into a phoenix, flying into the pure realm of true yang.

The preceding verse said the seven-reversion and nine-restoration require the completeness of the number of yin and yang; but to operate yin and yang requires that you recognize true yin and true yang. "Containing female substance within the male," in terms of the *I Ching* signs, is the emptiness in *fire* ☲; in people it is the conscious knowledge hidden in the human mind. "Bearing yin yet embracing yang," in terms of the signs, is the fullness in *water* ☵; in people it is the real knowledge inherent in the mind of Tao. Real knowledge and conscious knowledge, the two medicinal substances, must be combined before they can make the elixir.

The "yin spirit" has yang within yin, which is the "spirit" of real knowledge; the "yang spirit" has yin within yang, the "spirit" of conscious knowledge. "Slightness in the yin spirit" means slightness of yang; "predominance in the yang spirit" means excess of yin. When yang is slight and yin excessive, there is imbalance and the gold elixir does not form. Only when real knowledge and conscious knowledge join do the yin spirit and yang spirit return to correct balance, changing into true essence and true sense.

When yin and yang combine into one, the celestial order is clearly revealed; the innate knowledge and capacity which had been about to fade away in people is round and bright, clean and bare. A bead of gold elixir hangs in the center of vast space, lighting up the universe to view, unobstructed in all directions. When people ingest a grain of this elixir, they immediately become immortals; when snakes swallow a grain they become dragons, when chickens eat a grain they become phoenixes, and fly straight into the pure realm of true yang.

The "snake swallowing" and the "chicken eating" also fit the laws of alchemy: the snake is associated with fire, in the south, as *fire* ☲. The dragon is associated with wood, in the east, as *thunder* ☳. The chicken, in the west, associated with metal, is *lake* ☱. The phoenix is akin to water, in the north, as *water* ☵. The snake swallowing and becoming a dragon is producing wood in fire, the chicken eating and becoming a phoenix is the existence of metal in water. Producing wood in fire, producing metal in water, metal and wood join, water and fire balance each other; one energy undifferentiated, being and nonbeing do not stand, things and self return to emptiness, body and mind, both sublimated, enter sagehood, and their unknowability is called spirit. Escaping the ordinary world and living in the realm of pure yang are not empty words.

[8]

As soon as heaven and earth interact, with obstruction or tranquility, morning and evening you will discern difficulty and darkness. Spokes come together at the hub, water returns to the source; the wonder lies in the operation of extraction and addition. When you get the one, the myriad are all done; stop making divisions into south, north, east, west. Reducing and reducing, be careful with the foregoing achievement; the jewel of life is not to be treated lightly.

The path of the gold elixir is the path of creation; the path of creation is the path of alternation of yin and yang. In the first month of the year, the energy of heaven rises and the energy of earth descends: this makes *tranquility* ☷☰. In the sixth month, the energy of earth rises and the energy of heaven descends: this makes *obstruction* ☰☷. In a day, midnight is the beginning of morning; at midnight the yang energy moves within and the yin energy goes outside: this makes *difficulty* ☵☳. Noon is the beginning of evening; at noon the yang energy stops outside and the yin energy arises inside: this makes *darkness* ☶☲. *Obstruction* and *tranquility* mean the rising and descending of the yin and yang of spring and autumn in a year; *difficulty* and *darkness* mean the coming and going of the yin and yang of morning and evening in a day.

Observing the vicissitudes of *obstruction* and *tranquility* as heaven and earth interact, one will recognize the process of *difficulty* in the morning and *darkness* at night. This is because the waxing and waning of yin and yang in a day is like the waxing and waning of yin and yang in a year. But the yin and yang of a year and the yin and yang of a day are all operated by one energy coming and going. Practitioners of the Tao are guided by the seasons of *obstruction* and *tranquility* of heaven and earth, and follow the mechanism of *difficulty* and *darkness* of morning and evening: when yang is appropriate, they advance the yang fire, when yin is appropriate they operate the yin convergence. When the firm strength of yang and the yielding flexibility of yin are properly timed, there grows an accumulation of good, aggregating the five elements and blending the four forms, like thirty spokes coming together at the hub, forming a wheel, like a thousand streams all returning to the source and entering the ocean, integrating into one energy, so the gold elixir crystallizes.

However, the marvel of the crystallization of the gold elixir is all a matter of the operation of extraction and addition. Extraction means removing false yin and false yang, addition means adding true yin and true yang. When false yin is gone, true yin appears; when false yang vanishes, true yang arises. When true yin and true yang return to central balance, two yet joined into one, real knowledge and conscious knowledge, essence and sense, merge and again you see the original face of innate knowledge and innate capacity. The accomplishment of extraction and addition is indeed a wonder.

Overall, cultivating the elixir requires recognition of true yin and true yang, and also requires recognition of the primordial truly unified energy. This energy exists prior to the differentiation of chaos, when yin and yang are still undivided; when absorbed it is true emptiness, when activated it is ineffable existence. It is symbolized by metal in water, embodied as innate natural goodness, and functions as the vital unified mind of Tao. The rule of alchemy is just to take the uniform great medicine of the mind of Tao. Though this mind of Tao is uniform, it governs the energies of the five elements and contains the qualities of the five elements. This is because the mind of Tao is the manifestation of true unity. One is the first number; the mind of Tao is one yet contains five, five yet ultimately one. In reality, when the point of ultimate oneness is reached, we cannot even say it is the mind of Tao; we can only call it integration with the celestial design. Thus Confucianism calls integration with the celestial design the Great Ultimate, Taoism calls it the gold elixir, Buddhism calls it complete awareness. This is what the classic means when it says, "When you get the one, the myriad are all done."

If you get the one, this means the jewel of life is already in your hand; there is no need to distinguish south, north, east, and west, and use the method of aggregating. Just use the mind of Tao to ward off the human mentality, reducing and reducing it, eventually causing all the acquired influences in the human mind to vanish: when it is purified into flexible, harmonious conscious knowledge, then the human mind too turns into the mind of Tao.

The reason for this is that there is discrimination in the human mind, which carries the energies of senses and objects since time immemorial plus the accumulated habits of personal history, all joined in the aberrations of the individual temperament. If you do not eliminate each of these roots of ill, even the slightest residue will at some time act up, given the appropriate circumstances. Then the jewel of life will leak away, and the foregoing work will all be in vain. Therefore the text says to be careful with the foregoing achievement, and not treat the jewel of life lightly. An ancient immortal said that as long as there is any positive energy left one does not die, while as long as there is any negative energy left one does not become immortal. Therefore, after obtaining the elixir, it is necessary to eradicate entirely the seeds of the vicious circles that have been going on since time immemorial; only then can the jewel of life be one's own, forever indestructible.

[9]

At the winter solstice one yang returns; thirty days adds one yang line. Between moons the hexagram return *comes in on the tide of the morning of the first day of the month; after the fifteenth,* heaven *ends and* meeting *appears. A day is also divided into cold and hot: When yang is born,* return *arises in the middle of the night; at noon* meeting *symbolizes the arrival of one yin. When you refine the medicine you must know dusk and dawn.*

The preceding verse spoke of the work of extraction and addition; this teaches people to be guided by the evolution of dusk and dawn of heaven and earth. As for the dusk and dawn of a year, on the winter solstice, in the eleventh lunar month, one yang arises; each thirty days adds another yang line: so one yang arising in the eleventh month makes *return* ☷☳, the second yang arising in the twelfth month makes *overseeing* ☷☱, the third yang arising in the first month makes *tranquility* ☷☰, the fourth yang arising in the second month makes *great power* ☳☰, the fifth yang arising in the third month makes *parting* ☱☰, and the sixth yang arising in the fourth month makes *heaven* ☰☰. These are the six yang hexagrams.

In the fifth month, one yin arises, making *meeting* ☰☴, and the thirty days of each month add one yin line; in the sixth month the second yin arises, making *withdrawal* ☰☶, in the seventh month the third yin arises, making *obstruction* ☰☷, in the eighth month the fourth yin arises, making *observing* ☴☷, in the ninth month the fifth yin arises, making *stripping away* ☶☷, and in the tenth month the sixth yin arises, making *earth* ☷☷. These are the six yin hexagrams. The six yang months are the dawn, the six yin months are the dusk; this is the dusk and dawn of a year.

In between moons, in the interval of the ending of one month and the beginning of the next, sun and moon meet, the moon receives the sun's light, and on the third day the yang light first spews over the ocean; the tide responding to it makes *return*. Every two and a half days adds a yang line, until the fifteenth, when sun and moon face each other and the light is round and full, making *heaven*. From the first to the fifteenth days of the month are the six yang hexagrams.

After the full moon, *heaven* ends, and from the sixteenth to the eighteenth one yin arises; the yang light has waned, and *meeting* appears. Every two and a half days adds another yin line, until the thirtieth, when the moon is dark and the yang light is all gone; there is only a dark mass, making *earth*. From the sixteenth to the thirtieth days are the six yin hexagrams. Two and a half days are an interval, twelve intervals go through the six yang and six yin hexagrams: this is the dusk and dawn of a month.

The interval of a day is also divided into cold and hot. In the middle of the night, one yang arises, making *return*; every two hours adds one yang line, until the sixth yang arises in the 10 A.M.–12 noon interval, making *heaven*. At noon, one yin arises making *meeting*; every two hours adds a yin line, until the sixth yin arises in the 10 P.M.–12 midnight interval, making *earth*. The twenty-four hours go through twelve hexagrams, six yin and six yang; this is the dusk and dawn of a day.

Sages transfer a year's dusk and dawn of yin and yang into a month, transfer a month's dusk and dawn of yin and yang into a day, and transfer a day's dusk and dawn of yin and yang into an hour. An hour has eight intervals, and each interval has fifteen segments, so eight intervals have one hundred and twenty segments. The sixty segments of the first four intervals are the six yangs, the sixty segments of the last four intervals are the six yins. Also, the dusk and dawn of one hour is transferred into one interval, with fifteen segments; the first seven and a half segments are yang, the last seven and a half segments are yin.

In a single interval culling the great medicine, returning it to the crucible and furnace of evolution, operating the yang fire and yin convergence, refining it into elixir, is what is called "dividing midnight and noon in time without intervals, distinguishing *heaven* and *earth* in a hexagram without lines." It is only necessary to know the "dusk" and "dawn" which are the arising of yin and yang. When you know the dusk and dawn, then the evolution of a day, a month, a year is right in a single hour, a single interval. The blind of the world who practice sitting meditation at midnight and noon, or circulate energy at the new and full moon, or practice developmental exercises at the winter and summer solstices, do not know the principle of "dusk and dawn."

[10]

If you do not distinguish the five elements and four forms, how can you distinguish the cinnabar and mercury, lead and quicksilver? Without having even heard of the cultivation of the elixir and the firing process, you already call yourself a hermit? If you are unwilling to reflect on your own errors, and even teach others erroneous ways, you mislead others into perpetual confusion; how can you take such a deceiving mind lightly?

The preceding verse said that to refine the medicine requires knowledge of the dusk and dawn of yin and yang; this verse quickly follows up on the preceding, for those who don't know the dawn and dusk of yin and yang, bringing out the path of spiritual immortals. The basic aim is to develop others after developing oneself, to cultivate virtue after cultivating the Tao. People who are astray do not know the true principles of the five elements and four forms, do not understand the code words cinnabar, mercury, lead, and quicksilver, do not understand the medicinal substances, do not ask about the firing process; yet, having learned some minor teachings of sidetrack methods, they imagine they have the Tao, call themselves hermits, are unwilling to reflect on their own errors, and even teach others erroneous paths. This is the blind leading the blind, misleading others into confusion, never able to get out. This sort of deceiving, indulging mind will go to uninterrupted hell, never to emerge—how could there yet be any hope of attaining the Tao?

[11]

Cultivating over eight hundred virtuous practices, accumulating a full three thousand hidden deeds, equally saving self and others, friend and foe, only then do you accord with the original vow of spiritual mortals. Then tigers and rhinos, swords and soldiers, do not injure you, the burning house of impermanence cannot constrain you; after the precious descends, you go pay court to heaven, calmly riding a phoenix-drawn chariot.

The preceding verse said that sidetracked methods and aberrant procedures do not clarify the great Path but only damage virtue, and cannot develop virtue; this verse speaks of the need to practice virtue after practicing the Path.

Practicing the Path is for oneself, practicing virtue is for others. Practice of the Path has an end, but practice of virtue has no end. Therefore after spiritual immortals completed the Path, they always fulfilled three thousand meritorious deeds and eight hundred practices, forgetting both others and self, equanimous towards friend and foe, becoming coextensive with the universe, containing myriad things, embodying all the qualities of the Tao, thus finally according with their original vow.

When one reaches this stage, all is empty, inside and out; neither existence nor nonexistence remains, body and mind are both sublimated—tigers and rhinos cannot harm you, weapons cannot get at you, the burning house of impermanence cannot constrain you. The precious talisman comes down to summon you, and riding peacefully in a phoenix chariot you ascend in broad daylight.

[12]

The feelings of altair and vega are joined, their paths meet; the tortoise and snake act according to their nature. The moon and sun join their charms at the beginning of the month; the two energies operate sustained by each other. Basically it is the wondrous function of heaven and earth; who can comprehend this truth? If yin and yang are kept apart, they become malignant; how can you have the eternity of heaven and earth?

The preceding eleven verses all say the great way of cultivation of the gold elixir requires a combination of two medicines of the same kind, true yin and true yang, before the elixir can be made. People may wonder if it is made by forced effort, but it is not—it is all a natural operation. Therefore this verse sums up the meaning of the foregoing verses, to get students to thoroughly investigate the true principle.

It is like the stars Altair and Vega meeting on the seventh day of the seventh month, tortoise and snake associating through similarity, moon and sun meeting at the turn of the month—all of these represent the natural commingling of the two energies of yin and yang as they interact. This is the wondrous function of the creative operation of heaven and earth. The course of creation in heaven and earth is the course of alternation of yin and yang: yin and yang sustaining each other, one energy flows, yin to yang, yang to yin; as yin and yang come and go, the four seasons take place and all things grow. The mechanism of life never ceases, so it is always there, of old and now.

If practitioners of the Tao do not comprehend this truth, and abandon the principle of creation by yin and yang, they stick to emptiness or cling to forms, making forced endeavors which have the contrary effect of keeping yin and yang apart. This is not only of no help to essence and life, it even harms essence and life; malignancy cannot be avoided. Can you then still hope for the eternity of heaven and earth, to become an undying immortal?

The path of eternity of heaven and earth is the path of blending of true yin and true yang. When true yin and true yang are blended, the mechanism of life therein wells forth and congeals into a spiritual embryo, coming into being from nonbeing, from being into nonbeing, escaping the illusory body and bringing forth the real body: only then can one share the eternity of heaven and earth. If practitioners of Tao want to seek the eternity of heaven and earth, they will find no means without true yin and true yang.

There is one more poem on the moon over the West River, representing the intercalary month. According to the author's own preface, this verse and the following five verses are not part of the main body of *Understanding Reality*, but belong to the collection of additions; reflecting on the meaning of the words, this is the path of first cultivating life and afterwards cultivating essence. Three commentators include it in the main collection because it has an explanation of cultivating life, and I follow them here.

The elixir is the most precious treasure of the physical body; when cultivated to perfection, the transmutations are endless. One can go on to investigate the true source in the realm of essence, and ascertain the ineffable function of the birthless. Without awaiting another body in the next life, one attains the spiritual capacities of a Buddha in the present; after the Naga girl achieved this, who since then has been able to follow in her footsteps?

Yuan-tu-tzu said, "A point of positive vitality is hidden in the physical body; it is not in the heart or genitals, but in the opening of the mysterious pass." The point of positive vitality is the elixir; hidden in the physical body, it is the most precious treasure of the body. The elixir is nothing but the vitality of the primordial point of complete yang; it is also called the energy of primordial real unity, and it is also called the abundant sane energy. In storage it is called true emptiness, in action it is called ineffable existence. Its substance is natural wholesomeness, its function is the mind of Tao. This most precious treasure in the human body does not belong to the heart or genitals; it is stored in the mysterious pass.

The opening of the mysterious pass has no location, no form; this elixir also has no location and no form. Being equanimous in action and stillness, untrammeled by matter or voidness, lively and effervescent, if you operate the fire to forge it into something stable and solid, it is always responsive yet always tranquil, always tranquil yet always responsive, capable of endless transformations, with unfathomable spiritual marvels, unfathomable even to the spirits of heaven and earth. It abides in the physical body, yet can transform the physical body; this is what is called the spiritual body. Therefore the author says that the evolution of life is connected with the body, meaning connected with the spiritual body. When the spiritual body is achieved, the spiritual embryo is complete, the foundation of life is stable, striving ends and nonstriving appears, by which one can cultivate essence.

The true source of essence is the ineffable function of the birthless. Cultivation of life is the way to live long; cultivation of essence is the way to be birthless. With no birth there is no death; no birth, no death, united with Space, body and mind both sublimated, one is forever freed from transmigration, and transcends beyond heaven and earth. Without awaiting another body in the next life, one attains the spiritual capacities of a Buddha in the present. This is because the path of birthlessness is sudden enlightenment, completely pervading, all things empty, directly transcending to the beyond.

In ancient times when the Buddha was teaching at the assembly on the Spiritual Mountain, a seven-year-old Naga girl emerged from the earth, presented a jewel, and attained buddhahood on the spot. The author here cites this case of the Naga girl presenting a jewel to demonstrate cultivation of the essence of true emptiness. Cultivating the essence of true emptiness is the Naga girl presenting a jewel and realizing true emptiness, unborn and imperishable; this is attaining the spiritual capacities of a Buddha.

But before the principle of life has been practiced, the principle of essence is hard to comprehend. On the whole, if one can suddenly awaken to complete pervasion and can nurture the true essence, one still has not escaped coming and going within temporal conditioning; without having gone through the tempering of the great fire, as soon as there is any leak one can hardly avoid the trouble of reincarnation. If one cultivates essence after having cultivated life, one has already come forth from refinement in the furnace of the great fire, so that all pollution has been burnt away; proceeding from here to cultivate essence by practicing the path of nonstriving, going from gradual to sudden, one directly ascends to the stage of ineffable enlightenment of the supreme one vehicle. How can one be reincarnated then? This is why the text says one gains the spiritual capacities of a Buddha in the present, without awaiting another body in the next life. So we know the great path of the gold elixir first cultivates life before cultivating essence.

v. Five Verses, Representing the Five Elements: Metal, Wood, Water, Fire, Earth

[1]

Even if you understand the essence of the true thusness, you still have not escaped reincarnation; it is better to include cultivation of the great medicine, immediately transcend to nonleaking, and be a real human.

The essence of true thusness is naturally real being as is—there is no effort involved at all. It is not material, not void. It is what is called unconsciously following the laws of God. If you want to cultivate this essence, you must understand this essence; once you have understood this essence, you must take this essence and refine it into something indestructible—only thus can you attain salvation. If in spite of having understood it you do not know how to cultivate and refine it, your life does not depend on yourself and still depends on fate—when your time is up, you have no support, and cannot escape death and reincarnation.

Not giving up the work of gradual cultivation after sudden enlightenment, using the yang fire and yin convergence to cook and refine the great medicine, you dissolve aggregated conditioning, shed that which withers, and bring forth the real body. Then you can go into water without drowning, go into fire without getting burned; tigers and rhinos cannot injure you, weapons cannot harm you. Then you are a nonleaking real human.

In ancient times, after the sixth patriarch of Ch'an Buddhism had gotten the transmission of the fifth patriarch, he hid among hunters, mingling with ordinary folk, integrating his illumination, thus perfecting true attainment. Tzu-hsien realized complete pervasion suddenly, but he knew in himself it wasn't the ultimate, and he needed the transmission of Hsing-lin to attain the great achievement. People usually think it is just a matter of cultivating the great medicine, or that if one realizes true thusness this itself is enlightenment. Then what did the fifth patriarch transmit to the sixth patriarch, since the latter had already realized "there is originally not a single thing"? And why did Tzu-hsien seek out Hsing-lin after having suddenly realized complete pervasion?

So we know that all-at-once understanding and gradual cultivation are both necessary. It may happen that one suddenly understands first and then gradually practices, or one may first gradually cultivate and then suddenly understand. Essence and life must both be cultivated; the work requires two stages. This verse speaks of reaching life by way of essence, practicing the gradual from the sudden.

[2]

Entering the womb, usurping the house, moving the abode, living in an old residence—these are called followers of the four fruits. If you know how to conquer the dragon and subdue the tiger, real gold will make a dwelling that will never decay.

"Entering the womb" means first spotting a rich and noble family with a pregnant wife in her last month, so as to enter her womb. As for "usurping the house," when a pregnant woman is near delivery, there will always be a yin-soul waiting to enter an opening; to enter first, before the other does, is called usurping the house. "Moving the abode" means when the body declines and fails, to pick a vigorous living body and surreptitiously move into it. "Living in an old residence" means when a vigorous healthy person dies by violence, to borrow the still warm corpse, enter an opening, and live in this "old residence."

"Entering the womb" and "usurping the house" are more or less the same, "moving the abode" and "living in an old residence" are also more or less the same. All four refer to cultivating the yin spirit to be able to go in and out. Self-serving Buddhists are called followers of the four fruits; they are also called heretics. Derivatives of the teachings of the two lesser vehicles, they are not the supreme vehicle of Buddhism, which is realization of true thusness. They are only different from ordinary people in that transmigration is clear to them.

As for the great path of the gold elixir, this involves conquering the dragon of true essence in the eastern house, and subduing the tiger of true sense in the western house, returning sense to essence, nurturing sense by essence, so that sense and essence harmonize, dragon and tiger meet, producing the spiritual body, like building a house of real gold, which lasts as long as heaven and earth, never to decay. Then there is no transmigration.

[3]

The methods of mirror-gazing, imprisoning breath, and contemplating the spirit are hard for beginners, but later become easy. Even if one can suddenly roam myriad lands, nevertheless when the house gets old one changes the abode.

Mirror gazing is done by hanging a mirror on the wall and keeping the spirit in it; after a long time at this, the yin spirit comes out. Imprisoning the breath starts by not letting out one breath, two breaths, then ten breaths, a hundred breaths, gradually reaching the point where one never lets out the breath-energy, which then circulates internally by itself. Contemplating the spirit may be done by silently paying court to the supreme God, or climbing up into the clouds to discover the sages, or imagining the spirit emerging from the top of the head, or imagining the spirit going out from the "hall of brightness," an inch behind the middle of the brows. There are very many such practices; for beginners they are hard, but later the going is easy. After many years they enable one to project the yin-spirit. But it is only solitary yin: when the physical constitution deteriorates, it leaves this body and enters another—what benefit is this for essence and life?

[4]

Buddhists teach people to cultivate ultimate bliss: Just focusing on ultimate bliss is the direction of metal. Of all matter and form, only this is real; any other is unreal and vain to assay.

Ultimate Bliss is (the pure land) in the west; the west is the direction of metal, which in people is the firm sense of real knowledge. This sense is stable, uncompromising, perfectly pure, and cannot be moved by anything. It is like the hardness of metal, which never breaks down. Cultivating Ultimate Bliss is cultivating this true metal of real knowledge. When the true metal is forged to perfection, it has both firmness and flexibility; freed from all pollutants, it shines brightly and becomes a supreme treasure. In ancient times Dipankara cultivated this and made a clear jewel tower; Shakyamuni cultivated this and made a sixteen-foot-tall gold body. Of all matter and form, the only thing that is real is cultivating this firm, strong sense of real knowledge; anything else is unreal, not worth considering.

[5]

Ordinary expressions and common sayings accord with the path of sages; you should turn to them for careful research. If you use everyday activities to search in reverse, everything in the world turns to jewels.

The Tao is not far from people; what people consider the Tao is far from people. The Tao of essence and life is the eternal Tao, the eternal Tao is the Tao of daily life; it's just that while people use it daily they do not know it.

If you want to cultivate essence and life, you should thoroughly investigate the principles of the eternal Tao. If you can carefully investigate the principles, you do not need to read a thousand classics and ten thousand texts; there are great revelations of the celestial mechanism right in ordinary expressions and common sayings. For example, good people are called really genuine, truthful, conscientious, reasonable, respectable, aware of proper proportion, aware of when to go forward and when to withdraw, circumspect, perceptive, having their feet on the ground; bad people are said to be inhuman, lacking conscience, and unreasonable—they hurt others to benefit themselves, are self-deceived, violate nature and reason, take suffering for pleasure, take the false for the real, pick up one thing and forget another, without knowing death and life, without knowing good and bad, only knowing one and not two, only aware of the existence of themselves and not that of others.

Expressions like these are meaningless when said, but flavorful when reflected on. Why not pick out one or two of these common sayings and bore into them; in your ordinary activities, seeking against the tide, everything in the world is a jewel, everywhere is the Tao, everything is useful in this.

Ordinary scholars say the Tao cannot be spoken, so they will not make real efforts to examine the principles of essence and life. Also, they cannot humble themselves to ask help from teachers and friends; or if they do ask for help, they still do not truly recognize reality, and speak of searching for the treasure from nothing at all. Those who act like this will never accomplish anything even if they leave home and spend their lives traveling all over the world.

The Outer Collection

The outer collection of *Understanding Reality* is based on essence. After the author wrote *Understanding Reality*, he still feared that the essence of true awareness, which is the original source, might not yet be fully explored, so he wrote more poems and sayings and appended them as material for the path of twin cultivation of essence and life.

1. Four Four-line Verses

[1]

The subtle body of Buddha is omnipresent; myriad phenomena present no obstacle. If you understand the true reality eye which is completely pervasive, then you will know the triple world is your house.

The Buddha is the essence of true emptiness which comes from nowhere and goes nowhere. True emptiness is not empty; so its body is most subtle. The essence of true emptiness basically has no body, but because it includes subtle existence, that subtlety is its body. Emptiness without this subtlety is nihilistic, indifferent emptiness; it is not the real essence of Buddha. How can it be omnipresent, how can myriad phenomena present no obstacle? Because of its subtle nonvoidness, the body is omnipresent, all-pervasive; because it is empty yet real, myriad phenomena cannot obstruct it. Because it is omnipresent and unobstructed, it is also called the completely pervasive reality eye. Completeness means there is no head or tail, no back or front, no before or after, no above or below, no inside or outside—this is realization of suchness. Pervasion means being present in all places, manifest in all times. It is so great it fills the universe, so fine it enters a hair; this is the subtle body. Only completeness can be pervasive, only by pervasion is it complete. The light shines clear and bright, invulnerable to all situations; therefore it is called the reality eye. This is why it is called the treasury of the eye of truth. To understand this completely pervasive reality eye is to actually perceive the subtle body of Buddha, which is neither material nor void, yet is both matter and emptiness. Heaven and hell both swept away, the triple world is one house, the ten directions are the whole body.

[2]

Looking at it, you cannot see its form; but when you call, it responds. Do not say this sound is like a valley echo; if there is no valley, what sound is there?

"Looking at it, you cannot see its form" refers to emptiness; "call, and it responds" refers to existence. Because of emptiness there is existence, like an echo in a valley. Emptiness is not empty—such is the subtle body of Buddha. But the subtle body of Buddha is always empty, always existent, always existent, always empty—what need is there to call before there is response? Response to a call means there is still "emptiness," still "existence"—still constrained by emptiness, emptiness which is not pervasive does not equal the subtle body of Buddha. It is better to take this "empty" thing and smash it. Emptiness does not empty anything—where does the sound come from? Since there is no sound, there is naturally no emptiness. No emptiness, no sound, this is great liberation, which is fully alive. This is what is meant by the saying, "The man unmoving atop the hundred foot pole may have gained initiation, but it is not yet real: step forward from the hundred foot pole, and the universe is the whole body."

[3]

One thing contains seeing, hearing, perception, and cognition: The sense objects reveal its working. Even the one thing ever aware is not existent; what could the four be based on?

Seeing, hearing, perception, cognition—these four are all produced by one thing, the luminous aware discriminating mind. Since that one thing is ever aware, in the midst of sense data the four associate and activate one another, without a moment's rest. If one can eliminate the one thing which is ever aware, the four have no basis to rely on, and naturally vanish.

Deluded people cannot perceive the basic nature of enlightenment, which is truly empty yet subtly existent; they just take the luminous aware discriminating mind as real. They may empty this thing, or guard this thing, still not knowing this thing is the root of repeated birth and death, the seed of perpetual transmigration. If you don't root this out, how can you perceive the basic nature of enlightenment? This is what is meant by the saying, "The root of eons of birth and death, fools call the original Man."

[4]

Reaching India without moving a step, sitting straight, all places are present before the eyes. A halo behind the head is still a phantom; even when clouds rise beneath your feet you are still not an immortal.

The fundamental nature of enlightenment has no head or tail, no back or front; when you go toward it you do not see its head, when you follow it you do not see its back. If you say it exists, yet it seems not to; if you say it does not exist, yet it does. Not falling within descriptions in terms of existence or nonexistence, its light penetrates the hidden and reaches the revealed, able to illumine the universe. This is spontaneous ineffable awareness. Basically it is not produced by sitting; all those who study Ch'an and practice sitting, those who just play with the discriminating consciousness, think they have actually attained buddhahood when they see illusory scenes and unreal images, or dream they travel to India, or produce lights from their heads, or see things in trance, or walk in the clouds in ecstasy. They are far off. Those who aspire to the Tao should first sweep away all sidetracks and aberrated paths, then seek out the true ineffable awareness where there is no form or appearance. Only then can the fundamental nature be realized.

II. Verses on Various Themes

ON THE ESSENTIAL GROUND

The essence of buddhahood is not the same or different:
  A thousand lamps are together one light—
Adding lamps does not make more lights,
  removing lamps does not damage the light.
Neither grasping nor rejection impinges on it,
  neither fire nor water can obstruct it,
Nothing in perception or cognition can assess it.

The verse uses the term "essential ground" because the body of true essence is unmoving like the ground; be there sameness or difference, though circumstances and events be manifold and various, dealing with them all with an equanimous mind is like the shining of a thousand lamps, shining on all with a single light, the lamps not one but the light one. This essence has no increase or decrease, it has nothing to grasp or reject, it cannot be obstructed by fire or water. Also, just as the ground can sustain the weight of the mountains, and can take the thrust of the rivers, and can endure the injuries of myriad things, just as the ground is like this, so too the essence is like this. Perception and cognition have no existence in it; if we force a name on it, it is just emptiness. Emptiness doesn't mean extinction, but flexible adaptivity applied without minding.

ON BIRTH AND DEATH

When you seek life, there is fundamentally no birth;
If you fear death, when has there ever been extinction?
Seeing with the eyes is not as good as seeing with the ears;
How can talking with the mouth compare to talking with the nose?

The essence of enlightenment fundamentally has no birth or death; as for those who insist on life and fear death, when has there ever been life without death? When there is birth, there is death; only the birthless is deathless. Because that essence is birthless and deathless, it cannot be seen with the eyes, it can only be seen by the ears; it cannot be spoken of by the mouth, it can only be spoken of by the nose. What can be seen by the eyes and spoken of by the mouth is the nature which has birth and death; what is seen by the ears and spoken of by the nose is the nature which has no birth or death. Whatever can be seen by the eyes and spoken of by the mouth is not essence; what can be seen by the ears and spoken of by the nose, that is essence. Nonseeing seeing—that is true seeing; nonspoken speech is better than that which is spoken. Since this birthless deathless essence has no head or tail and no back or front, is neither existent nor nonexistent, is neither void nor material, what is there to see or tell? If you can see it or verbalize it, it is not the essence of true emptiness.

THE THREE REALMS ARE ONLY MIND

The subtle principle of the three realms as only mind:
Myriad things are not this, not that;
There is not a thing that is not my mind,
There is not a thing that is my self.

The three realms are the realm of form, the realm of desire, and the realm of no form. The realms of form and desire are realms of minding, the realm of no form is the realm of mindlessness. Neither minding nor mindlessness is the essence of buddhahood. The title of the verse says the three realms are only mind, but what is to be called the true mind is the unminding mind which is neither existent nor nonexistent, in which neither being nor nonbeing stands, and things and self are all ultimately empty. In the mind of the true mind, myriad things are one body, without division into "this" and "that." "There is nothing that is not my mind" refers to not clinging to voidness; "there is nothing that is my self" refers to not sticking to forms. Not clinging to voidness, not sticking to forms, there is just one mind; one mind is one essence, mind is Buddha and Buddha is mind.

SEEING MIND IN THINGS

Seeing things, you see the mind; without things,
   mind does not appear.

*In the ten directions, open or blocked, the true mind is
   omnipresent.
If you conceive intellectual interpretation, it turns into a false view.
If you can see objects without minding, then you will see the face
   of enlightenment.*

"Seeing things, you see the mind; without things, mind does not appear" refers to the human mind with perception and cognition. "In the ten directions, open or blocked, the true mind is omnipresent" refers to the true mind without perception or cognition. The human mind arises and vanishes according to the presence or absence of things; the spiritual light of the true mind is always bright, the same whether there are things or not—everywhere is it. It neither arises nor vanishes, and cannot be assessed by the human mind with its limited faculties of perception and cognition; if you try to understand the true mind by the intellect, you are recognizing a thief as your child—a false view and a serious error.

The true mind is round and bright, naked and free, not divorced from objects yet not attached to objects. If people can see objects without minding, this is true mind, this is the original face of enlightenment—there is no need to seek the original face of enlightenment anywhere else. In sum, when there is no human mind, only then can you see the true mind. Once the true mind is seen, you immediately realize enlightenment and suddenly transcend to the beyond.

Equalizing beings

*I am not different from other people; people's minds are themselves
   different.
For people there are friends and strangers; for me, no "that" or
   "this."
Creatures of water, land, and air, I view equally as one body;
Whether people are high or low in rank, their hands and feet
   are the same as mine.
I am not even me; how could there even be you?
"That" and "this" both nonexistent, myriad bubbles return
   to water.*

The title of this verse is "Equalizing beings," which means equally seeing others and self, friends and strangers, fish, animals, and birds, people in high and low ranks, as one body alone. The important point of this verse is in the line "I am not even me." The reason people of the world cannot see beings as equal is because they are egotistic. If one can be selfless, how can one know there is a second person? With "you" and "me" both forgotten, myriad beings all empty, they are equal of themselves without being equalized.

Mind itself is Buddha

Buddha is mind, mind is Buddha: "Mind" and "Buddha" are
  basically illusions.
If you know there is no Buddha and no mind, this at last is the
  real Buddha of true suchness.
The real Buddha has no likeness; a single round light engulfs
  myriad forms.
The bodyless body is the real body; the formless form is the
  true form.
Not material, not void, not nonvoid, not moving, not still,
  it does not come or go.
No differences, no sameness, no being or nonbeing, it cannot be
  grasped or abandoned, cannot be listened to or looked at.
Inside and outside, round and bright, it pervades everywhere:
One Buddha-land is in a grain of sand, one grain of sand contains
  a universe;
One body and mind, ten thousand are the same. Knowing this, you
  should understand the principle of unminding:
Not being conditioned or obsessed is pure work, not doing
  anything, good or bad, is paying honor to Kaśyapa.

The important point of this verse is in the line, "Knowing this, you should understand the principle of unminding." Unminding does not mean ignorance; if it were ignorant unminding, it would be the same as a wood carving or clay statue—how could it be said mind is Buddha? Generally speaking, the meaning of unminding is simply not sticking to forms and not sticking to voidness.

The true mind has no substance or form; originally there is not a single thing in it, so what form could it have? The light of the true mind engulfs myriad things, all-pervasive without obstruction—how could it be void? Not form, not void, round and bright, clean and naked, mind is Buddha, Buddha is mind, yet neither is "mind" or "Buddha." Therefore it says "mind is Buddha, Buddha is mind," and it also says "mind and Buddha are basically illusions." If you perceive mind is Buddha, and also know it is neither mind nor Buddha, the principle of unminding can avoid falling into nihilism.

UNMINDING

What a laugh my mind is—like a dunce, like a bumpkin,
Now unmoving, now ebullient, calmly letting things be as they may.
I do not know how to cultivate spiritual practice, yet do not do anything wrong.
I have never helped other people, yet am not self-serving either.
I do not keep any rules of discipline, nor do I follow taboos.
I do not know ritual or music, I do not practice benevolence and duty.
What people can do I do not understand at all.
When hungry, I eat, when thirsty, I drink,
When tired I sleep, waking, I act.
When it's hot I dress lightly, when cold, I put on more clothes.
Without thought or rumination, what sorrow, what joy?
No regret, no ambition, no memories, no ideas.
The ups and downs of ordinary life are just inns on a journey.
A tree in a forest where birds may perch also can be a simile;
It does not try to prevent their coming, and does not try to stop them when they leave.
Not avoiding, not seeking, no praise, no blame.
I do not dislike ugliness or envy beauty.
I do not run for a quiet room, or run away from the bustling city.
I do not speak of others' wrongs or boast when I am right.
I am not solicitous of the highly placed, nor do I slight the lowly or the young.
Friend and enemy, great and small, inside and outside,
Sadness and happiness, gain and loss, honor or insult, danger or ease—
My mind does not see dualistically, but is equanimous, all the same.
It does not lead to fortune, and does not start calamity;

Sensing, it responds, returning, it again arises.
I do not fear weapons, I am not scared of wild beasts.
I refer to whatever is at hand without being restricted by names.
My eyes do not go to forms, sounds do not enter my ears.
Whatever appearances there may be all belong to falsity.
The forms and voices of men and women are not fixed entities.
Mindless of physical appearances, I am not influenced or attached;
Wandering freely, nothing can get me down.
The sphere of light of ineffable awareness shines throughout, inside and out.
Enfolding the four quarters, without far or near.
The light is not light—it is like the moon in the water.
Since you cannot grasp it or throw it out, how can you compare it to anything?
When you understand this sublime function, you transcend to the beyond.
If anyone asks my religion, it is just this.

This lengthy poem just illustrates unminding. The marvel is in unminding, by which one can be beyond the world while in the world, roaming freely, untrammeled by things. Not a particle of dust is to be admitted into people's hearts, for whenever there is any dust within, endless human mentality emerges. Once human mentality arises, one becomes capricious and loses autonomy and independence, taking the servant for the master and considering the master a servant. How then can one be free? If one can be totally unminding, imperturbable and unshakable, then one is independent. When independent, one is autonomous. Myriad ruminations cease, entanglements do not arise; the sphere of light of ineffable awareness is all-pervasive and all-embracing, without distinction of far or near. This is true attainment of freedom, the sublime function of unminding.

On the *Heart Scripture*

The clusters, the truths, sense faculties and objects, void and form—
In none of these is there a single thing worth saying.
When perverted views are ended,
The body of tranquility is serene.

The clusters are the five clusters of matter, sensation, perception, patterning, and consciousness, which form the human being. The truths are the four truths of suffering, its cause, its end, and the way to end it. The sense faculties are the six organs of eyes, ears, nose, tongue, body, and intellect. The sense objects are the six fields of form, sound, smell, taste, tactile feeling, and phenomena. Voidness is extinction, form is attachment to appearances. The clusters, truths, sense faculties and objects, void and form are all phenomena projected by the mind, and all are related to perverted views. If you can sweep all away, then the body of mind is tranquil; this is the bodhisattva Independent Seer, this is nonbirth and nondeath. If anything among these remains, then there is birth and death, so you do not attain independence. If you arrive at constant independence with no birth and death, then everything is pure.

No sin or merit

Walking all day without ever walking, sitting all day without ever sitting,
Doing good does not make merit, doing evil involves no son.
If people today have not clarified the mind, do not act arbitrarily, clinging to these words:
After dying you will see the king of the underworld, and have trouble escaping being boiled or mashed.

The title says there is no sin or merit—what does this mean? Sin and merit both come from the mind: mindfully doing evil is mindfully committing sin; mindfully doing good is mindfully seeking merit. Good and evil, sin and merit, all exist dependent on mind; if you reach the state of mindlessness, you are not even conscious of walking or sitting—how could you be conscious of good and evil, sin and merit? This is why it says doing good does not make merit and doing evil does not involve sin. It is like a baby, unselfconsciously and unknowingly laughing happily and crying angrily, this all proceeding from mindlessness—what merit or sin is there?

Mindlessness means there is no human mentality; when there is no human mentality, there naturally is the true mind. The extent of the true mind is the same as the universe, containing everything; not thinking of good, not thinking of evil, it does not commit sin, does not seek merit. It does not conceive of merit or sin. If people have not clarified the true mind, and just let their ignorant, intransigent mind act up, doing all sorts of mischief, and tell themselves there is nothing wrong, how can they avoid being boiled or mashed as a result after they die?

Complete pervasion

When you have seen true emptiness, emptiness is not empty;
Complete illumination pervades everywhere.
Senses and objects, mind and phenomena—there is no thing at all;
Only by subtle function can you know how to assimilate.

The essence of true emptiness is all-pervasive, unobstructed; its light illumines everywhere, nothing can get by it. It is intrinsically empty without being emptied, empty yet not empty. It is just a matter of being ever responsive yet ever tranquil, ever tranquil yet ever responsive.

Going along with it

Myriad things, every which way, confront us;
Go along with them in action and repose, leave them to their devices:
Round and bright stability and wisdom are ultimately never defiled,
Just as water produces lotuses, yet the lotus itself is dry.

Though this verse has four lines, really the meaning is in the one line "round and bright stability and wisdom are ultimately never defiled." "Round and bright" means subtle being; "stability and wisdom" means true emptiness. True emptiness is naturally in myriad things, yet is not defiled by myriad things. Subtle being naturally encounters myriad things, and can respond to myriad things. Ever responsive, ever tranquil, going along yet at peace, one is like a lotus, which grows from the mud yet is not dirtied.

The jewel moon

The bright orb of the moon in the sky; its clear light is unobstructed in myriad lands.

It cannot be gathered or dispelled, it cannot be pushed forward or backward.

"There" is not far, "here" is not near; the exterior is not outside, the interior is not inside.

There is difference in sameness, sameness in difference; I ask you the mechanism—do you understand?

The essence of enlightenment, true emptiness, is complete pervasion of ineffable awareness, its light illumining all, like the bright moon in the sky shining everywhere equally. Gather it, and you do not see the light collect; dispel it, and you do not see the light disperse. Ahead, you do not see the light go forward; behind, you do not see the light recede. As it illumines "there" it does not seem far; as it illumines "here" it does not seem near. Illumining the exterior, the light is not outside; illumining the interior, the light is not inside. Gathering, dispelling, before, behind, forward, backward, there, here, far, near, exterior, interior, inside, outside—though there is difference in the illumination, the light is the same. There is difference in sameness, sameness in difference; one root ramifies into myriad differences, myriad differences return to the one root. Release it and it fills the universe, wrap it up and it hides in secrecy. Lively and active, it is like the mechanism of a marionette.

Picking up the pearl

The pearl in the poor one's clothes is originally round and bright;

If one does not know how to find it oneself, one will count others' treasures instead.

Counting others' treasures is after all of no benefit—it just makes you expend your labor in vain:

How can it compare to recognizing your own jewel, which is worth more than billions in gold?

The shine of this precious pearl is most great, as it lights up all worlds in the universe.

It has never been subject to diminution, but has been blocked by floating clouds.

After having recognized this jewel, who would care for ephemeral illusions anymore?

The pearl of Buddha is the same as one's own pearl; one's own essence returns to the ocean of the essence of Buddhahood.

*The pearl is not a pearl, the ocean is not an ocean. Equanimous, the
   measure of mind embraces the cosmos.
Let the dust and clamor fill your purview—stability and wisdom,
   round and bright, are always free.
This is not void, this is not material; inside and outside are clear,
   without obstruction.
The six psychic powers are subtle and inexhaustible, helping self
   and others without any end.
See and you understand, myriad tasks are done; beyond study, you
   pass the days without contrivance.
Calm as an infant without a set character, active or still according
   to situations, without fixation.
Neither stopping illusion nor cultivating truth, the ideas of truth
   and falsehood are all in the realm of dust.
Myriad things have always been signless; in signlessness there is
   the body of reality.
The body of reality is the naturally-so Buddha, neither a person nor
   a thing.
So vast as to fill the universe, it is rarified and ungraspable.
Filth cannot defile it, its light is inherently bright. There is nothing
   that is not born from mind;
If mind is unborn, things pass away. Then you know sin and merit
   are basically formless.
There is no Buddhahood to cultivate, no teaching to preach. The
   knowledge and insight of great people are naturally distinct;
When they speak, they make the roar of a lion, unlike jackals
   discussing birth and death.*

The important point in this poem is the line "If mind is unborn, things pass away." These "things" are the various thoughts and imaginations in the mind. If the mind is unborn, all things are empty, the pearl of essence is always shining, stability and wisdom are round and bright, inside and outside are clear; ephemeral illusions are not worthy of attachment, dust and clamor may fill the eyes but cannot be a hindrance. Beyond study, uncontrived, one is like an unformed infant, active or still according to circumstances, without illusory images of truth or falsehood, the body of reality always exposed, the naturally-so Buddha is manifest. Then it fills the universe, light shining on all worlds; what veil of floating clouds is there?

Pointing Out Errors in Meditation

The essence of enlightened meditation is like water: the substance still, the ripples roused by the wind spontaneously stop;
In action and repose tranquil and ever clear, it is not only thus when sitting.
People now sit quietly to get realization, and do not say it is all in seeing essence.
If essence is clear in seeing, seeing is stable in essence.
Stability makes wisdom, its use without end; this is called the spiritual power of buddhas.
If you want to study their substance and function, just see the space of the ten directions:
In space there is not a single thing, and there is no subtlety or trance.
Since subtlety or trance cannot be found, to look for them throws you off the track.
But do not grasp "off the track" as words to rely on; the original mind is like space—what has it to do with gain or loss?
Just clear away myriad things, clear them away without remainder,
And suddenly complete illumination will appear of itself, no different from the buddhas.
The physical body is a fetter to us, but thus we mix with the ordinary world.
Totally unminding in action, what right or wrong, glory or ignominy, is there to contest over?
The body is just a lodging; the innkeeper's name is Illuminator.
The Illuminator neither comes nor goes, so we know it has no more birth or death.
If you ask what the Illuminator is like, any description is wrong;
Every act and every thing we see is neither the same nor different.
Seeing these acts and things, each one is Buddha and disciple.
In terms of difference, myriad pipes all sound; in terms of sameness, one wind envelops all.
If you want to recognize the jewel, do not say you will know when you get the teaching:
When there is sickness, you use medicine to cure it; once the sickness is cured, why should medicine be dispensed anymore?

When the mind is deluded, use the teaching to reveal this; once the
   mind is enlightened, the teaching is no more necessary.
It is also like a clouded mirror getting polished, the stains
   encrusting it disappear.
Basically because things are deceptive, we are told to detach from
   appearances.
Detached from appearances, then what? This is called ultimate
   reality, unexcelled.
If you want to adorn a buddha land, practice compassion
   impartially, rescue the suffering.
Though the fundamental vow of enlightenment is deep, do not
   grasp within forms.
This is twin fulfillment of virtue and wisdom; the future assurance
   of enlightenment takes place beforehand.
If one is affected by any trace of nihilism or eternalism, one has no
   affinity with the buddhas.
Thinking back to the deluded clinging of the mundane, all are
   habituated to sensual attachments;
Because their feelings of craving are many, they remain bound to
   the world.
Study of the Tao requires fierceness, an unsentimental mind firm
   as iron.
Even our children and spouses are not different from other people.
Always maintain a single round light, not seeing any favor to be
   desired;
Once you have no attachments to anything, what hell or heaven is
   there to speak of?
After that, our destiny is up to us—there is no ascension or fall in
   emptiness.
Appearing and disappearing in the Buddha lands, never apart from
   the seat of enlightenment,
Kuan-yin has thirty-two adaptations, and we too should realize
   from this
That creative manifestations are inconceivable, all coming from
   the essence of freedom.
I am a mindless meditator, and do not know how to judge ordinary
   things, the black ox of before now is all white.
Sometimes I sing and laugh to myself, and bystanders say I am a
   halfwit.

How can they know this wool-cloaked figure enbosoms a priceless jewel within?
And if you see me talking about emptiness, it is like swallowing a date whole;
Only buddhas can know this truth—how can the ignorant express it?
There are also practitioners of Ch'an who only learn to argue
And boast of their swiftness in repartee, still basically ignorant of the true self.
It is because they pursue the branches and pick the leaves, not knowing how to find out the root.
When you get the root, the branches and leaves naturally flourish; without the root, branches and leaves cannot survive.
If they go on flaunting the spiritual pearl in their grip, it turns into discrimination between self and others, hard to remove:
That is very far away from the ineffable awareness of our spiritual source.
These people are pitiful, laughable, vainly talking of years of study,
Too proud to ask of others, wasting their whole lives unfulfilled.
This is the dullness of the ignorant and deluded, caused by false views and deep habits.
If you do not wake up in this life, how can you avoid sinking in the next?

The meaning of this whole poem is in the first four lines. The essence of enlightened nature is thoroughly pure, its clarity is like water. Not arousing waves, not being defiled, all action and repose is it; one is not stable only when sitting. If you take sitting to be meditation, that is not true meditation; it is nihilistic, indifferent meditation, and cannot match the essence of enlightened meditation. True meditation includes both stability and wisdom, subtly functioning endlessly; mind and phenomena both forgotten, detached from appearances, adorning a buddha land, impartially practicing compassion, harmonizing with ordinary society, in the world yet beyond the world, meditating without meditating, stable without stabilization. All those who sit quietly for realization and those who engage in verbal competition, wild foxes ignorant of the true self, who wake up after meditation stupor only to have their wakefulness cause confusion, cannot know there is a true essence of meditation, which is the ineffable awareness of the spiritual source.

Song on reading Ch'an master Hsueh-tou's *Anthology on Eminent Adepts*

The one water of Ch'an is divided into a thousand streams,
Illumining the past and clarifying the present, with no stagnation or blockage.
Students these days do not search out the source: They mistakenly point to a footprint and call it the ocean.
The teacher Hsueh-tou arrived at the true import; he beat the drum of truth with a thunderous sound:
When the lion king comes out of the cave and roars, all the beasts and deviants take fright.
With songs, poems, and sayings, he carefully guides people who are lost.
His manner of expression is free, his meanings are lofty and profound; his strikingly musical notes echo over the ages.
Nevertheless the deluded stop at chasing objects and consider only the literary style.
The true character of real suchness basically has no word—no low, no high, it has no bounds; not form, not void, not dual in substance, the countless lands in the ten directions are its single orb.
When has true stability ever divided speech and silence—it cannot be grasped, cannot be abandoned.
Just do not keep the mind on appearances; this is the true guideline of the Buddha.
To clear away false ideas, he counterposed the true; if falsehood does not arise, "truth" is invisible too.
If you can know truth and falsehood are both not so, then you will attain real mind without obstruction.
With no obstruction, you can be free; one enlightenment abruptly dissolves the evils of the ages.
Without exerting effort, you realize enlightenment and henceforth are forever removed from the ocean of birth and death.
Our teacher is near and his words are uplifting, left in the world as a model and guide.
Last night he was called forth by me, grabbed by the nose and stuck on a staff:

I asked him about the ultimate meaning, and he said all words deny it.

Though this song is a eulogy of the book *Anthology on Eminent Adepts*, in reality it is communicating characteristics of real suchness. Where it says, "Just don't keep the mind on appearances; this is the true guideline of the Buddha," these two phrases have already summed up the great meaning in the anthology. Not fixing the mind on appearances is unminding; when unminding, "true" and "false" do not arise. When true and false do not arise, there is no obstruction; when there is no obstruction, one attains freedom. When one attains freedom, reality is everpresent, and one is forever removed from the ocean of birth and death.

The line "Last night he was called forth by me, grabbed by the nose and stuck on a staff" indicates the author's intent outside words. Students are to think, in calling forth, what is called; and what does sticking the nose refer to? Calling forth means calling the essence of the true character of real suchness; piercing the nose means penetrating the mind which is neither form nor void. Understanding this essence, knowing this mind, the staff is in one's hands, supporting the heavens above and the earth below. No back, no front, round and bright, clean and bare, naked and free, this is the ultimate meaning of Ch'an—what more is there to say?

Interpretation of Discipline, Concentration, and Wisdom

Discipline, concentration, and wisdom are subtle functions in religion;
Though the buddhas and Ch'an adepts have spoken of them, those who do not as yet comprehend them have fixations:
So now I will briefly talk about them, to help people awaken.
When mind and objects are both forgotten and not a single thought stirs, this is called discipline.
Awareness being round and bright, thoroughly clear inside and out, is called concentration.
Dealing with things according to circumstances, subtle function inexhaustible, is called wisdom.
These three require each other to develop, and act as substance and function to one another.

*The three have never been separated: it is like the sun being able to
shine by light, light being able to illumine by shining—
If not for light, the sun cannot shine, if not for shining the light
cannot illumine.
When we look into the source of discipline, concentration, and
wisdom, they are based on one essence;
Light, shining, and illumination are based on one sun.
Since the one is not even one, how could the three be three?
Three and one both forgotten, there is profoundly calm purity.*

In this interpretation, the author has already entered absorption in discipline, concentration, and wisdom; the words are simple, the meaning clear. If students can put this into practice, they can directly ascend to the goal. However, though the author's words and meaning are clear, it may be that students are not very perceptive or may lack the necessary power, and be unable to proceed to understanding the fundamental, so I will add some footnotes, to guide people on behalf of the author, enabling them to enter from the shallows to the depths, and rise from lowliness to the heights. I hope this will be possible.

Discipline means to forget emotions when confronting experiences, and not to be affected by objects. Concentration means utter sincerity and truthfulness, without vagary, not moving or shifting. Wisdom means adapting efficiently according to events, without partiality or bias. To be disciplined, to be concentrated, to be wise, the three require one another. Going from effort to end up in spontaneity, they merge into one essence, ultimately leading to the state of nonconscious purity.

In reality, when you arrive at purity, even one essence is not it—how could there be three things, discipline, concentration, and wisdom? Therefore it says, "Three and one both forgotten, there is profoundly calm purity." Before arriving at purity, the three are necessary; having arrived at purity, the three merge and sublimate spontaneously. If the three and one are not forgotten, it still is not pure meditation. One of the verses says, "When the mind is astray, the Teaching must be used to reveal it; when the mind is enlightened, the Teaching is no longer necessary." It is so that mind and teaching both be forgotten that we are told to detach from all appearances. This seems to be the meaning of "Three and one both forgotten, there is profoundly calm purity."

The moon on the West River—twelve verses

[1]

Errant thought is not to be forcibly annihilated; why should true suchness be sought?
Buddhas equally act on the fundamental essence; delusion and enlightenment are not confined to before and after.
When enlightened, you become a buddha instantly; when deluded, you sink in the flow for myriad eons.
If you can accord with true practice for a moment, you annihilate the defilement of countless wrongs.

The fundamental essence is the essence of enlightenment, in which there is no errant thought, and no true suchness. It is only because people of the world have delusion and enlightenment that there are the terms "errant thought" and "true suchness." When you are deluded about essence, you conceive erroneous thoughts; when you realize essence, you return to true suchness. When you awaken to suchness, you instantly become a Buddha; when you conceive errant thoughts, you sink in their flow for eons. Errant thought or true suchness—it is simply a matter of the difference between delusion and enlightenment. If you try to forcibly annihilate errant thought and seek true suchness without enlightenment, how can you get to see true suchness? The concluding line says, "If you can accord with true practice for a moment, you annihilate the defilement of countless wrongs." Then you can be perfectly clear.

[2]

Fundamentally there is no origination or extinction, yet we insist on seeking divisions marking birth and death.

*As for sin and merit, these too are baseless; when has the subtle
  body ever increased or decreased?
I have a round clear mirror, which has hitherto always been
  covered;
Today I polish it so it reflects the universe, and myriad images are
  clearly revealed.*

The fundamental essence of enlightenment, true suchness, has no origination or extinction; there is no possibility of increasing or decreasing it. It is because of attachment to objects that there is origination and extinction, birth and death. This is just like a mirror being covered, that is all. If you can polish away the accumulated dust of past influences, it is round and bright, without defect. Using this to reflect the universe, myriad forms are clearly revealed. What producing or destroying them is there?

[3]

*The essence of the self enters the essence of the buddhas; the
  essence of buddhahood is everywhere thus.
From on high the cold light shines in the cold springs; one moon
  appears in a thousand ponds.
Its smallness is smaller than a hair, its greatness fills the universe;
High and low do not restrict it, it may be square or round; what
  long or short, deep or shallow can you say it has?*

The essence of the self, the essence of buddhahood, the essence of human beings in all nations and lands are all the same, not more in sages, not less in ordinary beings. It is like the single disc of the bright moon appearing in a thousand ponds. This essence can be small, can be great, can be high, can be low, can be square, can be round, can be shallow, can be deep, can be long, can be short—yet it is not confined to small or great, square or round, high or low, shallow or deep. It is just that ordinary people use it every day but do not know it.

[4]

*The principle governing the teaching fundamentally has no
  doctrine; the emptiness that empties emptiness also is not
  empty.*

*Quiet and clamor, speech and silence, are originally the
  same—why bother to talk of a dream in a dream?*
*There is no function in the function that has function; effort is
  applied in the effortless effort.*
*It is like the fruit naturally reddening as it ripens—do not ask how
  to cultivate the seed.*

The Buddhas' expositions of doctrine really have no dogma; when a Buddha speaks of emptiness, it is really not empty. The doctrineless doctrine is called true teaching; nonempty emptiness is called true emptiness. True teaching, true emptiness, quiet or clamor, speech or silence—it is just a matter of unconsciously following the laws of God; what doctrine is there to preach, what emptiness is there to expound? To insist on preaching doctrine and expounding emptiness is like talking of a dream in a dream—how can you know the essence of true teaching, true emptiness? Tranquil and unperturbed, yet sensitive and effective, sensitive and effective yet tranquil and unperturbed, this is "no function within function having function, applying effort within effortless effort." That there is "no function within function having function" means that the teaching is based on emptiness; that one "applies effort within effortless effort" means that there is teaching within emptiness. The teaching basically empty, emptiness having a teaching, it is neither true nor false, not existent nor nonexistent. Round and bright, unobscured, after a long time there is spontaneous release, just as fruit naturally ripens on a tree. This itself is cultivating the true seed of the essence of enlightenment—there is no more need to ask how to cultivate the seed.

[5]

*Good or bad—forget thoughts all at once; let neither prosperity nor
  decline concern the mind.*
*In dark and light, now concealed, now revealed, float or sink as you
  may; according to your lot, eat when hungry, drink when thirsty.*
*Spirit calm, serene, ever tranquil, one may sit or recline, sing or
  hum.*
*The autumn water in one pond is blue and deep; when the wind
  blows, do not be startled, let it be as it is.*

The overall meaning of this poem is in the lines "Spirit calm, serene, ever tranquil, one may sit or recline, sing or hum." Once the spirit is calm, good and bad, prosperity and decline, dark and light, obscurity and prominence, floating and sinking, do not enter the mind; passing the days according to circumstances, you sit and recline, sing and hum, untrammeled, free, without thought or worry, like the autumn water in a pond, blue and deep, without waves even when there is wind—what fear is there of vexation or upset?

[6]

No need to try to annihilate objects; enlightenment is an artificial definition.
Matter and voidness, light and dark, are basically equal; stop dividing reality and falsehood into two.
When you understand, it is called the Pure Land—there is no more India or Ts'ao Ch'i.
Who says paradise is the western heaven? When you understand, Amitabha appears in the world.

The essence of enlightenment is originally round and bright, clean and naked, bare and untrammeled, not matter, not void, not light, not dark, not real, not false. Those who understand this attain buddhahood on the spot—what's the need to try to extinguish feelings about objects? It is because so many people do not understand, that the Buddhas and bodhisattvas provisionally defined enlightenment, to get people to return to the immediate by way of the gradual, so as to realize buddhahood. Enlightenment means the true way, in that by returning from error to truth there is a gradual awakening.

[7]

Others, self, beings, lives; how can we divide that and this, high and low?
Reality spontaneously shines throughout, with no "I" or "they"—one need not seek it thought after thought.
Has seeing what is right ever been seeing what is right? Hearing what is wrong is not necessarily hearing what is wrong.

*Various functions have never controlled each other—in life and
  death, who can hinder you?*

Others, self, beings, lives, that, this, high, low, I, they, seeing, hearing, right, wrong—these are all artificial characterizations. If you can penetrate them all with shining awareness and see through them completely, not being concerned with them, then life is as is, death is as is, life is all right, death is all right too; life and death present no obstacle, and you naturally understand life and death.

[8]

*If you cultivate practices and charity while dwelling on
  appearances, the resulting rewards will be limited to celestial
  and human spheres.*
*It is like shooting an arrow up at the clouds; it will fall, simply
  because the force comes to an end.*
*How can that compare to unfabricated reality? Returning to the
  original, reverting to simplicity, going back to pristine purity,*
*Objects forgotten, feelings ended, going along with natural reality,
  thereby you realize acceptance of the truth of nonorigination.*

Formless form is true form. True form does not come from the fruits of practices or charity performed while dwelling on appearances. It comes from reverting to pristine purity and simplicity, forgetting objects and ending feelings. When you find the true form, every action, every stillness, is natural reality; you spontaneously attain acceptance of the truth of nonorigination. The *Śūraṅgama Sūtra* says, "This person thereupon attains acceptance of the truth of nonorigination." A commentary on the sutra says, "True suchness is called nonorigination. Truth has no contamination; knowledge of truth is called acceptance."

[9]

*Once you have caught the fish or the rabbit you naturally forget
  the net and the trap.*
*The raft to cross the river, the ladder to the heights: once you have
  reached the goal, they are abandoned.*

*Before you are enlightened, you need explanations; after
  enlightenment, verbalizations become wrong.
Even though these lines belong to noncontrivance, they too are
  to be shed.*

A net it a means to catch fish; once you get the fish, you can forget the net. A trap is a means to catch rabbits; when you get the rabbit, you can forget the trap. A raft is a means to cross a river; when you reach the shore, you can leave the raft. A ladder is a means to climb up high; when you reach the height you can leave the ladder. These are similes for words as a means to understand principles; when the principles are understood, one can forget the words. Though the lines about forgetting the net and trap, abandoning the raft and ladder, are telling people to understand true essence and fundamentally are in the realm of nondoing, one cannot immediately wind matters up with nihilistic inaction. By mere nihilistic inaction, how can one reach the state of sublime awareness of true thusness? It is necessary to shed this nondoing before one can deeply attain self-realization.

[10]

*After enlightenment, do not seek quiescence; guide the deluded
  according to conditions.
When views of annihilation and eternity are presented, there are
  expedients to guide back to reality.
Five eyes, three bodies, four knowledges, six perfections and
  myriad practices cultivated equally.
One orb of round light, a fine jewel helps others and can also save
  oneself.*

Buddhism considers realization of essence first, but that does not mean that after enlightenment there is then empty nothingness. It is necessary to take this empty essence back to reality; only this is the true essence of buddhahood. Therefore the text says not to seek quiescence or extinction after enlightenment, but to guide the deluded for the time according to conditions. Guiding the deluded is the reason for practicing expedients and doing good works.

The five eyes are the celestial eye, the eye of wisdom, the objective eye, the enlightened eye, and the physical eye. The three bodies are the pure body of reality, the complete body of reward, and the innumerable created bodies. The four knowledges are the great round mirror knowledge, the knowledge of essential equality, the subtly observing knowledge, and the knowledge of practical accomplishment. The six perfections are generosity, discipline, tolerance, diligence, meditation, and wisdom. The myriad practices are all expedients and good works. The five eyes, three bodies, four knowledges, six perfections, and myriad practices simultaneously cultivated inwardly and outwardly, the basic essence of true thusness becomes clearer and clearer with refinement, like a brilliant jewel, penetrating obscurity, bringing the hidden to light. Helping others as well as oneself, it is always useful—how could it be just emptiness alone?

[11]

I see people these days expounding essence who just boast of
   quickness in repartee;
But when they meet actual situations they are all the more
   deluded—how are they any different from the ignorant?
What is preached should be put into practice—only then is it called
   speech and action without defect.
If you can use the sword of wisdom to cut the jewel, this is called
   the true knowledge of the enlightened.

The important point of this verse is in the last line. The true knowledge of the enlightened is all-pervasive; this is the sword of wisdom. By that true knowledge one can get rid of error and return to truth, so it is called the sword of wisdom. Because that true knowledge is round and bright, unobscured, ever present, it is called a jewel. To cut the jewel does not mean to obliterate it but to take it in, not allowing the shining of the light to operate outside. When speaking in terms of substance it is called a jewel, when speaking in terms of function it is called the sword of wisdom. The sword of wisdom, the jewel, and true knowledge are all one, not three things.

This true knowledge is not obtained by talking; it can only be real if it is cultivated by personal practice. If one cannot personally practice it and only wants to talk about it, considering a quick wit to be insight, one will be confused in actual events—what will be accomplished? Therefore when it says "If you are able to use the sword of wisdom to cut the jewel, this is called the true knowledge of the enlightened," only when the words and actions are complete is it really true knowledge. Verbal quickness in repartee is not true knowledge.

[12]

If you want to understand the sublime path of birthlessness, it is all a matter of seeing the true mind for yourself.
The true body has no form, and no cause either; the pure spiritual body is just thus.
This path is not nonbeing and not being, not in between, not to be sought there either.
When both extremes are dismissed, abandon the middle; once you see it, this is called supreme.

Once you see the true mind, this is the sublime path; there is no need to seek the sublime path elsewhere. The true mind is unstained, unattached, unperturbed, unmoved, formless and soundless; this is also called the pure spiritual body. This mind, this body, is not existent, not nonexistent, yet both existent and nonexistent. It cannot be sought in being, cannot be sought in nonbeing, and cannot be found in neither being-nor-nonbeing. Since none of these three apply to it, try to think what it is. When you see this, you immediately transcend to birthlessness; this is called the sublime path of the supreme one vehicle.

The true body and true mind are originally one; in terms of substance it is called the true body, in terms of function it is called the true mind. Substance and function as one, body and mind forgotten, physically and spiritual sublimated, merging with the Tao in reality—isn't this what birthlessness means?

Glossary

ABERRANT ENERGY   Energy produced or activated by external influences, by inner emotions, or by arbitrary conceptions. It is called aberrant in the sense of being conditioned and obstructing autonomy or preventing realization of the true self.

ABSOLUTE ONE   The name of a god used to symbolize the unified mind.

ALTAIR AND VEGA   Stars whose meeting symbolizes union of yin and yang.

AMITABHA   A Buddha representative of compassion, infinite light and life, in the sphere of "Ultimate Bliss" (q.v.).

AUXILIARY TECHNIQUES   Exercises for producing health and bliss.

BAMBOO   A symbol of emptiness in the sense of emptying the mind of ordinary preoccupations in order to make it receptive to higher knowledge.

BATHING   A relaxation of intensive effort in spiritual practice, to prevent excess of striving from resulting in counterproductive impulses such as eagerness or unbalanced force. The term is also used to refer to "washing the mind," which is related to the former usage in the sense that concentration is held to also require "cleaning" out mental contaminants that may be retained or even exaggerated in the effort to focus the mind on something else.

BIRTH AND DEATH   The ongoing process of material and psychic change. A common Buddhist term, it is used to refer to attachments to transient particulars, with the resulting subjection to mental pressures and states caused by a conflict between the craving for stability and the actuality of evanescence. Hence the term is often used synonymously with bondage or suffering.

BIRTHLESS   Objectivity, this means "nonorigination," the principle that as all things are interrelated and have no independent existence in themselves, beginnings are a matter of definition and not of inherent reality. Subjectively, birthlessness means the mind is not compulsively aroused and does not fabricate illusions.

BLACK OX A Ch'an Buddhist term for the ignorant, unregenerate mind: the ox turns "white" as the mind is purified and illuminated.

BLACK TIGER A symbol of "true lead," which stands for the mind of Tao or the primal root of consciousness.

BODHIDHARMA The reputed founder of Ch'an Buddhism in China.

BODHISATTVA A Buddhist term for an awakened person who is consciously dedicated to the total welfare of all living beings.

BODY OF REALITY A Buddhist term for pure objectivity or pure awareness.

BOTH COUNTRIES Yin and yang, the mundane and the celestial, tranquility and action.

BUDDHA LAND The environment of fully awakened consciousness.

CELESTIAL AND HUMAN SPHERES In Buddhist terminology, as used here, celestial and human spheres refer to states of bliss and social order, considered as lesser rewards of ethical and religious practices which are not thoroughly purged of selfishness or attachment. It should be noted that "celestial" has quite different connotations in Buddhism and Taoism: in Buddhism, it can be almost derogatory, since it stands for blissful states which are considered a potential hindrance to enlightenment; in Taoism, it is positive, referring to the realm of enlightened consciousness.

CELESTIAL ESSENCE The original essence of consciousness, before being affected by mundane influences and confined within habit.

CELESTIAL IMMORTALITY A state of mental refinement in which emotional and intellectual attachments to objects of the world, including the ego, have been removed, and one is no longer ultimately identified subjectively with the individual body or personality, so that consciousness is "spacelike" and merged with objective reality.

CELESTIAL JEWEL The highest state of perfection envisioned by Taoist enlightenment.

CENTER   The point of balance, the state of mind before it is affected by feelings; it also stands for will, sincerity, intent, and truthfulness, as the hub of experience. The state of balance of the celestial and the earthly, of detachment and involvement, of firmness and flexibility.

CHANG CHIEN   A famous traveler, used in this treatise as a symbol for yang.

CHANG SAN-FENG   A famous Taoist adept of the Ming dynasty, traditionally considered an inventor of the popular exercise system known as T'ai Chi Ch'uan.

CINNABAR   Symbol of the energy of consciousness.

CINNABAR CRUCIBLE   The human mind.

CLOSED ROOM   This term refers to the practice of concentration in which the energy of awareness is not allowed to "leak" outside into distraction or emotive effervescence.

CONSCIOUS ESSENCE   The essence of mind or nature of awareness.

CONSCIOUS KNOWLEDGE   The range of awareness or data available to consciousness.

COUNTING OTHERS' TREASURES   A Buddhist expression for nonparticipatory study of the externals of a developmental system.

CRESCENT MOON FURNACE   The mind of Tao; the image of the crescent is often used to represent the emergence of the "light" of the primal mind from the "shadow" of acquired conditioning.

CRUCIBLE   The "vessel" in which the "elixir" is "cooked." It is variously defined: it can refer to mind (cf. *cinnabar crucible, gold crucible*), or to the qualities of firmness and flexibility, or determination and adaptability.

CULTURAL COOKING   The practice of "nonstriving" or "nondoing," which involves tranquil preservation of clarified consciousness to prevent it from scattering in distraction; calmly watching over the mind. "Cultural" means gentle, without force.

DARK   Symbol of unknowing: the human mind is said to be light outside and dark inside, in that its awareness plays on objects and not on inner essence; the mind of Tao is said to be dark outside and light inside, in that it is not fixed on externals but is aware of inner essence. Dark can thus mean unknowing in the sense of ignorance or in the sense of detachment.

DEATH-IMPULSE The force of mortality, impermanence, decay: associated with the dissipation of life energy, and with habituation to transient things.

DEMONS Obstructions on the path. According to Lu Yen in *Wu Chen Pao Fa Chiu Yu Ching*, anything can be the path, including demons, while anything can be a demon, including the path. There are said to be inner demons and outer demons; the way to overcome them is said to be to silence the mind and master thought.

DIPANKARA An ancient Buddha, symbol of primordial enlightenment.

DOING Practice involving conscious effort and striving, such as effort to escape the force of mental habit so as to experience the original mind and gain autonomy; striving to extract the primal energy of consciousness from accretions of experiential history.

DUST Sense objects, or the realm of the ordinary senses; often used in a general way to refer to the mundane world and/or the products of mental agitation arising from contact with the world in the absence of inner freedom.

EARTH The medium of the joining of the conscious human mind and the subconscious mind of Tao; referred to as intent, or will. Also associated with the "center," standing for sincerity, truthfulness, or faith, as a unifying force in the human being. Note that this is different from the *I Ching* sign *earth*, which is italicized in the text of the translation.

EARTHEN POT This term has the same meaning as "earth," but here is represented as a metaphysical container or locus in which various elements of mind are concentrated and unified. In psychosomatic Taoist yoga the "earthen pot" is assigned an actual physical location, in the region of the solar plexus, the center of the trunk, this spot being used as a focus of concentration.

EARTHLY SOUL Used in the present text to symbolize real knowledge. It is referred to as yang ("soul") within yin ("earth") because real knowledge is primordial (unconditioned) and hence yang, but is ordinarily hidden, hence yin.

EAST "In the east" means within oneself.

ELDER WATER   The unified energy of consciousness from which real knowledge is derived.

ELIXIR   A general word for the energy, capacity, and function of life and consciousness: various terms such as gold elixir, great elixir, outer elixir, inner elixir, and restored elixir are used in the context of different aspects or stages of the spiritual "alchemy."

EMBRYONIC BREATH   An ancient hibernation technique; also refers to a state of composure and profound tranquility, in which the breath is imperceptible and the mind does not give rise to any impulses.

EMPTINESS   Metaphysically, emptiness means that phenomena are not objectively just as they subjectively appear to be; practically speaking, it refers to a state of mind which is not prejudiced by subjective assessments, a state of clarity and directness. In Taoism this is referred to as "emptying the human mind."

ENLIVENING   Unification of mind, balanced combination of the various elements of mind in such a way that they complement each other and work together harmoniously and constructively.

ESSENCE   The essence or nature of mind.

EXTRACTION   This term has several meanings: (1) extraction of hardness of the mind of Tao; (2) extraction of excess conscious knowledge of the human mind; (3) extraction of false yin and yang. It thus is used to mean: (1) removal of vehemence of effort associated with bypassing the human mind and bringing forth the mind of Tao; (2) stilling of excess intellectual activity; (3) removal of undesirable qualities of weakness and aggression, or other analogous extremes of passive and active attitudes and behavior. In sum, extraction means lessening or removal of qualities or energies which inhibit balanced development at any given point in the process of the spiritual alchemy.

FALSE FEELING   Subjective feelings and emotions conditioned by physical states, thoughts, or external influences.

FALSE FIRE   Volatility, passion, intellectually or emotionally conditioned consciousness.

FALSE NATURE   The acquired temperament and personality formed by historical and environmental factors.

FALSE YIN AND YANG   Extreme, isolated, or unbalanced manifestations of passivity and activity. For example, weakness/force; cowardice/aggression; quietism/arbitrary action; vacillation/stubbornness.

FIRE   Consciousness, awareness; also, concentration.

FIRE AND WATER   Conscious knowledge in the human mind (fire) and real knowledge in the mind of Tao (water). These are represented by the corresponding *I Ching* trigrams ☲ and ☵. *Fire* ☲ has one yin in the center, representing the contaminant of mundane conditioning mixed into consciousness. *Water* ☵ has one yang in the center, representing the celestial or primordial hidden inside the mundane. The standard Chinese characters for fire and water are also used to stand for anger and lust, or for spirit and vitality.

FIRING PROCESS   A general term for procedure, course of practical work; also spoken of in terms of specific firing processes.

FIVE ENERGIES RETURNING TO THE ORIGIN   A state of mental and physical collection, used to recover the original energy. It is described as "The body unmoving, the mind unstirring, the nature tranquil, feelings forgotten, the physical elements in harmony." It is also said to be practiced by not using the external senses.

FIVE EYES   A Buddhist term for the range of potential perception available to humans: the flesh eye, which is the ordinary organ of sight; the celestial eye, which is the power of clairvoyance; the wisdom eye, which is the power of intuitive insight; the objective eye, which is the power to see things as they are in reality; and the enlightened eye, which is the power to see both absolute and relative truth, encompassing all the other eyes.

FLOATING CLOUDS   Thoughts, feelings, objects; the evanescent world.

FLOWER POND   Openness of consciousness.

FLOWING PEARL   Open awareness.

FOUR FORMS OR FOUR SIGNS   Metal and wood, water and fire; these stand for sense and essence, vitality and spirit. Hence combining the four forms means unification of the human being, with the mind of Tao and the human mind united, sense and essence joined, and energy and consciousness combined.

FOUR FRUITS   A Buddhist term for stages of development culminating in individual mental freedom. Various psychic powers are associated with attainment of these stages. The usage of the term in this text appears somewhat idiosyncratic.

FOUR KNOWLEDGES   A Buddhist term for complete consciousness; the round mirror knowledge, which means impartial awareness; knowledge of equality, which means insight into the relatively of all things; observational knowledge, which means discernment of particulars; practical knowledge, which is application of understanding in action.

FROG IN A WELL   The mind enclosed in narrow subjective views.

FURNACE   Variously defined: sometimes referred to as flexible obedience, in the sense of following proper procedure; as receptivity, in the sense of being aware of the qualities of each time so as to be able to adjust the "firing" accordingly; or as constant alert observation. See also *crescent moon furnace*.

FURNACE OF EVOLUTION   The inner energy of life, kept aglow by conscious attention; also the external world of change, used consciously for self-refinement.

GOLD CRUCIBLE   The mind in its original, uncontaminated state.

GOLD ELIXIR   The primordial energy of life; also referred to as a combination of innate capacity and innate knowledge.

GOLD IMMORTAL   One who has restored the original capacity and energy of life, and refined them so that they are free from contamination by mundane conditioning.

GREAT ELIXIR   The maturation of the spiritual state realized by unification of mind and recovery of potential.

GREAT ONE   A god used to symbolize unity.

GREAT ULTIMATE   Primordial unity of being.

GREAT VEHICLE   A Buddhist term for the overall endeavor leading to the perfection of both the individual and the community.

HALL OF BRIGHTNESS   A spot in the brain, used by some Taoists as a focus of attention in certain concentration exercises.

HEART SCRIPTURE   The Buddhist *Prajñāpāramitāhrdayasūtra*, the shortest Buddhist scripture, summarizing the emptiness of absolute existence.

HEAVENLY SOUL   Symbol of conscious knowledge, referred to as yin within yang, in the sense of mundane conditioning being mixed in with primordial consciousness.

HSING-LIN   A Taoist adept, disciple of Chang Po-tuan, author of *Wu Chen P'ien*.

HSUEH-TOU   An eminent Ch'an master (980–1052), especially noted for his poetry.

HUI-NENG   The sixth patriarch of Ch'an Buddhism (638–713).

HUNDRED-FOOT POLE   A Ch'an Buddhist term alluding to a transitional state of inner emptiness, stillness, and detachment.

INCREASING AND DECREASING   Increasing conscious access to the mind of Tao, decreasing the inhibiting conditioning of the human mind.

INCUBATION   A phase of practice associated with "nondoing" and "bathing" (*q.v.*), and the "cultural fire": concentration may at first be tainted with eagerness, anticipation, vehemence, and so on; thus the practice of "bathing" in the sense of purification is applied, removing contamination from intense concentration in the "martial" phase. This is called "incubation" in the sense of carefully nurturing the embryonic state of initial enlightenment to maturity.

INDEPENDENT SEER   Name of a bodhisattva (*q.v.*) in the Heart Scripture (*q.v.*).

INNER ELIXIR   The originally inherent potential which has been "recovered" after being "lost" to temporal conditioning and is refined after being "returned inside."

JACKALS   A Buddhism term for exponents of doctrines which hold to something relative as being absolute.

KAŚYAPA   The name of an outstanding disciple of the founder of Buddhism, said to have received the "special transmission outside the doctrine" from which Ch'an Buddhism is supposed to derive.

KUAN-YIN   Chinese name of Akalokiteśvara, a Buddhist bodhisattva representing the embodiment of compassion. In the *Saddharmapundarīkasūtra*, Kuan-yin is said to have thirty-two forms, or specific adaptations to the needs of those ready to be liberated. Kuan-yin is one name of the Independent Seer (*q.v.*), but two names are used in this text to indicate two specific contexts in which the associations evoked are different.

K'UN-LUN   A Central Asian mountain chain, representing: (1) west-metal-true sense, the mind of Tao; (2) primordial unified energy, the source of all being. In psychosomatic meditation systems of the "lesser vehicle" of Taoism, the K'un-lun also is used as a code word for the head.

LEAD CRUCIBLE   Lead stands for real knowledge and true sense; thus the lead crucible is the receptacle of this knowledge, the mind of Tao.

LEAK   In Buddhism, this term means psychological clinging or mental contamination; in Taoism, it means drainage of energy.

LIFE-IMPULSE   The essence of consciousness.

LION   A symbol of a Buddha, particularly associated with the power of transcendent wisdom; the roar of the lion means the refutation of all dogmatism, through the principle that whatever is conditioned and dependent is empty of inherent reality.

LIVING MIDNIGHT   Midnight symbolizes the state when the human mind and its discriminatory consciousness are silent; living means it is the point at which the potential of the mind of Tao is released. Living also means that properly accomplished "darkness"—cessation of the activity of the human mentality—is not oblivion, as open awareness remains as a channel of access to higher experience.

MARTIAL REFINING   Concentrated effort to master feelings, get rid of delusions, remove acquired conditioning, and restore the original mind.

MASTER LU   Lu Yen, also known as Lu Tung-pin, a T'ang–Five Dynasties Taoist adept, traditionally considered an ancestor of the Complete Reality schools. Regarded as a spiritual immortal and a functionary in the celestial hierarchy, Lu is believed to have retained sufficient energy after physical disintegration to be able to project manifestations of himself, and is said to have appeared repeatedly over the centuries. Many writings and sayings are attributed to him.

MASTER TS'UI   Ts'ui Chih-chen, a Taoist adept said to have lived in the Latter Han dynasty. His *Ju Yao Ching*, a treatise on spiritual alchemy, is esteemed in the Complete Reality tradition.

MEDICINAL SUBSTANCES Essence and life, essence and sense, real knowledge and consciousness, innate capacity and knowledge, vitality, energy, and spirit are all called medicinal substances, ingredients of the "elixir" of spiritual immortality.

MERCURY Symbol of the essence of consciousness. Also associated with flexibility and with instability, the mercurial nature of the human mind; hence it must be stabilized by combination with the "lead" of real knowledge of the mind of Tao.

METAL Being firm and strong, metal symbolizes the true sense of real knowledge, which is unequivocal.

METAL IN WATER Symbol of the primal root of consciousness, unified vitality or energy, real knowledge in the mind of Tao, innate natural goodness. It is referred to as yang within yin, represented by the trigram *water* ☵.

METAL MAN Symbol of the mind of Tao.

MID-AUTUMN The fifteenth day of the eighth lunar month; the full moon, representing pure yang as full illumination or revelation of the original state of the mind of Tao.

MIDNIGHT AND NOON Midnight, as the starting point of morning, represents the beginning of activation of yang, the real knowledge of the mind of Tao; noon, as the starting point of evening, represents the beginning of yin, the conscious knowledge of the human mind. Midnight is the mind of Tao emerging actively, noon is the human mind receiving it passively; midnight is the beginning of transcendence, noon is the beginning of reintegration with the world.

MIND-MONKEY The unruly mind, jumping from one object to another.

MORNING AND EVENING Active and passive phases of praxis. Active practice is referred to as doing, striving, and martial firing. Passive practice is referred to as nondoing, nonstriving, and cultural cooking. Hence morning and evening means breaking through the accidental or acquired to reach the essential or primal, then stabilizing and preserving this accomplishment.

GLOSSARY   *199*

MYSTERIOUS FEMALE   A representation of the combination of yin and yang, flexible receptivity and unequivocal sense. This term, from the *Tao Te Ching*, is one of those defined in many different ways. It is sometimes referred to as the basic mind, or open consciousness.

MYSTERIOUS PASS   This term, one of the most important in Taoist alchemy, has numerous definitions. Psychosomatic meditation systems associate it with particular points in the body, variously locating it behind the navel and in front of the kidneys, between the genitals and kidneys, in the umbilical region, on the top of the head, or on the forehead. These are considered lower or "sidetrack" systems: in the higher teachings the mysterious pass is referred to as the celestial mind, or the middle, and it is also said to be where yin and yang divide, where essence and life abide, the lair of spirit and energy, found only in profound abstraction. The opening of the mysterious pass is a critical experience in Complete Reality Taoism: descriptions of it resemble those of "seeing essence" (q.v.) in Ch'an Buddhism. In sum, the mysterious pass may be viewed as an orientation point in concentration practice: in auxiliary or elementary methods, it is concrete, while in advanced methods it is abstract.

NAGA GIRL   In the Buddhist *Saddharmapundarīkasūtra*, a young girl who attained sudden enlightenment; commonly used to represent transcendence of social and temporal distinctions.

NATURAL REAL FIRE or NATURAL FIRE OF REALITY   Spontaneous awareness without conscious effort; equated with the "cultural fire." It is called natural and real because it represents the consciousness purged of artificiality, the reality of the original mind.

NEGATIVITY   Mundane conditioning, bondage to things of the world.

NINEFOLD RESTORATION   Restoration of the original celestial mind, freed from bondage to accumulated habit and acquired personality.

NINE HEAVENS   Nine is the number of yang: thus nine heavens stands for pure yang, which is the celestial, unconditioned, primal state.

NINE-RESTORED GOLD LIQUID   Purified real knowledge.

NINE TRANSMUTATIONS   Transmutation of conscious energy into the celestial purified state, represented by the number nine, which stands for yang.

NINE YEARS   Some presentations of Taoist practice speak of "nine years facing a wall," a stage entered into after stabilization of consciousness, devoted to becoming thoroughly immune to the influences of objects and feelings.

NONLEAKING   In Buddhism, this term signifies freedom from mental contamination; in Taoism, it means that energy is not wasted.

NONORIGINATION   See *birthless*.

OTHER   This term may be used to mean an enlightened teacher, whose perspective is beyond the scope of self-centered subjectivity; it is also used to refer to everything outside oneself, from which one's "investment" of concern-energy needs to be recovered in order to gain autonomy. In sexual yoga it is used to refer to one's partner.

OTHER SHORE   A Buddhist term for consummation, attainment, and transcendence.

OUTER ELIXIR   This term may be used to refer to mineral or vegetable potions, or to the energy-circulation exercise known as the waterwheel. In the present commentary, "outer" is taken to refer to the condition of something vital in oneself being "lost," as it were, by becoming bound up in external objects.

OUTER FURNACE   This term refers to the use of action in the world as a means of self-refinement.

PEARL IN THE POOR ONE'S CLOTHES   An allusion to an allegory in the Buddhist *Saddharmapundarīkasūtra*: a benefactor sews a pearl into the clothes of a drunken sleeper. Unaware of this, the latter lives a life of poverty and hardship until he meets the benefactor again and has the hidden pearl pointed out to him. Discovering the pearl, he becomes wealthy. The pearl symbolizes the buddha-nature, the potential of enlightenment, said to be hidden beneath the "clothing" of acquired conditioning.

PHANTASMIC BODY.   The physical body, called phantasmic because it lacks permanent reality.

POLAR ENERGIES   Yin and yang.

POSITIVE   Yang, as that which is "celestial," unconditioned, primal.

POWER OF TAO   The *Tao Te Ching*, one of the most widely read classics of Taoism.

PUNISHMENT AND REWARD   Punishment is "repelling yin," getting rid of mundane conditioning. Repelling yin to the point of balance, being in the world yet not being controlled by things of the world, is symbolized by the autumn equinox, and by punishment and death. Reward is the emergence of the unconditioned primal mind; the spring equinox represents emergence to the point of balance, being free yet remaining in the world voluntarily.

QUICKSILVER   Another term for mercury, symbolizing the conscious knowledge in the human mind.

QUIETISM   The habit of taking quietude or detachment as an end rather than a means; this is diagnosed as a misunderstanding and an illness in both Ch'an Buddhism and Complete Reality Taoism.

REALITY BODY   The original unified essence of the human being.

REALITY EYE   A Buddhist term for objective awareness without distorting projections on the part of the observer.

REALM OF DUST   The realm of the senses; the ordinary world.

RECOGNIZING A THIEF AS YOUR CHILD   A Ch'an Buddhist expression meaning to mistake the conditioned portion of the mind as the true mind, or to take function for essence.

RETURN   Recovery of the original mind.

RIVER DIAGRAM   An ancient diagram of cosmology based on the five elements.

SAME ENERGY   Energy which is not influenced by external objects or by subjective thoughts and feelings.

SEEING ESSENCE   A Ch'an Buddhist term for direct experience of the original mind without the intervention of conceptualization.

SEVENFOLD REVERSION   Seven is associated with yang and fire, and fire with consciousness: sevenfold reversion, or seven-reversion, is a term for restoration of consciousness to reality, removal of subjective distortions.

SEVEN-REVERTED CINNABAR Stabilized consciousness, restored to its primal state.

SHAKYAMUNI Epithet of the founder of Buddhism.

SHUTTING THE COCCYX In sexual yoga, contraction of perineal muscles to stop the flow of semen and prevent ejaculation in the male is felt as pressure in the coccyx, one of the critical points on which attention is focused in the waterwheel exercise.

SIDETRACK METHODS Auxiliary techniques of limited scope, obsession with which diverts the practitioner and inhibits full development of human potential.

SIGNLESSNESS A Buddhist term meaning that things in reality are not identical to the descriptions projected on them by the mind which conceives of them.

SILVER A symbol of real knowledge.

SILVER WITHIN WATER Real knowledge concealed by temporal conditioning.

SIX PERFECTIONS Six modes of practice recommended in Buddhism for simultaneously developing oneself and benefiting others.

SIX PSYCHIC POWERS Capacities believed in Buddhism to be released in the process of liberation of the mind: clairvoyance, clairaudience, total recall, mental telepathy, psychic travel, and ability to terminate all contamination in the mind.

SPIRIT OF DISCRIMINATION The conceptualizing mind.

SPIRITUAL BODY The basic essence of consciousness.

SPIRITUAL SPROUTS The incipient activation of the living, creative potential of the original mind.

SUCHNESS A Buddhist term used to refer to objective reality and to the purified mind.

ŚŪRAṄGAMA SŪTRA A Buddhist scripture especially favored by Ch'an Buddhists and Complete Reality Taoists since the Sung dynasty.

SWALLOWING SALIVA A common Taoist hygiene practice for vitiating poisons naturally occurring in food.

THREE BASES Heaven, humanity, and earth: also associated with spirit, energy, and vitality, which are called the upper middle, and lower bases. These are considered fundamental elements of the macrocosm and microcosm.

THREE BODIES In Taoist usage, this term refers to the "real original body," corresponding to youth, the "strong body," corresponding to maturity, and the "declining body," corresponding to old age. In Buddhist usage (written differently in Chinese but ordinarily translated the same in English), the term refers to three aspects of the completed human being, corresponding to the physical presence and actions, the psychic presence of knowledge and bliss, and the most subtle presence of essence.

THREE COMPONENTS Heaven, earth, and humankind.

THREE FIELDS Three "fields of elixir" corresponding to the vitality, energy, and spirit. In psychosomatic exercises, these fields are assigned physical locations in the lower trunk, midtrunk, and head.

THREE FLOWERS GATHERED ON THE PEAK In psychosomatic Taoist practice, this refers to the unity of vitality, energy, and spirit in the upper field of elixir. In the present commentary it is used figuratively for a state of realization.

THREE REALMS A Buddhist term for three domains of mundane experience: the realm of desire, in which emotions are involved; the realm of form, purely aesthetic and intellectual, without emotion; and the formless realm, without desire, concept, or any sort of concrete form.

THREE VERMIN Consumptive or degenerative forces represented as vermin or parasites anciently said to be in the three fields of elixir and to eventually cause death; thus they represent dissipation of vitality, energy, and spirit.

THUSNESS Suchness (q.v.); being as is, without the imposition of artificial definitions; also called true thusness.

TRIPLE ANALOGUE *San Hsiang Lei,* a Taoist classic of the Latter Han dynasty.

TRIPLE WORLD The totality of the three realms (q.v.).

TRUE EMPTINESS A Buddhist term for pure potential, called "empty" because of absence of limitations, inconceivability, ungraspability, and openness.

TRUE LEAD   Symbol of real knowledge and primordial energy.

TRUE SEED   Real knowledge; same as true lead.

TS'AO CH'I   The place where Hui-neng, the sixth Ch'an Buddhist patriarch, taught in southern China; hence generally associated with Ch'an.

TZU-HSIEN   A Taoist adept in the third generation of the southern school of Complete Reality Taoism, disciple of Hsing-lin (*q.v.*).

ULTIMATE BLISS   A Buddhist paradise, said to be a realm free from the obstructions to enlightenment ordinarily encountered on earth; in Ch'an Buddhism it is said to be within oneself.

UNMINDING   A Ch'an Buddhist term for inner freedom and equanimity.

VALLEY SPIRIT   A symbol of open awareness.

WAR   Inner struggle against the compulsive force of personality and habit.

WATER OF CELESTIAL UNITY   In ancient cosmology the element of water was associated with the sky and the number one; this is used in alchemy as a symbol for the primal unity of being.

WAVES   Mental disturbance.

WESTERN HEAVEN   The "pure land" of Ultimate Bliss (*q.v.*), nominally said to be in the west, esoterically said to be in oneself.

WILD FOX   A Ch'an term for an aberrated practitioner.

WIND   External influences.

WIND AND THUNDER AT MIDNIGHT   Disturbance taking place at the critical juncture where the human mind quiesces and the mind of Tao emerges.

WINTER SOLSTICE   The point of quiescence of the habit-ridden human mentality and emergence of the mind of Tao; equivalent to midnight.

WOOD AND METAL   Symbols of essence and sense.

YELLOW FEMALE   True intent, or truthfulness, the medium or "go-between" through whose agency yin and yang are united.

YELLOW PATH   The "middle way" or "center" (*q.v.*), standing for balance.

YELLOW SPROUTS The emergence of the "living potential," or original energy of life, as it becomes freed from preemptive habit.

YUAN-TU-TZU A Taoist adept in the sixth generation of the northern branch of the Complete Reality school, teacher of the famous expositor Shang-yang-tzu.

Readings

For an extensive bibliography of works on Taoism and alchemy, see Joseph Needham's *Science and Civilization in China*, 5 vols. (Cambridge University Press).

For studies of Chang Po-tuan and his successors, including a translation of the *Wu Chen P'ien* from the point of view of chemistry, see the works of Tenney Davis in *Proceedings of the American Academy of Arts and Sciencies* 73 (1939–40), and *Journal of Chemical Education* 16 (1939).

For observations of contemporary Taoism in Taiwan, see the works of M. R. Saso; for historical and anthropological studies, see the works of H. Maspero and H. Welch.

For recent Chinese bibliographical and historical studies, see Ch'en Kuo-fu's *Tao Tsang Yuan Liu K'ao* (Hsiang Sheng Publishing Co., Taiwan, 1975) and Ch'en Yuan-an's *Nan Sung Ch'u Hopei Hsin Tao-chiao K'ao* (Hsin Wen Feng Publishing Co., Taiwan, 1976).

For information on Taoist meditation in contemporary Taiwan, see Li Lo-ch'iu's *Fang Tao Yu Lu* (Chen Shan Mei Publishing Co., Taiwan, 1965).

The works of Liu I-ming may be found in *Tao Shu Shih Er Chung* (Hsin Wen Feng Publishing Co., Taiwan, 1982).

Other commentaries on the *Wu Chen P'ien* may be found in volume 14 of *Tao Tsang Chi Yao* (Hsin Wen Feng Publishing Co., Taiwan, 1976).

A useful compendium of Complete Reality Taoist lore may be found in *Chung Ho Chi*, which is in volume 17 of *Tao Tsang Chi Yao*, and in volume 2 of *Tao T'ung Ta Ch'eng* (Hsin Wen Feng Publishing Co., Taiwan, 1974).

Information on the life of Chang Po-tuan may be found in *Hsuan Men Pi Tu* (Tzu Yu Publishing Co., Taiwan, 1965), and in *Li Tai Shen Hsien Shih* (Hsin Wen Feng Publishing Co., Taiwan, 1978).

Some information on Taoist alchemical terminology may be found in Tai Yuan-ch'ang's *Hsien Hsueh Tzu Tien* (Chen Shan Mei Publishing Co., Taiwan, 1961); somewhat less specialized is Li Shu-huan's *Tao Chiao Tzu Tien* (T'ien Tao Company, Hong Kong, 1980).

THE INNER TEACHINGS OF TAOISM

by CHANG PO-TUAN
Commentary by LIU I-MING

INTRODUCTION

Taoism is an ancient body of knowledge that has manifested itself in a multitude of diverse phenomena throughout Chinese history. So pervasive has the influence of Taoism been that it is difficult to name a single facet of Chinese civilization that has not been touched by it in some way. Politics, religion, science, medicine, psychology, art, music, literature, drama, dance, design, even warfare—in all these realms of endeavor are to be found phenomena bearing the characteristic stamp of Taoism.

There is an enormous body of specialist Taoist literature extant, containing a wide variety of technical lore. Much of this lore is couched in a number of esoteric languages, using such diverse formats as cosmology, mythology, religion, history, fiction, humor, magic, and alchemy. Needless to say, the problems of decoding this literature are formidable, for not only are there numerous codes, but even a single code may also be subject to a number of different interpretations.

The methods that have been employed in Taoist practice over the ages are also many and varied. Included in this vast range of techniques are physical, psychosomatic, and mental exercises, including special modes of movement, breathing, sexual intercourse, gazing, imagination and visualization, and dreaming. There are also many concentration exercises using such aids as special patterns of walking, thinking, and writing. Other exercises involve human service and the cultivation of certain types of social relations.

The earliest known Taoist text seems to be the *I ching*, well known as one of the fundamental Chinese classics, esteemed by both Confucians and Taoists. Composed in a time when divination was considered an integral part of the process of government, the core *I ching* writings have the outward form of oracles. Taoists consider the *I ching* one of the most detailed guides to human development, and the esoteric language of Taoist spiritual alchemy, a major teaching format, is largely based on the symbolism of the *I ching*.

After the *I ching*, the most famous and popular of Taoist classics is undoubtedly the *Tao te ching*. This text was compiled and recorded in a time of the decay of an ancient social order, time when all writing considered serious dealt with sociopolitical issues. Not surprisingly, therefore, much of the *Tao te ching* is presented in terms of advice to rulers. Taoists consider this a fundamental text, drawing from it models of basic meditation techniques and mental postures. A large body of commentary and derivative literature is based on the *Tao te ching*, including other writings and lore associated with Lao-tzu, the reputed transmitter of this early classic.

Another extremely popular Taoist classic, the *Chuang-tzu*, was also written in this time of political deterioration, which was characterized by growing militarism and the predominance of sheer force over social contract. The *Chuang-tzu* has an air of humorous abandon, anarchy, satire, and unleashed imagination, envisioning an entirely new consciousness beyond the scope of then-current conceptions. Perhaps the first work of fantasy in Chinese literature that did not profess to be dynastic history, the classic *Chuang-tzu*, a dramatic release of the spirit, is widely considered one of the greatest literary masterpieces of all time.

Another classic apparently composed or compiled around this same time was the *Sun-tzu*, a famous treatise on military strategy. Although it is not usually referred to as a Taoist text per se, the *Sun-tzu* is nevertheless widely recognized as largely Taoist-inspired. While basically pacifistic, Taoism is not sentimental and has always recognized the reality of war. Rather than simply make moralistic pronouncements against war, Taoism approaches this problem realistically, using two basic strategies. The first of these is preventive, minimizing the causes of war existing in the human psyche; the second is palliative, minimizing the trauma of war when it actually does take place. The *Sun-tzu* shows what is now referred to as guerrilla warfare as a Taoistic type of strategy based on this idea of minimization of the actual violence and overall stress of warfare.

With the founding of the Han dynasty in the late third century B.C.E., the centuries of strife from which emerged such great Taoist classics as the *Tao te ching*, *Chuang-tzu*, and *Sun-tzu* came to an end. Taoistic laissez-faire government, characteristic of several Han dynasty reigns, allowed the economy to recover from generations of warfare and oppression; a great deal of interest was taken in natural science, with marked developments in agriculture and technology. There was also extensive intercourse between Taoism and Confucianism, resulting in the incorporation of certain Taoistic elements into the Confucian outlook.

One of the major Taoist texts dating from the Han period is the *Huai-nan-tzu*, composed by a group of Taoists at one of the minor courts. The *Huai-nan-tzu* recasts a great deal of ancient lore in a form suitable for its time, presenting the natural, human, and supernatural realms as a continuum in which the affairs of each realm reflect and are reflected by those of the others.

This vision of interreflection enabled Taoists to integrate secular and transcendental concerns harmoniously, and the *Huai-nan-tzu* includes discussions of political and military strategy as well as higher human evolution. The correspondence of the microcosm and the macrocosm, a characteristic theme, is also employed in a subtle way in the *Huai-nan-tzu*, inner psychic processes being represented metaphorically by such outer natural processes as the progress of the seasons. This device in particular became very popular later in the literature of Taoist spiritual alchemy.

Another product of the Han dynasty, destined to become one of the most important Taoist texts, is the cryptic *Ts'an t'ung ch'i*, or *Triplex Unity*, by the adept Wei Po-yang. This manual of spiritual alchemy became a major sourcebook for practitioners of the Complete Reality School of Taoism, which arose approximately one thousand years after the composition of the *Triplex Unity*. This difficult but intriguing book is still referred to in modern Taoist literature as the ancestor of alchemical treatises and is held in highest esteem.

Toward the end of the Han dynasty, growing political corruption and repression fostered spreading alienation among the intelligentsia as well as the peasantry. One characteristic manifestation of Taoism that arose from these conditions was the formation of intellectual circles of "pure conversation" involved in the study of human character and the creation of a new libertarian literature. On the other end of the social spectrum was popular Taoist freemasonry, which produced vigorous movement in society by grassroots organization and violent uprising.

After the fall of the Han dynasty, China was politically fragmented, with much of the north and west eventually being taken under the rule of alien dynasties. The breakdown of the political and intellectual monolith of the Han provided leeway for the entry of new elements into Chinese culture from southern and central Asia. One of the most powerful forces to enter China at this time was Buddhism, which figured prominently in the eventual rebirth of Chinese civilization after the turmoil of the post-Han generations.

Over the centuries following the dissolution of the Han dynasty, Buddhist texts were translated into the Chinese language at a prodigious rate, and Buddhist monastic orders were established on Chinese soil. At the same time, a parallel development took place in Taoism; large numbers of Taoist scriptures resembling those of the Buddhists were composed, and cloisters of Taoist monks and nuns were eventually set up on the Buddhist model.

These Taoist scriptures were even classified after the manner of the Buddhist canon, and are often considered mere imitations of Buddhist scriptures, much like the Buddhicized Bon and Shinto writings of Tibet and Japan. The Taoist scriptures contain, however, certain elements whose parallels in Buddhism are to be found only in the esoteric forms of Tantric Buddhism, which never seem to have become very popular in China, in contrast to Tibet and Japan.

In addition to the great post-Han outflow of Taoist literature in religious garb, during this period there appeared two very famous classics employing older formats—the *Pao-p'u-tzu* and the *Lieh-tzu*. Both of these books go to great lengths to establish the idea that conventional knowledge is not ultimate, thus to expand the horizons of the human outlook; they approach the issue, however, from quite different angles.

The *Pao-p'u-tzu* places much emphasis on immortality and stresses the impossibility of assessing the question of the existence of immortals by ordinary standards based on common experience. The text contains a collection of alchemical recipes for elixirs that are supposed to transform human beings into immortals and transform base metals into gold.

It is by no means clear whether these recipes, obtained by the author of the *Pao-p'u-tzu* through extensive travel and research, were originally intended to be understood literally or metaphorically. There is ample evidence, however, that the supposed alchemical enterprise did involve considerable work and experimentation in chemistry and metallurgy as well as psychological development. The coexistence of material and spiritual alchemy was also paralleled in the West, and many outstanding personalities, such as Albertus Magnus, Ramon Lull, and Paracelsus, are associated with alchemy in Europe.

The author of the *Pao-p'u-tzu* was also a distinguished Confucian scholar who wrote many essays on social and political subjects. These writings are collected in the so-called outer chapters of the *Pao-p'u-tzu*, forming a large proportion of the book. The same scholar also collected and transmitted legends of immortals, who were believed to intervene in human affairs from time to time and whose existence has been the subject of lively interest in China since remote antiquity.

The contents of the *Lieh-tzu*, in contrast, range from cosmology and metaphysics to satire. Among the ideas emphasized in this text are the interrelation of all phenomena and the limited nature of mental constructs used by the intellect to describe reality. A number of stories in the *Lieh-tzu* are drawn from the earlier *Chuang-tzu*, which it greatly resembles in certain ways. Some of these tales passed into popular lore and appear even in modern political and educational writings.

By the end of the sixth century C.E., China had been reunified, under the short-lived Sui dynasty. Public Taoist institutions were now well established, drawing many Buddhist monks and nuns into their ranks. A degree of friction developed between Taoism and Buddhism on the institutional level and continued for the next two or three centuries, with the salutary effect of allowing neither to become too complacent for too long.

The Sui dynasty was soon replaced by the T'ang dynasty (618–906), under which Chinese civilization enjoyed a new golden age, extending its cultural and economic influence into the surrounding nations of Asia. During the T'ang dynasty, Buddhism flourished, with a number of great specialist schools emerging into prominence. Nevertheless, Taoism still enjoyed considerable official favor and support; for a time civil service examinations based on Taoist classics were even established alongside the traditional conventional examinations in Confucianism.

A curious episode in the history of T'ang dynasty Taoism is the death of two emperors after ingesting alchemical immortality potions. The *Pao-p'u-tzu* notwithstanding, material alchemy and the search for literal physical immortality had in fact been repudiated centuries before in such classics as the *Chuang-tzu* and *Ts'an t'ung ch'i*; but repeated denunciation of such practices in later literature suggests that they continued to exist.

The incongruity of the age-old search for alchemical gold and physical immortality with the widely recognized evidence ancient Taoists give of advanced knowledge of psychological and physical realities only recently rediscovered by modern science has often led to the question of whether there was any real connection between different forms of activity lumped together under the name of Taoism. Although Taoist literature openly acknowledges the existence of ignorant experimentation and fraudulent practices, nevertheless it has been suggested that imperial poisonings were not mere superstitious bungling but intentional assassination; and that behind alchemical experimentation associated with Taoism was a conscious ploy to harness human greed to human progress by using it to motivate research in the natural science.

After the fall of the T'ang dynasty, various sects of Taoism continued to thrive, with increasing organization of sacred texts, rites, and local settlements. A Taoist canon was compiled in 1013, and an encyclopedic digest of its contents was also composed by the editors of the canon.

Not long after this collection of Taoist scriptures into a canon, three new schools arose, giving a new face to Taoism. These were the Absolute One, the True Great Way, and the Complete Reality schools. Active in northern China under alien rule, these attracted many followers from all walks of life. Many Buddhist centers, abandoned by Chinese Buddhists in the years of turmoil brought by the northern conquerors, were now taken over by these new Taoists.

The Complete Reality School, a highly purified form of Taoism showing a strong affinity with Ch'an (Zen) Buddhism, was particularly powerful and prominent, noted for its humanitarian works as well as its production of mystics of high attainment. During the Yuan dynasty (1279–1368), Complete Reality Taoists were charged with a new compilation of the Taoist canon, and thus the present form of the canon contains many works by adepts of this school.

Two main formats were employed by Complete Reality teachers and writers: records of sayings or short essays similar to those of the

Ch'an Buddhist masters, and the ancient language of spiritual alchemy, largely based on the imagery of the *I ching*. Unlike Ch'an Buddhist works, however, the Complete Reality Taoist records of sayings, essays, and poetry include those of numerous female adepts; and unlike ancient alchemical texts, Complete Reality alchemical writings contain a considerable measure of explicit language.

One of the most important figures in the emergence of the Complete Reality movement was the eleventh-century adept Chang Po-tuan, who became known as the founder of the southern sect of the Complete Reality school. Chang is particularly known for his classic *Understanding Reality*, which has been a standard text of spiritual alchemy ever since, ranked on a par with the ancient *Triplex Unity*.

Born into a family of Confucian scholars, Chang Po-tuan continued in this tradition but eventually extended his interests into many fields, including astronomy, mathematics, and medicine. As his *Understanding Reality* attests, he also studied Ch'an Buddhism in depth and did extensive research in alchemical literature. According to his own statement, Chang was prompted to compose his alchemical treatises by the enormous confusion he found in the exegetical literature based on earlier alchemical works.

Although Chang spent many years associating with Buddhists and Taoists in search of transcendental knowledge, he was not to meet his real teacher until he was over eighty years of age. He then learned the Taoist secrets of restoration of vitality and energy, and ultimately mastered the spiritual teachings. He reached a high degree of mystic attainment and finally passed away at the age of ninety-nine after transmitting the inner teachings of Taoism through his writings and personal contacts.

Although Chang had a number of successful disciples, he is said to have been "punished by heaven" three times for passing on secrets of alchemy to unworthy people. After this he retired from the world and wrote his magnum opus, *Understanding Reality*, through which he said sincere people could learn the process of spiritual transformation.

Another of Chang's important writings, translated here as *The Inner Teachings of Taoism*, presents a summary of Taoist practice in the alchemical format. It is a simplified, condensed version of the teachings of *Understanding Reality*, giving the main outlines of the alchemical work in twenty short verses. This text is presented here with a modern explanation written by the great Taoist commentator Liu I-ming in 1808.

The Inner Teachings of Taoism became a very popular text, perhaps because of its brevity and accessibility. It was originally untitled, but later became known as *Four Hundred Words on the Gold Elixir.* According to Liu I-ming's introduction,

> The text is phrased in a simple and concise manner; the meaning is evident and clear. This work and Chang's *Understanding Reality* are like inside and outside: *Understanding Reality* gives a detailed breakdown of the "medicinal ingredients" and "firing process" of spiritual alchemy, whereas this treatise gives a general summary of the whole subject. The two works are one yet two, two yet one.
>
> Although this treatise has been annotated and explained many times since its composition in the Sung dynasty, these interpretations are either in terms of material alchemy or in terms of psychosomatic exercises: it is impossible to find a single commentary that conveys the reality, expresses the spirit, and reveals the hidden dimensions of this treatise.
>
> I could not bear to let this precious work of the Founder be buried away, so I have made a detailed explanation of it, section by section, analyzing the metaphors and clearly pointing out what the "crucible," "furnace," "medicines," "firing," "doing," and "nondoing" are. Every word is clarified, every phrase analyzed; I have torn away the shell to expose the pit, broken open the bones to reveal the marrow. The jewels of this treasure chest are set out clearly in the open, in hopes that readers will understand at a glance and not be deceived by misleading interpretations.

Following his verse-by-verse elucidation of Chang Po-tuan's text, Liu I-ming gives a summary in classic fashion with twenty verses of his own composition. Because of the general nature of Chang's text, Liu then adds notes on essentials of Taoist study and secrets of alchemy, to clarify practical procedure in an orderly fashion. He explains this appendix in his introduction:

> After finishing the explanation of Chang's text, I was still concerned that students might try to seek results without due re-

gard for process, mistakenly hoping for immediate effects. Therefore I have added twenty-four essentials and twenty-four secrets, to enable students to proceed in an orderly fashion, ascending from lowliness to the heights. Those who practice with their feet on solid ground will eventually reach profound attainment of self-realization without wasting any effort.

Liu I-ming was one of the foremost interpreters of Taoist classics in his time, and from a modern point of view his commentaries are unsurpassed in clarity. Deeply versed in both noumenal Confucianism and Ch'an Buddhism, he was dedicated to restoring the original principles and practices of Complete Reality Taoism. He believed that a point had been reached where there was more harm than benefit in the practice of veiling the Taoist teachings in esoteric language, and undertook to reveal the meaning of the alchemical classics in plain language. To this end, he not only elucidated the inner teachings of numerous ancient texts, but also composed a systematic study of important terminology; as he himself explains,

> Transmission of the true Tao has been lost for a long time, not just recently. After I had met genuine teachers, I compared the various alchemical classics and really found out the meaning of their symbolic language. Therefore I revealed what I had learned from my teachers in my explanations of the *Triplex Unity*, *Understanding Reality*, and other texts. Yet I still feared that students might have difficulty in gaining consistent and comprehensive understanding, so I wrote a treatise on symbolic language.

This exposition of Taoist symbolism is also presented in this volume, again with Liu's own poems summarizing each point under discussion.

Generally speaking, Liu's explanations consist of three distinct levels of presentation, and the key to reading his works in such a way as to extract the essence of Taoist teaching lies in distinguishing these three levels. The three types of presentation Liu uses may be described as illustration of traditional use of esoteric terminology in Complete Reality teaching, repudiation of interpretations considered spurious by Complete Reality Taoists, and revelation of inner meaning in plain language.

In the course of his explanations, Liu will often speak in symbols, thereby demonstrating didactic manipulation of the esoteric terminology of elements, yin and yang, *I ching* signs, and so on. Since ancient times this manner of expression has been used for several purposes: concealment, diversion, concentration, identification of initiates and imitators, and stimulation of thought.

The use of symbolism is therefore an expedient, as the ancient *Tao te ching* indicates, and its use depends on attendant circumstances. Liu's main purpose is to render esoteric language unnecessary, and the meaning of the teaching can be grasped without reference to these symbolic discourses. The value of Liu's symbolic presentations comes after the inner meaning is understood, as they can then be used as keys for unlocking the meanings of other alchemical texts.

Another secondary level of Liu's presentations is his repudiation of certain interpretations traditionally considered spurious by Complete Reality Taoists. These interpretations, and the practices based thereon, are generally referred to as "side doors" and are said to range from thoroughly aberrated and harmful "deviant paths" to useful but minor "auxiliary techniques" that may nevertheless sidetrack and injure untutored or obsessive enthusiasts. Liu explains:

> People of later times did not search out the meaning of the alchemical classics, but just stuck to the symbols: Confucians took them to be superstitious nonsense, while Taoists took them in a superficial manner. In extreme cases, people fixated on the symbols and arbitrarily invented all sorts of practices, getting caught up in sidetracks and deviant practices. Countless people have harmed themselves mentally and physically in this way. Surely this was not the intent of the ancients when they evoked images in symbolic language.

Repudiation of the "side doors" actually goes back at least as far as the *Chuang-tzu* and is even more explicit in the *Triplex Unity*, a millennium before the emergence of the Complete Reality School of Taoism. It is reiterated in many Complete Reality texts, but there are variations in the degree to which auxiliary techniques are accepted and applied by various teachers at various times.

In the southern sect of Complete Reality, founded by Chang Po-tuan, there is more emphasis on energy work than in the more austere northern sect, which Liu I-ming followed. This difference is explained by the advanced age of many initiates of the southern sect, beginning with Chang Po-tuan himself, who did not attain the Tao until he was in his eighties. Energy work, used for rejuvenation in order to sustain the spiritual work, is naturally often emphasized more, and in different forms, for older people than for younger people. In any case, these practices are said to be the most dangerous, and the need for expert guidance means that they may be publicly repudiated by those who practice them privately.

The critical aspect of Liu I-ming's work, rejecting the "side doors," may be viewed as representing the most radical form of the traditional Complete Reality distinction between the quintessence of Taoism and tangential physical or psychosomatic techniques. Two basic forms of the interpretations repudiated as spurious are false analogy and literal interpretation of symbolic expressions. While Liu also stressed the importance of vital energy and physical health, in interpreting Taoist symbolism he always rejected physical interpretations in favor of metaphysical interpretations.

The real marrow of Liu's texts, the main point of focus, generally follows symbolic discourses and precedes critiques of aberrations; this is when Liu shifts into plain language and provides an open explanation of the inner meaning of the passage under consideration. Sometimes these explanations are extremely brief, no more than a couple of sentences, but they provide the key to the whole book and present the points to look for in reading—what is known in Chinese as the "eye" of the work.

This small volume, when approached with these distinctions in mind, will yield an overall understanding of Taoism as it is presented in the alchemical format, in terms of three levels of realization: the reality, the appearance, and the illusion; or, in other words, the inner teachings, the outer husk, and the random spinoffs. In this sense, this volume is presented as an introductory study of a major manifestation of Taoism, including its principles, practices, and problems.

PART ONE
The Inner Teachings

[1]

True earth arrests true lead;
true lead controls true mercury.
Lead and mercury return to true earth;
body and mind are tranquil and still.

Earth dwells in the center, as the mother of myriad beings. It is possible thereby to blend the elementary forces, produce and nurture myriad beings. Earth is that whereby origin and completion are effected. The true earth referred to here is not material earth; it is the true intent of the human body, which has no location. True intent is the director of myriad affairs; it controls the vital spirit, sustains essence and life, occupies and guards the center of the being. Because it has functions similar to earth, it is called true earth. Insofar as it is truthful and whole, without fragmentation, it is also called true faith. Because it contains the impulse of life within it, it is also called the center. Because it encloses everything, it is also called the yellow court. Because it is one in action and repose, it is also called the medicinal spoon. Because it can harmonize yin and yang, it is also called the yellow woman. Because it holds the pattern of the noumenon, it is also called the crossroads. There are many different names, all describing one thing, this true intent.

Lead is dense and heavy, hard and strong, lasts long without disintegrating; what is called true lead here is not ordinary material lead, but is the formless, immaterial true sense of real knowledge in the human body. This true sense is outwardly dark but inwardly bright, strong and unbending, able to ward off external afflictions, able to stop internal aberrations. It is symbolized by lead and so is called the true lead. Because its strength and vigor are within, it is also called the black tiger; because its energy is associated with metal, it is also called the white tiger. Because it is not constrained by things, it is also called iron man. Because its light illumines myriad existents, it is also called the golden flower. Because it is the pivot of creation, it is also called the North Star. Because it conceals light within darkness, it is also called metal within water. Because it contains masculinity within femininity, it is also called the rabbit in the moon. There are many different names, all describing this one thing, true sense.

Mercury is something lively and active, light and buoyant, soft and yielding, easily running off. Here what is called true mercury is not ordinary material mercury, but the formless, immaterial spiritual essence of conscious knowledge in the human body. The spiritual essence is outwardly firm yet inwardly flexible, utterly empty and metaphysical, unfathomable in its changing manifestations; call and it responds, touch it and it moves. It is symbolized by mercury, so it is called true mercury. Because it goes out and in unpredictably, it is also called the dragon. Because its energy is associated with the east, it is also called the blue dragon. Because it is developed by passing through tempering by fire, it is also called the red dragon. Because its nature is soft and loving, it is also called the wood mother. Because it is yang outside and yin inside, it is also called the girl. Because it contains femininity within masculinity, it is also called the raven in the sun. Because its reality is hidden within fire, it is also called mercury within cinnabar. Because its light is penetrating, it is also called flowing pearl. There are many different names used to depict this one thing, spiritual essence.

True intent, true sense, and spiritual essence are the three jewels in our bodies, true earth, true lead, and true mercury. These three jewels have a primordial, whole, unified energy, which is complete, without any defect. This cannot be called intent, sense, or essence—it is all one reality. But then when it mixes with temporally acquired conditioning, and yang culminates, giving rise to yin, the single energy divides into three. Thus there come to be the terms *intent, sense,* and *essence.* Once the real divides, the false comes forth; the seeds of routine take command, sense faculties and data stir together, and habit energy grows day by day: true intent becomes adulterated with artificial intentions, true sense becomes adulterated with arbitrary feelings, and spiritual essence becomes adulterated with temperament. Aberration and sanity mix, the artificial confuses the real, essence and life are shaken; day by day, year by year, the real disappears and all becomes false. Positivity exhausted, negativity complete, how can death be avoided?

When the real people have taught others to return to the fundamental and go back to the original, thereby to preserve essence and life, they have all taught people to restore these three things to reality. The path of restoration starts with knowing the original true intent. When you know the true intent, if you give your mind to it, the jewel of faith is in your hand; instantly all existents are empty, and you observe everything with detachment. External things cannot move you, and sane energy gradually rises. When consciousness of reality is constantly present, arbitrary feelings evaporate and true sense emerges, always responsive yet always calm, like true earth grabbing true lead so that the lead does not sink.

Once true sense appears, not concealing, not deceiving, the original spirit is always present and the discriminating spirit does not arise; then the temperament sublimates and the spiritual essence becomes manifest. This is like true lead controlling true mercury, so that mercury does not fly up.

The method of arresting and controlling is not a matter of conscious contrivance; it is natural, spontaneous arresting and controlling, arresting without arresting, controlling without controlling. Because real truthfulness is in the center, the yin and yang of the sense of real knowledge and the essence of conscious knowledge cleave to one another, the two energies combine and congeal spontaneously.

What is difficult to accomplish in alchemy is the combination of essence and sense. The combination of essence and sense without imbalance is called centering. When the intent, essence, and sense meet, they are as before one energy; what had gone returns; what was lost is restored. This is like lead and mercury returning to the earth pot, stable and balanced, impervious to all conditioning influences. The illusory body and the stubborn mind naturally become quiet and still. The errant movements of the illusory body and the stubborn mind all come from separation of intent, essence, and sense; when these three are united, the real returns and the artificial quiesces—how could body and mind be stirred?

[2]

Nothingness produces white snow;
quiescence produces yellow sprouts.
The fire warm in the jade furnace,
over the crucible flies violet mist.

The previous section says that when mercury and lead return to true earth, body and mind do not stir; then one has entered the state of empty silence. But emptiness requires that emptiness reach the point where there is nothing to be emptied; only then is it called the ultimate of emptiness. Silence requires that silence reach the point of utter quiescence; only then is it called the ultimate of silence. When you reach nothingness, the primordial unity begins to emerge; when you attain quiescence, the primal true positive energy comes back. Therefore the text says that "white snow" and "yellow sprouts" are produced. White snow symbolizes the energy of the primordial unity; this is like the metaphor of "white light arising in the empty room." "Yellow sprouts" appear with the return of the living potential; they symbolize the existence of movement within stillness. The empty room produces white light; when stillness culminates, there is movement; within black there is white; within yin there is yang—the primordial energy comes back, and the gold elixir takes form.

Once the gold elixir has form, it is urgent to use a gentle fire to incubate it, without either neglect or force, not slacking off for a moment. The "jade furnace" is the furnace of the flexibility of earth, symbolizing the calm serenity of the work, not being hasty or excited. The crucible is the crucible of the firmness of heaven, symbolizing firmness and stability of will, not changing. The "purple mist flying" symbolizes the sudden opening up of knowledge and wisdom when the work is consummated. When the spiritual sprouts are first born, use gentle fire to warmly nurture them, without either obsession or indifference, guarding against danger; progressing from weakness to strength, rawness to ripeness; when the firing is complete and the elixir is made, the light of wisdom shoots out—this is like the violet mist flying up from the crucible when the medicine in the crucible is fully developed.

[3]

Lotuses bloom in the flower pond;
golden waves are quiet on the spiritual water.
Deep in the night, the moon just bright,
heaven and earth are in one round mirror.

The flower pond symbolizes the openness of consciousness; the spiritual water symbolizes true essence; the lotuses symbolize the light of wisdom; the golden waves symbolize objects of sense. When the spiritual sprouts have been warmly nurtured until their energy is complete, the flower of mind blooms and the light of wisdom arises. Therefore it says lotuses bloom in the flower pond. Once the light of wisdom arises, inwardly thoughts do not sprout, so essence is calm; then external things are not taken in and feelings are forgotten. Therefore the text says that the golden waves are quiet on the spiritual water. When essence is calm and feelings are forgotten, even if one is in the midst of myriad things, one is not deceived by myriad things. Round and bright, the mind is like the full moon shining deep in the night, its light pervading above and below, heaven and earth; the gold elixir crystallizes in the great void of space.

[4]

Red sand refines to positive energy;
liquid silver cooks into metal vitality.
Metal vitality and positive energy,
red sand and liquid silver.

The preceding three sections sum up the overall process of alchemy; from here on is a detailed analysis of the finer subtleties of the medicinal substances and firing process.

"Red sand" (cinnabar) is associated with the turbulence of the energy of fire and symbolizes volatility in people. "Liquid silver" (quicksilver) is associated with the movement natural to water and symbolizes the human mentality in people. Positive energy gives birth to beings; this symbolizes the real essence in people. The vitality of metal is luster; this symbolizes the consciousness of reality in people.

Lu Tsu said, "The seven-reversion restored elixir is a matter of people first refining themselves and awaiting the time." The classic *Understanding Reality (Wu chen p'ien)* says, "If you want to successfully cultivate the nine-reversion, you must first refine yourself and master your mind." Shang Yang Tzu said, "Restoring the elixir is very easy; refining the self is very hard." These statements all say that if you want to practice the great Tao, you must first refine yourself.

The essential point in self-refinement starts with controlling anger and desire. The energy of anger is the aberrant fire of the volatile nature, which erupts upon confrontation and is indifferent to life, like a conflagration burning up a mountain, which nothing can stop. If you do not exert effort to quell it, refining it into something without smoke or flame, it can easily obscure reality. "Red sand refines to positive energy" means taking this volatility and refining it into neutral true essence.

As for desire, when the discriminating spirit of the human mentality sees objects and encounters things, it flies up; the senses become active all at once, and the feelings and emotions arise, like a gang of bandits stealing valuables, whom none can defend against. If you do not exert effort to block it and cook it into something that does not move or stir, it can easily thwart the process of the Tao. "Liquid silver cooks into metal vitality" means taking the human mentality and cooking it into the mindless consciousness of reality.

The extinction of the volatile nature and the appearance of true sense are like red sand transmuting into positive energy, ever to be warm, gentle essence. The death of the human mentality and the presence of consciousness of reality are like liquid silver changing into metal vitality, ever to be luminous mind.

Since reality is always there inside falsehood, and falsehood is not outside reality, when this nature and this mind go through the cooking and refining of fire, they become the real essence and the consciousness of reality. So the red sand turns to positive energy, and the liquid silver turns into metal vitality; if they are not put through a refinement process, they will always be the volatile nature and the human mentality, and even positive energy will turn into red sand, even metal vitality will turn into liquid silver. Therefore the text says, "Metal vitality and positive energy, red sand and liquid silver." The false can become real, and the real can become false—the difference is a matter of refining or not refining. So practitioners should first quell anger and desire in order to refine the self. Restoring the elixir takes place momentarily; refining the self requires ten months. The work of refining the self is no small matter.

[5]

The solar yang soul, the fat of the jade rabbit;
the lunar yin soul, the marrow of the gold raven:
put them in the crucible and transmute them
into a flood of water.

The preceding section speaks of the work of refining the self; this one speaks of the secret of gathering the medicines. The solar yang soul and the gold raven symbolize the finest part of conscious knowledge; the jade rabbit and the lunar yin soul symbolize the light of wisdom of real knowledge. Without the light of real knowledge, conscious knowledge cannot perceive far; without the manifestation of conscious knowledge, real knowledge cannot convey its light. Therefore the text says, "The solar yang soul, the fat of the jade rabbit; the lunar yin soul, the marrow of the gold raven," indicating that these two true medicines are to be put into the metaphysical crucible and quickly refined by fierce cooking with the true fire of concentration, causing them to mix and combine so that they merge like a flood of water, without the slightest pollution. Only then is the work done.

Conscious knowledge is flighty, and real knowledge easily becomes concealed: as soon as they act up, one should immediately put them back in the crucible and make them stay there, not letting them leave. This crucible is not a material crucible with form; as explained before, it is the crucible of firmness of heaven. This is the firm, strong, sane energy of the positive yang of heaven. When the sane energy is always present, unified awareness pure and true, the mind is stable and the will is far-reaching, growing stronger as time goes on, and real knowledge and conscious knowledge are forged into one whole.

[6]

The medicines are produced in the occult opening;
the firing process arises in the yang furnace.
When the dragon and tiger have mated,
the gold crucible produces a mystic pearl.

The medicines are the medicines of real knowledge and conscious knowledge. The occult opening is an opening of profound subtlety, where yin and yang divide, and also where essence and life abide. This is what is called the opening of the mysterious pass. This opening has many different names—the opening of the mysterious female, the door of birth and death, the house of enlivening and killing, the opening of nothingness, the gate of myriad wonders. All these terms refer to the same thing.

This opening is not existent, not nonexistent, not material, not void; it has no location or form, but is in ecstasy and profound abstraction. It is not inside or outside. If you try to find it in terms of place or form, you will miss it by a long shot.

The firing process is the process of the work. The yang furnace is the work of intensive refinement by fierce cooking. It is not that there really is a furnace; because of the use of firing work to refine the medicines of real and conscious knowledge, it is called a furnace.

The dragon is associated with wood and symbolizes essence, emerging from conscious knowledge. The essence of conscious knowledge transforms unfathomably, so it is represented as a dragon. The tiger is associated with metal and symbolizes sense, emerging from real knowledge. The sense of real knowledge is firm and strong and unbending, so it is represented as a tiger.

There is temperamental nature, and there is innate essence; there is emotional feeling, and there is unerring sense. Temperamental nature is acquired, whereas innate essence is primal; emotional feeling is secondary, whereas unerring sense is inherent.

The gold crucible is the crucible of the firmness of heaven. The mystic pearl is another name for the gold elixir. Because the gold elixir pill is round and bright, it is represented as a pearl; because its spiritual subtlety is hard to express, it is also represented as a mystic pearl.

The preceding section said that the solar yang soul and the lunar yin soul transmute into one flood—the gold elixir is formed. But in alchemy the production of the medicines has its time and the operation of the fire has its process; if you do not know the time of the production of the medicines and the process of the operation of the fire, the gold elixir will not crystallize. In *Understanding Reality*, our author writes, "Even if you know the cinnabar and lead, it is useless if you do not know the firing process. It all depends on the power of practical application; the slightest deviation, and you will fail to crystallize the elixir."

When the two medicines, real knowledge and conscious knowledge, arise in the occult opening, one should take the opportunity to get to work, intensively refining them to burn away conditioned temperament and emotional feeling, overcome the ordinary dragon and ordinary tiger, and cause the true dragon and true tiger of primordial true essence and sense to mate in the gold crucible, becoming inseparably bound to one another, naturally producing a mystic pearl which is round and bright, pervading the universe without obstruction.

However, when these medicines arise in the occult opening, sharing the qualities of heaven and earth, sharing the light of sun and moon, sharing the order of the four seasons, they are difficult to obtain and easy to lose. When the firing process conforms to what is appropriate, the real solidifies while the false evaporates, and the gold elixir immediately crystallizes. If the firing process is even slightly off, the real departs while the false comes, and you stumble by even while it is right before you. The classic *Guide to Putting in the Medicine (Ju yao ching)* says, "Reception of energy is fortunate; prevent it from turning into disaster." It is necessary to be careful.

[7]

This opening is not an ordinary aperture:
made by heaven and earth together,
it is called the lair of spirit and energy;
within it are the vitalities of water and fire.

The preceding section said that the occult opening can produce the medicines. Because this opening is most abstruse and subtle, in ecstasy and deep abstraction, if you aim for it, you lose it; if you conceptualize it, that is not it. It is not one of the ordinary apertures in the body, which have form and shape and can be pointed to; it is formless, invisible, a sacred opening that cannot be pointed out. In the human body, this opening is not the "yellow court" (between the heart and navel), not the "crimson chamber" (at the solar plexus), not the "field of elixir" (below the navel), not the "ocean of energy" (below the navel), not the coccyx, not in front of the kidneys and behind the navel, not the space between the kidneys and the genitals, not the middle of the spine where the ribs join, not the active and passive energy channels, not the "luminous hall" (an inch behind the midpoint between the brows), not the "center of tranquillity" (in the midbrain), not the "celestial valley" (at the top of the head), not the "jade pillow" (at the back of the head), not the mouth and nose. Its creation has to do with the yin and yang energies of heaven and earth joining in the center of space.

HEAVEN ☰ is firm, associated with yang; EARTH ☷ is flexible, associated with yin: when the two energies, firm and flexible, join together, then there is this opening. When the two energies, firm and flexible, are separate, this opening does not exist. Metaphorically, the open space between heaven above and earth below is this occult opening.

If people have firmness without flexibility, or are only flexible and not firm, this is solitary yin or isolated yang—with the adulterated energy therein suffocatingly full, how can there be the occult opening? Since there is no occult opening, the dynamic of energy has ceased—how can it produce medicine? Therefore the text says the occult opening is made by HEAVEN and EARTH together.

Because it is made by combination of HEAVEN and EARTH, it is also called the lair of spirit and energy. Spirit is the subtlety of consciousness that is beyond conception; energy is the harmonious living potential. Spirit is yin within yang, represented as FIRE ☲ and as the sun. Energy is yang within yin, represented as WATER ☵ and as the moon.

Heaven and earth, yin and yang, join together, with an opening in the center space, wherein sun and moon come and go; when people's firmness and flexibility join together, there is an opening in the center space, wherein spirit and energy congeal. The principle is the same. Therefore it is called the lair of spiritual energy, with the vitalities of WATER and FIRE in it.

People are born endowed with the vitalities of sun and moon (yang and yin), so the spirit and energy in the body are the vitalities of WATER and FIRE.

This opening cannot be sought consciously, nor can it be grasped unconsciously. Though one depends on personal instruction from a teacher, still it must be realized by oneself. When you discover this opening, WATER and FIRE, the medicines, appear at hand and need not be sought externally. Right away you can cull them at will. It is too bad that students everywhere practice concentration on specific defined "apertures" in the head and torso—how can they stabilize spirit and energy and preserve essence and life that way?

[8]

Wood mercury, one dash of red;
metal lead, three pounds of black.
Mercury and lead combine into granules
that shine violet-gold.

The preceding section said that the occult opening has the vitalities of WATER and FIRE; it is by the vitalities of FIRE and WATER that the elixir can be formed. The vitality of fire is wood and mercury; wood and mercury are buoyant and symbolize spiritual essence. The vitality of water is metal lead; metal is dense and tends to sink, and symbolizes true sense. Spiritual essence, containing the fire of open awareness, is conscious knowledge, yang outside and yin inside. The yin is less than the yang; yin hides inside the yang. That inside yin is associated with fire, so it is called "one dash of red." True sense, containing stable sane energy, is real knowledge, yin outside and yang inside. The yang is less than the yin; yang hides inside the yin. That outside yin is associated with water, so it is called "three pounds of black."

"One dash of red" symbolizes a small amount; "three pounds of black" symbolizes a large amount—it is not that there really are measures of one dash and three pounds. The method of alchemy involves gathering the bit of true fire of open awareness within conscious knowledge and refining out the adulterating energy of confused feelings, then gathering the pure spiritual water of desirelessness within real knowledge and extinguishing the baseless burning of the temperament. When the true fire and spiritual water join into one, water and fire balance each other, true feeling and spiritual essence combine, and real knowledge and conscious knowledge cleave to one another; then sense is itself essence, and essence is itself sense. Utterly conscious of reality, consciousness utterly real, the unified energy functions the same as heaven and earth. This is likened to lead and mercury being forged into spiritual granules; when the firing is complete, the medicine is perfected and turns violet-gold, never again to change.

[9]

The home garden's scenery is beautiful;
the weather is that of spring.
Without working with plow and hoe,
the whole earth is golden.

The preceding section said that the elixir can be compounded with lead and mercury. People might suppose that this means it is made by forging ordinary material lead and mercury, but they still do not realize that these are not the ordinary material substances, but are the beautiful scenery of the home garden within oneself. Since real knowledge and conscious knowledge, which are one's own true lead and mercury, are naturally present in one's home, they need not be sought externally; the scenery is beautiful. Yin and yang being in harmony, the mechanism of life unceasing, is like the weather in spring; the medicinal sprouts grow, without needing the work of plow and hoe. White snow flies, filling the sky; everywhere there grow yellow sprouts, which you can gather as you go along—everything is the Tao; wherever you walk there is treasure at every step, as though the whole earth were gold.

[10]

True lead arises in water;
its function is in the palace of FIRE:
turning black to red,
fog is thick in the crucible.

The preceding section says the scenery is inherent in the home garden; nevertheless, though it is inherent, it is not your command without thoroughgoing work. Because the lead of real knowledge is sunken into yin, it is symbolized by the WATER trigram ☵, yin outside and yang inside, yang enclosed by yin, acquired influences covering up the inherent sane energy so that the sane energy cannot get out by itself. If you want to bring it out, the function is in the palace of FIRE ☲; conscious knowledge, solid outside and empty inside, is symbolized by the FIRE trigram, containing the true fire of open awareness. When you use this true fire to burn away acquired influences, then real knowledge appears and merges with conscious knowledge, turning black to red, real knowledge becoming conscious knowledge. Yang, capturing yin, obtains nurturance; yin and yang cleave to one another, producing a harmonious energy, like a thick fog staying inside the crucible without dispersing.

[11]

True mercury comes from fire;
its function is in water.
The maiden goes to the south garden;
her hand grips the jade balustrade.

The true mercury, conscious knowledge, secretes the adulterated energy of discriminatory awareness; it is symbolized by the trigram

FIRE ☲, being light outside and dark inside. The discriminatory awareness uses consciousness to produce illusions; seeing fire, it flies—without the lead of real knowledge to control it, the discriminating awareness would cause trouble, and it would be impossible to return to reality. Therefore, the function lies in WATER. WATER symbolizes real knowledge, which has the pure "water" of true unity. When you use this pure water to extinguish the aberrant fire of discriminatory awareness, after the aberrant fire goes out, conscious knowledge returns to reality. The "south garden" represents FIRE; the "jade balustrade" represents WATER; the "maiden" is another name for conscious knowledge, so called because conscious knowledge is yin within yang. When conscious knowledge is controlled by real knowledge, yin comes to yang and is not moved by external things; conscious knowledge cleaves to real knowledge, real knowledge cleaves to conscious knowledge. This is "the maiden going to the south garden, her hand gripping the jade balustrade," the functions balancing and completing one another.

[12]

Thunder and lake are not east and west;
water and fire are not north and south.
The handle of the dipper circles the heavens,
requiring people to understand how to aggregate.

The preceding sections speak of wood/mercury, metal/lead, water, and fire mixing together; people often imagine these terms to apply to forms and locations within the body, associating fire with the heart and the south, associating water with the genitals and the north, associating wood with THUNDER and the liver and the east, associating metal with LAKE and the lungs and the west. They just take the heart, genitals, liver, and lungs for WATER ☵, FIRE ☲, THUNDER ☳, and LAKE ☱, and have actually not gotten the true tradition. They still do not know that THUNDER stands for our true essence, LAKE stands for our true sense, WATER stands for our real knowledge, and FIRE stands for our conscious knowledge. These four are the primordial true "four forms" inherent in us; because of mixture with acquired adulterated energy, they each dwell in a separate place and cannot join. Now if you want to restore them to unity as one energy, this requires the work of aggregation.

The work of aggregation means turning the celestial mechanism of the dipper handle. The dipper handle is the fifth, sixth, and seventh stars of the Big Dipper. Where these stars sit is unlucky; what they point to is lucky. They turn, as it were, the constellations through the heavens in the course of a year. In the human body, this refers to the point of true sense of real knowledge. One name of true sense is the iron man, in that it is strong and unbending, able to give life and to kill; this is also like the dipper handle in the sky. After birth, it is polluted by external influences, seduced by external things; the dipper handle points outward, not inward; the enlivening energy is outside, the killing energy is inside. Following the course of nature, the young mature, the mature age, the aged die; this goes on and on in repetitious cycles, with no hope of escape. If one knows the mechanism of life and death and turns around the dipper handle, when one changes one's orientation, one arrives at one's homeland and can thereby take over the evolutionary cycle and thus join the four forms and five elemental energies, so that the elixir soon forms, without effort.

But most people cannot recognize the dipper handle of true sense; they mistakenly take physical locations in the four directions in the body to be THUNDER, LAKE, WATER, and FIRE, and indulge in bogus practices, vainly imagining formation of the elixir. Does no one wonder why they struggle all their lives, only to grow old with no attainment? Is this not to be lamented?

[13]

The firing process does not call for set times;
the winter solstice is not in December.
As for the rules for bathing, spring and autumn
are also metaphors without reality.

The preceding section states that THUNDER, LAKE, WATER, and FIRE have special meanings and are not east, west, south, north. Not only that; when it says in the alchemical classics to advance the yang fire in December, repel the yin convergence in May, and bathe in spring and autumn, these are all just metaphors, without literal reality. They do not really mean the four seasons.

In the course of nature's cycle, the time when yang energy first emerges from the earth is called the time of the rat, which corresponds to the month of December and the hour of midnight. The time when yin energy first emerges from the earth is called the time of the horse, which corresponds to the month of May and the hour of noon. The time when yang energy has risen midway between heaven and earth is called the time of the hare, which corresponds to the spring equinox and the hour of six A.M. The time when the yin energy has risen halfway between heaven and earth is called the time of the bird, which corresponds to the autumn equinox and the hour of six P.M. So the rat and the horse are the times when yin and yang have just arisen, and the hare and the bird are the times when yin and yang are level. These are the rat, horse, hare, and bird of the Tao of nature.

The Tao of alchemy takes the time of the rat as the time to advance the yang fire, because when a point of yang light appears in the body, it is like the winter solstice in December. When one yang subtly arises, one should quickly advance the fire and gather it, assisting this bit of faint yang to gradually grow and develop, not letting it fade away. This is what is called advancing the fire of yang in December, or at midnight, the time of the rat.

The time of the horse is taken to be the time for repelling the yin convergence because the arising in darkness of a point of yin energy in the body is like the summer solstice in May of the lunar calendar. When one yin comes to join, one should quickly work to repel it, suppressing this bit of false yin, evaporating it as it grows, not letting up for a moment. This is what is called operating the yin convergence.

In reality, yang and yin arise all the time. The arising of yang is the time of the rat; the arising of yin is the time of the horse. These are the living rat and horse within our bodies, not the dead rat and horse of the calendar and clock. Therefore it says that the process does not call for set times and the "winter solstice" is not in December. The reason it mentions the time of the rat (December/midnight) and not the time of the horse (May/noon) is that the horse is contained within the rat. An ancient immortal said, "No need to look for the rat and the horse in the season or time of day; within the body there is naturally one yang arising." Seeing this, we can know that the winter solstice is not in December.

The Tao of alchemy takes spring and autumn, or six A.M. and six P.M., as appropriate for bathing, because after the point of yang light in the body has returned, it gradually grows and harmonizes with yin energy, neither too much nor too little, returning to balance, and this is like the yang energy on earth in spring rising to midway between heaven and earth at the spring equinox; one should stop the firing and make the yin and yang equal and harmonious, not advancing the fire excessively—this is the reason for "bathing." It does not mean one should bathe at the spring equinox. And when the point of yin energy in the body comes to join, as it grows it recedes and joins with yang energy, without imbalance, entering the mean. It is also like the yin energy in autumn rising to midway between heaven and earth at the autumn equinox; one should stop working and balance the firmness and flexibility, not repelling the yin excessively—this is the reason for "bathing." It does not mean one should bathe at the autumn equinox. Therefore, the text says that in the rules for bathing, spring and autumn are also metaphors without reality.

Our author's *Understanding Reality* says, "When the moon in the east and west reaches its season, punishment and reward are at hand; medicine is patterned on this." So we know that when advance and recession in the growth of the medicine are spoken of in terms of spring and autumn, it does not mean literally that one should bathe in spring and autumn. Later people did not know the metaphorical language of the alchemical classics and supposed that they mean to advance yang in December and at midnight, the month and hour of the rat, and to repel yin in May and at noon, the month and hour of the horse, then to bathe at the spring equinox and six A.M. and at the autumn equinox and six P.M., the months and hours of the hare and bird. But if you use the calendar and clock to figure the rat, horse, hare, and bird, think of this: the terms *rat, horse, hare,* and *bird* are applied to years, months, days, and hours alike—which do you take for the rule? Isn't this a big mistake? When our author says that the winter equinox is not in December, and that spring and autumn are also empty metaphors, he gets rid of the misapprehensions of all those who have gone off on tangents, and tells students to make a careful distinction based on the real pattern. What can compare to that compassion?

[14]

The raven's liver and the rabbit's marrow—
grab them and put them back in one place.
Grain after grain, from vagueness to clarity.

The preceding section says that the firing process and bathing are not in the times of the rat, horse, hare, and bird; it is all a matter of teaching people to know the harmonization of essence and sense, the same energy of yin and yang. "The raven's liver" is the vitality of the sun; liver is dark, which is associated with wood, and so symbolizes the essence of conscious knowledge. The rabbit's marrow" is the light of the moon; marrow is white, which is associated with metal, so it symbolizes the sense of real knowledge. Conscious knowledge and real knowledge, true essence and true sense, are the great medicines used in cultivating the elixir. Taking these four and putting them together, operating the fire to cook and refine them, they transmute into one energy. One energy undifferentiated, the living potential is ever-present, unfailingly growing from one yang to gradually reach the pure wholeness of six yangs, going from vague to clear, the gold elixir developing naturally. Here, "grab" does not mean forced action or effort; it means causing them to remain and not letting them leave. When they stay put, mixed thoughts do not arise and external influences do not enter; the four are gathered in one place and do not conflict with one another. "Grain after grain" means that when the basis is established, the path develops and the yang energy gradually grows; it does not literally mean there is the form of grains.

[15]

The undifferentiated contains space;
Space contains the world:
when you look for the root source,
it is the size of a grain.

The preceding section said the elixir can be made by the raven's liver and the rabbit's marrow. This elixir is nothing but the energy of primordial true unity inherent in our original, undifferentiated beginning. This energy envelops space, and space envelops the world. Enveloping space and the world, its size is measureless; yet even though it is measureless, when you search out its root source, it is no bigger than a grain. And though it is said to be like a grain, yet it is imperceptible and ungraspable: "Vague and indefinable, therein is an image; indefinable and vague, therein is something. Dark and occult, therein is a vitality; that vitality is most real, therein is true experience. This image, this thing, this vitality, this experience, are all what is called the energy of primordial unity. This energy is the origin of heaven and earth, the mother of myriad things. It is truly empty yet contains ineffable existence, ineffably existing while inherently truly empty. It has nothing to do with great or small; it cannot be defined as being or nonbeing; it is neither material nor vacuous, yet both matter and emptiness. Let it go and it is everywhere; roll it up and it hides in mystery. Its concealment and revelation are unfathomable; its transmutations are unpredictable. How can any concrete object be compared to it? If you know the unitary energy within nondifferentiation, when you know the One, myriad tasks are done, and practicing the Tao is not difficult.

[16]

Heaven and earth share the liquid of reality;
sun and moon contain the vitality of reality.
When you understand the foundation of water and fire,
the world is in your body.

The preceding section said that one grain can contain space and the world. But the reality of this grain is inherent in our body and need not be sought elsewhere. It is only necessary to understand how to harmonize yin and yang. When yin and yang are not in harmony, the energy of primordial unity does not return and the gold elixir does not crystallize.

Observe how when heaven and earth mate, the liquid of reality descends and fosters the growth of myriad beings and things; when sun and moon mate, the vitality of reality circulates and brings about the four seasons. This is when yin does not leave yang and yang does not leave yin; yin and yang join, containing the liquid of reality and the vitality of reality—only then is there creation. Otherwise, solitary yin does not give birth, solitary yang does not foster growth; the mechanism of life has ceased, so where can creation and evolution come from?

Our conscious knowledge and real knowledge are the heaven and earth and sun and moon in our bodies. Conscious knowledge has the yang energy of heaven, so it is heaven. The light emanated by the yang energy is like the hollow in the FIRE trigram ☲, which hollow is the sun. Real knowledge has the yin energy of earth, so it is earth. The fine essence secreted by the yin energy is like the fullness in the WATER trigram ☵, which fullness is the moon. So heaven and earth, sun and moon, are all inherent in our bodies. It is just that people do not know how to harmonize them, so yin and yang are separated and the enlivening potential fades away, ultimately returning to the Great Flux.

If you understand that the foundation of WATER and FIRE of real knowledge and conscious knowledge originally belong to one energy, and if you cultivate them backward, inverting WATER and FIRE, using real knowledge to control conscious knowledge, using conscious knowledge to nurture real knowledge, water and fire balance each other, movement and stillness are as one; then mind is Tao, Tao is mind, mind is the mind of Tao, body is the body of Tao, sharing the qualities of heaven and earth, sharing the light of sun and moon, sharing the order of the seasons—the whole world is within one's own body.

[17]

The dragon comes from the eastern sea;
the tiger comes from the western mountains.
The two beasts have a battle
and turn into the marrow of heaven and earth.

The preceding section said that if you understand the foundation of WATER and FIRE, the great Tao can be attained. WATER and FIRE are symbols of real knowledge and conscious knowledge; if you want water and fire to balance and settle each other, it is necessary first to join metal and wood.

Essence is associated with wood; dwelling in the east, it is the property of the self, and because of its unfathomable fluidity it is likened to a dragon. Sense is associated with metal; dwelling in the west, it is the property of the other, and because of its unbending strength it is likened to a tiger.

However, essence and sense both have differences in terms of being true or false, primal or conditioned. The essence of round luminosity and the formless sense are the true primal; the temperament and feelings tied to objects are the false and conditioned. After we are born, the false mixes in with the true; the dragon becomes fierce, the tiger becomes wild, and they dwell apart, not communicating. Unless we get rid of the false and rescue the true, the great Tao is unattainable.

When the text says that "the dragon comes from the eastern sea," it means chasing the dragon to the tiger, using essence to seek sense. When it says that "the tiger comes from the western mountains," it means leading the tiger and riding the dragon, using sense to return to essence. When essence and sense meet, use sense to stabilize essence, use essence to control sense; when essence and sense are bound together, their fierceness and wildness become docility and harmony: the false vanishes and the true returns. Essence loves sense, obedient and dutiful; sense loves essence, kind and benevolent. When metal and wood, sense and essence, join together, this is the complete Original Face without defect. Therefore the text says that "the two beasts have a battle and turn into the marrow of heaven and earth."

The word *battle* has a deep meaning. Once people's primal yang culminates and mixes with temporal conditioning, the senses and their objects as they have been conditioned through history become active, and feelings and emotions run amok; add to this the acquired energies of habits accumulated in this life, and inside and outside are all yin, which cannot easily be stripped away. Without intense effort to strip away this conditioning acquired through cultural and personal history, how can it be extinguished? Properly speaking, *battle* means vigorous and intense refinement, which effort is not to be relaxed until yin is exhausted and yang is pure. "Turning into the marrow of heaven and earth" means pure unity without duality when essence and sense have been purged of all pollution; only then is the work done. The subtle meaning of this stage is expressed in our author's *Understanding Reality* in these lines: "The white tiger of the western mountains is very wild; the blue dragon of the eastern sea cannot stand up to it. Grabbing them with both hands, make them engage in mortal combat; they will change into a cluster of violet-gold frost."

Indeed, essence and sense are not easy to harmonize. It takes years of intense effort before it is possible to return to reality.

[18]

Gold flowers bloom with mercury petals;
jade stems grow on lead twigs.
Water and fire have never been separate;
how long do heaven and earth endure?

The preceding section is on the joining of metal and wood, the union of essence and sense; this section immediately follows up on that, expressing the effect of the joining of metal and wood.

"Gold flowers" and "lead twigs" are associated with yang, which is firm, and refer to true sense. "Mercury petals" and "jade stems" are associated with yin, which is flexible, and refer to true essence. The center of FIRE ☲ is open; openness is associated with yin, and is conscious knowledge. The center of WATER ☵ is full; fullness is associated with yang, and is real knowledge. "Gold flowers bloom with mercury petals" means there is flexibility within firmness, sense being none other than essence; "jade stems grow on lead twigs" means there is firmness within flexibility, essence being none other than sense. "WATER and FIRE have never been separate" means that fulfillment contains emptiness and emptiness contains fulfillment; real knowledge is conscious knowledge, and conscious knowledge is real knowledge.

Able to be firm, able to be flexible, able to be empty, able to be full, firmness and flexibility corresponding, emptiness and fulfillment including each other, tranquil and imperturbable yet sensitive and effective, sensitive and effective yet tranquil and imperturbable, going through the same processes as heaven and earth, thus one shares the eternity of heaven and earth—when will there ever be destruction?

[19]

Bathe and ward off danger,
extract and add, taking care.
In all, there are thirty thousand intervals;
beware of even the slightest slip.

The preceding section speaks of the merging of essence and feeling, the congealing of real knowledge and conscious knowledge, whereupon the elixir forms. But though the medicinal substances are easy to know, the firing process is most difficult. If you do not know the details of operating the fire, and slip up even a little bit, it will cause a tremendous miss and the gold elixir cannot be formed.

After the elixir has been restored, there is a time for bathing and a process of extraction and addition. Before the medicines are obtained, one must refine the self to gather medicine; after the elixir is obtained, one must bathe to incubate it. Bathing means the work of warding off danger.

An ancient immortal said, "The elixir is restored in a short time;

incubation requires ten months." In ten months there are thirty thousand intervals; during each interval one keeps attentive to ward off danger, like a hen sitting on an egg, like an oyster embracing a pearl, focusing single-mindedly on the sphere of attention. One also works on extracting lead and adding mercury, carefully guarding against any slip-up. If there is any slip-up, this produces falsehood within reality; external influences sneak in, and the gold elixir, once gained, is again lost, forms but then decays. Then the problem of burning the crucible cannot be avoided.

Therefore in alchemy the work of warding off danger is indispensable, start to finish. Warding off danger means preventing external influences from creeping in and taking care that the basis of the elixir is not damaged. When we speak of warding off danger, the work of extraction and addition is therein. Extraction means taking out the lead; addition means putting in the mercury. Before the elixir is crystallized, one must use true lead to control true mercury; once the mercury is inert and the elixir has crystallized, it is necessary to extract this lead energy again before the true mercury can become a spiritual jewel. This is because although the true lead of real knowledge is something primordial, being produced from within the temporal, it carries acquired energy. First one uses real knowledge to control and stabilize conscious knowledge, not letting conscious knowledge fly off outside; once conscious knowledge is stabilized, it is necessary to gradually remove the acquired pollutant energy carried by this real knowledge, so that eventually none is left at all. Only then is the elixir perfected. If any of that acquired energy is not extracted, not removed, conscious knowledge cannot become a round and bright jewel. When you take out one part of pollutant energy in real knowledge, you add one part of pure energy to conscious knowledge; when you take out one hundred percent of the polluted energy in real knowledge, you add one hundred percent pure energy to conscious knowledge. When polluted energy is exhausted and pure energy is stable, the firing is done and energy is sufficient; only then do you have the complete luminous jewel of real consciousness, round and bright, and nothing else.

Our author's *Understanding Reality* says, "When you use lead, do not use ordinary lead; and when you have finished using the true lead, that too is thrown away. This is the real secret of using lead. Using lead and not using it—these are veracious words." This is the meaning of extracting lead and adding mercury.

In essence, the work of extracting and adding is none other than the function of warding off danger; extracting and adding are precisely that whereby to ward off danger. Avoiding danger, extracting and adding, being careful for the ten months, not deviating from the correct process, how could the gold elixir not form?

As for the "thirty thousand intervals," it is not that there really is a period of ten months; it is just a metaphor for the process from the restoration of the elixir to the perfection of the elixir, when the spiritual embryo reaches complete maturity. Students should investigate the reality and not destroy the meaning by taking the words literally.

[20]

When husband and wife mate,
clouds and rain form in the secret room.
In a year they give birth to a child,
and each rides on a crane.

The foregoing section told of the medicines, the firing process, and the power of practice, in each case using similes from alchemy. The author feared that students would not understand the profound subtlety therein and would mistakenly enter the circuitous routes of auxiliary methods, so he added this section, using the ordinary relationship of man and woman, husband and wife, which is obvious and easy to see, as a metaphor to instruct people.

In the path of cultivating reality, the thousand classics and ten thousand texts just teach people to harmonize yin and yang, to cause yin and yang to merge and return to one energy. Observe how in the world husband and wife meet; when they mate, then they can produce a child. In cultivation of the Tao, yin and yang meet, and then when they mate, they can produce an immortal.

Our real knowledge is yang within yin; this is the "husband." Our conscious knowledge is yin within yang; this is the "wife." After the primal yang in people culminates, acquired conditioning takes over affairs, and the real gets lost outside, as though it lived in another house and did not belong to oneself. Though one may have conscious knowledge, the wife does not see the husband; yin being without the balance of yang, this consciousness has falsehood in it. If the husband, real knowledge, is recognized and called back home to meet the wife, conscious knowledge, and taken into the privacy of the secret room, the husband loves the wife and the wife loves the husband; husband and wife mate, sense and essence combine, so the primal energy comes forth from within nothingness and congeals into the spiritual embryo. Then, adding the work of ten months of incubation, when the energy is replete and the spirit complete, it emerges from the womb; there is a body outside the body, transcending yin and yang, untrammeled by natural process.

Then one goes on to advanced practice, again setting up the furnace and crucible, to carry on the subtle path of nondoing. The child gives birth to grandchildren, and the grandchildren also branch out, producing a thousand changes, ten thousand transformations. Each soars into the skies riding a crane, becoming immortals of the empyrean.

This path is entirely the Tao of yin and yang; giving birth to people and giving birth to immortals is not apart from yin and yang; the only difference is in whether the product is an immortal or an ordinary person. As the immortal San-feng put it, going along with the usual course of conditioning makes one an ordinary person, and going against it makes one an immortal; it is all a matter of reversing the process. The method of reversal cannot be known without a teacher. One who knows can form the elixir in a short time and need not spend three years nurturing it and nine years maturing it. But it is necessary to recognize the true yin and the true yang.

, , ,

The foregoing explanation has been divided into sections, omitting nothing of the meaning. Now, based on the lines of the original text, also according to the same sectioning, I present verses for explanatory notes, simply phrased but inclusive in meaning, cutting through the metaphors and images, to let students understand at a glance and be further able to comprehend the true interpretation without getting involved in speculation. Then most of the secret of cultivating reality can be grasped.

Explanatory Verses

[1]
True intent arouses real knowledge;
Conscious knowledge also spontaneously responds.

The three join as one,
And at once body and mind are settled.

[2]
The empty room produces light;
In quietude yang is restored:
Gather it and diligently refine it,
Transforming it into violet-gold frost.

[3]
In the spiritual opening the light of wisdom arises;
Essence appears, and feelings about objects vanish.
Clear and bright the jewel that glows in the dark;
Everywhere is bright and clean.

[4]
Volatility transmutes into true essence;
The human mind changes into the mind of Tao.
Without refinement by the spiritual fire,
How can gold be separated from the ore?

[5]
Real knowledge and conscious knowledge;
These two are originally the same energy.
Subjected to refinement by fire,
They merge without a trace of defect.

[6]
In the occult opening real consciousness appears;
Take the opportunity to get to work to nurture it.
When essence and sense cleave to one another,
They always produce the material for the elixir.

[7]
There is an opening of open awareness
Which is called the opening of the mysterious female;
Therein are stored spirit and energy,
Originally the root of the celestial and earthly souls.

[8]
Conscious knowledge is the vitality within fire;
Real knowledge is the jewel within water.
When negativity within water and fire vanishes,
The light is brilliant, truly sound.

[9]
The spiritual remedy is inherent in oneself;
What is the need to seek it outside?
Preserve the responsiveness of constant shining,
And everywhere you go becomes a forest of jewels.

[10]
Real knowledge is all real,
But it needs to be espoused by conscious knowledge.
Refining away the yin of acquired conditioning,
The two become one whole.

[11]
Conscious knowledge likes to wander outside
And needs to be governed by real knowledge;
When the "wife" follows the "husband,"
Water and fire balance each other.

[12]
Thunder, lake, water, and fire
Are symbols of vitality, spirit, sense, and essence;
If you know how to aggregate them,
You walk alone atop the mountains of the immortals.

[13]
The firing process is not related to hour or season;
Why bother to seek midnight and noon, winter and summer?
Bathing is washing the dusty mind;
How can spring and autumn govern it?

[14]
"Metal" sense and "wood" essence
Should not be unbalanced or disparate.
The two are as the same energy;
The spiritual root blooms of itself.

[15]
So great as to enfold space,
Yet small as a grain of rice;
If you ask about this root source,
It is the one reality alone.

[16]
The vitalities of heaven and earth, sun and moon,
Are fundamentally inherent in our bodies.
If reality and consciousness do not stray from each other,
Creation is always in the palm of your hand.

[17]
When essence arises, sense comes to stabilize it;
When sense arises, essence goes to lead it.
When their conflict and struggle are ended,
Then, as of yore, they are unconditioned.

[18]
Essence and sense merge;
Real and conscious knowledge join.
With fierce refinement and gentle cooking,
A crystal-clear temple is produced.

[19]
Controlling the mind is called bathing;
Incubation involves extraction and addition.
At every moment, forestall danger;
As accomplishment deepens, you naturally enter the mystery.

[20]
When you understand the principle of yin and yang,
The spiritual embryo is not hard to form;
Producing a child, also producing grandchildren,
Eternal life never ends.

Each section of this classic text on the essence of alchemy is sound; each line points to reality. The furnace and crucible, medicinal substances, firing process, order of practical cultivation, doing and nondoing, from start to finish, are all included. Although the text is brief, it contains the overall meaning of the whole text of *Understanding Reality*.

Now I have explained the symbols and metaphors in this text, breaking open the core to see the nucleus, splitting the bones to reveal the marrow, in order to shed some light for beginning students to guide them into the right path. But I fear that students may not know how actually to put it into practice and, not consummating the task of a student, may develop false imaginations about the great Tao and seek at random, deceiving themselves about the path ahead. So here, after having made these explanatory notes on the text, I also add Twenty-four Essentials for Students and Twenty-four Secrets of Alchemy. I phrase them very simply, so that what they refer to may be easily recognized, thereby bringing to light the secrets of which the ancient teachers did not speak.

If people of determination can use these essentials and secrets to study and understand the text itself, proceeding in order, then those who study the Tao will eventually understand the Tao, and those who practice the Tao will eventually accomplish the Tao. It is to be hoped that people will not waste the months and years rushing into byways.

Twenty-four Essentials for Students

[1]
See through things of the world.
If you cannot see through the things of the world,
You will sink into an ocean of suffering. How can you get out?

[2]
Cut off entanglements.
If you cannot cut off entanglements,
The vicious cycles of compulsive habit stand before you.

[3]
Thoroughly investigate principle and meaning.
If you do not know how to discern the principles of body and mind,
You cannot distinguish aberration and sanity, and miss the road.

[4]
Find a teacher and associates.
When you empty the mind, you can fill the belly;
If you are self-satisfied, you will grow old without development.

[5]
Make determination endure.
If you want to accomplish something that endures unchanging,
It requires work that endures unceasing.

[6]
Get rid of anger and hatred.
If you do not sweep yourself clean of anger and hatred,
You will be full of turbulence, which will obscure the truth.

[7]
Relinquish attachment to the physical body.
See the physical body as something temporary and artificial,
And naturally there will be a way to seek the real body.

[8]
Do not be afraid of hard work.
With strength of mind, one will be able to climb to the summit;
If you are afraid of hardship, you will never enter the real.

[9]
Tolerate ignominy and endure dishonor.
Tolerate ignominy, and though lowly you cannot be surpassed;
Endure dishonor, and through yielding you can be strong.

[10]
Forgive people and defer to others.
It is essential to humble oneself and honor others;
Equanimous deference is a good method.

[11]
Take possessions lightly; take life seriously.
Ask yourself—even if you pile up mountains of gold,
Can you buy off impermanence?

[12]
View others and self as the same.
Others and self have the same source, without high or low;
If you discriminate between "them" and "us," you raise dust.

[13]
Do not be deluded by alcohol or sex.
If you do not drink, your nature will not be deranged;
If you are chaste, your life force will be stable.

[14]
Accept hunger and cold as they come.
Dressing and eating according to circumstances, stop idle
    imagination;
If you are afraid of hunger and cold, your will won't be firm.

[15]
Leave life and death to destiny.
Two things, death and life, depend entirely on nature;
The one will to seek the Way is always up to oneself.

[16]
Do whatever you can to be helpful.
Wherever you are, continue to perform worthy deeds;
Seeing danger, exert your utmost power to help people.

[17]
Do not take a liking to excitement.
It is easy to lose the real in the midst of excitement and glamour;
In the realms of the senses you can derange your essential nature.

[18]
Do not be proud or complacent.
Arrogance arouses the hatred of others;
If you are self-satisfied, you cannot bear the Tao.

[19]
Do not crave fine food.
Superior people plan for the Way, not for food;
Inferior people nurture the palate, not the mind.

[20]
Do not talk about right and wrong.
Everyone should sweep the snow from his own door
And not be concerned about the frost on another's roof.

[21]
Do not use intellectual brilliance.
If you have talent, do not employ it; always be as if inept;
If you have knowledge, hide it, appearing to be ignorant.

[22]
Sleep less and work more.
Working by day, cautious by night, effort never ceasing,
Giving up sleep, forgetting to eat, the will must be firm.

[23]
Do not take a liking to fine things.
Pearls and jade, gold and silver, are things outside the body;
Vitality and spirit, essence and life, are the fundamental treasures.

[24]
Be consistent from beginning to end.
If you work without strength, it is hard to reach deep attainment;
Only when you die embracing the Tao do you see reality.

These twenty-four essentials are important passageways for students which must be put into actual practice. When you have passed through each one and applied them in your life, only then can you meet a real teacher and hear about the great Tao. If there is even one that you cannot practice and get through, even if you meet a real teacher and hear about the Tao, it is not certain to benefit you.

The teacher's function is to polish away errors, to clearly perceive and subtly test the student and see whether the student is genuine or false. A genuine, sincere person is like real gold, which has no fear of fire, become brighter the more it is refined in the fire, being appraised by an expert, certified and accepted.

Someone without will may start out diligently but eventually slacks off; outwardly obedient yet inwardly refractory, such people will greedily fantasize about the treasures of others without being able to carry out their own tasks. This is what is called not getting rid of temper, not changing the attitude, falling into the sea of vicious circles; even if you accumulate vast hordes of gold and jade, the spirits and immortals will laugh coldly and will not respond. Such people cannot even hear the Way, much less accomplish it.

Those who hear the Way are small sages; those who accomplish the Way are great sages. The affair of great sages is certainly not within the capabilities of empty obscurantists.

Twenty-four Secrets of Alchemy

[1]
Repair the alchemical workshop.
Nourish the temporal; strengthen the physical body.
To nourish the temporal is the point of departure;
When vitality, energy, and spirit are vigorous, one can bear hunger and cold.
Having cultivated the physical body until it is firm and strong,
Giving shelter from the rain and wind, it is good for refining the elixir.

[2]
Refine the self and set up the foundation.
Overcome anger and lust; conquer the self and return to normalcy.
Refining the self and mastering the mind are building the foundation;

Mundane feelings and idle thoughts are all to be thrown away.
When you have refined your self to where it does not exist,
You are imperturbable and unshakable, and cannot be deluded by things.

[3]
Set up the crucible and furnace.
Stabilize the will with firmness; do the work with flexibility.
Making the will firm and strong is setting up the crucible;
Gradually progressing in the work is setting up the furnace.
Firmness and flexibility are both used, without imbalance;
Having prepared, work the fire and the convergence according to the time.

[4]
Cull the medicines.
Seek the real in the artificial; pick the gold out of sand.
The great medicines are three—vitality, energy, spirit;
It is necessary first to distinguish the true from the false.
The division between right and wrong is slight;
Be careful not to mix them up.

[5]
Use lead to control mercury.
When real knowledge is not obscured, conscious knowledge is not flighty.
Another name for sense is true lead;
Essence, light and mercuric, is represented as mercury.
When you understand the method of bringing sense to stabilize essence,
The human mentality does not arise and the mind of Tao is complete.

[6]
The yellow woman harmonizes.
When true intent does not scatter, yin and yang naturally harmonize.
You should know that the true intent is the "yellow woman";
Truthfulness alone can harmonize the four forms,
Aggregating the five elements uses its power;
Perfecting the being and building life are not apart from it.

[7]
Lead and mercury intermingle.
Essence goes to seek sense; sense comes back to essence.
Putting the lead in the mercury, sense returns to essence;
Putting the mercury in the lead, essence cleaves to sense.
When sense and essence merge without obstruction,
There is no worry that the great Way will not be accomplished.

[8]
Work the fire to smelt and refine.
Activate sane energy; sweep out aberrant energy.
Gentle cooking and fierce refinement are the methods of immortals;
Fire comes forth in the spiritual furnace, yin and yang,
Burning away the thousand kinds of pollutants.
Naturally the great medicines emanate misty light.

[9]
The restored elixir congeals.
Firmness and flexibility balance each other; essence and sense are
    as one.
When essence and sense are unified, that is called the restored elixir;
Bright and clear, reality and consciousness join into one whole.
Having obtained the original priceless jewel,
Carefully guard it; practice observation of the spirit.

[10]
Bathe and incubate.
Do not let thoughts arise; do not let attention scatter.
Washing off defilement and dust is the method of bathing;
Do not be negligent, do not be forceful, join yin and yang.
When entanglements do not arise, the basis of the elixir is stable;
Nurturing the spiritual root, the flower buds are fragrant.

[11]
The basis of the elixir becomes mature.
Within black there is white; when quietude culminates, there is
    movement.
Within black there is white—the herb of long life.
Within darkness is concealed light—the life-prolonging tonic.
Refining it into something crystal-clear and pure,
It penetrates heaven and earth with a ray of light.

[12]
Ingest the gold elixir.
Gather the spirit into the room, transmuting earthliness.
The elixir ingested does not come from outside;
The refined real consciousness rests within.
The internal organs produce light; earthly energy is transmuted;
Without confusion or obscurity, obstacles are broken through.

[13]
Move the furnace and crucible.
The root source in hand, plant and nurture according to the time.
The gold elixir in hand, there is true transmission;
Moving the furnace and crucible is a mystery within mystery.
Henceforth carefully cook the great medicine,
Refining the primordial within the primordial opening.

[14]
Congeal the spiritual embryo.
All the spirit gathered, the five elements merge.
The five energies return to the origin and gather on the spiritual
    pedestal;
The primordial seed is already firmly planted.
As though an idiot, as though drunk, as though deep asleep,
In ecstasy and profound abstraction you congeal the spiritual embryo.

[15]
Difficulty in the morning, darkness at night.
Know the male, keep the female; refine with the natural fire.
Knowing the male, it is also necessary to keep the female.
Steaming with water and fire is not a matter of the hour.
There is naturally a pivot which turns over the trigrams;
What is the need to make conscious effort?

[16]
Incubate the embryo.
Like a hen sitting on an egg, like an oyster embracing a pearl.
Concentrate single-mindedly, like a hen sitting on an egg;
Be thoroughly sincere, like an oyster embracing a pearl.
Hour after hour quietly watch over the aperture of open awareness,
To avoid letting water and fire be isolated in the furnace.

[17]
Forestall danger.
Externally oblivious of the body, internally oblivious of the mind.
Before celestial energy is thoroughly pure, there is still danger;
As long as earthly energy is not exhausted, it is necessary to prevent peril.
If the pollution of acquired conditioning is dissolved away,
It can be guaranteed that the embryo will not be damaged.

[18]
In ten months the embryo is mature.
Primordial energy is pure; conditioning is evaporated.
After ten months of work, the embryo is finally mature;
When conditioning is all dissolved, the primal is complete.
Utterly pure and clean, there is nothing else;
It is one naturalness, neither form nor void.

[19]
Wait for the time to break free.
No thought, no doing, not obsessed, not indifferent.
Basically there is a time to break free, transformed;
It will not do to be too early or too late.
Truthfulness within reaches outside, not admitting force;
When a melon is ripe, it naturally separates from the stem.

[20]
The infant emerges.
Breaking through nondifferentiation, leaping into nothingness.
Keep still in the yellow court and nurture the valley spirit;
With body complete and energy replete, the fire is stopped—
With a peal of thunder, the gate of heaven opens,
And out leaps the indestructible immortal person.

[21]
Breast-feed for three years.
Enlightened but not shining, illumined but not using it.
When real consciousness is refined into a golden body,
It never ever falls into the dust.
Nursing it for three years, enlightened but not shining,
Knowing before and understanding after, the sage is spiritual.

[22]
Exiting and entering at will.
Body and spirit both sublimated, merging into reality with the Tao.
Body and spirit both sublimated, equal to space,
Merging in reality with the Tao, all things are penetrated.
Appearing, hiding, going against or along, no one can fathom it;
Clustered, there is form; dispersed, the wind.

[23]
Facing a wall for nine years.
Neither being nor nonbeing stand; the universe is ultimately empty.
Nine years facing a wall, who is there that knows?
The work of entering the room does not depend on thought.
The universe returns to emptiness; ordinary and holy are gone;
In the realm of silent serenity, the abode of immortals is built.

[24]
The child also produces grandchildren.
Transformation without end, unfathomable spiritual wonders.
The child also produces grandchildren; ordinary and sage are the
    same—
The only distinction is in going along or coming back in reverse.
Ancient immortals left the secret of a great elixir,
With endless transmutations, getting through everywhere.

These twenty-four secrets are steps of the process which must be thoroughly understood, as the slightest deviation produces a great miss. Since ancient times the immortals and real people usually have not clearly indicated the order of the process; concealing the mother and speaking of the children, they have just instructed people by means of metaphors and symbols, fearing pilferage by unsuitable people.

Since I have received spoken instruction from a teacher, at the risk of making a mistake I wish to reveal this teaching publicly to those who aspire to it. Even if one lacks the power to put it into practice, simply getting to hear about the great Way is a measureless blessing.

But such a great task requires people of great strength to carry it out; it also requires people to have great character in order to perform it. If one has great strength but lacks great character, there are likely to arise obstacles that will prevent accomplishment of the great Way.

Therefore, if one wants to traverse this path, one should first build character. For mediocre and lesser people, character is more important than the path, because if their virtue is not great, even if they can hear about the Way they cannot necessarily attain it. Students of the Tao should first recognize clearly what these topics mean, know the beginning and the end, when to hurry and when to relax; only then will they have certain insight and avoid wasting effort.

Glossary

BLACK AND WHITE   Primordial and temporal; nondifferentiation and differentiation; transcendence and immanence; detachment and involvement. *See also* Female and male.

ENTERING THE ROOM   Advanced attainment.

FACING A WALL   Practicing equanimity.

FEMALE AND MALE   Receptivity and creativity; tranquillity and action.

GATE OF HEAVEN   In psychophysical Taoist yoga, the center of the top of the head, the "opening" from which the spirit is projected; metaphysically, the apex of consciousness, through which one passes into enlightenment.

STEAMING   Permeation of the being with the combination of "water" and "fire." (See the introduction and text for the significations of water and fire and their combination.)

TURNING OVER THE TRIGRAMS   In the unregenerate human being, the order of the water and fire trigrams is thus:
FIRE ☲ Conscious knowledge: tends to "fly up," become dissociated from true reality.
WATER ☵ Real knowledge: tends to "flow off," remain unconscious and inaccessible.
For enlightenment, these are "turned over" or "inverted":
☵ Real knowledge controls conscious knowledge.
☲ Conscious knowledge rises to real knowledge.

VALLEY SPIRIT   Open awareness.

YELLOW COURT   In psychophysical Taoist yoga, the center of the torso; metaphysically, the "center" in the sense of intent (as the force that unifies the being), truthfulness, balance, faith.

PART TWO

Solving Symbolic Language

On Symbolic Language

The ancient classics on the science of cultivating reality often speak of the path of nondoing, but seldom speak of the path of doing. However, on the path of nondoing, only those of superior knowledge become suddenly enlightened and attain complete comprehension, understanding everything in one realization, immediately ascending into the realm of sages. Mediocre and lesser people, those who are dull, deeply conditioned, and lacking perceptivity, will find that their power is insufficient to practice the path of nondoing; they will not be able to transcend all objects and reach the goal directly.

During the latter Han dynasty (second century C.E.) Wei Po-yang, a Taoist adept, composed the *Triplex Unity (Ts'an t'ung ch'i)* to guide those of middling and lesser faculties. He used images to present the imageless, used forms to allude to the formless. This was the beginning of the term *gold elixir* and the technical symbolism of lead and mercury, sand and silver, raven and rabbit, dragon and tiger, the baby, the girl, medicinal substances, the furnace and cauldron, cooking and refining, and so on.

Later on, many real people who had attained the Tao composed alchemical treatises, all based on the *Triplex Unity*, to expound the subtle principles. Their intention was for students in later times to use the former to study the latter, and use the latter to understand the former.

Nevertheless, later students did not look into the meanings of the code words and did not figure out the principles of the symbols. Seeing talk of gold elixir, lead, mercury, cauldron, and furnace, they thought it referred to the preparation of potions to ingest, and they took to chemistry. Seeing talk of raven and rabbit, dragon and tiger, they thought it referred to the internal organs, and they took to visualization exercises. Seeing talk of other and self, yin and yang, male and female, they thought it referred to conjugal elixir, and they took to sexual yoga. Seeing talk of going along, reversing, and inverting, they thought it referred to forced effort, and they took to energy circulation practices. Seeing talk of nondoing to cultivate essence, they took it to mean utter quiescence, and they got involved in quietism. Seeing talk of doing to cultivate life, they thought it meant exercise, and came to cling to form. These and other schools arose, all taking a deer to be a horse, taking a crow for a phoenix, not only without benefit to essence and life, but even to the detriment of essence and life. Could this have been the intention of the ancient teachers in using symbolic language?

Symbols are representations, speaking of one thing to allude to something else. To take an example from the field of common knowledge and experience, consider the cooking and brewing of food and drink. The pot is the "cauldron"; the stove is the "furnace." Water is put in the pot; fire is kindled in the stove. The basic tendency of fire is to flame upward, that of water to flow downward; when we put the water in the pot above and the fire in the stove below, water and fire are thus "reversed"—they complement one another, so that the food and drink are cooked and brewed. This represents ordinary water and ordinary fire complementing each other.

The strength in people is impetuous and volatile, so it is associated with fire; flexibility is relaxed and calm, so it is associated with water. Using flexibility to nurture strength, using strength to complete flexibility, strength and flexibility match each other, so that there is neither haste nor dawdling, effecting a return to equipoise, with the result that the Tao is easy to accomplish. This is the principle of the mutual complementarity of psychological water and psychological fire. Using the image of complementarity of ordinary water and fire to represent the principle of complementarity of psychological water and fire, that principle is clear.

Let us consider another example. Suppose a man is originally prosperous, but becomes profligate and squanders his fortune; then, on the verge of destitution, he repents of his errors, struggles and labors for a living again, gradually accumulates substance, and eventually reestablishes his fortune. This symbolizes return to the origin. The vitality, spirit, and sacred energy in the human body are originally complete and full; mixing with temporal conditioning, going along with the process of creation, expends vitality and belabors the spirit, so that the basic energy declines and the source wanes. If, on the verge of exhaustion, one can turn back, quell anger and cupidity, get rid of falsehood and preserve truth, by gradual application of effort one can eventually return to the root and restore life. This is the principle of return to the origin. Using the image of restoration and recovery of a man in the world to represent the principle of return to the origin by practice of Tao, that principle is clear.

To take another example, when a man and a woman mate, they are able to produce children, who produce grandchildren; this represents the continuing birth of the human Tao. When the yin and yang in the human being match and unite, they can produce enlightened adepts; this is the principle of continuing birth in the alchemical Tao. Using the image of continuing birth of the human Tao to represent the principle of continuing birth in the alchemical Tao, that principle is clear.

The alchemical classics all use metaphors to illustrate principles; they are telling people to discern from the image the principle to be practiced, not to turn away from the principle and act on the image. It is a pity that people do not investigate the principles, only recognizing the images. There are very many symbolic expressions used in alchemical classics; students should proceed from the symbol to discover the principle. When you get the image, forget the words; when you get the intent, forget the image. Then you will be close.

On Going Along and Reversal

Everyone in the world knows the path of "going along," but not the path of "reverse operation." What is going along? It means going along with natural process. What is reversal? It means reversal of natural process. Going along with natural process gives birth to humans and other beings, the cycle of birth, aging, sickness, and death never ceasing. Reversing the natural process produces enlightened adepts who are neither born nor perish, having a life span equal to that of the universe.

Ordinarily, after people are born, as they grow up they become imbued with temporal conditioning; inwardly, emotions and desires distract them from reality, while outwardly objects and events tax their bodies. They take the false to be real, take the aberrant to be correct, take misery for pleasure; following their desires to any lengths, they deplete their original vitality, energy, and spirit almost to the point of exhaustion, and thoroughly obscure their inherent round and bright true essence, unwilling to stop until they die. Therefore they undergo birth after birth, death after death, sunk for myriad aeons; this is what is called throwing oneself to one's death even without having been called by the king of death.

People of great wisdom reverse the operation of the natural process; they are not bound by the natural process, not molded by yin and yang, not compelled by myriad things, not changed by myriad conditions. Planting lotuses in a fire, hauling a boat through mud and water, they make temporary use of things of the world to practice the principles of the Tao, by the human Tao completing the celestial Tao. They uproot the mundane senses conditioned by history and sweep away all acquired influences. They rule their own destinies and are not ruled by fate. Restoring the whole, original being, they avoid compulsive routine, transcend all worlds, and become incorruptible.

But this celestial mechanism of practicing reversal in the midst of accord has a secret which is communicated verbally and transmitted mentally; one must seek the guidance of a true teacher, for it cannot be known through arbitrary guesswork. Students all over the world use their own meager light and narrow views, memorize a few sayings, ponder a few mystical stories, and think they know the Tao; seeking no further for guidance, they become charlatans, self-appointed preachers who are blind themselves and take in others who are blind. It is wrong to do this.

There are also mixed-up people who cannot recognize true teachers and go from one imbecile to another learning a few minor techniques and imagine they have the Tao; then, when enlightened people appear before them, they are unwilling to humble themselves to learn. They perform various practices at random: some consider descent of the energy in the heart and ascent of the energy in the genitals to be the practice of reversal; some consider the circulation of energy up the spine and down the front of the body to be the practice of reversal; some consider sending the vitality up to boost the brain to be the practice of reversal; some consider holding the breath and steadying the spirit to be the practice of reversal; some consider taking sexual energy from women to vitalize men to be the practice of reversal; some consider having the man below and the woman above to be the practice of reversal. There are thousands of such methods; they are all contrary to the path of sages and are not reverse operation of the natural process. They are all ways to death, not to life.

What such people do not realize is that reversal means going back to the origin of life. It is like someone who has left home and gone far away turning around and returning home. Although it is called reverse action, in fact it is action in accord with principle, so it is great accord within reversal. It is called reversal because it goes contrary to the course of action of ordinary people. Those who have taken to auxiliary methods, with all their intricacies, have been confused by the word *reversal* and have come to do all sorts of practices in the physical sphere. In the end they will fall into emptiness. Is this not foolish?

On the Medicines

When the alchemical classics and writings of the masters speak of gathering medicines and refining gold elixir, they are referring to primordial, formless, immaterial realities, not to mundane, physical, material medicines and not to substances in the human body.

After people are born, they accept the false and lose the real, expending their naturally complete treasure to the point of exhaustion, so that the body becomes pure mundanity, full of aberrant energies, as if afflicted with a serious illness, death being just a matter of time. Because of this, if not for genuine effective "medicine," they have no way to restore the mundane to the celestial and preserve essence and life.

What is genuine effective medicine? It is primordial, true, unified energy; it is primordial vitality, energy, and spirit, the "three treasures." The primordial, true, unified energy is also called true seed. It does not descend into material form; it is ultimate nonbeing yet contains ultimate being, is ultimate emptiness yet contains ultimate fulfillment. Truly empty yet subtly existing, it governs the three treasures of vitality, energy, and spirit.

The three treasures are also not physical things but formless realities. As an ancient adept said, the vitality is not sexual vitality, the energy is not metabolic energy, the spirit is not the thinking mind. Though they are three, the treasures all return to one primordial energy; the three combine into one energy, the one energy differentiates into three.

Gathering medicines means gathering these three treasures of one energy; operating the fire of reality to refine them, one produces elixir which transmutes all mundane energies in a person returning to unadulterated celestial energy, the pure, undefiled original being. It is like a person with an illness using medicine to cure it and become well.

Medicine here is a metaphor, but students in later generations took the alchemical classics literally and thought the medicines were material substances; they gathered herbs in the mountains and compounded them into potions, vainly hoping for long life. Some gathered minerals and cooked them into elixirs, which they ingested, imagining they would thereby become able to fly aloft. What they did not realize was that material medicines can only cure physical ailments and cannot cure immaterial ailments. Immaterial sickness can only be cured by gathering the primordial, true, unified energy.

The *Triplex Unity* says, "It is easy to work with what is of the same species, hard to work with what is not of the same kind." *Understanding Reality* says, "When bamboo breaks, you need bamboo to mend it; if you want to hatch chickens, you need eggs. Whatever is not of the same kind is a waste of effort; how can that compare to true lead combining with the potential for sagehood?" The true lead is precisely this primordial, true, unified energy; all those who take ordinary drugs to be herbs of immortality should wake up when they read this.

On the Firing Process

The "firing process" spoken of in the alchemical classics and writings of the masters is a metaphor for the order of practical spiritual work. Generally speaking, in spiritual work there is that which comes first and that which comes later; there are times for relaxation and hurry, advance and withdrawal. It will not do to put off for later what must be done first, or to do first what must be done later; it will not do to relax when one should hurry, or to hurry when one should relax. It will not do to withdraw when one should advance, or to advance when one should withdraw. It is as when one cooks medicines over a fire, there are times for gentle firing, intense firing, and stopping at sufficiency. So the order of application of effort in cultivation of reality is represented as a "firing process."

However, the firing process of spiritual work is not a matter of years, months, days, or hours; it applies to every moment—doing first what should be done first, doing later what should be done later, hurrying when one should hurry, relaxing when one should relax, advancing when one should advance, withdrawing when one should withdraw, shifting effectively at the appropriate times.

What should be done first is to establish inward discipline; what should be done after that is to deflect externals. When one should hurry is when applying effort; when one should relax is when gently nurturing. When one should advance is when celestial energy is insufficient and should be advanced; when one should withdraw is when mundane energy arises and should be withdrawn.

This is the true principle of the firing process. It is not the yogins' theory of advancing the yang fire at midnight, withdrawing the yin convergence at noon, and bathing at six A.M. and six P.M. It is also not the theory of advancing the yang fire at the winter solstice, withdrawing the yin convergence at the summer solstice, and bathing at the vernal and autumnal equinoxes.

The natural world has its own times, and humans have their own times; the times of the natural world cannot be precisely identified with human times. Winter, summer, spring, fall, midnight, noon, six in the morning, and six in the evening—in the human being, these times are present at every juncture. An ancient classic says, "No need to look for midnight and noon in the sky; there is arising of yang within the body." The arising of yang is midnight / winter solstice; the arising of yin is noon / summer solstice. Yang joining yin is six A.M. / vernal equinox; yin joining yang is six P.M. / autumnal equinox. These are the living times and seasons, not the lifeless times and seasons of the calendar.

The firing process as explained in the sixty-four hexagrams of the *I ching* also indicates the principles of advancement and withdrawal of yin and yang, teaching people to make adjustments according to the situation, adapting effectively in application of effort; it does not teach people to practice according to the sequence of the sixty-four hexagrams. *Understanding Reality* says, "Setting up symbols in the hexagrams is based on descriptions of the modes; understanding the symbol, forget the words—the idea is clear of itself. The whole world is astray, only clinging to symbols, acting out the energies of the hexagrams in hopes of flying aloft."

When reading such books, you should understand the ancients' intent in choosing symbols and making verbal formulations; once the meaning is realized, the symbol can be forgotten. The thousands of books on the path of cultivating reality are all in symbolic language; though the images they choose are not the same, they are all used to clarify yin and yang, going along and reversing, the medicines, real and false, and the order of the firing process. They do not talk about anything other than this. Since I have truly understood the meanings in the symbols through the guidance of teachers, I dare not keep this knowledge to myself and want to make it public, for those of discernment. Therefore I have taken essential points from the alchemical classics and produced diagrams to communicate their reality, analyzing and clarifying right and wrong to resolve students' doubts. The rest may be deduced by analogy.

1. THE STATE IN THE WOMB

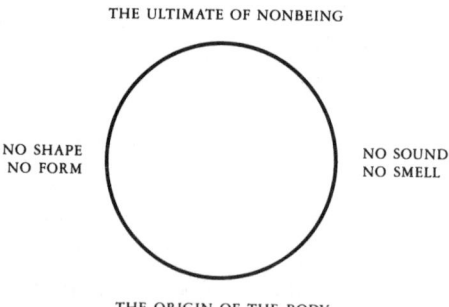

Before one's parents give birth to one's body, when the yin and yang energies of male and female interact, in the midst of darkness there is a point of living potential, which comes forth from nothing. This is what is called the primordial, true, unified generative energy. This energy enters into the sperm and ovum, fusing them into one: formless, it produces form; immaterial, it produces substance. The internal organs, the organs of sense, and the various parts of the body evolve, all becoming complete naturally. Even the mother who carries the unborn child does not know how this happens as it does.

Inexperienced students, unaware of this principle, imagine that when people are in the womb their umbilical cord conveys the mother's breath, so that the fetus exhales when the mother exhales and inhales when the mother inhales, gradually evolving and forming. This is not so. Respiration is acquired energy; how can acquired energy cause the sperm and ovum to evolve into a body? And how could breath enter into the womb? What they do not realize is that in the mother's womb there is only the primal point of generative energy, undifferentiated, which first causes the embryo to congeal, then nurtures the embryo, and eventually causes it to become complete. The whole process is accomplished by this generative energy, with nothing else mixed in.

At this point, though there is the human form, there is no human way; nothing in the world, not even water, fire, or weapons, can harm one here. Emotions and desires cannot reach one here. Ultimately, in reality there is just openness alone. When the ancient immortals taught people to practice the Tao to return to what they were like before their parents gave birth to them, they meant returning to the state of openness, beyond sense. Where there is no sense is the ultimate of nonbeing. The ultimate of nonbeing is the extreme of nothingness, where there is only nonbeing.

2. THE STATE OF THE INFANT

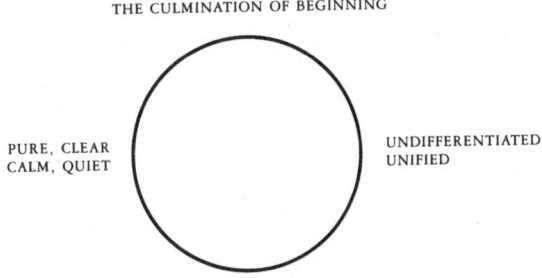

After ten months in the womb, the fetus is fully developed; like a ripe melon falling off the stem, the fetus breaks out of the amnion and emerges, feet toward the sky and head toward the earth. With a cry the infant first comes in contact with the air, breathing it in so that it mixes with the primordial original energy within. The primordial is the body; the temporal is the function. The temporal depends on the primordial to breathe in and out, while the primordial depends on the temporal to nurture the vascular system.

Furthermore, at the moment of that cry, the conscious spirit of the generations of history also enters into the opening and merges with the primordial original spirit. The original spirit depends on the conscious spirit to subsist, while the conscious spirit depends on the original spirit for effective awareness.

Nevertheless, though the newborn infant has acquired energy and acquired spirit, still the primordial governs the temporal and the temporal obeys the primordial. The primordial and the temporal merge into nondifferentiation; without discrimination or cognition, there is one reality alone.

When the ancient immortals taught people to find out the point of birth, they meant to find out the beginning of birth, which is to find out the appearance of the infant. Deluded people, not knowing this, have erroneously said that "the point of birth" means the woman's birth canal. This is wrong. The beginning of birth, the appearance of the infant, means pure clarity, without blemish; this is the germ and embryo of sages, the root and sprout of immortals and buddhas. Here one is ungraspable and invulnerable, because one is mindless.

Being mindless, one is not hindered by birth and death; there are no calamities, no troubles. This is the image of the culmination of beginning. The culmination of beginning is the final limit of beginning, before getting mixed up in temporal conditioning. Though merged with the temporal, it is the primordial alone which controls things. This is because it is at the culmination of beginning; it is beginning as it springs from nonbeing.

3. THE STATE OF THE CHILD

After a person has grown from infancy to the point where he can walk, speak, and follow others' directions, he is called a child. The infant has no discrimination or cognition, but the child already has discrimination and cognition, so it is as if floating clouds are dotting the sky. Having discrimination and cognition derives from the culmination of beginning eventually reaching the culmination of the great. The culmination of the great means the limit of the universal, which must be followed by the arising of the particular; when yang culminates, it must shift to yin. At this moment, however, the particular has not yet come, yin has not yet arisen; it is still the primordial that does things, while the acquired is latent. Though there is discrimination and cognition, the encrustation of the faculties has not yet taken place and acquired influences have not yet invaded; when hungry, one just eats, and when cold, one just puts on clothes. Joy, anger, sadness, and happiness come and go, vanishing as they arise; one does not know about differences of wealth and status, but is spontaneous and has no extraneous thoughts.

This, too, is the germ and embryo of sages, the root and sprout of immortals and buddhas. The ignorant consider the child to be the infant, but this is wrong. They both are imbued with natural reality, but they are different in terms of state, the infant being higher and the child lower, and they are also different in terms of intellectual knowledge, which the infant does not have but the child does. Therefore, to represent return to the origin, the ancient immortals chose the fundamental aspect of the infant and not the naive aspect of the child.

4. YIN AND YANG DIVIDE

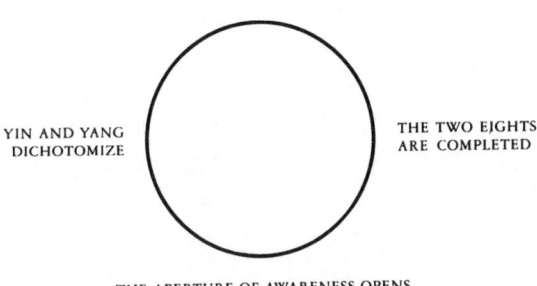

After people grow from childhood to the point where the energies of the two eights are complete, yang culminates and yin arises, opening an aperture; yin and yang divide, each dwelling on one side. Then there is artificiality within the real; here intellectual knowledge gradually develops, and good and bad are discriminated. This is the division of the culmination of the universal, dichotomizing yin and yang.

The completion of the energies of the two eights is like the upper and lower crescents of the moon joining into one shining orb, which symbolizes the culmination of primordial yang, like the culmination of the great, the culmination of the universal. When yang culminates, it must turn to yin, as when the universal culminates, unity divides into yin and yang, which separate as two.

The ignorant take such talk of two eights and production of yin to mean a boy's emission of yin vitality (semen) at the age of sixteen. This is wrong. Considering how some boys emit semen at fourteen or fifteen, some at sixteen or seventeen, and some at eighteen or nineteen, since there is no set age for this, we know that the two eights refer not to people's age but to the fullness of energy.

5. THE FIVE ELEMENTS SEPARATE

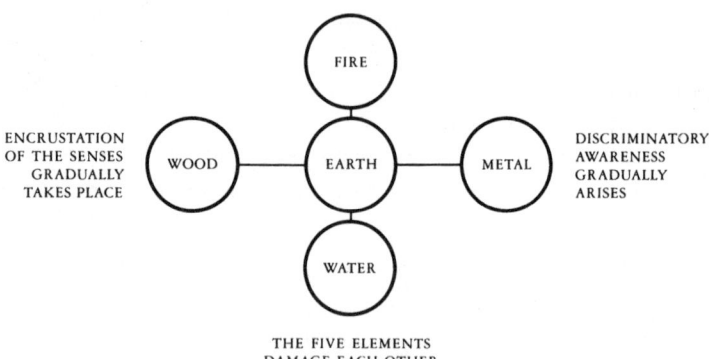

THE FIVE ELEMENTS
DAMAGE EACH OTHER

Once yin and yang divide, the five elements also become aberrated. The five elements—metal, wood, water, fire, and earth—represent sense, essence, vitality, spirit, and energy. In the primal state, these elements foster one another in harmonious union and are manifested in action as the five virtues of benevolence, justice, courtesy, wisdom, and truthfulness.

In the conditioned state, the five elements are imbalanced and damage each other; this manifests in action as the five rebels of joy, anger, sadness, happiness, and desire.

When the five elements are united, the five virtues are present and yin and yang are one. When the five elements are fragmented, the five rebels rise up and yin and yang are confused.

Once the five elements separate, discriminatory awareness gradually arises, and the encrustation of the senses gradually takes place; the real retreats and the artificial assumes authority. Now even the state of the child is lost.

The ignorant assign the five elements variously to five internal organs, but this is wrong. The five internal organs, having form and substance, are inns for the conditioned five elements, not the gardens of virtues of the primal five elements. If you identify the five organs with the five elements, how can the five organs divide and unite?

The five elements differ in being either primal or conditioned; the primal originate before birth, the conditioned emerge after birth. The primal produce sages, the conditioned produce ordinary people. Though the five elements are divided into primal and conditioned, they are all alive and do not have fixed positions.

6. ACQUIRED CONDITIONING RUNS AFFAIRS

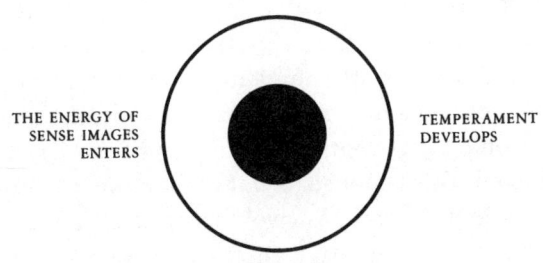

YIN IS PRODUCED WITHIN YANG

Yin and yang divided, the five elements separated, once conditioning mixes in, the primordial retreats; at this point the acquired temperament emerges, and external impacts come and condition the senses, which then beckon emotions and desires. Pristine purity is gradually invaded by mundane energy. Once mundane energy enters, it gradually grows, and celestial energy gradually wanes away. Indulgently pursuing desires, one eventually becomes totally subservient to them.

The ignorant think that the temperament is the real nature, but this is not so. The real nature is the nature as divinely decreed and belongs to the primordial; this is beneficial to people. The temperament is the nature created by people and emerges from acquired conditioning; this is harmful to people. How can acquired nature be identified with primal nature?

7. PURE MUNDANITY, NOTHING CELESTIAL

WHEN THE OIL IS USED UP,
THE LAMP GOES OUT

WHEN THE MARROW IS EXHAUSTED,
THE PERSON DIES

As acquired conditioning runs affairs, mundanity increases and the celestial retreats, day after day, year after year. Inwardly, myriad thoughts cause trouble; outwardly, myriad things coerce. Under inward and outward attack, the celestial energy wanes away and the whole being becomes totally mundane; as the three treasures are depleted, the life forces cannot be sustained, and death is inevitable.

Ignorant people think that when they end their days and die is a matter of fate, but this is not so. What human life depends on is positive energy; as long as any positive energy at all remains, one does not die. And as long as negative energy is incomplete, one does not die. If one goes along and lets the negative mundane energy extinguish the positive celestial energy, this is looking for the way to death on one's own—what has it got to do with fate?

The foregoing seven diagrams represent the process of producing humans, going along with the usual natural process: the next seven represent the process of producing immortals, reversing the usual natural process.

1. REFINING THE SELF, SETTING UP THE FOUNDATION

The path of cultivating reality is the path of restoration and return. Restoration means causing the self which has gone to come back;

return means regaining the celestial positivity which has been lost. This means restoration and return of the original, real celestial positivity in the midst of total mundanity.

Once people's conditioning runs affairs, they become totally mundane, so the primordial celestial energy wanes away to the verge of exhaustion. Without the work of restoration, how can that which is lacking be recovered, how can that which is lost be regained?

The work of restoration begins with refining the self and setting up the foundation. Refining the self means burning away temporal accretions encrusting the senses, temperamental biases, and all acquired energies with which one has become imbued by habituation. This means quelling anger and cupidity, conquering the self, and returning to order.

If one can quell anger and cupidity, conquer oneself, and return to order, one will be free from wishful thinking and rumination, and will be imperturbable and unwavering. This fundamental stability is like the necessity of building a foundation first when you build a house; when the foundation is strong and stable, it will be able to sustain the weight of the house as it is built. So self-refinement is in setting up the foundation; setting up the foundation is not other than self-refinement.

The ignorant think that refining the self means guarding the heart and that setting up the foundation means stopping the flow of semen. This is wrong. The work of self-refinement is only finished when mundanity is ended and the celestial is pure; until this is accomplished, the work cannot be stopped. If one thinks that guarding the heart and stopping the flow of semen are refining the self and setting up the foundation, how will one be able to complete the great work of the gold elixir?

An ancient immortal said, "Restoring the elixir takes place at once; refining the self requires ten months." So we know it is not a matter of guarding the heart and stopping the semen.

2. THE NATURAL, INNOCENT TRUE MIND

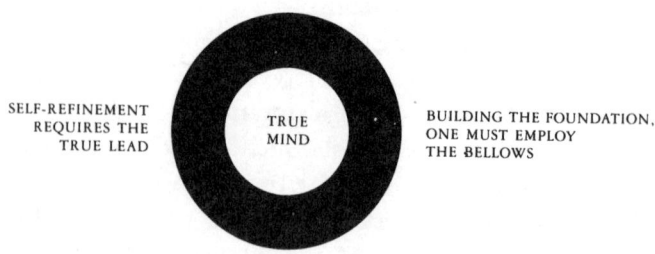

THERE IS WHITE WITHIN BLACK
MALE WITHIN FEMALE

Refining the self and setting up the foundation are not a matter of forced control, forced effort, or austere practices. What the work requires is first to recognize the natural, innocent true mind, and then to use this true mind to refine the self. Then a point of celestial energy emerges within the darkness; this is called true consciousness. When the true consciousness appears, right or wrong, false and true, are distinctly clear; one will not be compelled by desire for things and will not be influenced by sense objects, so self-refinement is very easy.

If one cannot find the true mind, then false and true will not be distinguished, right and wrong will not be clear; so even if one uses the mind to control the mind, after all it is the human mind at work, with repression and force. This is what is meant by the saying, "If you try to get rid of errant thoughts, that will increase the ailment; to try to head for reality is also amiss." How can one reach the selfless state in this way?

The ignorant mistake the human mentality for the true mind. This is wrong. The true mind is mindless; only the mindless mind is the naturally innocent mind. With this natural innocent mind, one will have no trouble mastering oneself. The *Hundred Character Inscription* says, "Knowing the original progenitor in action and repose, having no concern, who else do you seek?" San-feng said, "When building the foundation, you should use the bellows; when refining the self, you need the true lead." The original progenitor, the bellows, and the true lead, are all different names for the natural, innocent true mind.

Ah, but is the natural, innocent true mind easy to know? If you know it, then by attaining this one thing, myriad tasks are done.

3. THE CELESTIAL GROWS, THE MUNDANE WANES

Having found the natural, innocent true mind, the autonomous host sits peacefully in the center. Effort for the Tao decreases daily, while accomplishment increases daily. The celestial energy gradually grows; the force of mundanity gradually wanes. Growing and growing, waning and waning, until there can be no more growth or waning, this is the ultimate accomplishment.

The ignorant think that by sitting quietly, inactive, tranquil, indifferent, empty, the celestial energy will increase of itself and the force of mundanity will decrease of itself. This is wrong. The restored elixir is the restoration of the celestial within the mundane. If you want to restore the celestial by quiet sitting without action and tranquil indifference, how can the celestial return by itself, how can the mundane withdraw by itself?

Understanding Reality says, "Even if you know the cinnabar and lead, if you do not know the firing process, it is useless. It all depends on the power of practice; the slightest deviation, and you will fail to crystallize the elixir." By this we can know the way to foster the celestial and withdraw the mundane.

4. ASSEMBLING THE FIVE ELEMENTS

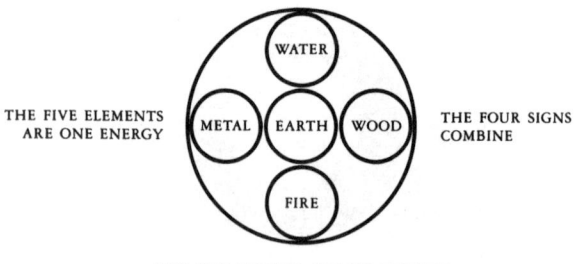

THE FIVE VIRTUES ARE ALL PRESENT
THE THREE TREASURES RETURN TO ONE

For the celestial to grow and the mundane to wane requires knowledge of assembling the five elements; when the five elements are assembled, the great Tao may be aspired to. The work of assembling is a matter of extracting the primordial five elements from the midst of the conditioned five elements. The conditioned five elements overcome one another, while the primordial five elements foster one another. When the five elements foster one another, they are integrated with the celestial design; this is the five elements as one energy, the combining of the four signs.

Ignorant people think that assembling the five elements means mentally drawing the energies of the heart and genitals up and down to mix with each other, and conveying the energies of the liver and lungs left and right to join each other. This is wrong. The energies of the internal organs are physical, and whatever is physical is acquired; it becomes, and so also decays. How can this crystallize the permanent, indestructible jewel of life?

5. YIN AND YANG MERGE

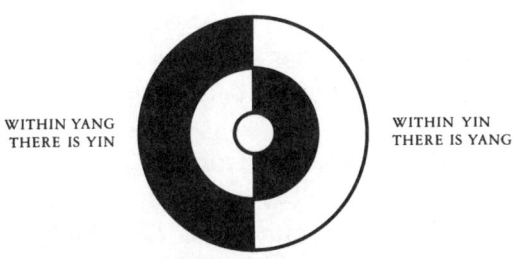

The five elements particularize from within yin and yang. When the five elements are assembled and united, this means yin and yang merge into one. When yin and yang merge, the gold elixir forms; this is the state of the child.

Nevertheless, the energy of acquired conditioning has still not disappeared. Yet even though the energy of acquired conditioning has not yet disappeared, since the primordial has been restored, conditioning submits to it and cannot cause harm. By doing yet another level of work from this point on, the gold elixir can be perfected.

The ignorant think that the merging of yin and yang means the mixing of the heart and genital energies, or the meeting of the active and passive energy channels, or the intercourse of man and woman. This is wrong. The gold elixir is made by the crystallization of the energy of primordial nothingness; it cannot be formed by temporal, physical substances.

6. UNIFIED ENERGY

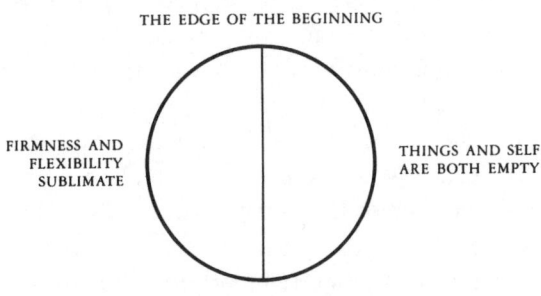

When yin and yang return to integral completeness, the state of the child is already restored; from this point on the natural fire of reality operates to burn away residual conditioning and return to the state where there is no discriminatory knowledge, where the spirit is secreted and the energy clusters. This is what is referred to as a man being pregnant, the "fetus" being the state of the infant. This is the point where the living body becomes imbued with energy; this is the edge of the beginning, and it is also called the universal One containing true energy.

Ignorant people think that formation of the spiritual embryo is done by ingesting mineral or vegetable substances. This is wrong. What is formed by ingesting mineral or vegetable substances is no more than clumps of blood or flesh. This only promotes death, and there is no hope of anything else.

7. ABSOLUTELY OPEN NOTHINGNESS

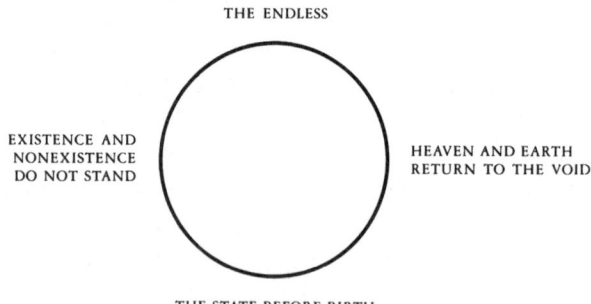

When the spiritual embryo has formed, then one applies ten months of incubation, the work of gently nurturing it, operating the natural fire of reality to forge and refine it from vagueness to clarity, from weakness to strength. When the cluster of mundanity has been stripped away, the embryo is fully developed, the elixir is done; like a ripe melon dropping off the vine, one suddenly breaks through the undifferentiated, bursts out with the pure spiritual body, leaps into the realm of absolutely open nothingness, and transcends the world. This is the state before birth, and is also the state of the endless. When the path leads back to the endless, body and mind are both sublimated and one merges in reality with the Tao. This is as much as a person can do.

The ignorant project the spirit by staring in mirrors, by silently concentrating on the top of the head, or by facing a wall and forgetting the body. This is wrong. The spirit liberated by the gold elixir is the celestial spirit, while the spirit projected by all the quietistic practices is the mundane spirit. The celestial spirit is eternal, unborn and unperishing; the mundane spirit, not having undergone refinement, is subject to reincarnation. Unless one attains the science of the gold elixir to transform it, even if one can project and recall the mundane spirit at will and can know the past and future, one cannot escape transmigration. This is referred to by the saying, "Even if you last thousands of aeons, in the end you will fall into utter destruction."

These last seven diagrams represent the process of producing immortals, reversing the usual natural process. The foregoing fourteen diagrams give a general idea of going along with creation and reversal of creation. Following this I will bring up essential symbolic terms, distinguish correct and erroneous interpretations, and give the true meanings, so that students may understand analogous terms.

THE GOLD ELIXIR

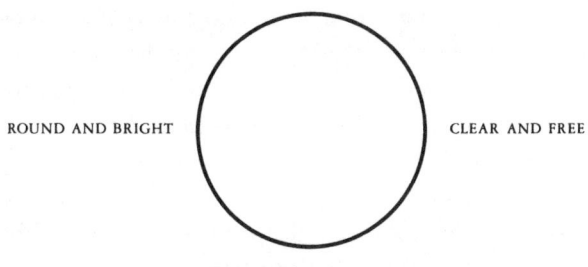

Gold is something stable and incorruptible; an elixir pill is something round, complete, luminous, pure, without defect. Ancient immortals used the term *gold elixir* as a metaphor of the essence of true consciousness, which is fundamentally complete and illumined.

In Confucianism, this essence is called the universal ultimate; in Buddhism, it is called complete awareness; in Taoism, it is called the gold elixir. Though there are three names, the reality is one. Confucians who cultivate this become sages; Buddhists who cultivate this become buddhas; Taoists who cultivate this become immortals. The adepts of all three teachings consider the fundamental true essence to be the basis of attainment of the Way.

The ignorant who do not know this consider the gold elixir to be a potion made from minerals. This is wrong. The true essence is matured through firing in the furnace of Creation, and lasts as long as heaven and earth, having the same light as sun and moon; how can it be made by mundane material substances?

THE HEART OF HEAVEN AND EARTH

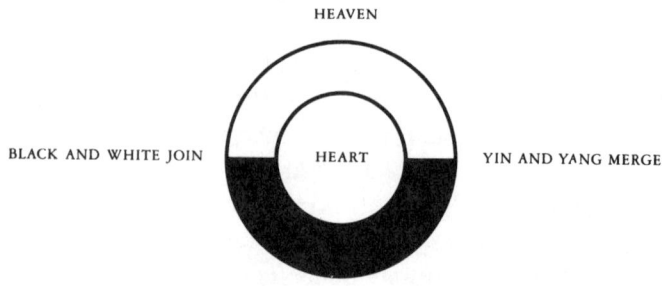

The first essential step in cultivating reality is to find the heart of heaven and earth. The heart of heaven and earth, the universal mind, is what has been previously referred to as the natural, innocent true mind. This mind is subtle and recondite, and is not easily manifested; it only shows a glimpse when "light appears in the empty room" and "within darkness, suddenly there is illumination."

Heaven is associated with yang, earth is associated with yin; the heart of heaven and earth is the mind in which yin is not separate from yang, yang is not separate from yin, yin and yang are merged. When yin and yang are conjoined, this mind is present; when yin and yang separate, this mind is absent. It is not form, not void, yet both form and void; it is not being, not nonbeing, yet both being and nonbeing. Form and void interpenetrate, being and nonbeing cannot be established; this is ineffable existence within true emptiness. When you know this mind and keep it intact, the overall basis is already established and the rest is easy.

The ignorant who do not know this all manipulate the avaricious physical heart; some consider the active mind the heart of heaven and earth, some consider the still mind the heart of heaven and earth, some think the mind dwelling on the middle of the torso is the heart of heaven and earth. This is all wrong. The avaricious heart is the conditioned human mind with personal desires; the active mind clings to existence, the still mind clings to nothingness, the dwelling mind fixes on form. These minds are as far from the heart of heaven and earth as mud is from the clouds.

The heart of heaven and earth is unified in action and stillness, is tranquil and unperturbed yet sensitive and effective, is sensitive and effective yet tranquil and unperturbed. How could it refer to the physical, avaricious heart?

THE CRESCENT MOON FURNACE

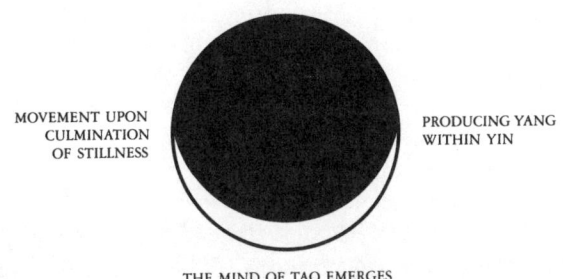

The crescent moon is the moon in the beginning of its phase, beginning to shine again after having become totally dark; this symbolizes the sudden manifestation of the celestial root in people when they have attained utter stillness. This celestial root is called the mind of Tao. A furnace is a vessel in which fire is used; because the mind of Tao has a celestial light which can be used to burn away a person's mundanity, the mind of Tao is also represented as a furnace. Actually, the mind of Tao is the heart of heaven and earth; in terms of substance it is called the heart of heaven and earth; in terms of function it is called the mind of Tao. The two names refer to the same thing.

The ignorant who do not know this observe the crescent shape of the Chinese character for *heart* and erroneously consider the physical heart to be the crescent moon furnace. Also, those who practice sexual yoga consider the vulva to be the crescent moon furnace. These interpretations are both wrong. The crescent moon furnace is the light of the mind of Tao shining; where this light shines, all falsehood vanishes and one can become a sage and an immortal.

Tz'u-yang said, "Stop wasting your time by an alchemical stove; to refine the elixir you must seek the crescent moon furnace." He also said, "In the crescent moon furnace, jade flowers grow; in the cinnabar crucible, mercury is level. After harmonious blending by the power of fire, the seeds have yellow sprouts which gradually grow and develop." By this we can know the meaning of the crescent moon furnace.

THE CINNABAR CRUCIBLE

Cinnabar is the color of fire. Because fire can refine things, getting rid of old encrustation and restoring them like new, the phenomenon of fire, represented by a cinnabar crucible, most efficacious, most miraculous, able to transmute things, symbolizes the spiritual illumination in people, which shines everywhere and accomplishes everything.

But there is the original spirit, and then there is the discriminating spirit. The discriminating spirit can frustrate the Tao, the original spirit can attain the Tao. Because of the encrustation of the faculties of the discriminating spirit through its history, it uses the awareness of the original spirit to create illusions, never stopping until the loss of essence and life.

Practice of the universal science requires using the original spirit to control the discriminating spirit. When the discriminating spirit does not arise, aberrant fire goes out; when aberrant fire goes out, true fire arises. When true fire arises, the harmonious energy is fertile and the mechanism of life does not cease; so there is hope of attaining the universal Tao.

The ignorant who do not know this mistake the conscious discriminating spirit for the original spirit. This is wrong. The original spirit is the nonpsychic spirit, its consciousness most real, its reality most conscious. The conscious discriminating spirit is the psychic spirit; though conscious, there is artificiality in it. Consciousness in the midst of artificiality is the seed of compulsive habit and routine. An ancient adept said, "The root of infinite ages of birth and death, the ignorant call the original being." The root of birth and death is this discriminating spirit.

THE OPENING OF THE MYSTERIOUS FEMALE

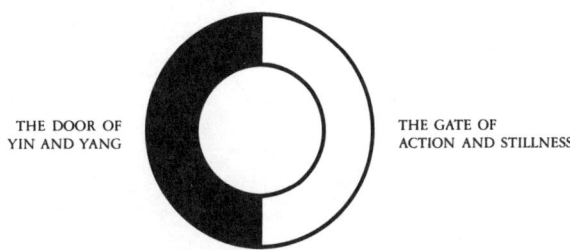

THE PLACE UNTOUCHED BY THE PHYSICAL ELEMENTS

Mysterious stands for yang, for strength, for action; *female* stands for yin, for flexibility, for stillness. The opening of the mysterious female is the aperture of yin and yang, the door of strength and flexibility, the gate of action and stillness; it has no direction, no location, no shape, no form. It is like an opening hung in space, where the five elements cannot reach, where the physical elements cannot touch. Ultimate nonbeing, it contains ultimate being; ultimate emptiness, it contains ultimate fulfillment. This is the opening within the conjunction of yin and yang.

The ignorant who do not know this take mouth and nose to be the mysterious female. This is wrong. The mouth and nose are the gate through which the breath exits and enters, not the gate through which yin and yang enter. When yin and yang conjoin, they produce immortals and buddhas; can the air breathed in and out produce immortals and buddhas? *Understanding Reality* says, "Few are they who know the opening of the mysterious female; do not act at random with the nose and mouth."

THE OPENING OF THE MYSTERIOUS PASS

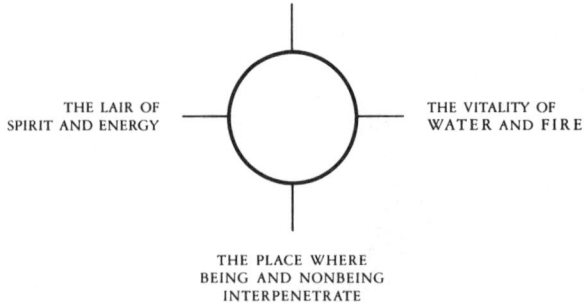

The mysterious pass is a most recondite and abstruse passageway. It is also called the door of life and death, the chamber of vivifying and killing, the border of divinity and humanity, the gate of punishment and reward, the opening of being and nonbeing, the lair of spirit and energy, the ground of emptiness and fulfillment, the crossroads, and many other names. All of these terms depict this one opening. The mysterious pass is another name for the mysterious female. Because its recondite subtlety is unfathomable, it is called the mysterious pass; because yin and yang are herein, it is called the mysterious female. Really it is just this one opening.

The ignorant who do not know this sometimes take the space below the heart and above the genitals to be the mysterious pass; some consider the center of the umbilical region to be the mysterious pass; some call the coccyx the mysterious pass; some take the center of the spine, where it joins the ribs, to be the mysterious pass. These are all wrong. The mysterious pass has no fixed position; if it had a fixed position, it would not be the mysterious pass.

Ch'en Hsu-pai referred to the point where thought arises as the mysterious pass; this seems to be correct, but really is not. The point where thought arises already has fallen into the realm of temporal form; how can it be considered the mysterious pass?

I now clearly point out to you that the mysterious pass lies in subtle abstraction, where being and nonbeing interpenetrate. *Understanding Reality* says, "Seek the image of being in the subtle; seek the true vitality in the recondite. From this being and nonbeing interpenetrate; before you have seen it, how can you imagine it?" Also, the *Four Hundred Words on the Gold Elixir* says, "This opening is not an ordinary aperture; made by HEAVEN and EARTH together, it is called the lair of spirit and energy. Within are the vitalities of WATER and FIRE." These passages truly point out the opening of the mysterious pass.

THE VALLEY SPIRIT

THE VALLEY IS FILLED WITH UNITY

The valley spirit is the spirit of open valleys. Between two high mountains is a valley; when people shout into it, the valley conveys their voices, so it is called the valley spirit. In Taoist practice this is used to symbolize the spirit of open awareness in people. This is because when the mind is open it is effectively aware; if it is not open, it is not effectively aware. The effective awareness comes from openness; this is called the valley spirit.

Spiritual means formless, imageless, ethereal, unfathomable. This spirit is that which is "tranquil and unperturbed, sensitive and effective." The so-called solidification of the spiritual embryo is also this spirit.

The ignorant who do not know this think that the valley spirit means the spirit focused on the "valley of heaven" (at the top of the head); some call concentration of the spirit in the "yellow court" (in the middle of the torso) nurturing the valley spirit. This is wrong. If you say the spirit focuses on the valley of heaven or concentrates in the yellow court, then it is not open; without openness, how can there be spirit? Not open, no spirit—how can it be called the valley spirit?

Understanding Reality says, "If you want to attain the eternal immortality of the valley spirit, you must set up the foundation on the mysterious female. When true vitality has returned to the golden room, a pearl of spiritual light never leaves." The mysterious female is integrated and open within; being open, true awareness is everpresent and does not become obscure. True vitality, spiritual light, and the valley spirit, all symbolize true awareness.

THE GOLD CRUCIBLE AND THE JADE FURNACE

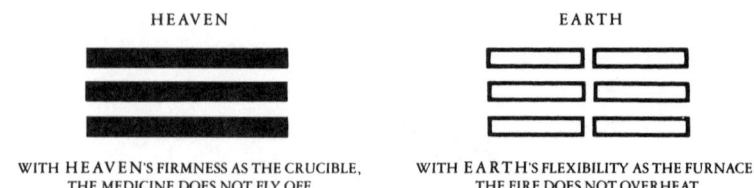

The gold crucible is something firm, strong, stable; this symbolizes single-minded concentration of will, by which one can bear the Tao. The jade furnace is something warm, flexible, even, peaceful; it symbolizes gradual progress of the work, by which one can persevere long and go far. The gold crucible is also called the crucible of HEAVEN; the jade furnace is also called the furnace of EARTH.

Ignorant people who do not know this cast iron crucibles, build clay stoves, and fire metals and minerals, vainly imagining that they will form the elixir in this way. This is wrong. This is because material furnaces and crucibles can only refine material medicines used for ordinary purposes; they cannot refine the immaterial elixir of immortality.

An ancient immortal said, "The crucible basically is no crucible, and the furnace is not a furnace either." What the furnace and crucible refer to is the fact that practice of the Tao can only be accomplished when firmness and flexibility are both employed. This is like a chemist needing a furnace for the crucible and needing a crucible for the furnace; only when equipped with both furnace and crucible can one make medicine.

THE MEDICINAL SUBSTANCES OF RAVEN AND RABBIT

There is a golden raven in the sun, which is the yin within yang; there is a jade rabbit in the moon, which is the yang within yin. Among the trigrams, the sun is FIRE ☲, yang outside and yin inside, symbolizing the presence of flexibility within strength. Among the trigrams, the moon is WATER ☵, yin outside and yang inside, symbolizing the presence of strength within flexibility. The science of spiritual alchemy is simply a matter of taking flexibility within strength and strength within flexibility, which are the two great medicines of true yin and true yang, and fusing them into one energy, thus forming the elixir. The reason that true yin and true yang are called medicines is that it is possible thereby to accomplish rejuvenation and extension of life. The so-called intertwining of tortoise and snake, and the mutual settling of water and fire, both represent this principle; it is just a matter of picking convenient images to represent the path of unification of true yin and true yang.

The ignorant who do not know this are confused by the words *raven* and *rabbit*, which conventionally stand for sun and moon; some practice the "inhalation" of sunlight and moonlight into the mouth; some practice taking in sunlight and moonlight with the eyes. This is wrong. In the sky there are the sun and moon of the sky; in humans there are the sun and moon of humans. The true yin and true yang of the human being are the raven and rabbit, sun and moon, of humans. The sun and moon in the sky are far away from us—how can their light be collected? Even supposing something is collected, it is external energy that can cause harm; if you do these practices of taking light into the mouth and eyes for a long time, they will result in swelling and blindness. So there is no benefit, but rather harm.

DRAGON AND TIGER MEET

THE DRAGON COMES FROM THE EASTERN SEA,
THE TIGER APPEARS IN THE WESTERN MOUNTAINS.
THE TWO BEASTS HAVE A BATTLE
AND TURN INTO THE MARROW OF HEAVEN AND EARTH.

The nature of the dragon is flexible; it enlivens beings. Associated with wood, among the trigrams it corresponds to THUNDER ☳. This symbolizes the flexible essence of human beings. THUNDER, though basically yang, is taken as a symbol of flexibility because there is less yang than yin. The nature of the tiger is strong; it kills beings. Associated with metal, among the trigrams it corresponds to LAKE ☱. This symbolizes firm sense in human beings. LAKE, though basically yin, is taken as a symbol of strength because there is more yang than yin.

When this essence and this sense are separated, they become temperament and emotion, resulting in injury. When they are conjoined they are true essence and true sense, enhancing life. The meeting of dragon and tiger is seeking sense through essence and returning sense to essence, meaning that essence and sense unite. Images such as the maid of the eastern house and the man of the western house joining in matrimony, the eldest son and the youngest daughter uniting, and metal and wood combining, all symbolize this merging of true essence and true sense.

The ignorant who do not know this consider the liver as the dragon and the lungs as the tiger, and say that the mating of the dragon and tiger means circulating the energies of liver and lungs in the umbilical center, in the lower abdomen, or in the middle of the torso. This is wrong. What they do not realize is that the energies of liver and lungs are conditioned physical energies; not only can they not be joined into one, but their forced aggregation will, if continued for a long time, produce an ailment that cannot be cured, hastening one's death. Is that not foolish?

INVERSION OF FIRE AND WATER

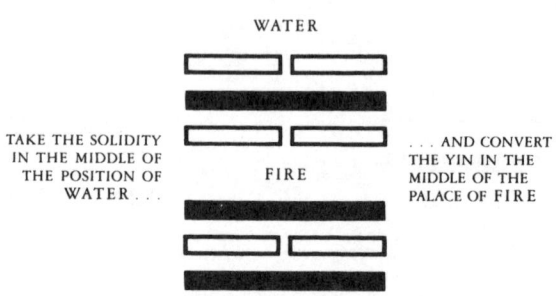

FIRE AND WATER SETTLE EACH OTHER

The trigram WATER ☵ is yin outside and yang inside; the trigram FIRE ☲ is yang outside and yin inside. Inner yang constitutes water; outer yang makes fire. The science of alchemy takes the yang in

WATER and fills in the yin in FIRE, using water to settle fire. This is called water rising and fire descending, water and fire being inverted. This symbolizes the spiritual water of real knowledge of the mind of Tao controlling the aberrant fire of conscious knowledge of the human mind.

Our real knowledge is dark outside and light inside, like WATER ☵ being yin outside and yang inside. Our conscious knowledge is light outside and dark inside, like FIRE ☲ being yang outside and yin inside. Controlling conscious knowledge by real knowledge, submitting to real knowledge by conscious knowledge, reality and consciousness are unified and crystallize into the elixir. This is likened to inverting WATER and FIRE so that water and fire settle each other. Such images as the boy and girl, the black lead and red mercury, also depict the uniting of real knowledge and conscious knowledge.

The ignorant who do not know this say the genitals are WATER and the heart is FIRE, and consider inversion of WATER and FIRE to mean conveying the energy of the genitals upward to combine with the heart, while the energy of the heart descends to the genitals. There are also those who gather the bedroom elixir, taking the boy and girl to actually mean a man and a woman, considering the inversion of WATER and FIRE to mean sexual intercourse with the man below and the woman above. Also, chemists take the inversion of WATER and FIRE to mean using lead to stabilize mercury, or to refer to building a fire in the furnace below while keeping water in the crucible above. These are all wrong. The part of cultivating reality is a matter of working on the reality; all aberrant practices and abominations dealing with form and polluted material substance are artificial, not real—how can one attain reality thereby?

REVERSAL OF THE FIVE ELEMENTS

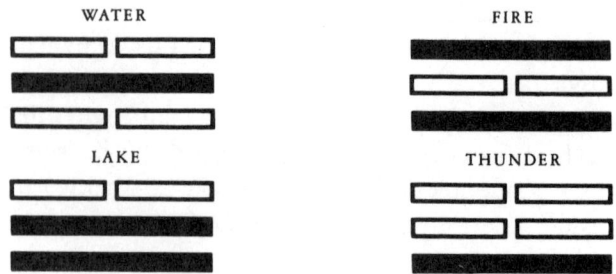

WHEN THE FIVE ELEMENTS DO NOT GO IN ORDER,
THE DRAGON EMERGES FROM THE FIRE;
WITH THE ART OF REVERSING THE FIVE ELEMENTS,
THE TIGER EMERGES IN THE WATER.

When the five elements go in order, wood produces fire, metal produces water; when the five elements are reversed, fire produces wood, water produces metal. The wood produced by fire is wood that never decays, like wood that is treated by fire to become charcoal and lasts forever in the ground. The metal produced by water is metal that never rusts, like gold in a smelting furnace liquefying, then forming an ingot with uncommon brilliance.

Fire producing wood symbolizes the fundamental essence of human beings refined in the furnace of evolution to become permanently stable essence. Water producing metal symbolizes the true sense in human beings crossing over the waves of the ocean of desire to become permanently undefiled sense. This is what is meant by the saying of the ancient immortals, "When the five elements go in order, the universe is a pit of fire; when the five elements are reversed, the whole world is made of jewels."

The ignorant who do not know this consider mental circulation of energy horizontally and vertically within the body to be the reversal of the five elements. This is wrong. What they do not realize is that the body is wholly mundane; the internal organs and external faculties are all temporary things, becoming a pile of stinking bones and flesh when respiration stops—where is there anything real? It is an impossible dream to be able to comprehend essence and life through these temporary things.

THE YELLOW WOMAN GO-BETWEEN

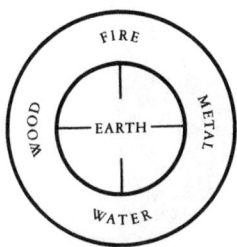

IF FIRE AND WATER DO NOT HAVE EARTH,
EVEN IF THEY INCLUDE THE FOUR FORMS,
THEY CANNOT FORM THE ELIXIR.

The "yellow woman" is the earth mother in the center, called the yellow woman because it can harmonize yin and yang and can combine the four forms. The alchemical treatises use this to symbolize the true faith within the true intent in people, which can harmonize essence and sense, and nurture vitality and energy. True intent and true faith are the yellow woman in our being; this is what is referred to as the central communicative principle.

Ignorant people who do not know this think the yellow woman go-between means mentally conveying the energies of the internal organs so that they conjoin. Then there are also mischief-makers who use glib procuresses to encourage sexual encounters so that they can take the first sexual fluids of virgins, and call this the yellow woman acting as go-between. This is wrong. The true earth has no position, true intent has no form; producing all things, containing all principles, it is possible thereby to join vitality, energy, and spirit, and to assemble the five elements—that is why it is called the yellow woman go-between. This term does not refer to mental gymnastics or to procuresses.

THE TWIN POLES OF THE TWO EIGHTS

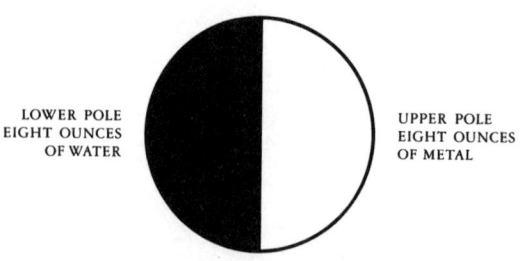

WHEN THE TWO POLES JOIN THEIR VITALITIES, THE BODY OF HEAVEN AND EARTH FORMS

From the time of the new moon, the moon communicates with the sun; on the third day of the lunar month, a slight light appears. Then on the eighth, the yang within yin is at the halfway point, like a strung bow; this is called the upper pole. On the sixteenth, the slight darkness of one yin appears on the full moon. Then on the twenty-third, the yin within yang is at the halfway point, again like a strung bow; this is called the lower pole.

At the upper pole is obtained eight ounces of the metal within water; at the lower pole is obtained eight ounces of the water within metal: the two eights making one pound, metal and water stabilizing each other, is a symbol of yin and yang joining. Alchemical texts use this to allude to the balance of strength and flexibility, without partiality, without bias, perfectly centered, correctly aligned.

Ignorant people who do not know this sometimes think a male reaching the age of sixteen is the full complement of the energies of the twin poles of the two eights, and then they stop emission of semen. Others take the two eights to mean eight ounces of lead and eight ounces of mercury, and cook these into a potion to ingest. Both are wrong. The two poles are yin and yang. The firm strength of HEAVEN ☰ is yang, and the yielding flexibility of EARTH ☷ is yin. When yin and yang mate, the body of HEAVEN and EARTH is formed, and the basis of the elixir forms. This is the meaning of the twin poles.

THE TINY PEARL

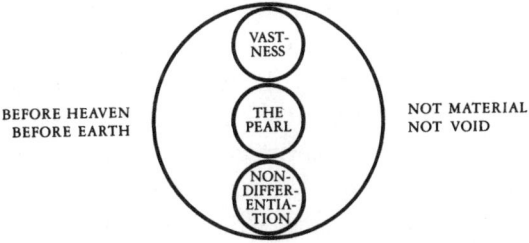

THE UNIVERSAL ONE CONTAINS THE TRUE ENERGY

Before people are born, when they are in the womb, there is an undifferentiated darkness; they are just in a swirl of unified energy, with nothing else. This is what is called the universal One containing the true energy. This energy is utterly spiritual, utterly ineffable, utterly open, utterly miraculous; it is ultimate nonbeing, yet contains ultimate being. The three bases, eight trigrams, four forms, and five elements, are all contained therein; so though it is formless, it can produce manifestations, which are endless—the organs and members of the body all develop naturally from it. Because it is utterly spiritual, utterly ineffable, utterly open, and utterly miraculous, it is also called true awareness, and it is also called the nonpsychological spirit.

In the womb, one energy containing reality is called the real energy; after leaving the womb, awareness containing the one energy is called conscious energy. One energy is the substance; this is real emptiness. True awareness is the function; this is ineffable existence. True energy, true awareness, real emptiness, ineffable existence—though the names are different, it is just one reality. This reality is formless, imperceptible, indescribable; it is so subtle that the ancient immortals called this reality a tiny pearl. Yet though they call it a tiny pearl, in reality it has no such shape; they call it thus because there is a point of conscious energy hidden in the center, and because that point of awareness contains the whole cosmos, space, and the universe. In reality it is the original energy which is prior to the bifurcation of the vast nondifferentiation of primal unity.

Ignorant people who do not know this take a blood clot of a girl's first menses to be the tiny pearl. Also, yogins take the tiny pearl to mean the outpouring of the light of the eyes after long concentration of the mind on the "hall of illumination," the spot one inch inside the point between the eyebrows. Both of these are wrong. The tiny pearl of primordial nondifferentiation is the jewel of consciousness which can produce saints and sages, immortals and buddhas—how could it be made by blood, or by the light of visualization?

The *Four Hundred Words on the Gold Elixir* says, "Primal unity contains space, space contains the universe; when you find the root source, it is the size of a tiny grain." San-feng said, "Who does not know, who does not understand, who does not act—all have gotten lost on the bead of primal nondifferentiation."

THE HEXAGRAM SIGNS OF THE FIRING PROCESS

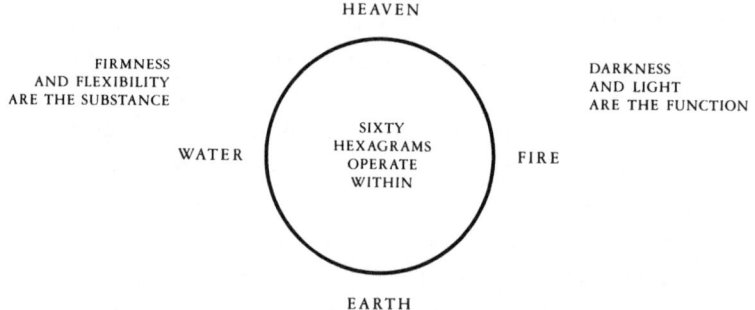

THE YANG FIRE HAS ITS TIME; THE YIN CONVERGENCE HAS ITS PERIOD.

The alchemical classics use the sixty-four hexagrams to represent the principles of the yang fire and the yin convergence. The two hexagrams HEAVEN ☰ and EARTH ☷ are taken for the crucible and furnace because the firmness of yang and the flexibility of yin are considered the substance. The two hexagrams WATER ☵ and FIRE ☲ are taken for the medicinal substances because the balance of firmness and flexibility is considered the function.

The two hexagrams RETURN ☳ and MEETING ☴ are the borders of intercourse of yin and yang; they are taken to illustrate that the use of firmness and the use of flexibility each have their time. The two hexagrams DIFFICULTY ☳ and DARKNESS ☶ are the beginning of evolution; they are taken to represent the necessity of using firmness when the fire is to be advanced and the necessity of using flexibility when the fire is to be withdrawn. SETTLED ☵ and UNSETTLED ☲ are the end of evolution; they are taken to represent how the use of firmness with the yang fire should not be excessive and the use of flexibility with the yin convergence should not be insufficient.

The remaining fifty-four hexagrams all follow HEAVEN, EARTH, WATER, FIRE, RETURN, MEETING, DIFFICULTY, DARKNESS, SETTLED, and UNSETTLED in their application, naturally being so. It is all a matter of the balancing and unification of yin and yang.

The ignorant who do not know this apply the sixty-four hexagrams to the terrestrial time of calendar and clock and perform forced practices on this framework. This is wrong. The creative energy of yin and yang of heaven and earth flows in cycles, without beginning or end, not according to the sequence of sixty-four hexagrams. The sixty-four hexagrams were made by a sage who observed heaven and earth and understood the evolution of yin and yang; the sixty-four hexagrams are just explanatory notes on the evolution of yin and yang. When the evolution of the human being and the evolution of heaven and earth are in concert, there are naturally the sixty-four hexagrams—one should not get mired in the words and cling to the symbols.

THE GATE OF BIRTH OF THE SELF

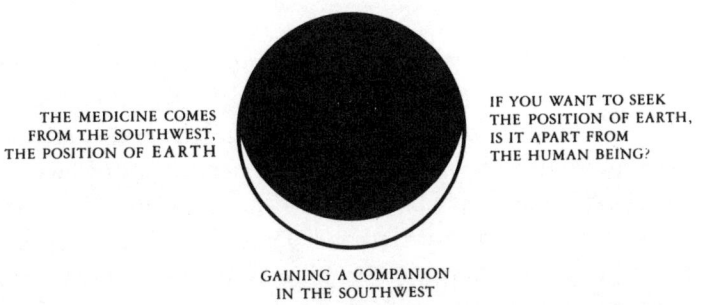

THE MEDICINE COMES FROM THE SOUTHWEST, THE POSITION OF EARTH

IF YOU WANT TO SEEK THE POSITION OF EARTH, IS IT APART FROM THE HUMAN BEING?

GAINING A COMPANION IN THE SOUTHWEST

When the moon reaches the southwest, darkness culminates and light is born. The southwest is associated with EARTH, which is pure yin. The arising of one yang at the bottom of pure yin has the form of EARTH ☷ above and THUNDER ☳ below, making the hexagram RETURN. In terms of the phases of the moon, this is the upturned crescent. These images both symbolize the sudden appearance of the celestial mind in the midst of extreme quiet. This is also called the mind of Tao and the natural, innocent true mind; it is what was referred to before as the crescent moon furnace.

If you see this mind, preserve it intact, and use it to promote the celestial and withdraw the mundane, with the sustained attention of a cat waiting to pounce on a mouse, you will naturally reach the point where the celestial gradually grows and the mundane gradually recedes. When mundanity is exhausted and the celestial is pure, one is an immortal. Therefore the southwest position of EARTH is called the gate of birth of the self, or the gate of giving life to the self.

The ignorant who do not know this think the gate of birth of the self is the female birth canal. This is wrong. The birth canal gives birth to humans—how can it give birth to immortals?

THE DOOR OF KILLING THE SELF

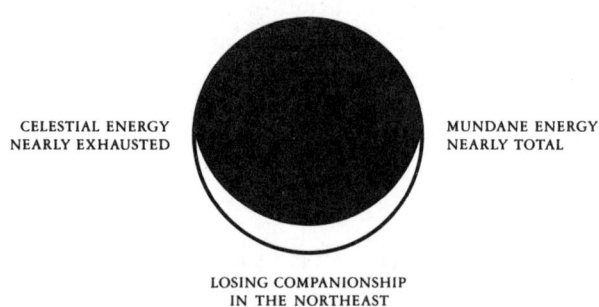

CELESTIAL ENERGY
NEARLY EXHAUSTED

MUNDANE ENERGY
NEARLY TOTAL

LOSING COMPANIONSHIP
IN THE NORTHEAST

From the northeast, the yang light of the moon is about to disappear. The northeast is associated with MOUNTAIN ☶, in which the yin energy is about to become total and the yang light is very slight. This stage is represented by the hexagram STRIPPING AWAY, which has MOUNTAIN ☶ above and EARTH ☷ below; in terms of the phases of the moon, this is the overturned bowl. These both symbolize external influences, acquired energies, stripping away the real, the original. Those of great power who suddenly awaken and turn around use this bit of remaining yang to break through darkness with light, applying effort to cultivate and sustain it; then it is not hard to return to the fundamental and restore the original.

Ordinary people who are deluded and unawakened go along with the force of mundanity as it strips away the celestial; then when the celestial is exhausted and the mundane is total, it is impossible not to die. The *I ching* calls this "losing companionship in the northeast." Alchemical texts also call it the door of killing the self.

The ignorant who do not know this think the birth canal of the female is the door of killing the self. This is wrong. The gate of birth and the door of death are both immaterial, formless passageways. By following mundanity one dies, by returning to the celestial one lives; hence the names *gate of birth* and *door of killing*. In reality, they are just one opening. When ancient immortals called this the pass of life and death, though they called it a pass, again this was just a matter of terminology—it has no location, no place.

Understanding Reality says, "Make the door of death the door of life; do not call the gate of life the gate of death. If you understand the killing mechanism and know how to reverse it, for the first time you will realize there is giving life within killing." Based on this, we can know the meaning of the gate of birth and the door of killing.

THE OPENING OF DOING

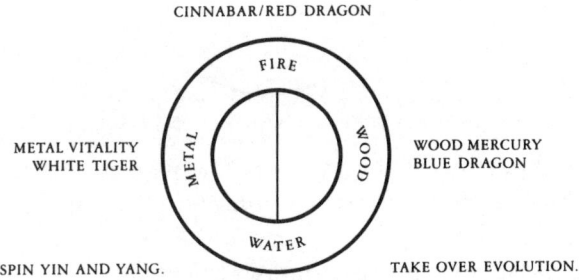

The path of doing is the work of "watching the opening with desire." Watching the opening means watching the opening of the evolution of yin and yang. The course of work, the orderly procedure—using the temporal to restore the primordial, combining the four forms, assembling the five elements, gathering the medicines, operating the fire, from restoring the elixir to forming the embryo—is all within that opening. Without the verbal communication and mental transmission of a true teacher, a slight miss causes a great loss.

The ignorant who do not know this take the path of doing to be manipulation of circulation in the temporal unreal physical body. This is wrong. The science of the gold elixir is the study of the primordial, whereby it is possible to spin yin and yang, take over evolution, reverse the mechanism of energy, invert heaven and earth, and be in primordial accord with nature. It cannot be accomplished by manipulation of the conditioned physical body.

Cheng-yang said, "Tears, saliva, gastric fluid, semen, air, blood, and lymph, the seven marvelous substances, are all mundane—if you take these things as the basis of the elixir, how can you fly aloft to the celestial realms?" Tz'u-yang said, "Saliva, semen, and breath are humanly manipulated. Only when you have elixir can you evolve. If there is no true seed in the crucible, it is like cooking with an empty pot." The adepts are those who recognize the real—the path of doing is not easy to know.

THE SUBTLETY OF NONDOING

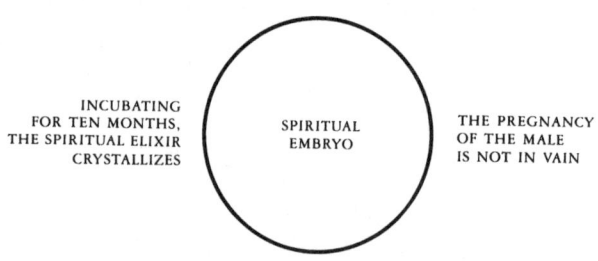

WITHOUT DESIRE, WATCH THE SUBTLETY.

The path of nondoing is the work of watching the subtlety without desire, and takes place after the formation of the spiritual embryo. This is calmly watching the subtlety of the development of the unified energy. After the spiritual embryo has formed, the temporal has been returned to the primordial; then one just uses the work of bathing and incubating, without either neglect or obsession, operating the natural real fire to bring about the transmutation by which the formless spontaneously produces form and the immaterial produces substance. When fully developed, the infant emerges, like a ripe melon falling from the vine; then the intense effort that had been hitherto applied is abandoned and no longer applied.

The ignorant who do not know this, without having found out what essence and life are and what practice of the Tao is, learn some auxiliary methods, roundabout routes, minor techniques, and immediately go into the mountains to practice quiet sitting, or shut off their senses and still their minds, and consider this to be nondoing. This is wrong.

Essence and life must be cultivated as a pair; the work requires two phases. The first of these two phases is doing, by which one comprehends life; next comes nondoing, by which one comprehends essence.

How can one comprehend essence and life by empty, quiet sitting and stilling the mind?

Understanding Reality says, "Before you have refined the restored elixir, do not go into the mountains; in the mountains, nothing within or without is real knowledge. This ultimate treasure is in everyone—it is just that the ignorant do not fully recognize it." It also says, "Beginning with doing, no one sees; when nondoing is reached, everyone knows. Only seeing nondoing as the essential marvel, do you not realize that doing is the foundation?" By this we can know that doing and nondoing each have their time, each have their function; they are very dissimilar.

MERGING WITH THE ORDINARY WORLD,
HARMONIZING ILLUMINATION

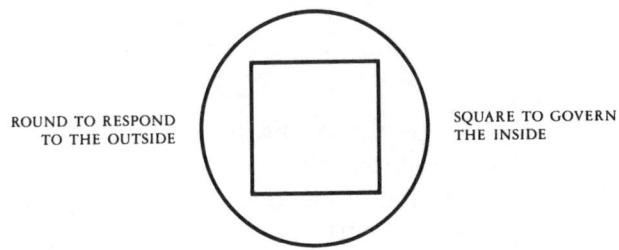

ROUND TO RESPOND TO THE OUTSIDE

SQUARE TO GOVERN THE INSIDE

MERGING WITH THE ORDINARY WORLD, PEOPLE DO NOT KNOW YOU;
HARMONIZING ILLUMINATION, THE TAO IS EASY TO COMPLETE.

Merging with the ordinary world and harmonizing illumination is the function of the great hermit who is concealed in the city. Merging with the ordinary world means mixing with the people without letting them know of one's real inner state; harmonizing illumination means harmonization without imitation, being in the world yet transcending the world. When able to mix with the ordinary world and harmonize enlightenment, one is outwardly round and able to respond to people, while inwardly square and autonomous. Using the phenomena of the world to practice the principles of the Tao, one may appear or disappear, rebel or conform, without hindrance; then practice of the Tao is very easy.

The ignorant who do not know this sometimes imagine that merging with the ordinary world and harmonizing illumination means dealing with affairs in the daytime and practicing quietude at night. This is wrong. This might be called following the ordinary world, but not merging with the world; it may be called concealing illumination, but not harmonizing illumination.

Merging with the ordinary world and harmonizing illumination has the power to take over the evolution of heaven and earth; it is the secret whereby one can appropriate the vivifying and killing of yin and yang. It is not easy to know, and not easy to do.

THE MEDICINE GOES BACK IN THE EARTH POT

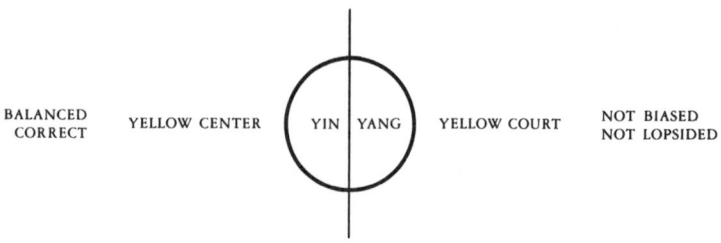

VITALITY, ENERGY, AND SPIRIT MERGE INTO ONE ENERGY.

The nature of earth is warm and soft; thus it can nurture beings. Cooking in a pot can complete things. Therefore a pot referred to as earth means a vessel which nurtures and completes. This is not ordinary earth, not an ordinary pot. The medicine going back in the earth pot is a symbol for the work of incubation, gentle nurturance, of the spiritual embryo formed by the joining of yin and yang.

Incubation of the spiritual embryo is all a matter of single-minded attention not scattering, persistently keeping to the center, yin and yang not being imbalanced. Therefore it is called the earth pot, since earth symbolizes the center; when you get down to the reality, it simply means central balance. If you keep to the center, yin and yang combine, the five elements assemble, and the spiritual embryo becomes complete. If you lose the center, yin and yang become lopsided, imbalanced, the five elements disintegrate, and the spiritual embryo is damaged. So keeping to the center, maintaining balance, is the secret of nurturing the spiritual embryo.

The ignorant who do not know this sometimes dig out earth ovens, heat up cinnabar, and take quicksilver from cinnabar, calling the earth oven the earth pot. Others melt lead in a clay oven with a reservoir of ash, and call the reservoir of ash the earth pot. They are all wrong.

Tzu-yeh said, "The true earth has no position, true intent has no form." It is because the "earth pot" which is the center has no form, no appearance, no location, no place, that it can develop and complete the spiritual embryo. It does not mean a clay vessel.

SOLIDIFYING THE SPIRITUAL EMBRYO

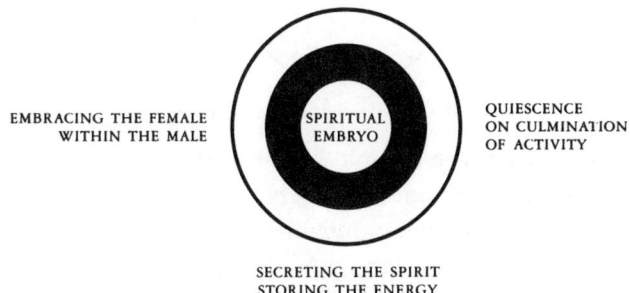

The spiritual embryo is the embryonic sage, the fundamental state of the infant, without discrimination or knowledge. When you reach the state of absence of discrimination or knowledge, the spirit is unified, objects disappear, and you enter into a state of profound trance without differentiation, entering from doing into nondoing.

Ignorant people who do not know this think that conveying the energies of heart and genitals to mix in the solar plexus region is the spiritual embryo; some consider concentration of the mind in the midtorso to be the spiritual embryo; some say the spiritual embryo means conveying energy up the spine and down the front of the body, finally dwelling in the lower abdomen. All of these are wrong. The spiritual embryo is formless and immaterial; though it is called an embryo, in reality there is no embryo to be seen. The term *embryo* just describes true awareness becoming solidified, stabilized, not scattering. If you forcibly coagulate a corpuscle of air and blood, that is a ghost embryo which hastens death, not the spiritual embryo of eternal life.

IN TEN MONTHS THE EMBRYO IS COMPLETE

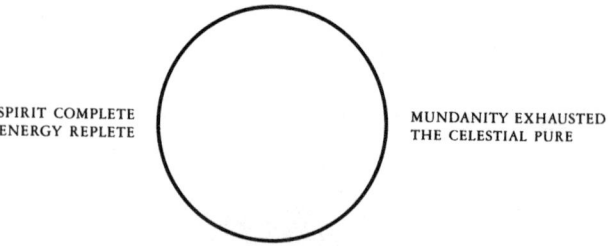

The completeness of the embryo in ten months is a symbol of completeness of spirit, repleteness of energy, mental accretions gone, acquired influences dissolved, mundanity exhausted, the celestial pure. It is like pregnancy being completed in ten lunar months; but when it is said that the method of the gold elixir is completed in ten months, this is just using the metaphor of pregnancy—it means that after the spiritual embryo is solidified, it is necessary to ward off danger and gently nurture it until it is fully developed, without any lack; it does not mean there is a fixed period of ten months.

The ignorant who do not know this are misled by the words *ten months*, and actually take ten months as a fixed period, during which they practice energy circulation, visualization, or mental freezing, by which they imagine they will solidify the embryo. This is wrong. The path of cultivation of reality, from gathering the medicines, refining them, crystallizing the elixir, solidifying the embryo, to release and transmutation, requires boundless effort—how could it be limited to ten months? By this we can know that *ten months* is just a symbolic term.

THE INFANT EMERGES

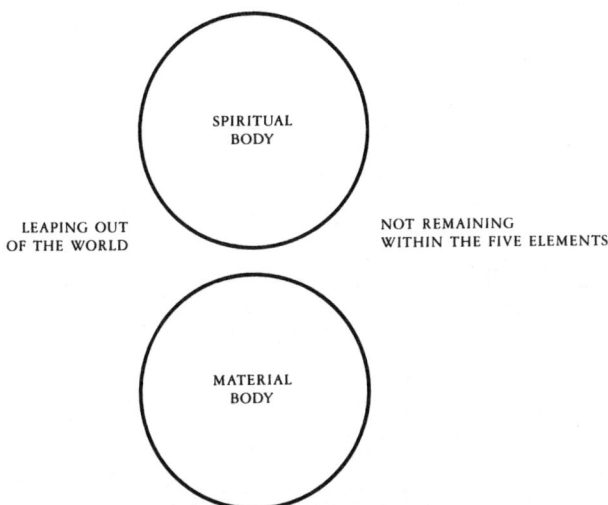

THERE IS A BODY OUTSIDE THE BODY.

The emergence of the infant means the release and transmutation of the spiritual embryo. The spiritual embryo means that within the material body there is also a spiritual body; release and transmutation mean that the spiritual body is born from the material body. Because a spiritual body is born from within the material body, this is likened to a woman giving birth after ten months of pregnancy, producing an infant. Therefore the spiritual body is called the infant. When the infant emerges, there is a body outside the body, leaping out of the world, not remaining within the five elements, avoiding transmigration, having the same life span as heaven and earth, the same age as sun and moon.

The ignorant who do not know this take the true yang within WATER ☵ to be the spiritual body, the infant; some take the vital energy in the genitals to be the spiritual-body infant. The infant within WATER is yang within yin; the spiritual-body infant is the reality of the merging and sublimation of yin and yang. As for the energy within the genitals, this is a wildfire in the genitals, and does not have the meaning of the infant at all. They should not be mixed up.

Understanding Reality says, "The infant is the unified true energy; in ten months the embryo is complete, entering the spiritual foundation." The *Four Hundred Words on the Gold Elixir* says,

"When husband and wife have intercourse, clouds and rain form in the bedroom. In a year is born an infant, and everyone rides on a crane." By this we can know what the infant of the spiritual body means.

SHIFTING THE FURNACE, CHANGING THE CRUCIBLE

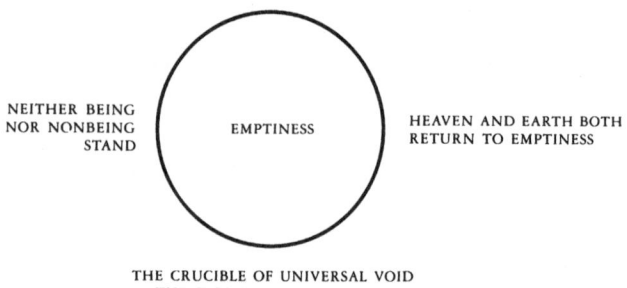

When the great Tao is completely attained, there is a body outside the body, one is physically and mentally sublimated, and one has reached the stage of a great sage, there is no further need for furnace and crucible—why should there be such a thing as shifting the furnace, changing the crucible? The reason for shifting the furnace and changing the crucible is to store the spiritual body and secretly develop spiritual powers.

What is shifted is the furnace, what is changed is the crucible. Using universal void for the crucible and nondoing for the furnace, the former crucible of HEAVEN and the furnace of EARTH, the cinnabar crucible and the crescent moon furnace, as well as the medicinal substances, are no longer used. All that is used is the spiritual body. The spiritual body transmutes spontaneously in emptiness, becoming increasingly effective with increasing openness, becoming increasingly marvelous with increasing voidness. Its marvelous efficacy unfathomable, its transmutations endless, is what is called the child also producing grandchildren, and the grandchildren also branching out. Getting to this state, ceasing effort, breaking through space, and leaping up to the supreme infinite celestial realm—this is the perfect attainment.

Students of later times who have not gotten the authentic tradition sometimes suppose that having a body outside the body is the consummation of the Tao. This is not so. *The Song of Tapping the Lines* says, "When not a single thing exists, that finally reveals the Tao; in the five directions comes through the countenance of the real person. Immortal boys and girls greet one on colored clouds, and in the five palaces of illumination, pronouncements of truth are transmitted." Seeing this, we know that the ultimate accomplishment is only when the spiritual body can transmute in countless ways.

PART THREE
Related Texts

Fifty Verses to Resolve Doubts

1. DETACHMENT FROM THE WORLD

Of worldly things, a thousandfold, not one is real;
The sentiments of mundane ties are most injurious to the being.
Cutting through with one stroke, there is nothing to bind you;
In the realm of liberation you become an independent person.

2. CULTIVATION AND SLEEP

Cutting down on sleep is really not removing the demon of sleep;
Forgetting to eat, neglecting to sleep, you cut through entanglements.
When entanglements are swept away and the mind is clear and calm,
You may sleep throughout the day and night—what is there to fear?

3. PRACTICE

Practice developing virtue is the greatest priority;
When achievement is great and practice profound, it moves heaven and earth.
Ridiculous are the foolish ones who only profit themselves;
With no achievement and little action, they dream of becoming immortals.

4. THE GOLD ELIXIR

The primordial basic essence is called the elixir;
In the furnace of the eight trigrams it is forged into a pill.
The deluded throughout the world vainly seek external medicines;
By taking these, they wrongly imagine they can ascend to the clouds.

5. THE MYSTERIOUS PASS

Few people know the opening of the mysterious pass;
Extremely subtle and recondite, it contains yin and yang.

Going along, you flow back into the road of affliction;
Coming back in reverse, this is the foundation of sages.

6. THE DISCRIMINATING SPIRIT

The consciousness which thinks is called the discriminating spirit;
The seed of transmigration, it carries the accretions of the senses.
The ignorant and deluded both play with the wandering soul;
After all, who can see the host behind it all?

7. THE CELESTIAL VITALITY

A point of celestial vitality is hidden in the physical being;
When you recognize the real, you can set your sights upon it.
It is not in the heart and not in the genitals;
Not void, not form, it is concealed in the mysterious pass.

8. PRIMORDIAL ENERGY

The primordial unified energy is in the vast undifferentiated;
It has no shape or form, yet does not fall into voidness.
When you recognize the true state of the beginning of life,
Only then will you know there is a host within yourself.

9. THE PRIMORDIAL AND THE CONDITIONED

Before birth is called the primordial;
Temperament comes along with emergence in the world.
The sages of yore and people of late are divided on two roads;
You should carefully distinguish the partial and complete.

10. THE BEGINNING OF THE COURSE

The beginning of the course is basically the primal treasure,
The subtle, recondite, true unified vitality.
It is something unadulterated, flawless, pure;
Do not misapply this term to menstrual blood.

11. THREE MEDICINES

The medicines are of three kinds—vitality, energy, and spirit;
Whatever has form is not the original reality.

Utterly pure, open and aware, these medicines
Are refined into the indestructible spiritual body.

12. ESSENCE AND LIFE

Essence and life are basically divided into primordial and temporal;
When the living body falls to the ground, it determines partial and complete.
Temporal essence and life follow the turns of fate;
Get hold of the primordial and you wield the authority yourself.

13. THE HEART OF HEAVEN AND EARTH

The heart of heaven and earth—where is it stored?
Yin and yang stimulate it to manifest a sphere of light.
Refining it in the crucible of openness and nonbeing,
Forever and ever it never wanes away.

14. THE MIND OF TAO AND THE HUMAN MIND

The human mind is like iron, the mind of Tao like gold;
One should assess them carefully in terms of subtlety and insecurity.
The spiritual capacity of transmutation has no high or low;
At the fountainhead, the living water distinguishes yang and yin.

15. BEFORE BIRTH

In the state before birth, who knows?
When silent, passive, undifferentiated,
The four forms and five elements do not reach;
The unified energy has no male or female.

16. AT BIRTH

The newborn state—what is it like?
The primordial and the temporal are one energy.
No discrimination, no knowledge, not a single stain—
The seed of buddhas and immortals, the lair of sages.

17. THE OTHER

The other is not another person;
If you mistake it for another, you are already way off.

Your child has wandered off outside—
Give it a call; when it sees your face, it will follow its parent.

18. OTHER AND SELF

The classics speak of other and self to distinguish yin and yang;
This is the realm of purity, neither material nor void.
Those who practice deviant techniques of sexual alchemy
Destroy their natural innocence in the brothels.

19. ASSOCIATES

Associates should be divided into inner and outer supports;
With two or three people as personal associates,
And outer associates likewise helping out,
Shed the dust of personal history.

20. PATRONS

People seek patrons, hoping to accomplish their practices;
Buying crucibles, smelting lead, they madly grasp for the wind.
How can they understand that the celestial mechanism transcends
    things of the world?
Depending on the power of others, they stick to their ignorance.

21. THE NINEFOLD CRUCIBLE

The number nine associated with HEAVEN is called pure yang;
The method of refining restored elixir in the ninefold crucible
Is interpreted by the deluded to refer to women as crucibles—
They will surely enter an inescapable impasse.

22. SUMMONING AND ABSORBING

There is a secret method of summoning and absorbing the primordial;
Beckoning fulfillment by emptiness, you see the emperor of the void:
In the clamor of form and sound, there is no obstruction;
Freely you spin the north star.

23. INVERSION

What difficulty is there in inverting yin and yang?
You should exercise spiritual observation in quietude.

When the mind of Tao is not obscured, the human mind vanishes;
Right away you ascend directly to the peak experience.

24. THE FIRING PROCESS

The work of operating the fire basically has no time;
Working by day, introspective by night, you kill the inner parasites.
Warding off danger, wary of peril, ever clear and calm,
In dealing with people you adjust without error.

25. THE HEXAGRAM IMAGES

For the firing process, the classics speak of the *I ching* hexagrams;
But it is wrong to ponder the lines and cling to the images.
It is all a matter of needing to understand the principle of yin and yang;
Advance or withdraw according to the time, as is indicated.

26. THE FURNACE AND CRUCIBLE OF HEAVEN AND EARTH

The crucible of HEAVEN and furnace of EARTH are in one's own body;
Stop inquiring externally after their basis.
When firmness and flexibility have no separation,
They forge the primal unified energy, the real.

27. THE CRESCENT MOON FURNACE

You ask what the crescent moon furnace is—
Within black there is white, returning after darkness.
Clearly I point out the matrix of the restored elixir
To waken the people of the time—do you know or not?

28. THE CINNABAR CRUCIBLE

Cultivation of reality depends on the cinnabar crucible;
It is not iron, not gold, not silver.
Recognizing the light of awareness, you take the fresh,
Replacing the old, you see original humanity.

29. THE EARTH POT

The earth pot is not made of earth;
The proper state of central balance is its true name.

Wood, metal, water, and fire, all gather herein,
Cultivating a mystic pearl that shines through the night.

30. THE DIPPER HANDLE

By watching the dipper handle as it turns in the sky,
You will realize that the mechanism of life is elsewhere.
Turning it around to retrieve autonomy within,
Then in the midst of the fire a golden lotus will appear.

31. THE TWO POLES

The lower pole is water, the upper pole metal;
It is just a matter of harmonious stabilization of yin and yang.
If you succeed in combining firmness and flexibility,
In the center appears the heart of nirvana.

32. CLEAR AND CLOUDY

Clear water is celestial, cloudy water mundane;
How many students make a close investigation?
Where the pivotal works moves, real and false are divided;
Getting rid of the cloudy and keeping the clear produces white gold.

33. SELF-REFINEMENT

Practicing self-refinement is the first priority;
Stopping craving, forgetting emotions, removing entanglements,
When all attachment to the senses is cut off,
There is a single field of elixir, completely clean and clear.

34. SETTING UP THE FOUNDATION

Stability of will is setting up the foundation;
Not wavering in body or mind is most excellent.
Rely on that in trouble and trial;
With no waves on still waters, there is no connection to things.

35. LEAD AND MERCURY

True mercury is not mercury of the mundane world;
True lead is not lead that comes from mines.

One is sense, one essence, the primordial medicines;
Refining them, returning to the root, there is a great restoration.

36. THE BOY AND GIRL

When the girl hides in FIRE, she is not real;
When the boy is in WATER, he cannot be followed.
But now that the opening of yin and yang has been explained,
By openness and solidity they give birth to the spiritual body.

37. WATER ☵ AND FIRE ☲

Do not seek WATER and FIRE in the north and south.
The nature of fire is to fly up; water flows down.
If you can invert the two things,
Water rises, fire descends, and they form the elixir.

38. THUNDER ☳ AND LAKE ☱

LAKE is not in the west, THUNDER not in the east;
When essence is disturbed and sense confused, their energies do not join.
When you attain the method of restoring sense to essence,
In a moment you see the true inner self.

39. MIDNIGHT AND NOON

Stop looking for midnight and noon in the night and day;
There is another indicator within the body.
There is yin and yang, movement and stillness, according to the time;
In the midst of concentration you always hear the note of high antiquity.

40. SIX A.M. AND SIX P.M.

The classics say that bathing is done at six in the morning and evening;
This describes two energies without the flaw of imbalance.
The ignorant who do not understand the meeting of yin and yang
Practice quiet sitting in the morning and at night.

41. THE YELLOW WOMAN

The pairing of female and male requires the yellow woman;
The central mediator forms the receptacle of creation.
If you ask for genuine information on the yellow woman,
Sincerity alone has the effect of harmonizing the five elements.

42. RESTORING THE ELIXIR

Why is cultivating the elixir called restoring the elixir?
When the five energies are separated, each is isolated;
When you know how to restore the original state, they all combine—
Mind and body unwavering, they form into a whole.

43. MATURATION OF THE ELIXIR

When the elixir has been restored, there is another method;
It does not require adjustment and further increase of yang.
The spiritual fire spontaneously burns in the furnace,
Sending forth a bead of light which suffuses the heavens.

44. THE SPIRITUAL EMBRYO

The spiritual embryo is not a corpuscle with form;
When energy clusters and spirit congeals, the true seed is planted.
Aware of perils, warding off danger, constantly taking care,
If you are too intent, it will surely cause disaster.

45. RELEASE FROM THE WOMB

When the spiritual embryo is released and transmuted, then it is completely real;
Ten months of work nurtures the valley spirit.
Celestial energy totally pure, the force of mundanity exhausted,
An immortal being leaps out in open space.

46. DOING

Doing is not manipulation of the physical body;
Forced gymnastics all result in injury.
How can you understand the true secret, mentally transmitted?
Unfathomed by ghosts or spirits, one revolves yin and yang.

47. NONDOING

Nondoing is not sticking to indifferent emptiness;
When you are able to avoid negligence and obsession both,
Rooting out the seeds of repeated birth and death,
Right in the center there is just one spiritual youth.

48. RETURN ☷☳ AND MEETING ☰☴

When yin culminates, returning to yang, advance the fire;
When yang is pure, on the verge of meeting, work the yin convergence.
When yin convergence and yang fire are used without error,
They forge the picture of the primordial absolute.

49. GENTLE AND VIGOROUS

Conquering demons by intense effort is vigorous cultivation;
Nurturing energy with empty mind is gentle development.
Knowing what is indicated and what is not, adapting to the time,
Everywhere gold shines, the eyes are clear.

50. HARMONIZING ILLUMINATION

Harmonizing illumination, merging with the ordinary world, is the secret celestial mechanism;
The spiritual achievement of the great function is truly rare.
Ever responsive, ever clear, ever independent,
According to the time one sheds the old and dons new clothing.

On the True Opening of the Mysterious Female

If students want to practice the great Tao and comprehend essence and life, first they should find the opening of the mysterious female. The opening of the mysterious female is the opening of the mysterious pass.

This opening has a double door, opening and closing. It is nine feet high and five feet wide. Outside is a spiritual officer on sentry; inside are a dragon and tiger standing guard. The central hall is one room which extends in all directions; in it dwells a true human, with unkempt hair and bare feet, wearing a patchwork garment of five colors and a belt of yellow silk, holding a scepter of golden light, sitting peacefully on the chair of spontaneity, leaning back without casting a shadow on the wall, a crystal lamp hung in front, eyes half closed, immobile, at rest, not impulsively looking around, not speaking at random. To the right there is a golden boy, to the left a jade girl.

Sometimes the true human opens its eyes and light fills the universe, illumining even the dark regions of the netherworld. Sometimes the true human opens its mouth and energy fills the universe, putting all demons to flight. The true human holds the power of evolution, the mechanism of yin and yang, the talisman of life and death, the handle of essence and life.

However, there are few people in the world who are in genuine earnest. Most cannot put forth intensive effort or endure long perseverance; also they do not seek out the fundamental true principles, but just think of the mysterious pass and mysterious female in terms of physical locations and do some minor techniques which are attached either to voidness or to form, falsely imagining that they will attain the Tao thereby. This is pitiful.

If one is a true stalwart, one can decisively set aside all entanglements, so that all objects are empty, and concentrate on the matter of most urgent importance, call on true teachers, form associations with worthy companions, never changing one's determination; then one can eventually come to know the mysterious pass, see the mysterious female, and finally comprehend essence and life. Students should work on this.

Essential Teachings for Cultivating Reality

The great Tao is uncontrived, based on spontaneity;
But until the work is complete, one cannot adapt with autonomy.
At the fork in the road, look for the true seed;
In the furnace of the eight trigrams, refine the heaven of essence.
The bottomless boat of method can cross the sea;
The medicines that come with the body can extend life.
Within punishment is hidden reward, which people can hardly fathom;
In harm arises blessing, which requires concentration.
The four forms blend, returning to the original state;
The five elements aggregate, growing a golden lotus.

Only when there is increase and decrease is it marvelous;
Only knowing what is indicated and what not can you enter the
    mystery.
Shedding all defiling things which bind and envelop,
You attain the state of completeness before birth.
Cultivating immortality, becoming enlightened, all depends on this;
Anything else is in vain, running to extremes.

THE BOOK OF BALANCE AND HARMONY

INTRODUCTION

The Book of Balance and Harmony is a famous anthology of writings by a thirteenth-century Taoist master of the School of Complete Reality, a movement begun a thousand years ago to restore the original principles and practices of Taoism. This collection, compiled by one of the master's disciples and still current in Taoist circles of East Asia, provides a most unusual compendium of the teachings of Complete Reality Taoism, including its theoretical and practical basis in classical Taoism.

Taoism is very difficult to define. Not only is the object of its attention by nature indefinable, but the manner of its expression varies so greatly that there is no conceptual framework that will encompass all the manifestations of thought and action commonly referred to as Taoist. Such unity as one finds in Taoism is believed by Taoists to be an internal rather than external coherence, a common source of inspiration and knowledge that expresses itself in any number of ways according to the circumstances in which it operates.

In this respect—the idea of inner unity in spite of outward diversity—Taoism closely resembles Buddhism and Sufism, both of which share many other points of similarity. Like Buddhism and Sufism, Taoism has produced giants in virtually ever field of human endeavor and lays claim to practical knowledge of the deepest secrets of mind and matter. The passage of time and the acquisition of knowledge through material science have if anything substantiated this claim to higher knowledge, even if they have not uncovered the most important point: the means by which this knowledge was acquired by the mystical scientists of ancient times.

The general idea of the Tao is beyond a doubt the most fundamental and pervasive concept to be found in Chinese thought, and as such it lends itself to use in almost any context. According to *Huainanzi*, one of the better-known classics of Taoism, the Tao is "that by virtue of which mountains are high, that by virtue of which oceans are deep, that by virtue of which animals run, that by virtue of which birds fly, that by virtue of which the sun and moon are bright." In short, the Tao is the general and specific law of the universe. Everything has its Tao, and every Tao is a reflection of the Great Tao, the universal Tao that underlies all things. So comprehensive is the meaning of the Tao that Confucius, the great educator, was able to say of the inconceivable fulfillment its understanding brings, "Hear the Tao in the morning, and you may well die that night."

It would, however, be oversimplifying matters to say that the totality of the bewildering variety of historical forms of Taoism represents a concealed unity, or that everything commonly classified under the broad rubric of Taoism partakes of this unity. It would be just as inaccurate to represent all forms of Taoism as part of a whole as it would be to represent Taoism as a welter of individual cults. There are several reasons for variety in Taoism: historical responses to different social and cultural situations, specialization in particular branches of Taoist arts and sciences, and encapsulation of spin-offs based on obsession with specific techniques.

One of the tasks taken up by the Complete Reality movement was to distinguish the source from the outgrowths and establish a practical basis for understanding and reliving the essence of Taoism. From this standpoint the Complete Reality adepts were able to uncover the place and function of all the different grades of authentic and spurious Taoism, revealing the inner workings of Taoism with unprecedented clarity and reestablishing the experience held to link all enlightened people of all times.

Ironically, one of the most comprehensive descriptions of Taoism as it is understood in advanced Taoist circles can be found in a Buddhist text, the *Avatamsaka-sutra* or *Flower Ornament Scripture*, which is held to contain the totality of all religion:

> The various methods and techniques of the enlightened adapt to worldly conditions in order to liberate people. The enlightened provoke deep faith by being in the world yet unaffected by it, just as the lotus grows in water yet water does not adhere to the lotus.
>
> With extraordinary thoughts and profound talent, as cultural leaders, like magicians the enlightened manifest all the various arts and crafts of the world, like song and dance, and conversation admired by the people.

Some become grandees, city elders; some become merchants, caravan leaders. Some become physicians and scientists, some become kings and officials.*

This Buddhist scripture uses the same idea to explain one of the most ancient associations of Taoism, that of the originators of civilization itself as people of higher knowledge attained through extradimensional awareness: "If they see a world just come into being, where the people do not yet have the tools for livelihood, the enlightened become craftsmen and teach them various skills." From this point of view, the Taoist vision of ancient Chinese culture heroes as esoteric adepts is more than a pleasant myth. In essence it means that Taoism is not, as usually thought, a product of Chinese civilization. Rather it is the other way about—Chinese civilization was originally a product of Taoism in the sense that like all successful original cultures it was initiated and guided by people in contact with the Tao or universal law.

Extravagant as this idea may seem to moderns who conceive of ancient humans as semiconscious primitives who somehow slowly evolved by fits and starts into civilized nations, it nevertheless explains something about the concentration of knowledge for which neither written history nor conventional psychology can account. It also means that the fundamental nature and mission of Taoism is not Chinese; again, as the *Flower Ornament Scripture* says "All-sided goodness abides by reality, not in a country."†

The earliest culture hero of China, one of the luminaries of the sacred Taoist sky, is Fu Xi (Fu Hsi), best known as the originator of the symbols of the ever-popular classic *Book of Changes*. Believed to have been a man of knowledge of very remote times, Fu Xi is said to have been the originator of animal husbandry and written symbols. Modern academics believe that the *Changes* signs were crude markers for use in divination, but Taoist tradition has it that special knowledge was put into the signs and extracted by civilizers of later eras of prehistory. Fu Xi is said to have obtained his knowledge by scientific study of natural, divine, and human phenomena, and the

---

*"Chief in Goodness," from Cleary, *The Flower Ornament Scripture*, vol. I (Boston: Shambhala Publications, 1984), pp. 330–67.
†"The Meditation of the Enlightening Being Universally Good," from *The Flower Ornament Scripture*, vol. I, pp. 176–81.

tradition of including these elements as parts of a curriculum of higher studies has been maintained by Taoists ever since.

Fu Xi is classically thought of as the first of the Three August Ones, the founders of Chinese civilization. After Fu Xi was Shennong, the August One who taught the people agriculture and horticulture, while his wife taught them sericulture. The third of the August Ones was Huang Di, popularly called the Yellow Emperor, who arose among people of a different race that had come into contact with the people descended from Fu Xi and Shennong.

The character of Huang Di is rather different from those of Fu Xi and Shennong, and he plays a larger part in Taoist lore. Before turning to this figure, however, there are two women of remote antiquity who made monumental contributions to early Chinese civilization and deserve special mention, one known as Guonu and one known commonly as the Golden Mother or Queen Mother of the West.

Guonu is a very mysterious figure whose great importance seems to relate to a crisis period accompanying the end of an immemorial migration. According to legend, she is most famous for having remedied serious dislocations in the psychic makeup of her people; from this operation is said to have emerged the science of the five elements or five forces, shadows of which pervade most of later Chinese thought. Guonu is supposed to have established the idea of homeland and to have introduced countermeasures to the savage rapacity that had emerged through the breakdown of the intuitive order of the human mind.

In contrast to Guonu as a figure of remote prehistory, the Queen Mother of the West is thought of as prehistorical, as living in the historical past, and as existing in the eternal present. The Queen Mother of the West is sometimes considered the first woman of civilized times to attain permanent consciousness, figuratively represented as immortality. She is of the premier rank in the sacred Taoist sky and is in charge of all female seers, both those who leave the world and those who remain in the world. The Queen Mother herself is believed to live in the Kunlun Mountains, abode of immortals living on earth and fabled repository of esoteric knowledge. There are many fascinating stories of the doings of the Queen Mother of the West and her wards in the interstices of history.

The figure of Huang Di, the Yellow Emperor, stands like a colossus on the border of prehistory. Unlike the earliest civilizers, Huang Di is represented as having assumed his political leadership while still in ignorance of higher laws. His enlightenment came about not only through his own efforts and divine inspiration, but through his studies with other human teachers. Among the most famous of Huang Di's teachers were the Original Woman of the Nine Heavens, who taught him magical arts of warfare and mastery of occult energies, which he used to overcome violent tribes; the Plain Woman, who taught him the science of sexual energetics; the Man at the Crossroads, who taught him internal medicine; and the Master of Expanded Development, who taught him the art of immortality.

Huang Di is of such importance in Taoist tradition that Taoism is sometimes even named after him. To him is attributed one of the greatest of Taoist texts, perhaps the first to be put into words, the *Yin Convergence Classic.* The earliest commentary on this text is said to have been written prior to 1100 BC, with many more to come over the next two millennia. Typical of Taoist texts, this classic has widely varying interpretations, both martial and cultural. It is very highly valued among Taoists of the Complete Reality tradition (who typically give it a purely spiritual interpretation) and is placed in the first rank of Taoist literature by the founder of the Southern School of Complete Reality in his own latter-day classic *Understanding Reality,* * in turn one of the main sourcebooks for *The Book of Balance and Harmony.*

There are also a number of key stories about the Yellow Emperor in popular Taoist literature—the classic *Liezi,* for example, *The Book of Master Lie*—which emphasize the Taoist view of politics as a lower art than self-cultivation. The fact that throughout history Taoists have taken diverse positions with regard to political matters—now passive, now aggressive, now aloof, now involved—should not obscure the central belief that there is a certain balance between higher and lower affairs that should be maintained for optimum efficiency of the human experience and must be restored when lost.

The importance of personal cultivation before assumption of leadership in society is also emphasized in the short classic *Guangchengzi* (*Book of the Master of Expanded Development*), represented as the teaching given by this illuminate to the Yellow Emperor after nearly

---

*See Cleary, *Understanding Reality* (Honolulu: University of Hawaii Press, 1987), II, 58.

two decades of the emperor's earthly rule had passed but the physical, social, and psychological condition of his person and his realm was deteriorating unnaturally. This establishment of priorities then serves as an introduction to the science of physical longevity and spiritual immortality, the former being the result of the practices conducive to the latter.

This teaching is put in terms consistent with basic meditation practices found throughout Taoism and Buddhism: "The essence of the ultimate Tao is mysterious and obscure; the furthest reach of the supreme Way is dark and silent. Without looking or listening, embrace spirit to become quiet, and the body will correct itself. Be quiet, be clear; don't strain your body, don't upset your vitality, and you can live long. When eyes see nothing, ears hear nothing, and mind knows nothing, your spirit will preserve your body, and your body will live long. Be careful of what is inside you, shut out what is outside you; being a busybody will destroy you.... I preserve unity, thus to participate in its harmony.... I share the lights of the sun and moon, I share the eternity of heaven and earth."

A commentary on the *Guangchengzi* by the illustrious poet, statesman, and mystic Su Shi notes the statement of another ancient text that the Master of Expanded Development, teacher of the Yellow Emperor, had mastered the *I Ching* hexagrams DIFFICULTY and DARKNESS. These two hexagrams are traditionally used in Complete Reality Taoism to represent practice, and the claim that this adept of remote antiquity had mastered them illustrates another common Taoist idea that is not shared by secular scholars—the idea that the full elaborations of the hexagrams antedate the kings who wrote the words to the *I Ching* and in fact derive from the original signs of Fu Xi himself. This claim is made, not on the basis of the archaeological or historical record, but on the basis of the signs themselves.

In any case, there is no doubt that the *I Ching*, the *Book of Changes*, has been regarded as a basic text by Taoists since ancient times. Early Confucian commentaries were at some point incorporated into the received text of the *I Ching*, and Confucians prized it for the sociological and political lessons they found there. Even today there are those who believe that the *I Ching* is a Confucian rather than a Taoist text. Taoists, however, regard pristine Confucianism as a branch of Taoism and have been able to use the *I Ching* for their inner teachings without contradicting the exoteric "Confucian" usage.

There are numerous programs for Taoist use of the *I Ching*, ranging from the "sudden enlightenment" understanding of the "uncharted" or "unmarked" signless process of "nondoing" to the "gradual enlightenment" understanding of the entire text as a representation of the total process of "doing," or structured praxis. Among the most distinguished contributions of esoteric Taoism to *I Ching* learning is the *I Ching* mandalas,* the body of diagrams and arcana attributed to Taoist methodologists (*fangshi*) of the Han dynasty (206 BC–AD 219) that became public during the Song dynasty (960–1278). These mandalas are said to contain both the practical meditative lore behind the *I Ching* and structured programs for reading the text.

The original written text of the *I Ching*, articulating readings of the meanings of the ancient signs of Fu Xi, is traditionally ascribed to King Wen and the Duke of Zhou, two ancient leaders who founded the Zhou dynasty shortly before the beginning of the first millennium BC. The Zhou dynasty is noted for its transition from the slave economy of the preceding Shang dynasty (1766–1122 BC) to a feudal economy.

Shang barbarism, characterized by state-sponsored superstition, dehumanization of common classes, and sheer lust for possessions, to the Taoist mind represented a deterioration of the human condition typical of societies where myth has deposed true science and material force has replaced spiritual power. The mind of the Zhou dynasty, by contrast, ushered in by revelation of the meaning of the ancient lore in the *I Ching*, is more humanistic and approaches nature and spirit with respect rather than fear.

The Zhou dynasty lasted in name for some eight hundred years, but after the first few centuries the political reality had changed drastically. The various feudal states under the Zhou suzerainty lost the ritual and ethical cohesion of earlier times; gradually at first, later at a raging pace, they began to vie with one another for preeminence, eventually ushering in a long period of warring states.

The degeneration of the Zhou order encouraged the flowering of public and semipublic philosophical and spiritual schools in the middle of the first millennium BC. With this general period are associated

*See Cleary, *I Ching Mandalas* (Boston: Shambhala Publications, 1989).

such illustrious names as Confucius, the great educator, and Li Er, the "ancient master" Lao-tzu or Laozi, believed to have transmitted a famous collection of key Taoist lore. Both of these figures are greatly honored by Taoists, and the remains of their teachings—Confucius' *Analects* and Li Er's *The Way and Its Power*—are perhaps the two most popular and influential books in the mental history of China.

Somewhat later came the great Confucian Mencius and the great Taoist Zhuangzi, who also left books that became extremely popular classics. Both Confucius and Mencius are claimed by Taoist tradition, but the latter's connection to the Taoist stream is often considered to be more obvious. The Song dynasty neo-Confucians of the School of Inner Design, who revived the inner element of original Confucianism, especially emphasize this aspect of Mencius.

Mencius dealt with political and ethical questions in a manner typical of the sociological bent of the Confucian specialization within Taoism. In contrast to the manifest sobriety of Mencius, Zhuangzi took the vehicle of humor and the flight of the imagination in order to convey certain sensibilities to the people of his time, an age of rapidly growing militarism. It may not be too much to say, in fact, that Zhuangzi and his school originated fiction as an overt operation in Chinese literature; and throughout the ages since, the most inspired and sophisticated novelists and poets have all steeped their minds in Taoism.

Other outstanding figures of approximately the same era who are also claimed by unitarian Taoist tradition are Mozi, the Tattooed One, and Master Sun the Martialist. The Tattooed One was at once a spiritualist and an engineer who preached universal love, leveling of society through elimination of luxurious living among the upper classes, and the connection of conscience to divine will. His response to the militarism of his time was to organize a group of humanitarian warriors and military engineers who traveled about constantly to defend the weak against the depredations of the strong. Sun the Martialist, on the other hand, taught the anatomy of conflict, both material and psychological, geared toward obviating the necessity for actual violence and minimizing it when it does occur.*

The final dissolution of the Zhou dynasty in both name and reality took place at the hands of the First Emperor of Qin (Ch'in). One of

---

*See Cleary, *The Art of War* (Boston: Shambhala Publications, 1988).

the most controversial figures in Chinese history, the First Emperor is also linked by some to the celestial court of Taoist inner government through his tutelage under legalist Confucian and immortalist Taoist teachers. The legalist Confucians believed that since human rule had become insufficient due to population growth and gradual loss of pristine conscience and morale, the rule of law was now needed to supersede individual will. Under the rule of the First Emperor, China was unified with respect to its writing system, its laws, and its weights and measures. Communications were opened, travel and commerce were encouraged. Private ownership and alienation of land by commoners was legalized, abolishing the ancient feudal system of the Zhou.

The short but momentous Qin dynasty was superseded by the Han. Although Western and Middle Eastern nations derive their names for China from the Qin dynasty, China's majority race derives its name for itself from this Han dynasty, so strong is the stamp of its four-century-long rule on the mind of Chinese history. The Han dynasty lasted from 206 BC to AD 9, when it was briefly overthrown by reformers in favor of the Xin or "New" dynasty, but reasserted itself in AD 25 to last until 229. The early Han dynasty is often called the Former Han, while the continuation is known as the Latter Han. An early emperor of the Former Han was persuaded by a certain scholar to authorize the creation of an intellectual orthodoxy—a combination of all the major trends of thought under the rubric of Confucianism. This enterprise led to the creation of state organs for the maintenance of this orthodoxy, which in turn produced a larger educated class than had ever before existed.

A typical member of this educated class might concentrate on one or another branch of Chinese science at different times, largely depending on one's time of life. If employed by the state as an administrative official or a professor, one would appear to be a Confucian in the daytime, but when at home at night or unemployed or in retirement one would more likely be a Taoist of one sort or another. Many women of the noble families, for example, excluded from public life yet free from the necessity of doing housework and taking care of children personally, became outstanding adepts in Taoist immortalism.

After the establishment of the Han dynasty and the ending of the early wars and conquests, a number of Han emperors took a Taoist approach to government, allowing the people to recuperate their energy and develop themselves with a minimum of interference. This Taoist influence added strength to the dynasty itself, yet paradoxically it produced an undertow of new thought and knowledge that the mental structure of the Han dynasty ultimately could not encompass. Such was the eventual deterioration of the Latter Han that hundreds of orthodox Confucian college students were openly massacred for expressing their desire to return to the way of Confucius and Mencius.

As early as Zhuang Zhou (Zhuangzi) the famous Taoist master of the fourth to third centuries BC to whom is attributed the classic *Chuang-tzu,* one finds evidence of the fragmentation of ancient Taoist knowledge and practice. Many of the "real people," whom Taoists believe guide the true progress of humankind, are said to have gone into hiding during the prolonged warfare that ravaged the ancient homeland of the Yellow Emperor. In the absence of general knowledge of the realities of Taoism the fragmentation of Taoism in both its social and esoteric forms continued apace through the Han dynasty. The arcane *Triplex Unity,* written shortly after the demise of the Han to elaborate on a laconic text of the late Han, devotes an entire chapter to specific obsessions leading misguided Taoists into aberration.

There was, nevertheless, a wider stream of Taoism running through the Han dynasty, evidenced by the great Taoist classic *Huainanzi* of the early Former Han and its early exegetical works of the Latter Han. Compiled by a king of the Liu family, the imperial clan of the Han dynasty, in concert with a small circle of Taoist practitioners and a group of Confucian practitioners, *Huainanzi,* or *Masters of Huainan,* ranges over many subjects from politics to spiritual alchemy. The *Huainanzi* book approaches the problem of Taoism's degeneration by unifying its scattered lore, and such is its scope that it is said the depths of Taoism cannot be known without delving into the *Huainanzi.* There is much in this book, however, that is heavily veiled, a compromise between the need for a more comprehensive presentation than one-track cults and the need for security in matters of power.

The end of the Han dynasty was heralded by massive uprisings, some of which were Taoist inspired. During the Latter Han, a spiritual and social movement called the Way of Great Peace appears to have stirred into action; somewhat later the Way of the Celestial Teachers appeared, as charismatics using their magical gifts for healing and social harmonization gained political independence for their settlements. The radical insurgency ending the Han dynasty tended to sort out different powers in both the exoteric and esoteric worlds. At times, esoteric kingdoms and magical freemasonries became semipublic, the more easily accepted for the disturbances caused by smaller nomadic and seminomadic nations taking over political control in what had for centuries been Han territory.

With the end of the Han dynasty, the barriers that had been set up by the self-reflection of the Han mind lowered sufficiently to allow the expression of both the fruits and the bewilderments of centuries of occult studies. For the next few centuries Buddhism flooded into China, and Confucians, Taoists, and Buddhists all worked together, sometimes by argument, sometimes by cooperation, to produce whole new skies of Chinese thought.

Three great Taoist texts mark the transition period ushering in this era, when Buddhism was still a foreign cult: the *Triplex Unity*, the *Book of Master Lie*, and the *Book of the Simpleton*. The *Triplex Unity* is said to be the first public revelation of the inner meaning of the *I Ching*, or *Book of Changes*, but it is in many places so arcane itself that nearly a thousand years elapsed before it became widely appreciated. It is closely related to a simpler late Han dynasty work.

The *Book of Master Lie* (Liezi or Lieh-tzu) is a compilation of Taoist lore ranging from abstract descriptions of the origin of awareness, perception, and thought to colorful stories illustrating complex psychological processes and jokes explaining metaphysical truths. This classic is to this day one of the most popular sources of folk wisdom.

The *Book of the Simpleton*, written nearly a century after the end of the Han, is largely devoted to the many questions involved in the studies of immortalism, alchemy, and government. One of the interesting features of this text is that it emphasizes the original inclusion of Confucianism within Taoism six centuries after the pre-Han rift that left many Confucian occultists without direction, and six centuries before the recollection of unity that characterized the Song dynasty under the influence of Buddhist panhumanism.

The interaction of Buddhism with Taoism over the following centuries produced greatly expanded Taoist canons and rites, as Taoist churches organized mass meditations like those of the rapidly growing Buddhist churches. Many Buddhist texts that were unused by mainstream Chinese Buddhism in its mature years seem to have left their traces most clearly in this great body of "religious" Taoist literature.

Nevertheless, this literature does not seem to be an imitation of the Buddhist lore so much as a reexperience of it in the native Taoist-Chinese cultural domain.

The religious or church Taoist canon is generally divided into three parts with four supplements, known as the Three Open Channels and Four Auxiliaries. The Three Open Channels are the Open Channel to Reality, the Open Channel to Mysteries, and the Open Channel to Spirits. The Four Auxiliaries are called Absolute Mystery, Absolute Peace, Absolute Purity, and Correct Unification.*

The Open Channel to Reality contains the so-called Supreme Purity scriptures, the Open Channel to Mysteries contains the so-called Spiritual Jewel scriptures, and the Open Channel to Spirits contains the so-called Three August Ones scriptures. According to old writings recapitulated in a famous Taoist encyclopedia, the open channel of communication with reality is pure spirituality, the open channel of communication with mysteries deals with the mysteries of creation and life, and the open channel of communication of spirits deals with the summoning and control of lesser forces.

In practical terms, the encyclopedist notes that the open channel of communication with reality becomes accessible through "the high energy of whole clarity, absolutely unmaterialized." The open channel of communication with mysteries becomes accessible through "the energy of highly fluid openness, aware wholeness not reifying or being possessive of anything." The open channel of communication with spirits becomes accessible through the "energy of highly fluid openness to original nothingness, reaching the hidden by profound abstraction and quieting of the senses."

Among the Four Auxiliaries, the section on Absolute Mystery is auxiliary to the Open Channel to Reality; it is based on the ancient Taoist classic called *The Way and Its Power* transmitted by the an-

---

*The idea of the open channel, according to a recapitulation of a Song dynasty Taoist encyclopedist, is associated with communication. The Chinese word that is used commonly means cavern or vault, but in Taoist lore these mystic caverns prove to contain skies even vaster than those in the ordinary world outside; they are also pictured as passages to worlds of vast skies and luxuriant earths.

cient master Li Er or Lao-tzu. The section on Absolute Peace is auxiliary to the Open Channel to Mysteries; it is based on scriptures strongly oriented toward ethical reflections of Taoism in politics and society. The section on Absolute Purity is auxiliary to the Open Channel to Spirits; it deals with alchemy. The section on Correct Unification is auxiliary to all three Open Channels; it contains recapitulations of the old teachings of the Way of the Celestial Masters, a hospitaler freemasonry turned Taocracy that normally included spiritual, social, and magical practices in unison.

The disturbance and disunion of the centuries after the fall of the Han dynasty ended with the Sui and Tang dynasties. Like the first unifying imperial dynasty of the Qin, the Sui dynasty was meteoric and monumental, laying the foundation for the three centuries of the Tang dynasty, the third latter-day golden age of China. This period is marked by the development of the major schools of Chinese Buddhism and the further codification of church Taoism. It also seems to be the final age for the academic Confucian style of the Han and for the proliferation of Taoist chemistry books.

Political struggles among certain followers of Taoism, Confucianism, and Buddhism were fostered by some of the highly placed members of the ruling house of the Tang to minimize their various threats to the established order, but other followers of the three Ways were already beginning the great reunification that was to mark the following Song dynasty. Prepared by their own practices, Taoists had absorbed much of the inspiration of Buddhism between the Han and the Sui dynasties; now Buddhism, reemerging in forms adapted to China, used Taoist sciences in their own teachings, just as early translators and interpreters had used Taoist terms to render Buddhist scriptures into Chinese.

The Pure Land school is the first of the major schools to be distinguished in China. Its origins midway between the Han and Tang dynasties coincide with the early development of the Three Open Channels literature in Taoism, and its prayer, meditation, and visualization practices have much in common with religious Taoism. Throughout Chinese history, there has always been a close affinity between the idea of the Buddhist Pure Land and the sacred skies of the Taoists where the immortals dwell.

One of the early Buddhist Pure Land patriarchs was originally a student of Taoist immortalist alchemy, but he was won over to the immortality of the vision of the Buddha of Infinite Light. Half a millennium later, the Complete Reality Taoists said the alchemical literature of that time had been confused, misunderstood; now one of the Taoist patriarchs was originally an enlightened Chan Buddhist who came to Taoism for the recovered science of life.

After the Pure Land school, the next to distinguish itself was the Tiantai school, a vast and comprehensive teaching based in theory on the "crown jewel" of Buddhism, the Lotus Sutra. In practice it was based on the sutras of transcendent wisdom with the meditations of the school variously known as the School of the Middle Way, the School of Openness, or the School of Essence, based on the teachings of the Indian sage Nagarjuna on *sunyata* or emptiness. The Tiantai school has a theoretical place for all the manifestations of Taoism in the Lotus Sutra's teaching about universal compassion; it has a practical place in its meditation teachings, where Taoist medical science is adopted to cure illnesses that the practitioner is not advanced enough to heal metaphysically.

Three more major schools appeared in the early Tang dynasty. The Chan school, the precursor of Zen that traced its origins back to the turn of the fifth century, emerged into public view during the vigorous seventh century with large independent organizations that sent developed individuals out into communities all over China to harmonize enlightenment with local conditions. Chan Buddhism is well known for using basic Taoist meditation techniques in the attempt to experience communion with the Dharmakaya, or reality body, considered most fundamental to Buddhist enlightenment. Later, Complete Reality Taoism recovered these techniques from Chan Buddhists and used them with great effect in unlocking lost mysteries of Taoism. In turn, eventually Chan Buddhists regularly adopted Taoist knowledge of medicine and exercise, while Taoists for their part attribute some of their own lore to the Indian founder of Chan Buddhism in China.

The Huayan school also became prominent during the early Tang dynasty. Immense in scope and comprehensive as the Tiantai school, Huayan Buddhism is based on the *Flower Ornament Scripture*; the teachings of Vijnanavada or the Buddhist School of Consciousness play an important part in the praxis. Both the theoretical and practical place of all sorts of Taoism in pan-Buddhist terms are represented in the *Flower Ornament Scripture*, while the Taoist idea of celestial government intervening on earth corresponds with the scripture's unifying theme of Universal Good in infinite manifestations.

The esoteric Zhenyan or Mantra school of Buddhism, which flourished briefly during the Tang dynasty, made extensive use of ritual, incantation, visualization, and other techniques close to those used by religious Taoists. There is reason to believe that pre-Tang esoteric Buddhism had found its way into Taoist circles during the formative centuries of religious Taoism, and there is no doubt that Central Asian esoteric Buddhism was again absorbed by some Taoists, notably those of the Southern School of Complete Reality.

In terms of thought and practice, Buddhism and Taoism were well prepared for the rediscovery of common ground that was to mark the Song dynasty following the Tang. Politically, the waxing and waning fortunes of the two religions during the Tang dynasty went from temporary installations of classical Taoist studies as an alternative route to civil service on a par with Confucianism, on the one hand, to persecution of Buddhism near the end of the dynasty with such severity that only the Chan and Pure Land schools survived. The Tang dynasty's political backlash against Buddhism, however, actually brought the three Ways closer together, as Confucianism and Taoism themselves were permanently altered by the Buddhist elements they included within their own praxes.

Within the context of Taoism, one of the greatest figures in the reamalgamation of the three Ways was the immortal Lu Yan, also called Lu Dongbin ("Visitor of the Hollow") or Luzu ("Ancestor Lu"). Traditionally said to have been a man of the Tang dynasty, according to legend Lu was a Confucian scholar with an advanced degree who turned to Taoism after having met one of the ancient adepts. Lu's teacher, Zhongli Quan, is said to have been a man of the Tang dynasty, but it is also claimed that he had been a general during the Han dynasty who retired into the mountains to learn the secrets of immortality.

Zhongli Quan and Lu Yan are both included among the most familiar immortals in popular Chinese folklore, but it is the latter in particular who stands out in Taoist tradition. All sorts of texts are attributed to Lu Yan as one of the functionaries of the Taoist esoteric government, believed to reappear on earth from time to time and to be accessible to mortals through mediums or automatic writers. The works associated with Lu Yan cover an unusually wide range of Taoist lore, but their most general mark is the idea of the unity of the three Ways of Taoism, Buddhism, and Confucianism.

As "Ancestor Lu," Lu Yan is considered the ancestor of the Complete Reality school of Taoism, for his disciple Liu Cao was the teacher of Zhang Boduan (983–1082), founder of the Southern school, and both Lu and Liu were teachers of Wang Zhe (1113–1171), founder of the Northern school. While so much lore has been attributed to later appearances or communications of Lu Yan that it is at times difficult to extract the early form of his teaching, the case of his disciple Liu Cao is much simpler. There are a few works attributed to Liu, including *Song of the Ultimate Way*, giving a summary of his teaching in which the affinity with Chan Buddhism is clearly evident, prefiguring the essence of the Complete Reality movement in Taoism.

"The body of illumination lasts forever," writes Liu in his song, "empty yet not empty; the mirror of awareness contains the sky, accommodating all things." Using Buddhistic terminology, this song shows the characteristic Complete Reality understanding of immortalism on an essentially spiritual plane. Liu then follows with a classic prescription for attainment that is common to Chan Buddhism and ancient Taoism: "When the home is empty and peaceful, the spirit naturally stays there," referring in typical metaphor to the practice of inward silence ordinarily used to break the force of mundane conditioning. Liu also emphasizes the common Chan Buddhist practice of mindlessness, which in Taoist terms means freedom from the compulsions of the human mentality: "Respond to people without minding, and spiritual transformation will be swift. The mindless mind is the real mind; when movement and stillness are both forgotten, that is dispassion."

This basic practice of inner silence and mindlessness figures prominently in certain kinds of Buddhist and Taoist lore, but like the "hollow" concept of older Taoism as an open channel to a vaster realm of experience, it is considered a prelude to life beyond. Complete Reality Taoism emphasizes a quasi-duality—essence and life—within the Tao. In terms that would become standard in the school, Liu Cao writes, "Spirit is essence, energy is life; when spirit does not run outside, energy is naturally stable."

The unification of essence and life, or spirit and energy, is considered of utmost importance in Complete Reality Taoism; indeed, degeneration in both Buddhism and Taoism is commonly attributed to imbalance between spirit and energy practices. Liu writes, "Don't think holding your breath is a true exercise; even counting breaths and contemplating designs are not. Even if you have cast off external concerns, if you still have inner mental entanglements, what is the difference in either case? Just observe the baby in the womb—does it know how to make subconscious calculations? Unify your energy and make it flexible, and the spirit will be permanently stabilized. The true breath going and coming is naturally unhurried, an extended continuum traveling around, returning to original life. Then even though you do not draw on it, the spiritual spring spontaneously flows at all times."

The science of essence or spirit, which is common to Complete Reality Taoism and Chan Buddhism, is held to be utterly simple, accessible to everyone, and said to be possible to accomplish on one's own, though its path is not without characteristic pitfalls. The science of life or energy, on the other hand, has a great range of complexities, contains much that is kept secret, and requires the instruction of a teacher. Complete Reality literature contains no end of criticisms of infatuated practitioners of mechanical regimens of mental and physical exercises—cultists generally characterized as being sidetracked in fragments of the science of life without the underlying science of essence.

In Liu Cao's *Song of the Ultimate Way* the balance of essence and life is maintained in a manner that came to be characteristic of Complete Reality Taoism, through what in alchemical terms is called pouring spirit and energy into each other. On the literary plane this is accomplished by a combination of images representing the use of energy leading into spirit and the effects of spirit emerging in the experience and use of energy.

"The great work takes thirty-six thousand microyears," the song continues, "in which are seasons of yin and yang." This statement refers to the idea of one year containing thirty-six thousand intervals of attention, in each of which are found the wax and wane of spirit and energy. This was considered the gestation period of the new human being. Continuous attention to the development of this mental "sacred embryo" throughout these thirty-six thousand years of normal awareness.

This process is supposed to produce a whole new being with a body based on energy rather than matter: "The steaming relaxes the passes and channels, changing the sinews and bones; everywhere is radiant light, penetrating everything. Parasites run out of the house of the earthly body." Liu then goes on to describe the climax and subsiding of the healing and renewing ecstasy followed by a return to essence, saying that you now find you have "just been on the terrace of awareness all along." In the aftermath of the rejuvenating experience, however, perception is opened: "In past years the clouds and fog obscured the Way; today, on meeting, the eye of the Way opens."

Liu continues with a characteristic reemphasis on cultivation of essence within life practice: "This is not done in a day and a night. This is our original reality, not a technique. In the dead of winter firm as iron and stone, fight back demons of mundanity, apply the power of insight. This all depends on being empty and aloof; return to purity and wholeness, and this is the clear calm land of Utopia."

The science of essence is associated with the Taoist practice of nondoing, as emphasized here and throughout Taoist literature, but the Complete Reality tradition emphasizes the ordinary need for effort to reach the state of nondoing, which in turn releases inconceivable potential. As Liu says, "In the beginning, what do you use to set up the foundation? When you reach the point of nondoing, nothing is not done." This effort does not necessarily mean formal exercise, but inner purification. Liu says: "Images of objects in thoughts should be removed, vitality and spirit in dreams held fast. Not moving and yet not being still is the great essential; not being square and yet not being round is the ultimate Way. When the original harmony is cultivated inwardly, you become real; when breathing is pursued outwardly, in the end you won't understand."

True to their Chan-like rigor in matters of essence and spirit, in matters of life and energy as well, rather than fix upon gross manifestations as did the cultists they criticized, the Complete Reality Taoists directed their attention to the source, going from the old physiopsychology to a new psychophysiology. Liu writes: "If the basic energy is not stabilized, the spirit is insecure. Let insects eat away the roots of a tree, and the leaves dry up. Stop talking about mucus, saliva, semen, and blood—when you get to the basis and find out the original source, they are all the same. When has this thing ever had a fixed location? It changes according to the time, according to mind and ideas. In the body it becomes perspiration when feeling heat, in the eyes it becomes tears when feeling sadness, in the genitals it becomes semen when feeling attention, in the nose it becomes mucus when feeling cold. It flows all over, moistening the whole body; ultimately it is nothing more than the spiritual water."

The term "spiritual water" is used symbolically for fundamental vitality and awareness; here the phrase echoes the idea that spirit and energy, the subtle forms of mind and body, are originally one. It is through the practical expression of this identity that the spiritual healing of both mind and body was accomplished by Taoist adepts. Liu says: "The spiritual water is hard to talk about; those who know it are rare. It sustains life in everything, and derives from the true energy. If you just know how to be peaceful and detached, without thought or worry, disciplined in consumption and behavior, moderate in speech, then ambrosia of the finest flavor will eliminate your hunger and thirst, and you will see the real Elemental."

The two most famous disciples of Liu Cao were the nominal founders of the main branches of Complete Reality Taoism. In the eleventh century, the middle of the Song dynasty, Zhang Boduan (Chang Po-tuan) elaborated on the inner cultivation of the subtle body, hinted at in Liu Cao's song, and clarified the spiritual essence of alchemical tradition, laying the foundation of the Southern School of Complete Reality. His writings on alchemy, especially *Understanding Reality*,* are still classics of this Taoist genre.

The inner cultivation of the subtle body is the art of opening the "passes and channels," subtle organs of spirit/energy accumulation and transmission visualized in the body. In Complete Reality custom, this exercise is a quintessential, stripped-down version of certain Taoist techniques that had been practiced through the medium of elaborate rituals in older religious schools of Taoism. The system of the subtle passes and channels is akin to certain formulations of esoteric Buddhism, which is always noted for its affinity to the Southern School of Complete Reality Taoism.

Zhang's classic *Understanding Reality* still contained a great deal of crypticism to prevent certain meanings from falling into the wrong hands, so a considerable body of exegetical literature grew up around it, beginning among Zhang's own heirs. During the twelfth century a kindred but independent movement began with Liu Cao's other fa-

*For other writings of Zhang Boduan, see Cleary, *The Inner Teachings of Taoism* (Boston: Shambhala Publications, 1986).

mous disciple, Wang Zhe. This, the Northern branch, deemphasized energetics and took up *Understanding Reality* with great interest from the point of view of their primary interest in essence and spirit.

The emphasis of the Southern school is conventionally said to approach essence through life, while that of the Northern school is said to approach life through essence. One explanation for this difference is that the Southern approach is for older people whose energy is depleted, while the Northern approach is for younger people who have an excess of energy. In either case, *Understanding Reality* has always been regarded as a classic by both branches of the Complete Reality school, and it is one of the main sources for *The Book of Balance and Harmony*.

In the commentary on *Understanding Reality* by Shangyangzi, one of the Great Yuan dynasty writers of the Northern school, there is a list of metaphors for the two ingredients of dual spiritual alchemy, useful for relating the various alchemical works on this plane. The original text says, "When the two things join, sense and essence merge," and Shangyangzi notes that these "two things" may be called heaven and earth, being and nonbeing, sense and essence, fire and water, sun and moon, man and woman, dragon and tiger, lead and mercury, opening and subtlety, mystery and female, higher earth and lower earth, raven and rabbit, vitality and energy, turtle and snake, other and self, mind and body, metal and wood, host and guest, floating and sinking, hard and soft, lyre and sword, yin and yang. Most of these terms are used in *The Book of Balance and Harmony*, providing keys to understanding its alchemical teachings.

Generally speaking, *The Book of Balance and Harmony* follows *Understanding Reality* in its lineage and sources: the ancient *Book of Changes* and its early commentaries; the perennial Taoist classic *The Way and Its Power* and associated texts; the transcendent wisdom teachings of Buddhism, especially as practiced in Chan Buddhism; the tradition of alchemical immortalism deriving from the classic *Triplex Unity* elucidation of the *Book of Changes* that was brought to its full flower in *Understanding Reality*; and certain parts of the early Confucian classics and traditions.

The Book of Balance and Harmony also follows the tradition of *Chuang-tzu*, *Triplex Unity*, and *Understanding Reality* in repudiating certain practices as quasi-Taoist aberrations. In this it goes even further than earlier texts in its inventory of practices as well as in its classifications. The author of *The Book of Balance and Harmony*, Li Daoqun, had studied with sixteen or more teachers and is said to have learned the final secret from a mysterious personage in Central Asia. He evidently was therefore broadly familiar with the range of Taoist and Taoistic teachings and practices current in his time, including those of the Great Way and Absolute One schools, two other Taoist movements that arose in the same era as the Complete Reality school.

The first section of the book, as compiled by one of Li's disciples, is devoted to fundamental principles. The unity of the three Ways—Buddhism, Confucianism, and Taoism—is affirmed in respect to the plane of the absolute, or complete awareness. Then the central theme of balance and harmony is introduced from the *Record of Rites*, one of the early manuals of Zhou dynasty civilization, and the *Scripture of Purity and Clarity*, a short popular text ascribed to Lao-tzu, identified with Li Er, the transmitter of *The Way and Its Power*. The text then turns to the basic postures of Taoist practice. The section concludes with an introduction to the theme of the two minds: the real mind (the mind of Tao) and the errant mind (the human mind). A famous expression from the *Documents*, another early Confucian classic, is used to introduce this idea here as elsewhere in Complete Reality literature: "The mind of Tao is subtle, the human mind is insecure." It is the purpose of Taoist praxis to bring the subtle mind of Tao from the vagueness of the subconscious to the forefront of awareness in order to stabilize the human mind and eliminate its insecurity.

The second section of the book consists of a series of statements guiding the reader through an abstract visualization of evolution. Evolution has a twin meaning. It refers to the natural growth, development, and wane of all beings and also to conscious evolution said to be accomplished by evading unnecessary conditioning and taking direct recourse to the source. The first kind of evolution is referred to as going along; the second kind is called going in reverse. These are fundamental concepts of complete Taoist praxis, and basic understandings of the key ideas of essence and life are accordingly introduced in this section.

The third section of the book is devoted to meditations on nature, events, and oneself through the principles of the *Book of Changes*. The pervasive themes of change, rhythm, poise, perception, and adaptation are established in the consciousness of the contemplator through a series of meditation themes. Here again the author connects the pristine Confucian work on the *Book of Changes* with the tradition of the *Scripture of Purity and Clarity* so highly prized in Complete Reality Taoism.

The fourth section of the book goes into the science of the "gold pill," the alchemy of vitality, energy, and spirit. This section is divided into two parts, one corresponding to the science of essence and the other to the science of life. The alchemy of life is called the outer medicine and deals with matters of the physical body—energy, health, and longevity. The alchemy of essence is called the inner medicine and deals with the metaphysical body. The combination of these practices is held to produce mental and physical refinement and, ultimately, transcendence of space and time in awareness.

The fifth section of the book takes up a central formulation of the Complete Reality school known as the "three fives." This formula, taken from the classic *Understanding Reality*, is based on the diagrammatic arcana of the *Book of Changes*. The term "three fives" is a codified reference to three central concepts: the three bases or fundamentals, the five elements or forces, and the one energy. The three bases or fundamentals—vitality, energy, and spirit—are also called the three treasures, or the medicinal ingredients of the gold pill, the elixir of immortality. The five elements or forces are essence and sense, spirit and vitality, and will. The compounding of these five elements is one of the major operations of spiritual alchemy. The one energy is the fundamental energy of the universe, the source of the differentiated elements and bases of the alchemical human. This "compounding" process is explained as the unification of mind, body, and will—a cornerstone of Taoist praxis supposed to produce what are commonly called "real humans."

The sixth and seventh sections of the book deal with the central issue of the "mysterious pass"—the critical initiatory experience by which Taoists transcend the ordinary world. In the Complete Reality practice of seeking and opening the mysterious pass is one of the strongest signs of Chan Buddhist affinity within this school of Taoism. Other schools place the mysterious pass at various locations in the body or head, but Complete Reality purists insist there is no such location. Rather, in the opening of the metaphysical mysterious pass the Taoists of the Complete Reality schools found an experience of overwhelming importance that changed their outlook on the many yogic techniques in common practice.

The eighth, ninth, and tenth sections of the book present a compendium of practices in a hierarchic arrangement. In Complete Reality Taoism it is commonly said, particularly in reference to the mysterious pass, that there are thirty-six hundred practices, none of which is directly connected to the ultimate enlightenment. This book mentions many exercises and classifies them according to their effect, showing how the same terminology has different meanings according to the system of interpretation. These sections refer to the teachings of many unnamed sects. The scheme of categorization into lower, middle, and higher teachings is common to Buddhism and religious Taoism; the highest grade of practice in this scheme, presented in the tenth section, is little different from Chan Buddhism.

The eleventh, twelfth, and thirteenth sections consist of questions and answers. The eleventh section, on the underlying unity of Taoism, Confucianism, and Buddhism, uses the metaphysics of the *Book of Changes*, certain key passages from early Confucian classics, and some of the basic lore of Chan Buddhism to establish the esoteric connection among the three Ways. The twelfth section explains the practice symbolized by the alchemy of the gold pill in the teachings of the *Book of Changes, The Way and Its Power,* and *Understanding Reality*. The thirteenth section, focusing on alchemy, defines a number of important terms commonly used in alchemical texts.

The fourteenth and fifteenth sections present synopses of live teachings from the school of the author. These are teachings on the refinement of vitality, energy, and spirit, using practices based on the *Book of Changes* and *The Way and Its Power*.

The sixteenth section consists of two short discourses. The first concerns the subject of essence and life, the two basic facets of Taoist science, emphasizing the need for integration and completeness. The text notes that Buddhists of the time were fixated on essence whereas Taoists were fixated on life. This is a pattern to be seen again and again in the history of the confluence and divergence of these two Ways—a pattern which the Complete Reality school strove to eliminate in their praxis. The second discourse, on the symbolism of the signs in the *Book of Changes*, reconciles the direct formless practice, known as the highest alchemy that has no signs or lines, with the formal gradual practice traditionally encoded in the *I Ching*'s symbols. Here again the author follows the classic *Understanding Reality* and the pattern of Chan Buddhism.

The seventeenth section consists of two short discourses on basic meditation technique. These discourses are based on the teachings of *The Way and Its Power*, the *Scripture of Purity and Clarity*, and the *Book of Changes*.

The eighteenth and nineteenth sections contain songs and poems recapitulating the Complete Reality teachings. These works combine the vocabulary and imagery of ancient Taoism, alchemical Taoism, and Chan Buddhism. Poetry and song are among the best-known media of Taoist expression, and many works are written entirely in these forms.

The twentieth and final section, consisting of three essays on the three Ways of Buddhism, Taoism, and Confucianism, sums up the book with an inquiry into the essential theoretical and practical issues underlying the Ways. The main theme of these essays is transcendence of creation and change—the establishment of higher awareness beyond the vicissitudes of ordinary life and death.

[1]
THE SOURCE MESSAGE OF THE MYSTIC SCHOOL

> When you are calm and stable, careful of attention, the celestial design is always clear, open awareness is unobscured; then you have autonomy in action and can deal with whatever arises.

The Absolute

The absolute is movement and stillness without beginning, yin and yang without beginning.

Buddhists call this complete awareness, Taoists call it the gold pill, Confucians call it the absolute. What is called the infinite absolute means the limit of the unlimited. Buddha called it "as is, immutable, ever clearly aware." The *I Ching* says, "tranquil and unperturbed, yet sensitive and effective." An alchemical text says, "Body and mind unstirring, subsequently there is yet an endless real potential." These all refer to the subtle root of the absolute.

So we know that what the three teachings of Buddhism, Taoism, and Confucianism esteem is calm stability. This is what a Confucian master called being based on calm. When the human mind is calm and stable, before it is affected by things, it is merged in the celestial design; this is the subtlety of the absolute. Once it is affected by things, then there is partiality; this is change of the absolute.

When you are calm and stable, careful of attention, the celestial design is always clear, open awareness is unobscured; then you have autonomy in action and can deal with whatever arises. With the maturation of practice of calm stability, one spontaneously arrives at this true restoration of the infinite, where the subtle responsive function of the absolute is clear and the design of the universe and all things is complete in oneself.

Balance and Harmony

Balance and harmony are the four directions centered on reality; in action all is balanced.

The *Record of Rites* says, "When emotions have not yet emerged, that is called balance; when they are active yet all in proportion, that is called harmony." Not having emerged means being careful of attention in the midst of calm stability; therefore it is called balance. Kept in attention yet immaterial, it is therefore called the root of the world. Proportion in action means being careful of what is manifested in action; therefore it is called harmony. Balanced in all actions, it is called arrival at the Way for the world.

Truly if one can be balanced and harmonious in oneself, then the being which is fundamentally so is clear and aware, awake in quietude, accurate in action; thus one can respond to the endless changes in the world.

Lao-tzu said, 'If people can be clear and calm, heaven and earth will come to them." This means the same thing as the saying, "Effect balance and harmony, and heaven and earth are in place, myriad beings grow."

Balance and harmony are the subtle functions of sensitive efficiency, the essential workings of response to change, the totality of the cyclic movement and stillness of the flow of production and growth spoken of in the *I Ching*.

Allowing and Following

Allow the body to be tranquil, the mind to be clear, society to be integrated, events to be spontaneous. Then body, mind, society, and events follow the order, way, time, and design of nature, in responding to people, things, changes, and opportunities.

Body, mind, society, and events are called the four conditions. All worldly people make these into entangling bonds; only those who allow and follow can deal with them. Always dealing with them, yet always calm, one is no longer entangled.

What is allowing? It means allowing the body to be tranquil, allowing the mind to be clear, allowing society to be integrated, allowing events to be spontaneous. What is following? It means following the order of nature, following the way of nature, following the timing of nature, following the design of nature.

When the body follows the order of nature, one can therefore respond to people. When the mind follows the way of nature, one can therefore respond to things. When society follows the timing of nature, it is therefore possible to respond to change. When events follow the design of nature, it is therefore possible to respond to opportunities.

When one can allow, can follow, and can respond, then one is free and clear in the midst of the four conditions. Those who see this way are always responsive yet always calm, always clear, and always pure.

Shining and Wandering

The shining mind is always calm; in action, it responds to myriad changes. Even when active, it is essentially always calm.

The wandering mind is always stirring; in quietude it produces myriad thoughts. Even when quiet, it is basically always astir.

Of old it has been said, always extinguish the stirring mind, don't extinguish the shining mind. The unstirring mind is the shining mind; the mind which does not stop is the wandering mind.

The shining mind is the mind of Tao, the wandering mind is the human mind. When it is said that the mind of Tao is vague, this means it is subtle and difficult to see. When it is said that the human mind is in peril, this means it is insecure and uneasy.

Even in the human mind there is the mind of Tao; even in the mind of Tao there is the human mind. It is a matter of persistently keeping centered and balanced in activity and stillness, so that the shining mind is always present and the wandering mind does not stir. Then what was insecure will become peaceful, and what was vague will become clear.

At this point, the errant mind comes back, and the error-free Tao is accomplished. This is what the *I Ching* calls "coming back to see the heart of heaven and earth."

[2]
Statements

Forms all contribute to one another, beings are immanent in one another; thus evolution and development go on without end.

The Tao is basically utterly open. Utter openness has no substance. It ends in endlessness, begins in beginninglessness.

, , ,

When openness culminates, it transforms into spirit; spirit changes to produce energy; energy masses into form—the one divides into two.

, , ,

With duality, there is sensing: with sensing there is pairing of yin and yang in mutual interaction. The creative and the receptive establish their positions, movement and stillness alternate unceasingly; creativity, receptivity, vitality, and spirit interdepend, the active and passive take over from one another. At this point, creativity, receptivity, desire, awareness, movement, stillness, attraction, and accord connect with the operation of essence, sense, spirit, vitality, and will, so that there is consistency, establishing the seasons of the life cycle.

, , ,

A harmonious process of distillation sustains origination and production: in heaven, it distributes the myriad forms; on earth, it nurtures all living beings.

, , ,

Forms all contribute to one another, beings are immanent in one another; thus evolution and development go on without end.

, , ,

Everything in the world arises in being; being arises in nonbeing. Being and nonbeing interpenetrate, concealing and revealing each other in mutual interdependence.

, , ,

Getting to the source of their beginning, we find all existents are based on energy. Discerning their end, we find all beings convert to form.

, , ,

Thus we know that all beings are basically one form and one energy. Form and energy are basically one spirit. Spirit is basically utter openness. The Tao is basically ultimate nonbeing. Change is therein.

, , ,

The position of heaven is above, the position of earth is below. Humans and other beings abide in the middle, spontaneously fluxing and evolving. Energy is therein.

, , ,

Heaven and earth are the greatest of beings; humans are the most intelligent of animals. Heaven and humans are one; the universe is in their hands, myriad developments arise in their bodies. Transformation is therein.

, , ,

The consummation of humanity is to establish life in the center of heaven and earth, to make essence of the endowment of open awareness. Establishing essence and life, spirit is therein.

, , ,

Life is connected to energy; essence is connected to spirit. Plunge the spirit into the mind, gather energy in the body. The Tao is therein.

, , ,

The enlightened make their energy and spirit complete. Through repeated harmonization they naturally become real.

, , ,

The real within the real, the mysterious within the mysterious, the insubstantial producing substantiality—this is called the embryonic immortal.

, , ,

If you want to reach the Tao, whence does it proceed? Be calm, be open, and there is hope of embryonic immortality.

, , ,

When open, there is no obstruction; when calm, there is no desire. When openness is complete and calmness profound, observe the process of nature and know its cycles.

, , ,

Let action proceed from calm, be filled by maintaining openness. These two principles are complementary; spirit and Tao are together.

, , ,

The Tao is the host of the spirit, the spirit is the host of energy, energy is the host of the body, the body is the host of impulse. When there is no impulsiveness, the body rests; when the body rests, energy rests; when energy rests, spirit rests; when spirit rests, it does not dwell on anything—this is abiding without abode.

, , ,

When the jewel of life is crystallized and the pearl of essence is bright, the original spirit is aware and the embryonic immortal is complete; then the path of open spontaneity is finished. How great is the spirit, the basis of transformation and evolution.

[3]
Secret Meanings

To master change, nothing is more important than to know the time; to know the time, nothing is more important than to understand inner design; to understand inner design, nothing is more important than open calm.

Images of Change

Change that can change is not eternal Change, images that can be imagined are not the Great Image. Eternal Change does not change, the Great Image is imageless. Eternal Change is change before delineation; changing change is change after delineation.

Eternal Change unchanging is the body of the absolute; changeable change is the basis of creation. The Great Image is the beginning of movement and stillness; that which can be imagined is the mother of form and name.

What is ever quiescent is eternal Change; that which never ceases is changing change. What is ultimately open and bodyless is the Great Image; what appears according to events is what can be imagined.

There is no way to find out the beginning or determine the end of the eternal; it is what clearly exists uniquely throughout all time. The Great outwardly contains heaven and earth, inwardly fills the universe; it is what pervades all worlds, profoundly still and perfectly complete.

Because eternal Change does not change, it can encompass the endless changes that take place in the world. Because the Great Image is imageless, it can describe the endless phenomena that occur in the world. Change and Image are the basis of the Tao.

Eternity and Change

Eternal Change does not change; changing change is not eternal. Because the eternal does not change, it can adapt to change; because the changing is not eternal, it can embody eternity. Never changing is the eternity of Change; the transiency of movement and stillness is the change of change.

Being invariably independent attains the eternal; going everywhere indefatigably masters the changing. Without knowing the eternal, one cannot master change; without mastering change, one cannot know the eternal. Eternity and Change are the basis of transformation.

Substance and Function

Eternity is the substance of Change, change is the function of Change. What never changes is the substance of Change; what changes with time is the function of Change.

Freedom from cognition and contrivance is the substance of Change; sensitive adaptation is the function of Change. Knowing the function, one can find out the substance; preserving the substance, one can sharpen the function.

Sages gaze above and examine below, search afar and apprehend the near, to realize the substance; developed people advance in quality, accomplish works, carry out tasks, and create tools, based on the function.

Investigating truth, fulfilling human nature, taking pleasure in the celestial, knowing the meaning of life, cultivating harmony and peace, and arranging the social order are all within Change. Preserving the substance of Change is the way to know the eternal; sharpening the function of Change is the way to master adaptation.

Movement and Stillness

The alternation of the firm and the yielding is the movement and stillness of Change. The rise and descent of yin and yang is the movement and stillness of energy. The coming and going of energy is the movement and stillness of things. Rising and retiring by day and night is the movement and stillness of the body.

The advancement and retirement of the individual, the arising and disappearing of thoughts, the fortune and misfortune of the world, the success and failure of affairs—all are alternations of movement and stillness. By observing their movement and stillness, the changes of events and the conditions of beings can be seen.

When there is attention in stillness, there is perceptivity in action. When there is autonomy in stillness, action can be decisive. When there is certitude in stillness, actions are auspicious. Stillness is the foundation of action, action is the potential of stillness. When action and stillness are always as they should be, one's path is illumined.

Contraction and Expansion

The coming and going of heat and cold is the contraction and expansion of a year. The coming and going of the sun and moon is the contraction and expansion of energy. The coming and going of past and present is the contraction and expansion of time.

The interdependence of being and nonbeing, difficulty and ease, long and short, high and low—all are the principle of contraction and expansion. If one knows the way of mutual influence of contraction and expansion, then one can comprehend endless benefits in the world.

Waxing and Waning

Waxing is the beginning of waning; waning is the end of waxing. Waxing is the massing of energy; waning is the dissolution of matter. Growth and development is called waxing; returning to the root, submitting to destiny, is called waning.

Origin and growth are the waxing of change, fruition and consummation are the waning of change. Spring and summer are the waxing of the year, autumn and winter are the waning of the year. Youth and maturity are the waxing of the body, aging and death are the waning of the body. Going from nonbeing to being is the waxing of things, going from being to nonbeing is the waning of things.

Waxing is the cohort of life, waning is the cohort of death. Ever since the first division of positive and negative energies, there has never been a pattern of waning without waxing, and there has never been anything that waxed without waning. Those who realize this are clearly aware of truth.

Spirit and Potential

What abides in the center is spirit, what emerges accurately is potential. What is silent and unstirring is spirit, what is sensitive and effective is potential. What appears and disappears unfathomably is spirit, what works responsively without convention is potential.

Potential is stored in the body, spirit is extended to myriad things. Potential foreshadows good and ill, spirit is ever fluid. Potential contains the qualities of creativity, development, fruition, and completion. Those who continually grow stronger are those who preserve this spirit. Those who comprehend heaven, earth, and humanity, functioning responsively without end, are those who use this potential.

Knowledge and Action

Knowledge is profound knowledge of principle, action is powerful practice of the Way. Profound knowledge of principle knows without seeing, powerful practice of the Way accomplishes without striving.

To "know without going out the door, see the Way of Heaven without looking out the window" is profound knowledge. To "grow ever stronger, adapting to all situations," is powerful practice.

To "be aware of disturbance before disturbance, be aware of danger before danger, be aware of destruction before destruction, be aware of calamity before calamity" is profound knowledge. "Preservation in the body without being burdened by the body, action in the mind without being used by the mind, working in the world without being affected by the world, carrying out tasks without being obstructed by tasks" is powerful practice.

By profound knowledge of principle one can change disturbance into order, change danger into safety, change destruction into survival, change calamity into fortune. By powerful practice of the Way, one can bring the body to the realm of longevity, bring the mind to the sphere of mystery, bring the world to great peace, bring tasks to great fulfillment. Who can reach this but those of great knowledge and great action?

Understanding the Time

To master change, nothing is more important than to know the time; to know the time, nothing is more important than to understand inner design; to understand inner design, nothing is more important than open calm.

Openness means awareness, calm means clarity. When one is imbued with clear awareness, the celestial design is evident.

The transformations of heaven can be seen by observing change; the trends of the times in the world can be checked by observing images; the sincerity or falsehood of people can be discerned by observing concrete manifestations.

That which cleaves to concrete manifestations cannot but correspond to something; that which takes place in the material realm cannot be without distinguishing characteristics. When it is going to rain, there must be moisture in the air; when a mountain is going to crumble, the lower part must give way first; when people are going to render help or harm, their faces first change.

It is like knowing how windy it is from watching a bird's nest, knowing how much it has rained by seeing a puddle in a hole. Insects respond to the season, and when leaves fall we know it is autumn. It is also like a caravan using a pheasant's tail feather to forecast the weather: if it's going to remain clear the tail stands straight up; when it's going to rain the tail droops.

Even inanimate things are this predictable; people are even more so. Those who do not know the changes of the times have not yet clearly perceived their inner design.

Correcting oneself

To promote worthy qualities and accomplish works, nothing is more important than correcting oneself. Once the self is correct, everything is correct. Forms and names cannot stand but for correctness, tasks cannot succeed but for correctness.

All activities start from oneself. Therefore developmental work requires self-correction as a foundation. When one deals with people after having corrected oneself, then people too will become correct. When one manages affairs after having corrected oneself, affairs too become correct. When one responds to things after having corrected oneself, things too become correct.

Only a unified correctness in the world is able to master the myriad changes in the world. So we know that correcting oneself is the great function of developmental work, and the stairway into sagehood.

Meditation

Clearing the mind, dissolving preoccupations, purifying thought, forgetting feelings, minimizing self, lessening desire, seeing the basic, embracing the fundamental—this is meditation of the Transformative Way. When the mind is clear and freed of preoccupations, it is possible to fathom the design of reality; when thoughts are ended and feelings forgotten, it is possible to fathom the essence of reality. When selfishness and desire disappear, it is possible to arrive at the Tao; when one is plain and simple, pure and whole, it is possible to know the celestial.

Sensing and Response

Comprehension in a state of quiescence, accomplishment without striving, knowing without seeing—this is the sensing and response of the Transformative Way. Comprehension in a state of quiescence can comprehend anything, accomplishment without striving can accomplish anything, knowing without seeing can know anything.

To sense and comprehend after action is not worthy of being called comprehension; to accomplish after striving is not worthy of being called accomplishment; to know after seeing is not worthy of being called knowing. These three are far from the way of sensing and response.

Indeed, to be able to do something before it exists, sense something before it becomes active, see something before it sprouts, are three abilities which develop interdependently. Then nothing is sensed but is comprehended, nothing is undertaken without response, nowhere does one go without benefit.

Three Kinds of I Ching

The three kinds of *I Ching* (*Book of Changes*) are that of the sages, that of heaven, and that of the mind. The Changes of heaven consist of the principles of transformation, the Changes of the sages consist of representations of transformation, and the Changes of mind consist of methods of transformation.

To view the Changes of the sages, it is important to understand the representations, for when the representations are clear you gain access to sagacity. To view the Changes of heaven, it is important to investigate principles, for when principles are investigated thoroughly you come to know the celestial. To view the Changes of mind, it is important to practice the Tao, for when the Tao is practiced you complete the mind.

If you do not read the Changes of the sages, you will understand the Changes of heaven. If you do not understand the Changes of heaven, then you do not know the Changes of mind. If you do not know the Changes of mind, you cannot adequately master change. So we know the *I Ching*, The Changes, is a book for mastering change.

Solving Confusion

The waning and waxing of energy, the rise and fall of the times, the presence and absence of opportunity, the welfare and impasses of society—these are changes of heaven.

Auspicious and inauspicious signs, advantageous and disadvantageous elements, expressions of danger and ease, symbols of rectitude and obscurity—these are changes recorded by sages.

Impasses and achievements in life, advancement and withdrawal in status, success and failure in society, safety and danger in position—these are changes of mind.

If you have deep understanding of changes of heaven, you know the forces and momentum of the times. If you have deep understanding of the changes recorded by the sages, you know transformations and developments. If you have deep understanding of mental changes, you know essence and life.

One understands the changes recorded by sages through mental changes; one infers the changes in heaven by the changes recorded by sages. One looks into the mental changes by means of the celestial changes. One who realizes the single pervasive thread is called a person with will.

Resolving Doubts

Change and movement have their times; safety and danger are in oneself. Calamity and fortune, gain and loss, all start from oneself. Therefore those who master change are those who address themselves to the time. For those who address themselves to the time, even danger is safe; for those who master change, even disturbance is orderly.

Those who do not lose their control manage to get through even in an impasse; those who are not careful of their actions are befuddled even by wealth.

Those who conceal their illumination are unharmed even in the absence of understanding; those who rely on what they have dwell on great possession and are sure to suffer harm.

Those who can respond even while very distant have the same will; those who have nothing to do with each other though very near have conflicting intentions.

Those who are most weak yet can prevail have their underpinnings; those who are most strong yet have no excesses are imbued with the Tao.

Beneficial use of bad things solves difficulty; averting the gaze from evil people avoids resentment.

Those who are not constant in virtue have no tolerance; those who do not do their own tasks benefit no one.

Those who stand alone with pride in themselves accomplish nothing; those who are cautious and practice self-awareness gain fortune.

Others benefit those who benefit others; others help those who help others; others trust those who trust others; others are generous to those who are generous to others.

Those who beware of evil have no evil; those who beware of error have no error.

To those who beware of calamity, fortune will come; to those who slight fortune, calamity will come.

How can it be doubted that safety and danger are in oneself?

The Accomplishment of Sages

The reason sages are sages is because of their application of the Changes. The means whereby application of the Changes produces accomplishment are openness and calm.

When open, one takes in all; when calm, one perceives all. When open, one can accept people; when calm, one can deal with events. When openness and calm are practiced for a long time, the awareness is clarified.

Openness is the image of heaven, calm is the image of earth. Spontaneous strengthening without cease is the openness of heaven, rich virtue supporting beings is the calm of earth. Empty vastness without bound is the openness of heaven; universal breadth without limit is the calm of earth.

The Tao of heaven and earth is this openness, this calm. When openness and calm are in oneself, then heaven and earth are in oneself. This is what is meant by the saying in Taoist scripture, "If people can always be clear and calm, all heaven and earth will come to them." Clarity is openness; openness and calm are the sages' accomplishment of spiritual qualities.

[4]
Secrets of the Gold Pill

The outer medicine is perfecting life, the inner medicine is perfecting essence. When the two medicines are complete, one is physically and mentally sublimated.

Stabilization of the furnace

Supporting the universe, the great unknown;
Who gives it the name of the jade furnace?
Having gone through refinement herein,
One can leave nonbeing and enter being at will.

Setting up the cauldron

It is not nonbeing, not being, not in between;
Outside is void, inside is empty;
The decisive and energetic overturn it and see—
All along *that* has always been aglow.

Restored elixir

It is originally clear, before history;
Obscurities are all due to fixation on illusory forms.
When you pick out the elixir,
It is round, open awareness.

Reverted elixir

The Tao is originally uncontrived, patterned on nature;
Sages set up images, a sphere of temporary names.
In everyday life it is completely manifest,
But only when you break through do you know the primordial.

THE SPOKEN SECRET

Take the real consciousness out of the overlay of conditioning that obscures it, and use it to make awareness complete, restoring the celestial. With the pure creative root of life stabilized, the pearl of immaterial essence is perfect.

As a sensitive receiver, one preserves the celestial design; detached from objects, one accords with the highest meditation. When one knows how to go about gathering real knowledge, in three stages one activates the embryonic immortal.

When the mind does not stir, the energy is naturally stable. When the will does not waver, the spirit is naturally aware. When the body is not restless, the vitality is naturally stable.

METAPHORS

Vitality in the body is yang within yin; refine vitality into energy. Energy in the mind is yin within yang; refine energy into spirit. The original spirit is formless; refine spirit into openness.

Outer and Inner Medicines

The outer medicine can be used to cure illness and prolong life. The inner medicine can be used to transcend being and enter into nonbeing.

Learning the Tao usually should start from the outer medicine; after that you come to know the inner medicine on your own. Advanced people who have already developed basic worthy qualities know it spontaneously, so they cultivate the inner medicine without cultivating the outer medicine.

The inner medicine involves no doing, but there is nothing it does not do; the outer medicine involves doing, and there is a way to do it.

The inner medicine has no form or substance, yet it really exists; the outer medicine has body and function, yet it really does not exist.

The outer medicine pertains to the physical body; the inner medicine pertains to the metaphysical body.

The outer medicine is perfecting life, the inner medicine is perfecting essence. When the two medicines are complete, one is physically and mentally sublimated.

THE OUTER MEDICINE

At the first pass, refining vitality into energy, it is first necessary to recognize the time when the primal vitality arises, and then quickly gather it.

At the middle pass, refining energy into spirit, one harmonizes the true breath, the inner pulse of life, so that it flows everywhere. From the bottom of the torso it flows backward up the spine to the head, where it mixes with the spirit. After that it descends to the solar plexus and enters the middle of the torso. When spirit and energy mate, a point of conscious energy appears in the center of the thorax.

At the upper pass, you refine spirit back into spacelike openness. Refining thought by mind is called seven-reversion; sense coming back to essence is called nine-restoration.

THE INNER MEDICINE

The inner medicine is essential for refining the spirit. When body and mind are both sublimated, merging in reality with the Tao takes place.

The inner medicine is the primordial point of true yang, the celestial. It is likened to the center line in the *I Ching* trigram HEAVEN ☰. When it mates with EARTH ☷, that forms WATER ☵. The center line represents true inner sense, which is firm and hence symbolized by metal, so it is also called metal in water. These are all names for ultimate vitality. When the ultimate vitality is stable, it reverts to generative energy.

The generative energy is the primordial, immaterial, unreified, real, unified, basic energy. It does not refer to oxygen in respiration. When the central line of HEAVEN ☰ has been injected into EARTH ☷, making WATER ☵, the central yin of EARTH is injected into HEAVEN, making FIRE ☲. The central yin of FIRE represents flexibility in consciousness; since it originates in EARTH, it is called mercury in sand.

The Tao produces one, one produces two, two produce three, three produce myriad beings: openness changes into spirit, spirit changes into energy, energy changes into vitality, vitality changes into form. This is called "going along."

Myriad beings are included in three (heaven, earth, beings), the three return to two (yin and yang), the two return to one: refine the ultimate vitality, and vitality turns to energy, energy turns to spirit. This is called "reversal."

Alchemical texts say "going along" produces people, "reversal" produces the elixir of immortality.

The three superior medicines are vitality, energy, and spirit. Their body is one, their functions are two. What is the body? It is the original great matter of the three bases. What are the functions? They are the inner and outer applications.

The inner medicines are primordial ultimate vitality, immaterial open energy, incorruptible fundamental spirit. The outer medicines are sexual vitality, the energy of breath, and the thinking spirit.

Refining Vitality into Energy
The first pass involves doing, taking from WATER ☵ to fill in FIRE ☲.

Taking to the Tao is seeking the mystery in the province of water, which represents vitality on the primal plane and desire on the temporal plane. Alchemical texts say, "When vitality arises, gather it at once; if you look afar, you can't taste it." Gathering is nongathering gathering; were there really something gathered, how could the central line in WATER, which represents something intangible, ever rise?

Vitality is an emanation of the primordial ultimate awareness: based on its action, the body comes to be; the ultimate vitality in the body is yang. "Gathering" means gathering this. This may be symbolically represented as HEAVEN ☰ being the primordial ultimate awareness; by one initial movement it mixes with EARTH ☷ and produces WATER ☵. This is a representation of the ultimate awareness emanating the fundamental vitality into the earthly plane.

The alchemical term "gathering lead" refers to gathering the inner sense of the vitality emanated by primal awareness. As this sense is firm and unequivocal, it is symbolized by metal and called "true lead." The experience of "gathering lead" is hard to describe. It is possible to understand much of it by pondering this statement from the *I Ching*: "THUNDER (movement) is in EARTH (stillness): RETURN. Kings of yore shut the gates on the winter solstice; the caravans did not travel, the lords did not inspect the regions." This means that the return of the movement of the primal vitality emerges from stillness; when it first arises, it is important to remain calmly attentive and not dissipate it by excitement or impulsiveness. The precise details of the process are secret, in that they must be passed on personally, according to individual circumstances.

Refining Energy into Spirit
In the middle pass, being and nonbeing interpenetrate; movement and stillness open and close.

Buddhists cultivate concentration in the chamber of FIRE, or conscious awareness. Taoist literature says, "Will stabilizes inner sense, inner sense stabilizes conscious knowing. When inner sense and conscious knowing submit to will, body and mind are tranquil." This statement is exhaustive. Once you find the true inner sense, there is no worry that consciousness will not be stabilized.

In refining energy, movement is essential: opening and closing, coming and going, rising and descending, without stopping. At first this is done consciously; later it becomes spontaneous. One exhalation and inhalation takes the place of the evolution of a year. This is the meaning of Lao-tzu's saying, "The door of the mysterious female is called the root of heaven and earth. Continuously there as such, use of it is unforced."

If people focus their minds on the opening of the changes of movement and stillness, when movement emerges from stillness and when movement culminates and begins to revert to stillness, they will find the essentials of refining energy are all there.

Refining Spirit Back into Openness
In the upper pass there is no doing. When the work arrives at this stage, not a single word applies.

These three levels of work are one when accomplished. If you can perceive this with unified vision, then the great concern of Taoism, Buddhism, and Confucianism is done.

[5]
Explanation of the Three Fives

Collecting body and mind is gathering medicine.

The alchemical classic *Understanding Reality*, by the adept Ziyang, says, "Those who understand the three words 'three, five, one' have always been truly rare. The east three plus the south two make five; the north one and the west four join; the production number of the center earth is five. When these three sets meet, they form an infant. The infant is unity imbued with true energy. In ten months the embryo is complete, entering the foundation of enlightenment."

These lines penetrate all the schools of philosophy, the alchemical classics, and the writings of the adepts. If you can see what is behind them, your study is done; if not, consider the following explanation.

"Three, five, one" refers to the three bases, the five forces, and one energy. The three bases are basic vitality, basic energy, and basic spirit. The five forces, or five elements, are essence, sense, spirit, vitality, and will.

The five forces are symbolized by wood, metal, fire, water, and earth; each of these is further associated with specific directions and numbers. "East three" stands for essence, "south two" stands for spirit. Essence and spirit relate to mind, so they are regarded as a family or set. "North one" stands for vitality, "west four" stands for sense. Vitality is the basis of the body, the body is the connector of sense. Vitality and sense relate to the body, so they are regarded as set. The center, the number five, and the element earth all stand for will. Will is the director of the five forces; it has no partner and forms a set in itself.

So the five forces comprise three sets; the representative numbers of the members of each set add up to five, so these sets are called the three fives.

When the practitioner collects body, mind, and will, then the three bases and five forces naturally combine into one. This is what is meant when alchemical texts say, "Collecting body and mind is gathering medicine."

The essence of collecting body and mind is an openness and calm. Empty and open the mind, and spirit and essence join. Calm the body, and vitality and sense are still. When the will is greatly stabilized, the three bases—vitality, energy, and spirit—merge into one. This is called "the three flowers gathering on the peak," "the five energies returning to the source," and "the spiritual embryo congealing."

Sense uniting with essence is called "metal and wood joining." Vitality uniting with spirit is called "water and fire mixing." Great stabilization of will is called "completing the five forces."

Alchemical literature says, "Refining vitality into energy is the first pass—the body is not agitated. Refining energy into spirit is the middle pass—the mind is not agitated. Refining spirit back into openness is the upper pass—the will is not agitated."

The mind being undisturbed is what is meant by "east three plus south two make five." The body being undisturbed is what is meant by "north one and west four join." The will being undisturbed is what is meant by "the production number of center earth is five." Body, mind, and will uniting is "the three sets meet, and form an infant."

The meeting of the three sets means the three bases and five forces combine into one. Therefore it says that when these three sets meet they form an infant. The term infant means pure unity. Therefore it says the infant is unity imbued with true energy.

"In ten months the embryo is complete, entering the foundation of enlightenment." In three hundred days the two medicines in the embryo, conscious essence and true sense, in equal proportion, are refined and matured. This is the great accomplishment of transcending the ordinary and entering into sagehood, so it is called entering the foundation of enlightenment.

For those who see this, the task of spiritual alchemy is done, the great affair of spiritual immortality is completed. The various symbols and terms of alchemical texts do not refer to anything outside of body, mind, and will.

Body, mind, and will are called the three sets or three families. Vitality, energy, and spirit are called the three bases. Vitality, spirit, higher soul, lower soul, and will are called the five energies. The meeting of the three sets is called perfection of the embryo. Unification of the three bases is called completion of the elixir.

[6]
THE OPENING OF THE MYSTERIOUS PASS

> The body is like a puppet; the strings of the puppet are like the mysterious pass. The person controlling the puppet is like the innermost self.

The opening of the mysterious pass is the most abstruse and most essential mechanism. It is not, as various practitioners of yoga say, in the forehead, or the navel, or the bladder, or the genitals, or between the kidneys and navel, or between the kidneys and genitals. From head to heels, any spot of the body you may focus on is not it. Yet it is not to be sought externally, apart from the body.

Therefore sages just used the word "center" to point out the opening of the mysterious pass. This "center" is it. Let me give you a convenient simile. When a puppet moves its hands and feet and gesticulates in a hundred ways, it is not that the puppet can move—it is moved by pulling strings. And though it is a strong device, it is the person controlling the puppet who pulls the strings.

Do you know this person who controls the puppet? The puppet is like the body, the strings are like the mysterious pass; the person controlling the puppet is like the innermost self. The movements of the body are not done by the body; it is the mysterious pass that makes it move. But though it is the action of the mysterious pass, still it is the innermost self that activates the mysterious pass. If you can recognize this activating mechanism, without a doubt you can become a wizard.

[7]
The Gold-Testing Stone

> There are thirty-six hundred methods in Taoism; people each cling to one and consider it fundamental. Who knows this opening of the mysterious pass is not in the thirty-six hundred methods?

The gold pill has open nonreification for its substance, clear calm for its function; it is an unexcelled, subtle way to reality. Few people in the world know this, few cultivate it; therefore sages, using their power of skillful means, have opened up good avenues of introduction, setting up terminology and imagery, writing alchemical treatises to guide students. If people who want to approach will familiarize themselves with these writings, understand their principles, intuitively recognize them and inwardly comprehend them, then when they apply them they will at once transcend into the realm of reality.

Nevertheless, people of later times, failing to search out the inner design, have clung to the superficialities of the presentation, bringing in all sorts of irrelevant issues, resulting in fragmentation of the Way into byways and sidetracks, as many as thirty-six hundred of them. This is because they have not received transmission of the Way.

Even more mistaken are the ignorant shallow students of today who arbitrarily write misinterpretations of the meaning of the classics of the sages. This is certainly wrong, for those of the future will then be unable to distinguish the false and the true, no matter how hard they try. They are to be pitied.

It is because of these facts that I have composed this Gold-Testing Stone to distinguish the real from the spurious, so that students will not be confused but will settle all doubts and leap directly to the shore of the Tao.

An enlightened teacher has said, "There are thirty-six hundred methods in Taoism; people each cling to one and consider it fundamental. Who knows this opening of the mysterious pass is not in the thirty-six hundred methods?"

It seems to me that the teacher said this out of kindness. For anyone who can see in this way, the whole earth is gold. Otherwise, if you cannot see, you should make a test, so I have written it here.

[8]
NINE GRADES OF PRACTICES
Sidetracks and Auxiliary Methods

> Some imagine the basic spirit going out and in through the top of the head. Some travel to the realms of wizards in dreams. Some silently pay court to the supreme god. Some consider oblivion to be entry into trance. Some consider counting breaths to be the firing process. Some imagine black and white energies of the heart and genitals merging.

Three Lower Grades

1. LOWEST OF THE LOW: FALSE PATHS

These methods include seventy-two schools of sexual play, and in the vocabulary of these schools technical terms of alchemy are given sexual and quasi-sexual connotations. For example, some regard woman as the alchemical cauldron, and some use nine women as the "nine-cauldron." Some regard the first menses as medicine, some take menstrual fluid in general as the "ultimate treasure" and gather it to ingest it. Some take semen and menstrual blood as the bases of the great elixir; some have a virgin boy and girl copulate, and then gather their first sexual fluids as a tonic. There are over three hundred such practices. This is what is called "mud and water alchemy." These are paths of confusion, misleading paths.

2. MIDDLE-GRADE LOW PATHS: OUTSIDE PATHS

These methods include eighty-four other schools of sexual intercourse, with thirty-six modes of culling the female principle. There are also such practices as ingesting placenta, ingesting hormones distilled from urine, and ingesting one's own sexual fluid.

Here too technical terms are given biological associations: placenta is called the "violet energy cycle," ingesting one's own semen is called "return to the source," prevention of ejaculation during sexual intercourse is called "nonleaking," menstrual blood is called the "red pill."

Some people also feed a certain mineral compound to a woman so that she gives birth to a mass of flesh, and then they eat this as supreme medicine. Such fallacious techniques number over three hundred. They are outside paths, deviations from the Way.

3. UPPER-GRADE LOW: OUTSIDE PATHS

There are also over four hundred recipes for material alchemy to make potions to be ingested. These are outside paths.

These three low paths comprise over one thousand items. They are practiced by people who are lustful and greedy.

Three Middle Grades

1. LOWER MIDDLE GRADE

Practices of the lower middle grade include abstention from grain, enduring cold, eating filth, eating the berries of the prickly ash, lying on ice with the back exposed, eating only once a day, and fasting completely. Being able to eat a lot may be considered a marvel, or drinking wine without becoming drunk may be considered miraculous. Some reduce their intake of food and call that "adding and subtracting." Some avoid flavoring and eat only bland foods. Some do not eat cooked food. Some drink wine and eat meat without concern for their health and claim to be uncontrived. Some perform various strange feats. These are the lowest of the middle grade.

2. MIDDLE MIDDLE GRADE

The middle middle grade includes practices such as swallowing fog, ingesting vapor, culling the light of the sun and moon, drinking the lights of the stars, taking in the energies of the five directions, and culling the energies of water and fire. Some concentrate on imagination of traveling throughout the world. Some imagine the two energies of yin and yang in the body turning into a woman and a man engaging in sexual intercourse. All sorts of artificial visualizations are in the middle middle grade.

3. UPPER MIDDLE GRADE

These methods include formal religious practices such as transmission of initiation and precepts, readings, recitations, and preaching. Also included are such practices as stargazing, bowing to the stars, keeping silent, doing hard labor, and maintaining outward virtues.

These doings are the highest of the middle grade, gradually approaching the Tao. Beyond these are three upper grades.

Three Upper Grades

1. LOWER UPPER GRADE

These methods include such practices as mirror gazing, meditative breathing, massage, physical exercises, extended pronunciation of certain sounds for therapeutic purposes, mentally gazing at the top of the head, keeping the attention on the navel, and swallowing copious amounts of saliva.

Some consider the term "firing process" to mean massaging the body to make it warm. Some seek long life by making nine massage strokes for one forceful exhalation in a rhythmic massage-breathing exercise. Some work up copious saliva and consider that to be what is meant by the technical term "true seed." Some consider a thousand mouthfuls of saliva to be what is meant by the term "enlivening." Some keep the mind on the "elixir fields" in the torso and head, some stare at the nose.

2. MIDDLE UPPER GRADE

These methods include such practices as holding the breath and circulating psychosomatic energy, bending and stretching exercises, massaging the lower back and kidneys, focusing the mind on the forehead, exercising the eyes, twisting the spine, and keeping the mind on the umbilical region.

Some call the eyes "sun and moon." Some consider the point between the eyebrows to be the "mysterious pass." Some chatter the teeth, a concentration exercise, and call that the "gate of heaven." Some imagine the basic spirit going out and in through the top of the head. Some silently pay court to the supreme god. Some consider oblivion to be entry into trance. Some consider counting the breaths to be the "firing process." Some imagine black and white energies of the heart and genitals merging.

3. HIGHER UPPER GRADE

These methods include such practices as exercising vitality and energy, tuning the internal organs, visualizing pure lands, fixedly concentrating on the elixir fields, swallowing the noon sunlight, circulating psychophysical energy through the three elixir fields, rerouting vitality aroused by sexual intercourse or inner concentration so that it travels up the spine to boost the brain, and inward gazing.

There are over a thousand practices in the upper three grades. Mediocre practitioners perform them, and they can thereby ward off sickness. Beyond these are three vehicles of gradual method.

[9]
Three Vehicles of Gradual Method

Refining thought by mind is the firing process. Ceasing thought is nurturing the fire. Keeping brilliance to oneself is stabilization. Conquering inner demons is "battle in the field." Body, mind, and will are the three essentials. The heart of heaven is the mysterious pass.

Lower Vehicle

In the terminology of this vehicle, body and mind are the alchemical cauldron and furnace, vitality and energy are the medicinal ingredients, heart and genitals are fire and water, five internal organs are the five forces, the liver and lungs are the dragon and tiger, semen is the true seed.

In this system, the "firing process" is carried out in terms of year, month, day, and hour. Swallowing saliva to irrigate the digestive system is called "bathing." The mouth and nostrils are considered the "three essentials." The space in front of the kidneys and behind the navel is considered the "mysterious pass." The merging of the five forces is considered completion of the "elixir pill."

This is a method of comfort and bliss that includes over a hundred operations. If one can forget feelings, this can also nurture life. This is somewhat similar to the higher three grades mentioned above, but the application is different.

Middle Vehicle

According to the usage of this vehicle, HEAVEN ☰ and EARTH ☷ are the cauldron and furnace, WATER ☵ and FIRE ☲ are water and fire, sun and moon are the medicinal ingredients. The five forces are vitality, spirit, higher soul, lower soul, and will. The tiger and dragon are body and mind. Energy is the true seed.

The seasons of cold and heat of a year are the firing process. Showering with holy water is bathing. Inward states not going out, eternal objects not getting in, is "stabilization." The head, solar plexus, and pubis are the three essentials. The top center of the brain is the mysterious pass. The merging of vitality and spirit is the completion of the elixir pill.

This middle vehicle is a method for nurturing life; it includes dozens of operations. It is much like the lower vehicle. Practiced diligently, it can prolong life.

Higher Vehicle

According to the usage of this vehicle, heaven and earth are the cauldron and furnace, sun and moon are fire and water, yin and yang are the mechanism of evolution. "Lead," "mercury," "silver," "sand," and "earth" are the five elements. Essence and sense are the dragon and tiger. Thought is the true seed.

Refining thought by mind is the firing process. Ceasing thought is nurturing the fire. Keeping brilliance to oneself is "stabilization." Conquering inner demons is "battle in the field." Body, mind, and will are the three essentials. The heart of heaven is the mysterious pass. Sense coming back to essence is completion of the elixir pill. Being suffused with harmonious energy is bathing.

This is the higher-vehicle path of extending life. There are resemblances to the middle vehicle in it, but the application is not the same. There are a dozen or so items involved. When superior practitioners carry this out consistently from beginning to end, they can realize the Way of immortals.

[10]
THE HIGHEST VEHICLE

> When accomplishment is fulfilled, character is well developed, and one directly transcends to completion all at once; physically and spiritually sublimated, one merges with the Tao in reality.

The highest vehicle is the ineffable Way of supreme ultimate reality. Here cosmic space is the cauldron, the absolute is the furnace. Clear serenity is the foundation of the elixir pill, nondoing is the matrix of the elixir pill.

Essence and life are the lead and mercury. Concentration and insight are water and fire, controlling desire and anger is the mixing of water and fire. Unification of essence and sense is the combining of metal and wood. Cleaning the mind is bathing. Maintaining sincerity and settling the will is stabilization.

Discipline, concentration, and insight are the three essentials. The center is the mysterious pass. Clarifying the mind is miraculous experience. Seeing the essence of mind is crystallization. Merging of the three bases into one is the spiritual embryo. Unification of essence and life is the completion of the elixir pill. Having a body outside the body is release from the matrix. Breaking through space is perfect attainment.

The subtlety of this supreme vehicle can be practiced by the most developed people. When accomplishment is fulfilled, character is well developed and one directly transcends to completion all at once; physically and spiritually sublimated, one merges with the Tao in reality.

[11]
Dialogues
The Underlying Unity of Taoism, Confucianism, and Buddhism

> Forgetting feelings to nurture essence, emptying the mind to nurture the spirit, myriad entanglements cease at once, a hundred thoughts clear up. Body and mind unstirring, the spirit congeals and energy crystallizes—this is called the alchemical foundation, and is also metaphorically referred to as the spiritual embryo.

One night the Master of the Brilliant Moon was sitting peacefully in the moon cave. The cold light and clear air were pure and pleasant. His disciple, Master of the Jadelike Moon, was reflecting intensely on the importance of the matter of life and death, the necessity of respectfully seeking out spiritual immortals, and the need for concentrated cultivation. He asked the teacher, "I have heard that the elevated sages, the lofty realized ones, the immortal teachers since ancient times, have all attained the Tao by cultivation of reality and have always considered lead and mercury the root and stem of the gold pill. What are lead and mercury?"

The teacher said, "Lead and mercury are the beginning of heaven and earth, the mother of myriad beings, the basis of the gold pill. They are not the metals ordinarily referred to by these names.

"Nevertheless, people in error, ignorant of the true mystery, thinking in terms of their own arbitrary ideas, have confused and ruined later students, so that they have wasted their lives. This is a great pity. Without the guidance of a genuine teacher, whatever you do is arbitrary. This is what the adept Ziyang meant when he wrote, 'Even if you are exceptionally intelligent, if you do not meet a real teacher, don't indulge in guesswork.'

"Now I will point out to you the true lead and true mercury—they are body and mind. A wise teacher said, 'Body and mind are the medicine and fire.' Also, 'If you want to know the river source where the medicine is produced, it's just in the southwest—this is its homeland.' Southwest is the direction associated with the *I Ching* trigram EARTH ☷. EARTH is associated with the body. The vitality in the body is yang within yin. This is likened to the center line of HEAVEN ☰ entering EARTH ☷ to make WATER ☵. Yin outside, yang inside—there is the metal of HEAVEN in WATER, so it is called metal in water. This stands for sense in vitality.

"Now mercury is the energy in the mind, yin within yang. It is likened to the center line of EARTH ☷ entering HEAVEN ☰ to make FIRE ☲. Yang outside, yin inside, firm outside, flexible inside, HEAVEN outside, EARTH inside—there is EARTH within FIRE, so it is called mercury in cinnabar. This stands for essence in consciousness.

"It is because of the subtlety of the psychic combination of vitality and energy that the images of lead and mercury are used symbolically. It is just to make the student aware that there are substance and function. Thinking along these lines, it is all a matter of body and mind. After body and mind are united, there is no more 'lead and mercury.' "

QUESTION: What is "extracting and adding"?
ANSWER: When the body does not stir, the energy is settled; this is called "extraction." When the mind does not stir, the spirit is settled; this is called "addition." When body and mind do not stir, the spirit congeals and the energy crystallizes; this is called "returning to the basis."

Therefore "extracting lead and adding mercury" means taking the yang in the center of WATER ☵ to fill in the yin in the center of FIRE ☲, thus forming HEAVEN ☰. That means taking the true sense submerged in the earthly out of the earthly in order to eliminate the mundanity which has invaded the essence of mind through conditioning, thus resulting in restoration of the primal celestial state of conscious energy.

QUESTION: What is "cooking and refining"?
ANSWER: When body and mind are on the verge of unification, if there is the slightest disturbance, then you use a firm, resolute mind to oppose it; this is called "martial refining." Once body and mind are

unified, after vitality and energy have commingled, you use a flexible, peaceful mind to preserve this; this is called "cultural cooking."

The principle of this is nothing but conquering body and mind—this is what is called "cooking lead and refining mercury." Forgetting feelings to nurture essence, emptying the mind to nurture the spirit, myriad entanglements cease at once, a hundred thoughts clear up. Body and mind unstirring, the spirit congeals and energy crystallizes—this is called the alchemical foundation and is also metaphorically referred to as the spiritual embryo.

The different terms mentioned above simply refer to using essence to concentrate sense. When your nature is tranquil, feelings are forgotten; you see the original, embrace the fundamental, revert to openness, go back to the root, return to Life. This is called completion of the elixir pill and is metaphorically called release from the matrix.

QUESTION: The alchemical classics say that the essence of the work is in the mysterious pass. Where is the mysterious pass?
ANSWER: The mysterious pass is the most recondite and subtle mechanism. How could it have a fixed position? If you place it in the body, that is wrong; yet it is also wrong to seek it outside the body. To cling to the body is to be fixated on the physical form; to cling to externals is to be fixated on things.

The mysterious pass is just the point where the physical elements and five forces do not adhere. Let me give you a simile to facilitate understanding. The movements of a marionette are a matter of the mechanism at the top of the strings, which is operated by the puppeteer. The marionette is like the physical body, the strings are like the mysterious pass, and the puppeteer working the strings is like the original true nature.

Without the strings, the marionette cannot move; without the mysterious pass, people cannot move. You should concentrate twenty-four hours a day, throughout all your activities, on inwardly searching for this: what is it that speaks, is silent, looks and listens?

If body and mind are tranquil and settled, and the heart is still, you will naturally see the mysterious pass where the true potential subtly responds. When the *I Ching* says "tranquil and unstirring," it is referring to the essence of the mysterious pass; when it says "sensitive and effective," it is referring to the function of the mysterious pass.

Having seen the mysterious pass, once you attain it you have attained it forever. The medicines, the firing process, the three bases, and the eight trigrams are all therein.

If people today consider some physical location to be the mysterious pass, they will not attain, no matter how hard they work. I would like to point it out directly, but I'm afraid you wouldn't believe and wouldn't be able to use it. You must see it for yourself.

It is like the learning of the primordial in Confucianism—it is necessary to recognize it tacitly. Mencius said, "The vast energy fills the universe—it is hard to tell of." Isn't the subtlety that is hard to tell of the mysterious pass?

In Buddhism, the special transmission outside doctrine, which does not establish literal formulation, requires people to take it in with the spirit and understand it in the mind—this is called the incommunicable subtlety. If you know this principle, you can merge all through one penetration.

QUESTION: Some say that by practice of Buddhism and Taoism one can end birth and death and get out of routine existence, but by studying Confucianism one can fulfill social ethics yet not understand birth and death. Is this not the difference between Buddhism and Taoism on the one hand and Confucianism on the other?
ANSWER: How can those who arrive at truth worry about birth and death? There is a Confucian saying, "Find out truth and fulfill human nature, thereby arriving at the destiny of life; getting to the root of beginnings, returning to ends, knowledge encompasses myriad things." This is talking about knowing birth and death. What in Taoism is called the study of essence and life is actually the true message of Confucianism, where it is called the study of human nature and destiny.

Furthermore, when the ancient sage chieftain Fu Xi first wrote the *I Ching* signs, setting up teaching embodying the celestial, using the Tao to develop people, there was no division into three teachings. Therefore it is said, "The Supreme Celestial has not two ways, sages have not two minds."

The first line drawn by Fu Xi represents the absolute. When there is one, then there are two; this represents the two modes, one yang, one yin. "One yin and one yang—this is called the Tao." Looking up, gazing at the sky, Fu Xi wrote a line to represent heaven; looking down, examining the earth, he wrote a line to represent earth. In between he wrote a line to represent humankind.

Therefore three solid lines form the trigram HEAVEN, representing the "three components"—heaven, earth, and humanity. Two HEAVENS separated, making three broken lines, form EARTH, representing the six parts—the members of the body and the directions of space.

So it is said that the Tao establishing heaven is yin and yang, the Tao establishing earth is flexibility and firmness, and the Tao establishing humankind is benevolence and justice. The three components each have two aspects, so six lines form EARTH.

Speaking in terms of the person, the Tao establishing heaven being yin and yang refers to the spirit and energy of the mind; the Tao establishing earth being flexibility and firmness refers to the form and substances of the body; the Tao establishing humankind being benevolence and justice refers to the essence and sense of the will.

Mind, body, and will are represented by the three components of HEAVEN; spirit, energy, essence, sense, form, and substance are represented by the six parts of EARTH. This is what the *I Ching* means when it says, "Find it afar in things, find it nearby in the body."

QUESTION: The Connected Sayings commentary in the *I Ching* says six lines make a hexagram; why do you say six lines make the trigram EARTH?

ANSWER: When it says six lines make a hexagram, it refers to the hexagrams which the ancient King Wen made by doubling the trigrams invented by Fu Xi in high antiquity. But it cannot be said that there were no three components and six parts before King Wen doubled the trigrams into hexagrams.

A sage of yore said that "the Tao establishing heaven is yin and yang" refers to the HEAVEN and EARTH of the celestial plane, "the Tao establishing earth is flexibility and firmness" refers to the HEAVEN and EARTH of the terrestrial plane, and "the Tao establishing humankind is humanity and justice" refers to the HEAVEN and EARTH of the human dimension.

If you think along these lines, the three components and six parts are contained in the two trigrams HEAVEN and EARTH. The statement that six lines make a hexagram means after the doubling of the trigrams; this is called the temporal dimension.

QUESTION: You may say the three components and six parts were there before the hexagrams, but the *I Ching* commentary says that the *I Ching* images are important for fashioning instruments: were the images established based on instruments, or were instruments fashioned based on the images?
ANSWER: Instruments were fashioned based on the images.

QUESTION: After the august chieftains of high antiquity, later sages of ancient times fashioned instruments, but in each case the *I Ching* commentary refers to it in terms of the hexagrams. You say instruments were fashioned based on the images of the hexagrams, but were the names of the hexagrams in existence before King Wen doubled the trigrams?
ANSWER: You're on the wrong track. A past sage said, "You should believe that there were the Changes to begin with, before the diagrams." So the sixty-four hexagrams represented in the *I Ching* were all there in reality itself before King Wen doubled the trigrams.

QUESTION: If there are sixty-four hexagrams without doubling the trigrams, then why did King Wen double them?
ANSWER: The permutation into sixty-four hexagrams without doubling trigrams is the mental teaching of Fu Xi, the true transmission of the unifying thread of the Tao, leading students of all times to the door of enlightenment.

The production of the sixty-four hexagrams by doubling the trigrams is the consummation of the social studies of King Wen, his son the Duke of Zhou, and the great educator Confucius. Their purpose was to correct human standards, so that people of the world would take to the good and avoid the bad, establishing a stable structure of social relations.

Though one dare not carelessly express the science of essence and life, or human nature and destiny, nevertheless it is unacceptable to conceal this Tao. Confucius revealed it slightly in his *I Ching* commentaries, and the Taoist-Confucian noumenalist Zhou Dunyi clarified it in his writing on the absolute. They wanted people to think carefully and thoroughly and understand it for themselves. This is the kind of study that keeps the knowledge alive.

QUESTION: How do you explain the statement, "One yin and one yang constitute the Tao"?

ANSWER: Yin and yang are HEAVEN and EARTH. HEAVEN and EARTH come from the absolute; the absolute bifurcates into the two modes; the two modes are the celestial and the terrestrial.

QUESTION: HEAVEN ☰ is yang, EARTH ☷ is yin; why do you also speak of the celestial and terrestrial using the ordinary terms for heaven and earth?
ANSWER: The celestial and the terrestrial are HEAVEN and EARTH; HEAVEN and EARTH are yin and yang; yin and yang are one absolute; the absolute is basically infinite.

When we speak in terms of the absolute, we say "celestial" and "terrestrial." When we speak in terms of the Changes as represented by the *I Ching*, we say HEAVEN and EARTH. When we speak in terms of the Tao we say yin and yang.

In terms of the human being, the celestial and the terrestrial are form and substance, HEAVEN and EARTH are sense and essence, yin and yang are spirit and energy.

In terms of technical symbolism, the celestial is called the dragon, the terrestrial is called the tiger; HEAVEN is called the horse, EARTH is called the cow; yang is called the raven, yin is called the rabbit.

In terms of alchemy, the celestial is the cauldron, the terrestrial is the furnace; HEAVEN is metal, EARTH is earth; yin is mercury, yang is lead.

Spoken of separately, there are various different names, but in sum they are one yin and one yang. When people who cultivate immortality forge lead and mercury into a pill of the elixir immortality, this means that the body and mind combine and return to the beginning, yin and yang combine and revert to the absolute.

QUESTION: A commentary in the *I Ching* says, "Heaven and earth establish their positions, and the Changes go on therein." What does this mean?
ANSWER: Heaven and earth establish their positions, humankind is born therein; these are called the three components. Therefore people and things are born again and again, without cease. The reason it does not say people and things, but instead says the Changes, is that the sages say HEAVEN and EARTH are the door of the Changes, and the Tao is followed by adapting to the time.

In alchemy, HEAVEN and EARTH are called the cauldron and furnace—this is "heaven and earth establishing their positions." Yin and yang are called the evolutionary mechanism—this is "the Changes going on therein." Gathering medicine from the origin endlessly is carrying out the firing process unceasingly.

QUESTION: It is also written, "Opening the door is called HEAVEN, closing the door is called EARTH; one opening and one closing is called Change." What does this mean?
ANSWER: One opening and one closing" is one movement and one stillness. The yang of HEAVEN and the yin of EARTH are like the opening and closing of a door; this is the passageway of Changes of HEAVEN and EARTH.

Yin and yang alternate movement and stillness, work and rest go on and on; origin, development, fruition, and consummation establish the four seasons and make a year. Change means transformation.

The ultimate Tao and spirit and energy, as an undifferentiated unity, pervade the universe and all beings, opening and closing endlessly, producing the macrocosm and the microcosm.

Speaking in terms of the human body, this is breathing. Breathing out, one contacts the root of heaven—this is called opening. Breathing in, one contacts the root of earth—this is called closing. One exhalation and one inhalation produce the "gold liquid," the combination of energy and spirit—this is called change.

Opening and closing, breathing out and breathing in, are the "door of the mysterious female," the root of heaven and earth. Here "breathing out" and "breathing in" do not refer to exhalation and inhalation through the nose, but rather to the opening and closing of the true breath, the inner pulse of life, the movement of energy and stillness of spirit.

QUESTION: It is written, "The metaphysical is called the Tao, the physical is called the vessel." What does this mean?
ANSWER: The metaphysical has no form or substance. The physical has body and function. That which has no form or substance is connected to essence; this is called "mercury." That which has body and function is connected to life; this is called "lead." In sum, these are no more than body and mind.

QUESTION: It is written, "The sages used the Changes to clean their hearts, and withdrew into recondite secrecy." What does this mean?

ANSWER: It is the consummation of sincerity and truthfulness. The principles of the Changes extend throughout the macrocosm and the microcosm; sages ponder the principles of the Changes to clean their hearts and thoughts, and store them in ultimate sincerity.

QUESTION: The Classic of Documents says, "The human mind is perilous, the mind of Tao is subtle. Precise and unified, hold to the center." How does one hold to the center?
ANSWER: "Holding" refers to consistent stability. The "center" is the balance of straightforwardness. The mind of Tao is subtle and hard to see, the human mind is perilous and unstable. Even perfected people have the human mind, and even ignoramuses have the mind of Tao. If one can keep the mind constantly balanced in straightforwardness, this is what makes it subtle and hard to see. If the mind is even slightly biased and unbalanced, this is what makes it perilous and unstable.

Students of immortality discern unity and keep to it without vacillation, always holding to the center. Then naturally the perilous becomes safe and the subtle becomes obvious. This is also the reason why in spiritual alchemy the center is taken to be the mysterious pass.

QUESTION: It is written, "The work of heaven above is imperceptible." What does this mean?
ANSWER: The manifestation of truth may be imperceptible, but the Way of Heaven cannot be hidden either. When Taoist scripture speaks of the profound mystery of the macrocosm, this too is in reference to the supreme reality.

QUESTION: What is "unconsciously following the laws of God"?
ANSWER: Sages know it by nature and follow it silently. The celestial design is what is called the natural Tao in which noncontrivance is attained, which is realized without thought and reached without striving. This is what the classic on Equilibrium in the Center calls truthfulness and illumination.

When those who study the Tao already have the capacity, they directly comprehend essence and naturally comprehend life. This is knowing by nature. Those of shallower capacity are unable to comprehend essence directly; they penetrate it by way of teaching, going from being into nonbeing, from the coarse to the subtle. Therefore they first comprehend life and then comprehend essence afterward. This is knowing by learning.

QUESTION: It is said that Confucius was happy even in poverty—wherein lay his happiness?
ANSWER: Confucius was pleased with heaven and knew destiny. Therefore he did not worry. Even when oppressed he still enjoyed himself with music and song. He had attained a state not far from realization of the Changes. He also cultivated himself to restore vision of the heart of heaven and earth, and investigated truth to fulfill human nature and arrive at the meaning of life. This is the marvel of spiritual alchemy.

QUESTION: What about Confucius' great pupil Yan Hui's happiness in poverty?
ANSWER: Yan Hui had learned Confucius' way of satisfaction with the celestial design, knowledge of destiny, and freedom from anxiety. Therefore nothing affected his happiness. So he was like a simpleton, practicing psychological fasting, sitting and forgetting, getting rid of idle intellectualism, nearly becoming empty repeatedly. This too is the marvel of spiritual alchemy.

QUESTION: Zi Lu, another disciple, asked Confucius about death, and Confucius replied, "As long as you don't know life, how can you know death?" What does this mean?
ANSWER: Life and death are like the regularity of day and night; when you know there is day, you know there is night. The *I Ching* speaks of finding out the beginning and returning to the end; thus do we know about death and life.

Alchemical literature says that the state before birth is the basis of the gold pill. Buddhism has us ask where our essence was before our bodies existed.

Looking at it in this way, we see that the point of entry of Confucianism, Taoism, and Buddhism just requires us to find out the beginning, whereupon we will spontaneously know the end, to go back to the source and know the source.

If people can find out where this being comes from, they will naturally know the whole of life and death.

Consider the absolute: prior to the bifurcation of the absolute into yin and yang, what is this? If you can penetrate this, then you will know the state before embodiment. Finding out the beginning, you can thereby comprehend the end.

QUESTION: Before the absolute bifurcates, its form is like an egg. What is outside the egg?
ANSWER: The great void. When people receive energy, and their form and substance are still undifferentiated, they are also like eggs. After they are born, human nature and destiny are established. Outside the body is all the great void.

QUESTION: Confucius said, "My way is permeated by unity." What does this mean?
ANSWER: Sages say the unique celestial design in one's being permeates the universe, including all philosophies and religions and all things. This is like the Buddhist principle of nonabsoluteness of self, person, being, and soul. It is also like the Taoist teaching of comprehending everything by comprehending one. In all of these there is a pervasive unity.

QUESTION: According to the legend of the founding of Chan Buddhism, once Buddha held up a flower before an assembly, and his disciple Mahakasyapa alone smiled. Buddha said, "I have the treasury of vision of truth, the ineffable mind of nirvana—this I entrust to Mahakasyapa." What was this smile?
ANSWER: When Buddha held up the flower before the assembly, no one but Mahakasyapa saw the enlightened mind; that is why he smiled. Therefore Buddha entrusted to Mahakasyapa the marvel that is beyond doctrine.

QUESTION: Bodhidharma, the founder of Chan Buddhism in China, came to China from India and directly pointed to mind, without setting up verbal formulations, so people would see essence and attain enlightenment. What is seeing essence?
ANSWER: Bodhidharma pointed directly to mind with the subtle principle of true emptiness. Seeing essence makes people turn things around so that feelings are empty and they spontaneously see the essence of mind. It cannot be communicated in words.

QUESTION: Confucians have the primordial *I Ching*, Buddhists have the Perfection of Wisdom scriptures, and Taoists have the Spiritual Jewel scriptures—are these not words?

ANSWER: No. They are all cases of sages using the wordless to make formulations in words revealing the true eternal Tao. The Buddhist canon and records of sayings of adepts, the Confucian classics, traditions, and philosophical treatises, and the Taoist scriptures and alchemical texts are all pathways for entry into the Tao, ladders for climbing into the transcendental. If you reach the ultimate point, then not even a single word can be applied.

Your questioning about these various matters is also like a raft to cross a river—the transcendent experience should be sought outside of verbal formulations. If you encounter it, understand it, and penetrate it, you return to the absolute, with complete illumined awareness shining, unobstructed penetrating consciousness. Once essence and life are both complete, form and spirit both sublimated, being one with space, on a par with immortals and Buddhas, will not be hard.

QUESTION: I gratefully accept your revelation of the unifying principle of the three teachings of Buddhism, Taoism, and Confucianism, but it seems to me that there is a difference between Buddhist nirvana and Taoist "release from the matrix."

ANSWER: Nirvana and release from the matrix are but one principle. Release from the matrix means shedding the matrix of mundanity—isn't this nirvana? Taoists refine vitality into energy, refine energy into spirit, refine spirit into emptiness, then embrace the fundamental and return to openness—this is the same principle as the Buddhist teaching of ultimate emptiness, no different.

QUESTION: Is there still evolution after release from the matrix?

ANSWER: There is evolution. A sage has said, "Having a body outside the body is still no marvel; only when space is shattered is complete reality revealed." So after release from the matrix, one should tread the ground of reality until one unites with space.

When Buddhists speak of true emptiness, Confucians of noncontrivance, and Taoists of spontaneity, all are referring to embracing the fundamental, returning to the origin, and uniting with cosmic space. People with fixations cannot know this Way that is permeated with unity.

[12]
QUESTIONS AND ANSWERS

> Use action and stillness for the cauldron and furnace, vitality and energy for water and fire, body and mind for the evolutionary mechanism, essence and sense for the medicinal ingredients.

The teacher said to Zhao Ding-an, "The teachers of former generations, the elevated realized ones, the exalted sages, had a way to supreme reality, and left traditions on it in the world to liberate people—do you know?"

Ding-an said, "I have just entered the mystic school and am completely ignorant. I am very fortunate to have been taken on as a disciple. I really do not know the Tao of supreme true reality, and hope you will teach me."

The teacher said, "The Tao of supreme true reality has no limit that can be surpassed. It is the mystery of mysteries; no image can describe it. It is so without affirmation. It refers to the ultimate, supreme wonder. Sages have called it the Tao.

"All of the superior immortals since antiquity have realized mastery by way of this Tao; their practice and experience have always been based on this. The teaching of spiritual alchemy, which has been handed on privately, through verbal instruction and mind-to-mind communication by enlightened teachers over the generations, is this sublime Tao of supreme true reality."

QUESTION: What is the reason for using the image of a "gold pill" to symbolize the marvel of supreme true reality?
ANSWER: "Gold" means stability, the "pill" means roundness. Buddhists represent this as complete awareness, Confucians represent it as the absolute. It is nothing but the original unified consciousness. Its fundamental true essence, like the stability of gold, like the round-

ness of a pill, never ever decays. The more it is refined, the brighter it becomes. This is symbolized by a circle, which Buddhists call true suchness, Confucians call the absolute, and we Taoists call the gold pill. The names are different, but the essence is the same.

The *I Ching* says Change has an absolute, which gives birth to two modes. The absolute refers to open nonreified nature; the two modes are yin and yang. Yin and yang are heaven and earth, and humanity lives between heaven and earth. These are called the three components.

The Tao of the three components is inherent in one body: the absolute is the basic spirit, the two modes are body and mind. In terms of alchemy, the absolute is the matrix of the pill, the two modes are true lead and true mercury, the sense of real knowledge and the essence of conscious knowledge.

What we call lead and mercury do not refer to substances such as quicksilver, cinnabar, sulfur, tin, or vegetable matter. Nor are they semen, saliva, or the energy and blood of the genitals and heart. They are the basic spirit in the body and the basic energy in the body.

When the body is not agitated, the vital energy congeals; this is represented as an elixir pill. The so-called elixir pill is the body. What is represented by the empty circle is the essence, the true essence: taking the essence from the elixir is called the completion of the pill. The elixir pill is not made with anything external; it is made of the basis of life. This is truly real.

Few people know this. Many do not get the right information and seek externals, pursuing the false and turning their backs on the true. Therefore there are many who study but few who attain.

Some work with minerals, some work with external vapors such as clouds and fog, some work with sunlight and moonlight, some gather starlight, some "make elixir" by visualizing nine pills in the sky, some visualize something in the abdomen and call that the elixir pill, some keep their minds on the point between the eyebrows, some drive the vitality up the spine to boost the brain, some convey energy into the umbilical region.

And there are many other practices—ingesting filth, drinking semen and menstrual blood, breathing exercises, physical exercises, psychosomatic exercises, refining hormones from urine, bending and stretching and massage, silently paying court to the supreme god, circulating energy through the torso and head—there are more than a thousand such minor techniques, which will not accomplish the great result even if practiced diligently. This is what is meant by the classic statement, "Correct method is hard to find—many miss the true way and many enter abberant schools."

The essentials of arriving at reality are utterly simple, utterly easy; difficult to find, but easy to accomplish. None would fail to achieve it if they were guided by perfected people.

QUESTION: Please instruct me.
ANSWER: Refining the gold pill is all a matter of taking over the creative evolution of heaven and earth. Use action and stillness for the cauldron and furnace, vitality and energy for water and fire, body and mind for the evolutionary mechanism, essence and sense for the medicinal ingredients. Keep centered on mindfulness of the celestial, find the mysterious pass, gather the vital energy of the sense of essence at the appropriate time, then withdraw into watchful passivity in the proper manner.

Unify essence, sense, spirit, vitality, and will. Keep a balanced proportion of firmness and flexibility, creativity and receptivity, movement and stillness. With a combination of will and the inner sense of true essence, return to the fundamental, go back to the basis, revert to the root, and return to Life. When the work is complete and the spirit is prepared, the ordinary is shed and one becomes an immortal. This is called the completion of the elixir pill.

The most hidden and subtle mechanism is the mysterious pass. Why don't the alchemical classics say just where the mysterious pass is? It is for the very reason that it is indescribable and inexplicable that it is called the mysterious pass. Therefore sages have just used the word "center" to point it out to people. The mysterious pass is indicated by the word "center."

This "center" does not mean center in the sense of inside as opposed to outside, nor does it mean center in terms of location in the center of the four directions. Buddhists say, "When you don't think good or bad, what are you basically like?" This is the center of Chan. Confucians say, "When emotions are not active, this is called the center." This is the center of Confucianism. Taoists say, "Where thoughts do not arise is called the center." This is the center of Taoism. This is the center as applied by the three teachings.

When the *I Ching* says "tranquil, unperturbed," this is the substance of the center; "sensitive and effective" is the function of the center.

Lao-tzu says, "Effecting utter emptiness, keeping complete silence, as myriad things act in concert, I thereby watch the return."

The *I Ching* says, "Return means seeing the heart of heaven and earth."

The *I Ching* hexagram RETURN ☷☳ consists of one yang —— arising under five yins — —: yin is quietude, yang is movement; when quietude reaches its consummation, it gives rise to movement. It is this point of movement that is the mysterious pass.

Just apply your attention to the point where you rouse the mind and activate thought, concentrating on this constantly—then the mysterious pass will spontaneously appear. When you see the mysterious pass, then the medicinal ingredients, the firing process, the operation, extracting and adding, all the way to release from the matrix and spiritual transformation, are all in this one opening.

Gathering medicine means gathering the true sense of the essence of consciousness within oneself. This is done by first quieting the mind to still the impulses of arbitrary feelings; when stillness is perfected, there is a movement of unconditioned energy. This is the energy of true sense, and its first movement arising from stillness is called the return of yang. This is to be fostered until sense and essence, energy and spirit, are united. After that, withdraw into watchful passivity, because if you persist in intensive concentration after the point of sufficiency, your work will be wasted.

Thus the cycle of work goes from movement to stillness to movement to stillness. With long perseverance in practice, there takes place a gradual solidification, a gradual crystallization, which is the stabilization of real consciousness. This is described as nonsubstance producing substance, and it is represented as a spiritual embryo. This is called completion of the elixir.

QUESTION: You have told me about the process of the work, but I don't know all the different terms—please instruct me.
ANSWER: The different terms are just symbols—none are beyond body and mind. When you are working, stilling the senses and tuning the breath, physically immobile, and you cause the vitality, spirit, higher soul, lower soul, and will each to rest in its own proper place, this is called the "five energies returning to the basis."

When the mind does not move, this is called "the dragon howling." When the body does not move, this is called "the tiger roaring." Not moving physically or mentally is called "overcoming the dragon and subduing the tiger." When the dragon howls, the energy is stable; when the tiger roars, the vitality is stable.

Vitality and energy are symbolized by a snake and a tortoise, body and mind by a tiger and a dragon. Uniting these is called "combining the four signs."

Concentrating sense through essence is called "metal and wood joining." Controlling energy by vitality is called "water and fire mixing."

Wood and fire have the same source, their natures are one; their associated numbers add up to five. Water and metal have the same source, their natures are one; their associated numbers also add up to five. The chamber of earth, in the center, is assigned the number five. When mind, body, and will unite, these three sets meet and form the "infant." This is called the merging of the three fives.

Refining vitality into energy, refining energy into spirit, refining spirit back into openness—this is called "the three flowers gathered on the peak." It is also called the three passes.

Many students now refer to the coccyx, midspine, and back of the head as the three passes. This is just a method of practice, in which the attention is focused on these three sensitive areas and psychic energy is sent through them along the spinal column. This is not quintessential.

The point of arousing the mind and activating thought is the "mysterious female." People who refer to the mysterious female as the mouth and nose, relating it to ordinary respiration, are incorrect.

Body, mind, and will are the three essentials. The essence in the mind is called "mercury within cinnabar." The energy in the body is called "metal in water."

Not letting external objects in, not letting inner states out—this is called "stable settlement."

Being tranquil and unperturbed is called "nurturing the fire." Open, nonreifying spontaneity is called "operation."

Maintaining sincerity and focusing the will is called "guarding the castle."

Conquering inner demons is called "battle in the field."

True mercury is called the girl, true lead is called the boy. The embryonic breath is called the go-between. Essence and sense are called husband and wife.

Cleaning the mind and stabilizing the will, the essence is tranquil and the spirit is aware; yin and yang combine, the three bases convene—this is called "completing the embryo."

Carefully protecting the spiritual root is called "incubation." Incubation is like a dragon nurturing a pearl, like a hen sitting on her eggs; one carefully guards against straying, for with the slightest slip all the work that has gone before is wasted.

Luminous spirit emerging from the shell is called "release from the matrix." Returning to the root, returning to Life, going back to the original beginning, is called "transcendent liberation." Breaking through space is called "perfect attainment."

QUESTION: When the gold pill is completed, can it be seen?
ANSWER: It can be seen.

QUESTION: Does it have form?
ANSWER: It has no form.

QUESTION: If it has no form, how can it be seen?
ANSWER: "Gold pill' is just a name. How could it have form? I say it can be seen, but it cannot be seen with the eyes. In Buddhism it is said, "In not seeing, one sees intimately; in intimate seeing, one does not see." A Taoist scripture says, "When you look at it, you don't see it; when you listen for it, you don't hear it. This is called the Tao."

Looking at it, you don't see it, yet never are you not seeing it; listening for it, you don't hear it, yet never are you not hearing it. To say it can be seen and heard does not mean it is within the reach of eye and ear—it is only seen by the mind, heard by the will.

For a simile, let us take the example of the wind: in the mountains it makes the trees sway, on the water it rouses waves, so we cannot say it is not there; yet we cannot see it or grasp it, so in that sense we cannot say it is there.

So it is also with the substance of the gold pill. Therefore in the beginning of refinement of the pill elixir, being and nonbeing work together, movement and stillness need each other. Then when you accomplish the work, all entanglements abruptly cease, all things are empty, movement and stillness are both forgotten, being and nonbeing are both gone.

Now the mystic pearl takes shape, and the great unity returns to reality. Essence and life both complete, physically and mentally sublimated, one leaves reification and enters nonreification, roams in the clouds, and realizes incorruptible immortality.

Thus the scriptures and alchemical writings use various different terms to lead students from the crude to the subtle, so that they may gradually enter a state of beatitude and then see essence and realize openness.

The actuality is not on paper; writings are like a boat to ferry people across a river—once the people are on the other shore, the boat has no more use. This is the point of the saying of the ancient sage Zhuangzi, "When you catch the rabbit you forget the trap, when you snare the fish you forget the net."

And now that I have said all this to you, you should not cling to the words; just savor the meaning thoroughly and search out the root source. If your mind opens up at a word, it will not be hard to enter right into the realm of noncontrivance.

But there is still a mechanism beyond, which is not easy to set forth lightly—you should seek it outside words.

[13]
Some Questions on Alchemy

The three passes are the workings of the three bases. Refining vitality into energy is the first pass, refining energy into spirit is the middle pass, refining spirit back into openness is the upper pass.

Of all the commentaries of people of later times on the alchemical classics and writings of the adepts, none are useful. Some are attached to physical forms, some cling to verbal formulations, some consider clear purity to be the emptiness of suffering, some think mercury and lead have form. Their views are not the same—how could people who came after them not be confused? They still do not know the ultimate Tao is one—how could there be two?

Moreover, what are compiled in alchemical books of recent times are mostly sidetracks; their interpretations of "seven-reversion," "nine-restoration," and numerical sequences, for example, are mistaken. So here I have taken the essence of alchemical literature and assembled a number of questions to break through confusion.

QUESTION: What does "nine-restoration" mean?
ANSWER: Nine is the number associated with metal, which symbolizes sense. Restoration means return to the basis. So "nine-restoration" means using essence to concentrate sense. This is what alchemical literature means when it says, "When metal first returns to essence, then it can be called restored elixir." "Nine-restoration" does not refer to an enumeration of a series.

QUESTION: What does "seven-reversion" mean?
ANSWER: Seven is the number associated with fire, which symbolizes the spirit. Reversion means reversion to the fundamental. So "seven-reversion" means refining the spirit back into openness. Here again,

"seven-reversion" does not mean enumeration of a series. This is what the classic *Understanding Reality* means when it says, "Stop enumeration, just get the five forces in proper order."

QUESTION: What are the "three passes"?
ANSWER: The three passes are the workings of the three bases. Refining vitality into energy is the first pass, refining energy into spirit is the middle pass, refining spirit back into openness is the upper pass.

Some call the coccyx, midspine, and back of the head the "three passes," but this just refers to a method of practice and is not utterly essential. That which is essential to ascend to reality is in the three passes—how could they have fixed locations? It is a matter for personal instruction.

QUESTION: What is the "mysterious pass"?
ANSWER: The mysterious pass is the most abstruse, most subtle mechanism. It has no fixed location. Nowadays many people indicate the umbilical sphere, or the top of the head, or the forehead, or the space between the kidneys and genitals, or the space in front of the kidneys and behind the navel. These are all sidetracks.

An alchemical text says, "The opening of the mysterious pass is not to the right or the left, not in front or back, not above or below, not on the inside or outside, not on either side, not in the middle. It is the point where the physical elements and five forces do not adhere."

QUESTION: What are the "three chambers"?
ANSWER: The three chambers are the abodes of the three bases. Spirit resides in the chamber of HEAVEN, energy resides in the central chamber, and vitality resides in the chamber of EARTH. The chamber of HEAVEN, the abode of spirit, is also called the chamber of the purple climax; the central chamber is also called the yellow room; the chamber of EARTH, the abode of vitality, is also called the mansion on the crimson hill. People nowadays who define the three chambers as the "three elixir fields" in the lower abdomen, solar plexus, and brain are incorrect.

QUESTION: What are the "three essentials"?
ANSWER: The three essentials are the opening of returning to the root, the pass of returning to Life, and the valley of open nonreification.

QUESTION: What is the "mysterious female"?
ANSWER: As the *Tao Te Ching* says, "The valley spirit not dying is called the mysterious female." The adept Ziyang said, "The place where thought arises is called the mysterious female." This is correct. I say the place where thought arises is the root of birth and death—is this not the mysterious female? Even so, this only indicates a method of practice; the supreme vehicle is a matter for personal instruction.

QUESTION: What is the "true seed"?
ANSWER: The true seed is the point of spiritual light which is prior to the dichotomization of heaven and earth. Some say people are born from energy, and therefore consider energy the true seed. Some say this body exists due to thought, so they consider thought to be the true seed. Some say this body exists due to reception of the female and male vitalities, so they consider vitality to be the true seed. These three explanations seem right, but actually are wrong. This is what Buddhists mean by the saying, "What the ignorant call the original reality is in fact the root of infinite eons of birth and death."

QUESTION: What are the "crucible" and "furnace"?
ANSWER: Mind and body are the crucible and furnace. An alchemical text says, "First take HEAVEN and EARTH for the crucible and furnace, then take the medicines of the raven and rabbit and cook them." HEAVEN is the mind, EARTH is the body. People nowadays who set up an external furnace and crucible are mistaken.

QUESTION: What are the "medicinal ingredients"?
ANSWER: The medicinal ingredients are true lead and true mercury. These are just the original two things, yin and yang. They may be taken to refer to body and mind, sense and essence, or real knowledge and conscious knowledge.

QUESTION: What is "inner medicine," what is "outer medicine"?
ANSWER: The inner and outer medicines are refining vitality, energy, and spirit. The substance is one, but there are two functions. Sexual vitality, metabolic energy, and thinking spirit are all outer medicine. The primordial essential vitality, the energy of open nonreified spaciousness, and the undecaying basic spirit are inner medicine. This is

what is meant by the dual function, inner and outer, mentioned in alchemical literature.

QUESTION: The classic *Understanding Reality* says, "Knock on bamboo to call the tortoise to ingest jade mushroom." What does this mean?
ANSWER: Knocking on bamboo means stilling energy; calling the tortoise means concentrating vitality. Refining vitality into energy, using energy to concentrate vitality, vitality and energy merge and crystallize into a "jade mushroom." Ingesting this preserves life.

QUESTION: *Understanding Reality* says, "Strum the lute to call the phoenix to drink from the medicinal spoon." What does this mean?
ANSWER: Strumming the lute means emptying the mind; calling the phoenix means nurturing the spirit. When you empty the mind and nurture the spirit, the mind is clear, the spirit is transformed. The medicinal spoon is formed by conjunction of the celestial will and the earthly will; drinking from this makes essence complete and clear.

QUESTION: What is "the five energies returning to the source"?
ANSWER: When the body is not agitated, the vitality is stable—this is represented as water returning to the source. When the mind is not agitated, the energy is stable—this is represented as fire returning to the source. When the essence of consciousness is still, the higher soul remains within—this is represented as metal returning to the source. When the physical constitution is in harmony, the will is settled—this is represented as earth returning to the source. This total state is called the five energies returning to the source.

QUESTION: What is the "yellow woman"?
ANSWER: Yellow is the color associated with the center; woman refers to mother. Myriad beings are born from earth, so earth is the mother of myriad beings, and thus is called the yellow woman. In humans, this is called the embryonic breath, which means the combination of spirit and energy. It also refers to the true will, which stands in the center of mind and body, heaven and earth, and joins them in harmonious union.

QUESTION: What is the "metal man"?
ANSWER: The metal man is another term for true lead, or the firm sense of real knowledge.

QUESTION: What is "real gold"?
ANSWER: Gold is the basic spirit. It never decays, and becomes brighter the more it is refined, so it is called real gold.

QUESTION: What are "child and mother"?
ANSWER: The spirit is the mother of the body. The spirit being hidden in the body is represented as the mother being concealed within the child.

QUESTION: What are "guest and host"?
ANSWER: Essence is the host of the body, the body is the guest. Now we use this body to nurture this essence, so we let body be the host. This is what the classic *Understanding Reality* means when it says, "Let the other be the host, oneself be the guest."

QUESTION: What is "the primordial one energy"?
ANSWER: Before heaven and earth dichotomize, there is just one awareness; this is the point of true yang in the body. Because it is prior to the separation of the celestial and the earthly, it is called primordial.

QUESTION: What are "water and fire"?
ANSWER: In the sky, the moon and the sun are water and fire; in the *I Ching*, peril and awareness are water and fire; in Chan Buddhism, concentration and insight are water and fire. Confucian sages consider luster and luminosity water and fire; medical science refers to the genitals and heart as water and fire; alchemy takes vitality and energy as water and fire.

I now clearly point out that whatever in one's body flames upward is considered fire, and whatever descends and moistens is considered water. All the various names are metaphors used to foster direct experience in learners.

QUESTION: How is it that there is water in fire?
ANSWER: Water stands for the spirit, fire for awareness; water in fire is the spirit in awareness.

QUESTION: How is it that there is fire in water?
ANSWER: Fire in water, in terms of the body, is the energy within vitality.

QUESTION: What is being "settled"?
ANSWER: When water rises and fire descends, that is called being settled. The *I Ching* says, "There is a lake below a mountain, diminishing: thus does the superior person stop anger and craving." This is the method of settlement: stop anger and fire descends, stop craving and water rises.

QUESTION: What is being "unsettled"?
ANSWER: When you can't stop anger, fire flames upward; when you can't stop craving, water wets below: the fire of ignorance blazes, the waves of the ocean of suffering roll; the water of desire and the fire of intelligence do not mix. This is called being unsettled.

QUESTION: What is "metal and wood joining"?
ANSWER: Sense coming back to essence is called joining. Sense is associated with metal, essence with wood.

QUESTION: What is "separation"?
ANSWER: When feelings pursue things and consciousness follows thoughts, sense and essence diverge—this is called separation.

QUESTION: What are "clarity" and "turbulence"?
ANSWER: Clarity is when the mind does not stir; turbulence is when the mind stirs.

QUESTION: What are the "two eights"?
ANSWER: The contents of one pound—eight ounces of lead, eight ounces of mercury. It is not really a matter of pounds and ounces—the point is that the two things must be equal. An alchemical text says, "After the prior crescent, before the latter crescent, the medicinal ingredients are equal, the power of the fire is complete." This means balanced proportion of yin and yang—the earthly and the celestial, flexibility and firmness, conscious knowledge and real knowledge. This is also represented by the equality of day and night at the equinoxes.

QUESTION: What is "bathing"?
ANSWER: Washing the mind, cleaning out thoughts—this is called bathing.

QUESTION: What is "completion of the elixir pill"?
ANSWER: When body and mind unite, spirit and energy merge, and sense and essence conjoin—this is called completion of the elixir pill. It is represented as a spiritual embryo.

QUESTION: What is "nurturing the fire"?
ANSWER: Stopping thoughts is nurturing the fire.

QUESTION: What is "release from the matrix"?
ANSWER: Having a body outside the body is release from the matrix.

QUESTION: What is "perfect attainment"?
ANSWER: Merging with cosmic space is called perfect attainment. Evolution beyond things is not easy to speak of—it is a matter of people attaining it themselves.

[14]
LIVE TEACHINGS ON COMPLETE REALITY

> Learning the science of spiritual immortality does not require a lot of doing; the elixir is just a matter of refining the three treasures of vitality, energy, and spirit.

People on the path of Complete Reality should practice the path of Complete Reality. Complete Reality means keeping the basic reality complete. Only when you keep vitality, energy, and spirit complete can it be called complete reality: as soon as there is any lack, it is not complete; as soon as there is any defilement, it is not real.

, , ,

By keeping vitality complete you can preserve the body. To keep vitality complete first requires that the body be settled. When settled, there is no desire, so vitality is complete.

, , ,

By keeping energy complete you can nurture the mind. To keep energy complete first requires that the mind be clear and calm. When clear and calm, there are no thoughts, so energy is complete.

, , ,

By keeping spirit complete you can return to openness. To keep spirit complete first requires that the will be sincere. When the will is sincere, body and mind combine and return to openness.

, , ,

Therefore vitality, energy, and spirit are the three basic medicines; body, mind, and will are the three basic essentials.

, , ,

Learning the science of spiritual immortality does not require a lot of doing; the elixir pill is just a matter of refining the three treasures of vitality, energy, and spirit. When the three treasures are combined in the central chamber, the gold pill is completed. It is easy to know, not hard to practice. What is hard to practice and hard to know is fallacious, mere deception.

, , ,

The essential point in refining vitality is in the body. When the body is not agitated, "wind rises at the tiger's roar," "the dark tortoise hides away," and the basic vitality solidifies.

, , ,

The essential point in refining energy is in the mind. When the mind is not agitated, "clouds rise at the dragon's howl," "the red sparrow folds its wings," and the basic energy rests.

, , ,

The essential point in refining spirit is in the will. When the will does not waver, the celestial and the earthly combine, the three bases merge into one, and the spiritual embryo is complete.

, , ,

The cauldron and furnace of HEAVEN and EARTH, the medicinal ingredients of WATER and FIRE, the eight trigrams, three bases, five forces, and four forms are all no more than body, mind, and will.

, , ,

The consummation of complete reality is not outside of body and mind; whatever is apart from body and mind is an aberrant path. Yet even so, you should not get fixated on body or mind, for as soon as you get fixated on body or mind, you are burdened by body and mind. You must be one with their function, yet detached from their function.

, , ,

"Body and mind" do not mean the illusory body and physical brain; they are the invisible body and mind. What are the invisible body and mind? "Clouds rise from the mountains, the moon is in the heart of the waves."

, , ,

The "body" is the pure serene body of all time, subtle being within nonbeing. The "mind" is the root of spiritual subtlety before imagination, true nonbeing within being. Being within nonbeing is represented by the *I Ching* trigram WATER ☵, nonbeing within being is represented by the trigram FIRE ☲.

, , ,

Ziyang, one of the founders of the Complete Reality path, says in his classic *Understanding Reality*, "Take the solid heart in the center of WATER ☵ and change the yin inside FIRE ☲. From this it changes into the healthy body of HEAVEN ☰. Then to lie hidden or to leap into flight is entirely up to the mind." So there can be no doubt that body and mind are the point of consummation of complete reality.

, , ,

The point of spiritual alchemy is a matter of essence and life only. Anything apart from essence and life is a sidetrack. Clinging to one side is bias.

, , ,

One of the founding teachers said, "Spirit is essence, energy is life." This is what I am talking about.

, , ,

Refining energy is a matter of preserving the body, refining spirit is a matter of preserving the mind. When the body does not stir, "the tiger roars"; when the mind does not stir, "the dragon howls." When the tiger roars, lead goes into mercury; when the dragon howls, mercury goes into lead.

, , ,

Lead and mercury are different names for WATER and FIRE. The yang —— in WATER ☵ is the ultimate vitality in the body; the yin — — in FIRE ☲ is the basic energy in the mind. To refine vitality into energy is the way to first preserve the body; to refine energy into spirit is the way to first preserve the mind.

⁂

When the body is settled, one is physically firm; when physically firm, one perfects life. When the mind is settled, the spirit is complete; when the spirit is complete, one perfects essence. When body and mind unite, essence and life are complete, and one is physically and spiritually sublimated, this is called completion of the elixir.

⁂

When vitality turns into energy and energy turns into spirit, this is not yet wonderful. Why? There is still the subtlety of refining the spirit, which is not easy to speak of.

⁂

What I have spoken of is the general outline of spiritual alchemy. If you have insight, you will believe the great matter is not on paper. Otherwise, you should know where to set to work. Once you know where to set to work, then practice accordingly, beginning with refinement of vitality. After vitality is stabilized, then refine energy. After energy is stabilized, then refine spirit. After spirit is stabilized, then return to openness. When empty and open, you are imbued with the qualities of the Tao.

⁂

Refining vitality is a matter of knowing the time. In this context, "time" does not mean terrestrial time. If you cling to terrestrial time, that is not it. But if you say there is no time, how do you set to work? The ancients said that when the time arrives the spirit knows. One of the founding teachers said, "When lead sees winter, you should hasten to gather it." These words tell all: lead is true sense, winter is utter stillness; stilling conditioned feelings allows true sense to emerge—when true sense emerges, gather it at once.

⁂

Refining energy is a matter of harmonization. Harmonization means harmonization of the true breath and the true basis. Lao-tzu said, "The door of the mysterious female is called the root of heaven and earth. Continuously there as such, using it is not forced." This is the essential point of harmonization.

, , ,

The mysterious female is the mechanism of opening and closing of heaven and earth. The *I Ching* says, "Closing the door is called EARTH, opening the door is called HEAVEN; alternate closing and opening is called change." Alternating closing and opening is alternating stillness and movement. This is the meaning of Lao-tzu's statement "using it is not forced."

, , ,

An alchemical text says, "Breathing out contacts the root of heaven, breathing in contacts the root of earth. On breathing out, the dragon howls, clouds arise; on breathing in, the tiger roars, wind arises." I say that "breathing out contacts the root of heaven, breathing in contacts the root of earth" is the same as "closing the door is called EARTH, opening the door is called HEAVEN." "On breathing out, the dragon howls, clouds arise; on breathing in, the tiger roars, wind arises" is the same as "the alternation of closing and opening is called change." It is also the meaning of "using it is not forced." The breathing referred to here is the endless coming and going of the true breath, the pulse of life within the cyclic changes of the macrocosm and the microcosm.

[15]
Spoken Teachings

> The functions of vitality, energy, and spirit are twofold, but their substance is one. In terms of the outer medicine, first sexual vitality must not be used compulsively. Then the energy of breath must be very subtle, until there is no noticeable breathing. Then the spirit of thought should be calm and quiet.

The coming and going of external yin and yang is the outer medicine; the combining of internal WATER and FIRE is the inner medicine. The outer involves active application, the inner is spontaneous.

, , ,

The functions of vitality, energy, and spirit are twofold, but their substance is one. In terms of the outer medicine, first sexual vitality must not be used compulsively; then the energy of breath must be very subtle, until there is no noticeable breathing; then the spirit of thought should be calm and quiet.

, , ,

In terms of the inner medicine, refining vitality means refining the basic vitality, taking the primordial awareness out of the mundane context. This is represented as taking the basic yang out of WATER ☵. When the basic vitality is stabilized, then sexual vitality is naturally not compulsive.

, , ,

Refining energy means refining the basic energy, taking the conditioning out of ordinary consciousness. This is represented as filling in the yin inside FIRE ☲. When the basic energy is stabilized, the energy of breath naturally does not go out and in.

Refining spirit means refining the basic spirit, combining subconscious real knowledge with conscious ordinary knowledge. This is represented as combining WATER ☵ and FIRE ☲ to make HEAVEN ☰. When the basic spirit is stabilized, the spirit of thought is at peace.

, , ,

Beyond this, there is still the stage of refining spaciousness, which is not easy to speak of; it is best understood tacitly. Work on this.

[16]
Discourses

> If those who cultivate life do not understand essence, how can they escape the movement of time? If those who see essence do not know life, where will they wind up in the end?

On Essence and Life

"Essence" refers to the primordial, utterly inconceivable spirit. "Life" refers to the primordial, utterly vital energy. Vitality and spirit are the root of essence and life.

, , ,

The development of essence relates to mind; the development of life relates to the body.

, , ,

Understanding and knowledge come from the mind; with thought and imagination, the mind employs essence. Actions and reactions come from the body; with speech and silence, looking and listening, the body burdens life.

, , ,

When life is burdened by the body, there is birth and death. When essence is employed by the mind, there is coming and going.

, , ,

So we know body and mind are the abodes of vitality and spirit, vitality and spirit are the bases of essence and life.

, , ,

Essence cannot be there without life, life cannot be there without essence. Though there are two names, in principle they are one.

It is a pity that students today—Buddhists and Taoists—divide essence and life into two, each fixated on one side. Buddhists are fixated on essence, Taoists on life; criticizing each other, they do not realize that neither solitary yin nor isolated yang can fulfill the great work.

If those who cultivate life do not understand essence, how can they escape the movement of time? If those who see essence do not know life, where will they wind up in the end?

An immortal teacher said, "Refining the gold elixir pill without realizing essence is the number one sickness of practice; but if you just cultivate the true essence and not the elixir, the yin spirit cannot enter enlightenment for myriad eons." How true these words are!

Highly developed people master both essence and life. First they open their minds by discipline, concentration, and insight; then they preserve their bodies by refining vitality, energy, and spirit.

When the vitality is settled, the foundation of life is permanently stabilized; when the mind is open and clear, the basis of essence is completely illumined.

When essence is completely illumined, there is no coming or going; when life is stabilized, there is no death or birth.

At the point of complete unification, one enters right into noncontrivance; essence and life both complete, one is physically and mentally sublimated.

Still, it cannot be said that essence and life are fundamentally two; yet they cannot be explained as one matter either. They are fundamentally one, but the function is twofold.

Those who are fixated and partial, each setting up one aspect to enter into, are those who do not understand essence and life. If you do not understand essence and life, then there is dichotomization. As long as essence and life are not preserving each other, it is impossible to attain reality.

On the Symbolism of the I Ching Signs

The adept Haiqiong said that in the highest type of spiritual alchemy there are no signs or lines. So why do the alchemical books all use signs and lines from the *I Ching?* It is because all the sages set up teachings to illustrate the Tao. This is the meaning of the ancient saying, "There are no words for the Tao, but without words we cannot reveal the Tao."

, , ,

The signs are like signs hung in the sky to show people something, just as nature gives signs of what bodes well and ill, so people can easily see. Symbols represent this; the lines are similitudes.

, , ,

The trigram signs have three lines; these represent heaven, earth, and humanity, which are our three bases. The six lines of the hexagram signs represent the six directions of space, which are our head, feet, chest, back, and hands.

, , ,

The reason why alchemical texts use the *I Ching* signs and their lines is so that students will set up the "furnace" based on the pattern of the symbols and foster the "fire" according to the lines; these provide readily accessible guidelines. The reason Haiqiong said there are no signs or lines is to warn people not to get mired in the lines and symbols, to actualize the function in a detached way.

, , ,

For example, before this body is born, as-is-ness is unmoving—this is the time before the dichotomization of the absolute. Establishing essence and life based on the existence of this body is the absolute producing the two modes of yin and yang. When there are form and substance, then there are essence and sense—this is the two modes producing the four signs. Ultimately the vitality, spirit, higher soul, lower soul, will, energy, body, and mind are all complete—this is the four signs producing the eight trigrams.

, , ,

A sage of old said, "Buddhists cultivate concentration in the chamber of FIRE, Taoists seek the mystery in the domain of WATER." These are said to be the essential points in refining essence and life.

, , ,

Cultivating concentration in the chamber of FIRE means practicing discipline, concentration, and insight, not allowing sense objects to influence one, so that myriad existents are void. This is getting rid of the yin in the center of FIRE ☲, which means removing mundane conditioning from consciousness.

, , ,

Seeking the mystery in the domain of WATER means refining vitality, energy, and spirit, causing the three flowers to assemble on the peak and the five energies to return to the source. This is keeping the yang in the center of WATER ☵, which means preserving the primordial awareness underlying the original vitality of life.

, , ,

Exceptionally accomplished people master both principles, bearing yin and embracing yang, emptying the mind of compulsive conditioning and filling the being with primal energy. This is represented as taking the yang in the center of WATER and using it to fill the yin in the center of FIRE, thus producing once again the body of HEAVEN. This is what Ziyang's classic *Understanding Reality* means when it says, "Take the fullness in the center of WATER to change the yin in FIRE, thus transforming it into the whole body of HEAVEN. Then to lie hidden or to leap into flight is entirely up to the mind."

, , ,

As for using the signs and lines in carrying out the firing process, in the two hexagrams HEAVEN ☰ and EARTH ☷, strength and gentility depend on each other, coming and going alternately, establishing the four seasons, making a year, with the operation of the four qualities of creativity, development, fruition, and consummation going on endlessly. The firing process, with its advance and withdrawal, extraction and addition, increasing and decreasing, is modeled on and represented by this, concentrating a year into a month, concentrating a month into a day, concentrating a day into an hour, concentrating an hour into one breath. From a world-age on the macrocosmic scale down to a single breath on the microcosmic scale, everything has a cyclic movement. Those who understand this principle get the essence of the active and passive phases of the alchemical process.

* * *

But even though spiritual alchemy uses signs and its firing process uses their lines, these are all just symbols, and you should not get fixated on the signs and lines. You should know that you may need a raft to cross a river, but you do not need a boat when you get to the other shore; when you have caught the fish, forget the net, when you have caught the rabbit, forget the trap. This is what Ziyang meant when he wrote in his *Understanding Reality*, "When you get the meaning here, stop looking for symbols; if you study the lines, you are using your mind in vain," and "Distinguish midnight and noon within unmarked time, determine HEAVEN and EARTH in lineless signs."

* * *

I say that those born knowing realize on their own without seeking, hit the mark without trying—they do not need inductive teachings, so the highest type of spiritual alchemy does not use signs and lines. Mediocre and lesser people cannot understand directly and must enter gradually; therefore the alchemical texts all use *I Ching* lines and signs as guidelines for method. Those with understanding can comprehend them by themselves through contemplation.

[17]

Explanatory Talks

> If you do not cling to appearances, appearances will not cling to you. If you are not obsessed with anything, nothing will hold you.

Death and Life

Lao-tzu said people think lightly of death because of their eagerness for life. He also said that only those who do not make a fuss about life are wise in terms of valuing life.

⸫

This means that when you look for life, after all you cannot find it—then how can there be death? When there is life, then there is death; if there is no death, there is no life.

⸫

So we know that in the great matter of essence and life, death and life are important.

⸫

If you want to know death, you must first know life. When you know life, then you naturally know death. When Tzu-lu asked Confucius about death, Confucius said, "As long as you do not know life, how can you know death?" How great are the words of a sage! This seems to be what the *I Ching* means by the expression, "Find out the beginning, comprehend the end, thereby know the explanation of death and life."

⸫

I say that when those who study the Tao want to comprehend the end, they first find out the beginning; when they want to know the final end, they investigate the immediate present. If you are free right now, you will be free at the end; if you are independent right now, you will be independent at the end.

, , ,

The ability of the enlightened ones of all times to shed the mundane, become spiritually transformed, and adapt to changes endlessly, comes from their having purified themselves beforehand; thus at the end they rose lightly. If people can see through all situations in everyday life and get past them, not being blinded by things, not being compelled by entanglements, then in the end nothing will be able to blind them, no emotional entanglements will be able to hold them.

, , ,

I see people practicing meditation nowadays who drift into all sorts of imaginations as soon as they close their eyes. Once they have entered the realm of deception, they become one with their delusions, quite unawares. Sometimes they become aware of it, but are not able to drive delusions away. They become like zombies—they have all their ordinary sense faculties, but they are not able to use them freely; they are confused by imaginations and are unable to put them aside. Since they cannot be free right now, how can they be free on the border of life and death?

, , ,

If you are stable and strong, then it will be the same whether your eyes are open or closed—you will not be affected by any illusory states. Coming and going unhindered, you will have great freedom. If you are free now, why worry about not being free at the end?

, , ,

The work you do right now is itself the great matter of the end. The immediate present is the cause, the end is the result. All present thoughts lead into mundanity, all illusory reifications are in the realm of deception. If you can clear them away in ordinary life, then you will not be confused by them at the end.

, , ,

Random or confused thoughts should be gotten rid of by reason, illusory reifications should be cut off by will. When thoughts end, mundanity vanishes; when illusory reifications are empty, deceptions disappear. This is how the celestial emerges. After long long practice, the mundane is exhausted and the celestial is total—this is called immortality.

When conditions increasing thoughts arise, and you let your mind follow along, then mundanity grows and deception is strong. This is how the celestial fades away. If this goes on habitually for a long long time, until the celestial is exhausted and mundanity is total, you die.

, , ,

As long as any mundanity is left in those engaged in the great work, they do not become immortal; as long as any of the celestial is left in ordinary people, they do not die. Those who see this are of high rank in the mystic school.

, , ,

Establish firm resolve, keep the mind free from doubt; directly bring about bare clean open clarity, not allowing any defiling attachment or fixation—then this is the pure spiritual body.

If you do not cling to appearances, appearances will not cling to you. If you are not obsessed with anything, nothing will hold you. If you do not watch anyone, no one will watch you. If you do not mind anything, nothing will mind you. If you do not focus on any sensations, no sensations will focus on you.

, , ,

When sense data do not enter, the senses are pure; form, sensation, conception, conditioning, and consciousness are all empty. Then both ordinary and extraordinary perceptive capacities become complete and clear. When you reach this point, the senses perform each other's functions, and the whole body becomes an eye. Mundanities end, and the whole being is purely celestial. Essence and life are both complete, and one merges with the Tao in reality. What more death or life are there to transcend? There is no cause, no result, no combination; you reach great ease, great freedom. Herein is consummated the wonder of acquiescence in beginninglessness.

Movement and Stillness

Lao-tzu said, "Effecting utter emptiness, keeping utterly still, as myriad beings act in concert, I thereby watch the return." This means movement takes place when stillness culminates. Lao-tzu goes on to say, "Beings are manifold, but each returns to the root. Returning to the root is called stillness; this means reverting to Life itself." This means that when movement culminates it reverts to stillness.

, , ,

Lao-tzu also said, "Returning to Life is called the constant." This means that stillness turning to movement and movement turning to stillness is the constant of the Tao.

, , ,

If movement is taken to be movement, and stillness is taken to be stillness, this is normal for beings. An ancient sage has said, "Still, yet in movement; in movement, yet still—this is spirit. Moving without stillness, still without movement—this is an ordinary being."

, , ,

What is essential for preserving body and mind is not beyond movement and stillness. Students of the Tao collect body and mind, effect utter emptiness, and keep utter stillness; then they can watch return. The *I Ching* says, "Return means seeing the heart of heaven and earth."

, , ,

The *I Ching* sign RETURN ☷☳ represents returning from EARTH ☷☷; that is, moving from stillness. Five yins — — are in the sign, standing for utter stillness; one yang —— moves below them—this is called "return." This is movement upon the culmination of stillness.

, , ,

Watching return is knowing transformation; knowing transformation is not being subject to it; not being subject to transformation is returning to the root. "Returning to the root is called stillness; this means reverting to Life itself." This is reversion to stillness upon the culmination of movement.

′ ′ ′

The Connected Sayings commentary in the *I Ching* says, "Closing the door is called EARTH, opening the door is called HEAVEN. Alternate closing and opening is called change. Coming and going endlessly is called attainment." Alternate closing and opening are alternate stillness and movement; coming and going endlessly is stillness and movement unceasing. Alternating stillness and movement, the working goes on unceasingly, motivating, developing, creating, completing. This is called change. To carry this forth, adapting to changes endlessly, is called attainment.

′ ′ ′

Lao-tzu said, "The valley spirit undying is called the mysterious female." This means that when open awareness is not obscured, then the mechanism of movement and stillness cannot be inhibited. Lao-tzu also said, "The door of the mysterious female is called the root of heaven and earth." This refers to the opening and closing of the yang of HEAVEN and the yin of EARTH producing change and evolution.

′ ′ ′

Lao-tzu also said, "Continuously there as such, using it is not forced." This means the same thing as "coming and going endlessly is called attainment." The opening and closing of heaven and earth is like a person's breathing. Breathing out contacts the root of heaven; this is called opening. Breathing in contacts the root of earth; this is called closing. On breathing out, the dragon howls, clouds arise; on breathing in, the tiger roars, wind arises—this is called change. Wind and clouds meet, the dragon and tiger interact, movement and stillness depend on each other, the obvious and subtle unseparated—this is called attainment.

′ ′ ′

What I call breathing is not a matter of mouth and nose. It means the true breath coming and going continuously without ceasing, the pulse of Life, the drumming and dancing of heaven and earth.

′ ′ ′

Those who know that the change and movement of heaven and earth are the doing of spirit are called developed people. Those who comprehend this principle then realize that the power of the path of HEAVEN that does not cease is identical to the movement of one's own mind, with uncontrived work going on endlessly; and the richness of the path of EARTH that supports beings is identical to the stillness of one's own body, with function responding to things inexhaustibly.

, , ,

The mind is patterned on heaven, so it is clear; the body is patterned on earth, so it is tranquil. When always clear and always tranquil, the mechanism of opening and closing of heaven and earth is one's own domain. This is what is meant by the scriptural saying, "Clarity is the source of turbidity, movement is the foundation of stillness; if people can always be clear and serene, heaven and earth will come to them."

, , ,

Here I have dealt with the essential points of preserving body and mind in terms of movement and stillness. The intention is that people will collect body and mind, in the process of emulating heaven and earth. Preserving the body is a matter of harmonious attunement; preserving the mind is a matter of careful concentration.

, , ,

For harmonious attunement, movement is valuable; for careful concentration, stillness is valuable. Movement is patterned on heaven, stillness is patterned on earth; when body and mind are both calm, heaven and earth join.

, , ,

At the consummation of utter stillness, there is nonordinary movement of the spontaneous true potential responding inconceivably. It is precisely this mechanism of movement that is the celestial mind. Once the celestial mind is seen, the mysterious pass is penetrated; and once the mysterious pass is penetrated, the cauldron and furnace are herein, the firing process is herein, the three bases, eight trigrams, four signs, five forces, and all sorts of functions are all complete herein.

, , ,

When the work reaches this point, body and mind merge, movement and stillness complement each other, and the mechanism of opening and closing of heaven and earth is entirely within oneself. Eventually the mind returns to open quiescence and the body enters nondoing; movement and stillness are both forgotten, vitality stabilizes, and energy transmutes.

At this point, vitality naturally turns into energy, energy naturally turns into spirit, and spirit naturally turns into openness, uniting with cosmic space. This is called going back to the root, returning to the origin. Here the path of everlasting life and eternal vision is completed.

[18]
Songs

> When emptiness is complete and open, the basic energy stabilizes; with serenity in the midst of stillness, the celestial comes back.

On Finding out the Tao

If mystics go through the mystic pass,
It is not hard to ascend through experience to reality.
But this minute aperture confuses people,
So they are as though separated from it by myriad mountains.
There may be alchemists in the world,
But most of them are literalists and cling to things.
Even those who struggle with the teachings
Are still like a stupid cat staying in an empty den.
Some take minerals for the matrix of the elixir,
Some say the mouth and nose are the mystic female,
Some say the heart and genitals are fire and water,
Some say blood and semen are yin and yang—
Wearying and torturing the body, wasting vitality and spirit,
They stray from the subtle basis and fail to develop.
Even when the spiritual spring is exhausted,
They still cling, unregenerate.
Everyone naturally has what's essential for immortality;
The rule of Tao obeys humanity, but humanity is unworthy—
Illusions confuse them, who looks within?
Delusions control their feelings, who reflects back?
As I see real adepts,
They penetrate both Taoism and Buddhism
And shed the constraints of attachment to religious forms;
They have the courage to withdraw from worldly ambitions
To seek the hidden Way.

It is to such sympathetic friends
That I divulge the celestial mechanism.

The primordial true awareness
Should be brought to the center of consciousness.
When a statement of the mind of Tao
Is spoken to the wise,
There is no more need for arbitrary speculation.
At the peak of illumination, watch the mind absorb vitality;
Clearly the celestial intent reveals truth.
When you understand this mechanism,
You know how to gather medicine:
When primal consciousness emerges from stillness, foster it;
In a while concentrated sense will reveal essence—
Myriad energies all arrive, and there is true bliss.
Take the reflection of truth in the world
And store it in the mind;
With active effort and detached attention,
When the power of the work arrives
It produces being within nonbeing,
Crystallizing the mystic pearl.
Yet getting the mystic pearl is still not the marvel;
Tuning the spirit and nurturing it is still more profound.
If the body is agitated or the mind is volatile,
There may be an excess of craving or irritation.
In the firing cycle, you must recognize when enough is enough;
Still and settle the three bases, and the great treasure develops.
Breaking out of the top of the head, the spirit goes free—
Then we'll walk together
To visit the abodes of immortals.

On Cultivating Openness

The Tao is fundamentally utterly open;
Open nonreification produces energy,
One energy divides into two modes:
The one above, clear, is called heaven;
The one below, opaque, is called earth.
Heaven is round and moving;

The north star, never shifting, governs motion.
Earth is square and still;
The eastward flow, never exhausted, governs stillness.
The "north star" is the heart of heaven and earth,
The "eastward flow" is the energy of heaven and earth.
When the heart is nurtured by openness,
It thereby becomes still;
When energy is nurtured by openness,
It thereby circulates.
When the human mind is calm and quiet,
Like the north star not shifting,
The spirit is most open and aware.
For one who sees this
The celestial Tao is within oneself.
The one is physically and mentally sublimated,
And cannot be compelled to change by yin and yang,
Thus transcending the process of creation.

So we know openness
Is the substance of the great Tao,
The beginning of heaven and earth:
Movement and stillness come from this,
Yin and yang operate through this,
Myriad beings are born from this.

So openness is the great root of the world.
This may be symbolized by bamboo:
Dealing with events directly,
Dealing with the world adaptably,
Managing the mind with flexibility,
Managing the body with calmness—
This is like the resilient strength of bamboo.
Forgetting emotions in action,
Forgetting thoughts in stillness,
Forgetting self in dealing with events,
Forgetting things in adapting to change—
This is like the inner emptiness of bamboo.
Establishing certain resolve,
Keeping the mind free from doubt,

Completely pervading inside and out,
Unchanging beginning to end—
This is like the endurance of bamboo.
Widely calling on adepts,
Visiting enlightened teachers everywhere,
Extending hospitality to religious mendicants,
Synthesizing Taoism, Buddhism, and Confucianism—
This is like the clustering of bamboo.
Add to this seeing the basic, embracing the fundamental,
Minimizing selfishness and desire,
Tuning the breath, exercising sincerity,
Observing transformation, knowing return—
Who can do this unless utterly open?

Taoism, Buddhism, Confucianism—
All simply transmit one openness.
Throughout all time, those who have transcended
Have done the work from within openness.
Openness and sincerity are the essence of alchemy,
Learning Buddhism is meditation plunging into openness;
And as for learning the affairs of Confucian sages,
Selflessness in openness clarifies the celestial design.

The substance of Tao, open emptiness,
Is infinitely subtle;
With HEAVEN and EARTH operating in openness,
Energy is whole and fluid.
The creation and transformation of yin and yang
Alternate in openness.
If people plunge into openness,
They will comprehend successful adaptation.

The miracle of the restorative elixir
Is in setting to work
In the valley of open nonreification,
To effect utter emptiness
And keep utter stillness.
When emptiness is complete and open,
The basic energy stabilizes;

With serenity in the midst of stillness,
The celestial comes back.
Emptying the mind, filling the middle,
Is the formulation of the path;
When you don't obscure open awareness,
That is the time for gathering the medicine.
Emptying oneself and responding to situations
Is true ordinary activity;
Union with cosmic space is greatness.

Gathering real knowledge in open serenity
Is done without contrivance;
Promoting the fire of consciousness
Is done with openness as the bellows.
Extracting and adding,
Increasing and decreasing,
All depend on openness;
Upon shattering space,
One attains great awakening.

Ultimately the Tao is applied with gentility:
Shedding superficialities
And breaking down excess intensity
Must be practiced together;
Harmonizing enlightenment to mix with the world,
One forgets others and self.

That which is prior to the reign of images
Can only be known intuitively—
How can there by symbols without signs?
HEAVEN is not above, EARTH is not below;
In the middle is a point of pure awareness.
Crystal clear on all sides, there is no gap;
Thoroughly solid in all respects,
It is completely whole:
This is the door of the mysterious female,
Open in the center.

If you act in nonempty openness,
Opening and closing will spontaneously accord

With HEAVEN and EARTH.
When the door of the mysterious female opens,
The work is consummated;
The spirit goes out through here,
And also comes in through here.
Going out again and again,
Coming in again and again,
Returning to openness,
From equanimous calm, energy bursts forth.
When energy goes into action,
Heaven and earth open,
And from openness springs forth
A sphere of brilliant light,
Shining without lack of excess.

Responding to the time and people,
One rests the spirit in openness,
Acts in openness,
Reveals the state of openness in speech.
When openness reaches the point
Where there is not even any "openness,"
Then all logic ends.
When you plunge into openness,
Heaven and earth come to you.
With open heart and upright bearing,
Be like the green bamboo;
This is the foremost device
For cultivating openness.

Breaking Up Confusion

Worldly alchemists are lamentable—
There are many different types.
Clinging to symbols literally,
Performing practices randomly,
They waste their strength
On superficialities and spin-offs.

Taking in sunlight, sipping moonlight,
Absorbing light, drinking air and fog,

Practicing various contortions,
Rolling and massaging the eyes,
Swallowing large quantities of saliva,
Pressing the coccyx and midspine,
Concentrating on imagination and sustaining thoughts,
Staring at the tip of the nose,
Ingesting feces and urine,
Maintaining quietistic aloofness,
Falling into indifferent emptiness,
Practicing impulsively, now still, now active,
Practicing massage and counting breaths—
All of these are different
From the principle of the gold pill.

Calisthenics, six-sound breathing, avoiding grains—
What do these accomplish?
Obsession with sexual practices to gather yin,
Considering "nine shallow strokes, one deep"
To be "advancing and withdrawing,"
Relaxing the waist and cupping the testicles in the hand
To "protect the door of life,"
Bending and stretching to circulate energy,
Performing mental gymnastics,
Strengthening military arts—
Schools such as this
Are not worth talking about.

Then there are those who hold their breath,
Stretch like a bear
And contract their limbs like birds,
Causing useless strain.
Devotees who massage their waists
Are warm in the belly;
Practitioners who circulate breath
Are red in the face.
Tapping the back of the head,
Cradling the skull in the arms,
Chattering the teeth to "gather the spirits,"
Gazing at the top of the head—

Empty echoes are taken to be
The roar of the male tiger,
Rumbling in the belly is said to be
The howl of the female dragon.
Warming the lower abdomen
Adjusts a boiling sea;
Those who go sleepless day and night
Struggle to keep their eyes open.
Wearing a single robe, going barefoot,
Suffering from burning heat,
Lack in past life
Is paid back by hunger and cold.

Continually not talking is idle vanity;
How can one ascend to immortality
By silently paying court to the lord on high?
Sporting the "golden lance,"
Holding up the "golden well,"
Taking a beautiful woman as the cauldron of the elixir,
Calling sexual fluids the true lead—
Losing original harmony, they are still unaware.

Some babble on about Zen,
Loquaciously showing off their ability to speak;
Pointing to the sky, they talk of voidness,
Making a useless fuss.
Raising a fist, holding up a finger,
They do not know the source;
Bringing up sayings and contemplative methods,
They quip and jabber.
They deal with students by picking up a gavel,
Or by holding up a whisk;
Winking the eyes and raising the eyebrows
They consider awakening.
They consider studying stories
To be pure concentration.
A genuine highly developed Buddhist
Is never like those
Who consider rationalization wisdom,

Who will never clarify the mind
Or see its essence.

Taoist, Confucian, Buddhist—stop clinging!
Turn the attention inward to illumine within,
Think for yourself.
Suddenly you will find your nose is pointed,
And then you will finally realize
That you have been wrong all along.

Students of immortality—stop discussion,
Find out the basis of initial reception of energy.
Formalities and reified quests do not stand;
Have no more to do with formlessness either.

The heart is not fire, the genitals not water;
Ordinary vitality cannot be called the natural vitality.
The yellow woman is not in the spleen;
Stop saying the mysterious female is in the mouth and nose.
Six A.M. is not the rabbit,
Six P.M. is not the rooster;
Midnight is not water, noon is not fire.
The first yang is not in numbers,
Keeping full is not fixed to the time of the full moon.
The liver is not the dragon, the lungs not the tiger;
How can sexual fluids be called the matrix of the elixir?
The five forces are basically just one yin and yang,
The four signs are not apart from the dual mysterious female.
The river source where medicine is gathered
Is not easy to know;
Essence is always within oneself,
Sense has to be recovered from externals.
In the abode of consciousness,
The higher soul, the solar soul, is the "girl";
In the abode of vitality,
The lower soul, the lunar soul, is the "boy."

Doing or nondoing,
Studying or not studying,

Self-centered practitioners
Are all in an ivory tower.

Now I reveal the device
Completely in one statement:
Body and mind are the fire and medicine;
When body and mind are stable and settled,
The mystic teaching is mastered;
Vitality, energy, and spirit
Merge in open spontaneity.
In three hundred days,
The embryonic spirit is released;
Turning about,
One shatters cosmic space.

On the Mystic Principle

Though the supreme Tao has no location,
Still it is necessary that an adept transmit guidelines.
Effort and innocence are symbolically associated
With morning and evening;
Transitions from stillness to movement and movement to stillness
Are provisionally labeled midnight and noon.
Promoting the fire is refining the great elixir
Within nonreification;
Settling the furnace is seeking the true will
Within concentration.
When body, mind, and will are settled,
They join the three sets:
Sense and vitality,
Essence and spirit,
Together with will—
All have the same ancestor.
Increasing the celestial and reducing the mundane
According to the time,
There is an orderly process.
Guarding the castle is in oneself
Distinguishing host and guest.
Essence is in the mind,

Sense is in the body:
When the two medicinal ingredients merge,
Vitality and energy flow into and out of one another.

Directly transcending to ultimate reality,
One betakes oneself to the Great Vehicle.
Immediate understanding with complete pervasion
Is no small boon;
Inner understanding of the true potential
Is basically spontaneous.

Pitiful are the petty techniques upheld at random;
The glib of tongue boast of their abilities.
Who can even look at them
In their vanity and conceit?
They do not know how to plunge their minds
Into profound abstraction—
Why should they bother to set goals
And live in sanctuaries?
Beginners who do not seek teachers
Grow old without attainment,
Bringing misery upon themselves.

Accumulate accomplishments and deeds,
Be of service to humanity.
Turn the attention inward as well
To find receptivity and creativity.
Rouse the awareness within,
And the tiger roars wind;
Wash away dust from the senses,
And the dragon makes rain.
Action and illumination need the polar star
Of constant, unwavering insight;
Fostering the true and removing the false
Is up to stillness, the warrior of darkness.
By the time conscious essence
Comes from the abode of spirit,
The sense of reality has already reached
The abode of vitality.

When one pill of the great elixir
Forms in the furnace,
The embryonic immortal in the room
Dances three leaps.
The four signs and five energies
All combine harmoniously,
The nine-restoration and seven-reversion
Complete the work cycle.
The radiant form of the moon appears from the hut,
The shining light illumines the universe.

In governing human affairs
And serving the celestial,
It is best to be sparing;
This is called piling up virtue.
Too much introspection into the sky of essence
Increases defilement of sense;
Too much reasoning
Increases habituated consciousness.
Intellectual brilliance is not as good
As being simpleminded;
Eloquence and lofty talk
Are not as good as silence.
Cutting off rumination, forgetting impulses,
Then there are no judgments;
Hiding one's light,
Keeping one's development concealed,
One is aloof from sound and form.
When desire and taste are minimized,
Basic goodness arrives;
When affairs are reduced, involvements simplified,
The root of virtue is planted.

In a moment of perfect fluidity,
Myriad thoughts are cleared;
Passing through mundane and transmundane mindfulness,
All entanglements cease.
On careful examination of the writings
Of the sages of the three teachings,

I find the word "stopping"
Most simple and direct.
If you can work on the basis of stopping,
It will not be hard to become an enlightened wizard.
Stopping entanglements and arriving at the source
Is the mechanism of Chan Buddhism;
Stopping the mind and clarifying noumenon
Is the consummation of Confucianism;
Stopping energy and stabilizing spirit
Is the mystery of Taoism.
These three stoppings
Are interdependent, overcoming all;
To thoroughly investigate your own mind
Is the guiding principle.

The Inner Design of Essence

When the two modes first differentiate,
They distinguish three poles:
HEAVEN is focused on directness,
EARTH opens and closes;
Between heaven and earth,
The door of the mysterious female—
In its movement is increasing outflow,
In its stillness, increasing penetration.
The accurate transmission
Of the guiding basis of Tao
Points the way to the ultimate.

Sense goes with the body,
Essence goes with the mind;
Energy fosters awareness,
Vitality nurtures life.
In eliciting knowledge
By investigating phenomena,
There are typical constants;
On entering sagehood,
Transcending the ordinary,

There are no longer ranks.
Developed people live in the midst of change,
Awaiting the direction of Life;
Inwardly aware, unafflicted,
What worry is there?
Effecting function, promoting illumination,
Is the mechanism of enlivening freedom
And killing slavery to compulsion:
Remembering the ultimate end of the body,
Volatility and aggression disappear.
Turning the attention around,
You see through the dream body
And directly throw over
The raft of ancient books.

Polish the light, remove accretions,
Dissolve accumulated burdens,
Clarify the mind,
Be free of addictive habituation.
Submerge the mind in the subtle,
Sense and penetrate;
You will drink an endless river
In a single gulp.

No need to refine the essence of gold
In the crucible of HEAVEN,
Or cook jade broth
On the stove of EARTH—
On passing through, penetrating
Before the creation of symbols,
The world, when taken in,
Lies hidden in a tiny grain.

THE FIRING PROCESS

If you want to reach the mystery of mysteries,
You need to be careful when alone.
The mechanism of the work is in the eye:
Cut off the dust of form

And you will be impeccable;
The clear open heart
Will shine like jade.

Bring about utter emptiness,
Keep stillness steady;
Within stillness, a moving yang of creative energy returns.
At the first yang, the hidden dragon should be under control;
Then when you get to seeing the dragon, do not be hasty.
As soon as you experience "working hard," light illumines within;
When "sometimes leaping, in the abyss," then bathe.
At the fifth yang, the flying dragon
Effects evolution and development.
Then when yang peaks, yin arises,
Necessitating withdrawal, preventing insidious inroads.

At the first yin of EARTH,
Withdraw to where sense joins essence.
At the third yin, "it won't do to glorify with emolument."
After "closing the bag," the spiritual elixir is ripe;
If you meet with "battle in the field,"
Set your will on locking up tight.

When the mundane is stripped away
And the celestial is pure,
Then the firing is sufficient;
A tiny pearl is swallowed into the belly,
Producing a complete real member of the immortals.
Yin and yang are always in harmony,
Their combinations proportionate
In accordance with the time.
Essence and sense live together,
Conscious knowledge and real knowledge spontaneously join.
Having finished making space into an unconstructed abode,
This host is truly no ordinary worldling.
The mountain crags hiding the clouds,
Heaven and earth are clear;
The shining light of the moon
Illumines the open valley.

The Dragon and the Tiger

PREFACE

Dragon and tiger are different names for yin and yang; the process of yin and yang is sublimely subtle, unfathomable, so it is symbolized by the dragon and tiger.

The Connected Sayings in the *I Ching* say, "One yin, one yang—this is called Tao. The unfathomability of yin and yang is called spiritual." Alchemical literature says, "Unbalanced yin and unbalanced yang are called illnesses."

Yin and yang are the stillness and movement of the absolute. The One divided into two, the clear rises while the opaque sinks. Both the macrocosm and all microcosms have forms and descriptions due to the two energies of yin and yang. Therefore there is nothing in the world, large or small, that is outside yin and yang.

The various different names in the alchemical classics and writings of the adepts all refer only to yin and yang. Generations of immortality teachers, borrowing names to set up images, have symbolized yin and yang as a dragon and a tiger. This was to enable students to get an easy grip on the pattern whereby to accomplish the work.

The image of dragon and tiger is that of countless changes and transformations, marvelous subtlety difficult to comprehend. Therefore they are called medicinal substances. When speaking in terms of "setting up," they are referred to as the cauldron and furnace; when speaking in terms of being "put into operation," they are referred to as the firing process. They are compared to WATER and FIRE, represented as wood and metal, named woman and man, paired as wife and husband.

All of these different terms refer to subtle functions of the dragon and tiger. Because of their miraculous effect, they are called medicinal substances. Because they make things, they are called cauldron and furnace. Because they transmute, they are called the firing process. Because they interact for balance, they are called WATER and FIRE. Because they are straight and firm, they are called wood and metal. Because of their subtle communion, they are called wife and husband. What else but dragon and tiger could comprehend all this?

A literary work says, "Clouds follow a dragon, wind follows a tiger;

sages create, while all beings watch." This illustrates the quality of creative organization, which is represented by the fifth yang in the hexagram HEAVEN. We know that the subtlety of the dragon and tiger cannot be attained but for the spiritual qualities and the accomplishments of sages.

When you look for the dragon and tiger in yourself, they are essence and sense; transmuted and adjusted, they are mind and body, higher and lower souls, spirit and vitality. Carry them forth in action, and they are the door of the mysterious female, the mechanism of opening and closing.

Lao-tzu said, "The valley spirit not dying is called the mysterious female. The door of the mysterious female is called the root of heaven and earth. Continuously there as such, using it is not forced."

The *I Ching* says, "Closing the door is called EARTH, opening the door is called HEAVEN; one closing, one opening—this is called change. Coming and going endlessly is called attainment."

An alchemical text says, "Breathing out, you touch the root of heaven; breathing in, you touch the root of earth." This is the mechanism of opening and closing. "When you breathe out, the dragon bellows, clouds arise; when you breathe in, the tiger roars, wind arises." This is opening and closing referred to as change. "Wind and clouds sense each other and combine, producing gold liquid." This is coming and going endlessly referred to as attainment.

When the "gold liquid" of spiritual energy is restored, it crystallizes into the great elixir pill. Therefore the pill is provisionally labeled the great dragon-tiger pill. Take it and you will live long and see forever.

The breathing referred to here is not ordinary respiration; it is the door of exit and entry of the subtle interactions of the real potential.

If you actually penetrate through here, the dragon-tiger pill is completed, and there is hope for spiritual immortality. If true cultivators of reality can really gain lucid, penetrating understanding of the dragon and tiger, even though the real eternal Tao is said to be most mysterious and subtle, still it can be attained.

As for the matter of performing worthwhile actions to nurture the embryo of enlightenment, there are none that are accomplished without understanding the dragon and tiger.

The adept Ziyang said collecting body and mind is called conquering the dragon and subduing the tiger. When the mind does not move, the dragon bellows; when the body does not move, the tiger roars. When the dragon bellows, the energy is stabilized; when the tiger roars, the vitality is solidified.

When the basic vitality is solidified, this is sufficient to preserve the physical. When the basic energy is stabilized, this is sufficient to solidify the spiritual. Physically and spiritually sublimated, merging in reality with the Tao, the task of spiritual immortality is done.

Zhao Shu-zai was a courtier when he was young, and served in middle-level official capacities. Through the revolving of heaven and earth he saw through the evanescent life, so he gave up ambition and took to seeking the essence of the Tao. Though he lives in the ordinary world, in reality his mind rests in the mystic realm, and he is actually one who has shed the burden of worldly affairs.

Wishing to unify and solidify the spirit, he has therefore been concentrating on the dragon and tiger. One day he brought a diagram to show me, and asked me to add some words. I could not refuse, so I have written this to satisfy his request.

I said to him, "The ancients set up images based on the Tao; now I have set up words based on images. It is important to exercise clear perception and see through to the real point. Do not make the mistake of sticking to the zero point of the scale. If you can understand the meaning through words, and get the message by contemplating diagrams, then you know the real dragon and tiger are not on paper, but in oneself. When words and images are both forgotten, the qualities of Tao are all there.

"Yes, the real dragon and real tiger are not hard to seek—it just requires using yang to complement yin. Then the four qualities of origination, development, fruition, and consummation operate, powerful, true, and unceasing; hidden, flying, appearing, leaping—it is all up to the mind. But even so, this is still rousing waves on even ground, thunder in a clear sky. Work on this."

THE SONG

The real dragon and real tiger
Originally have no image—
Who can create a model of them
To convey what they are like?

If you understand them in formlessness,
You still fall into extremism
And wind up dissolute.
It is so clear,
Clear as the sun in the blue sky—
But even this is making waves
Where there is no wind.

If people now want to know,
The real dragon and tiger
Are not in the province of being or nonbeing,
Or the realm of midnight or noon.

Don't swallow the two things mixed up;
Just count the five forces backward.
The root and stem are originally
The chamber of utter mystery;
Creative evolution is in the crimson hill mansion,
The abode of the primordial vitality.

Though application involves deliberate conscious extension,
Ultimately open awareness has no fixed locus.
The unique universal Tao requires mental penetration;
The minute spiritual working is not visible to the eye.
When it suddenly bursts out
And opens the top of your head,
You see that sense and essence
Have the same one mother.

On the loftiest heights the celestial mind
Surveys all around;
The dipper of precise attention
Draws from the silver river of energy.

Congealing energy depends on concentration;
Insight and action emerge from profound stillness.
In a flash the celestial and the earthly commune;
Instantly reason and desire complement one another.

The tiger produces a clear sense of real knowledge,
The dragon showers the sweet rain of conscious essence:
Clouds roll, rain enriches, all the world is at peace—
Operating the creative dragon power, the work is completed.

People say heaven can be brought under control
By six dragons—
Who knows one dragon is the true host?
People say that five tigers
Get through the mysterious pass—
Who knows one tiger produces real will?

When you understand the normal harmony
Of the association of the dragon and tiger,
Then you know the tortoise and snake of energy and vitality
Swallow and spit out one another.

Sages set up symbols as a means to point to traces;
Understand outside of symbols, and you get to the mystical.
You must find the intent of adepts outside words;
Originally the absolute has no sphere.
To forget the symbol once you get the idea is still nothing special;
Forgetting even the idea is the ultimate rule.

Nothingness and Oneness

The Tao, basically open and nonreified,
Produces the absolute:
The absolute changes and there is the first one;
One divides into two, two produce three,
And the four signs and five forces emerge from here.

The nonreified One is the root of heaven and earth;
In the mystic teaching, One is the door of all subtleties.
The *I Ching* distinguishes creation and evolution from within One,
The human mind employs general norms on the basis of One.

When heaven attains oneness it is clear,
When earth attains oneness it is peaceful;

A valley is thereby filled,
Spirit is thereby aware.
Things are made by it,
Humans are born from it;
If leaders and rulers get it,
The country is secure.

Chan transmits true guidance within One,
Confucianism distinguishes opening and closing from One,
Taoism expounds true eternity by means of One.
The Confucian "Unique One" is immeasurably subtle;
Taoism has three vehicles, Chan has five branches:
Ultimately a thousand lamps are all one light.

Embrace the fundamental, preserve oneness,
Go through the mystic opening;
Thoroughly unified, understand
The teaching of sages.

The great mystery, the real One,
Is the gateway to restoration of Life;
So we know that the One
Is the real eternal Way.

Stop saying when One is attained everything is done;
Attaining oneness, keep One, preserve it without loss.
Once you penetrate, all merges,
And the celestial design is clear.

All phenomena are ultimately one,
But this is still nothing extraordinary;
The beginning is one Nonbeing,
Which produces all beings.
With nonbeing and being working together,
It is possible to last long.

If you can really return all to One, without partner,
You will know how to face south to see the north star.
When you attain this, you gain oneness

And then forget the One:
Now you can appear and disappear
The same as the basis of creation.

If you cling to One and can't forget it,
You're like a stupid cat staying in an empty cave.
When the three fives merge into one,
The one returns to emptiness.
After returning to emptiness,
There isn't even any emptiness.
With even nonbeing nonexistent,
There is profound tranquility.

People today call nothingness nothing,
And as dissolute nihilists get into dreadful ways.
People today call oneness one,
And with biased clinging waste effort.

When you understand nothingness that is not nothing,
Then in preserving oneness you'll know there is no One.
When One and Nothing are both overturned,
The great task of nothingness and oneness is done.

On Embracing Unity

When the Infinite culminates
It becomes the Absolute;
Circulation of the Absolute's subtlety
Begins in the One.

The One divided into two,
Producing yin and yang;
Myriad species, heaven, earth, and humans,
All emerge from here.

Originally the true One
Is utterly open, aware;
There is no change
Throughout all time.

But due to becoming substance,
Spirit emanates cognition,
Differentiating circumstances
Into good and bad.

Following feelings pursuing illusions
Increases suffering;
Fragrance, flavor, form, and sound—
All dazzle and confuse.

If you can truly find
The root source in the One,
You return to the origin,
Go back to the fundamental,
Without wasting effort.

Yin and yang commune in concentration;
Their combinations are gotten in nothingness.
The three bases and eight trigrams join in the will;
The four signs and five forces return to utter quiescence.
Suddenly bursting forth through the top of the head,
A brilliant gold light fills the spiritual room.

The valley of open nonreification
Is spontaneously cleared;
The door of the mysterious female
Opens and closes itself.

The wonder of the return of the celestial
Can never be exhausted;
The four qualities of creativity
Never ever cease.

Extending the energy
and stabilizing the spirit
In deep abstraction
Going from being into nonbeing
In a state of ecstasy,
What is the ruler within?

It is the original purpose
Of arriving at one's aim.

The Sword of Wisdom

Ever since adepts handed on
The secret of the sword,
The true imperative has been upheld
Completely, truly adamant.

If someone asks me about
Looking for its origin,
I say it is not ordinary iron.
This lump of iron
Comes from receptive stillness;
When you obtain it, it rises up.

Forging it in a glowing fire,
Through repeated efforts
It is refined
And forged into steel.

When students of the Tao
Know this secret,
The spirit of light is intensely powerful,
And devils of darkness vanish.

The subtle function of spiritual work
Is truly hard to measure;
I now give an explanation for you.
In telling you about it,
I divulge the celestial mechanism.

Setting to work when one yang comes back,
First have the six yangs pump the furnace bellows;
Then the six yins work the tongs and hammer.
When the work of firing is complete,
It produces the sword;

When it is first done,
It flashes like lightning.

Brandish it horizontally
And a cold clear breeze arises;
Hold it upright,
And the shining bright moon appears.
When the bright moon appears,
Auspicious light illumines heaven and earth;
Sprites and ghosts are distressed.

It stops turbidity, brings out clarity,
Sweeps away weird defilements;
It slays volatility,
Cuts down aggressiveness,
Destroys monsters:
Influences draining away
Vitality, energy, and spirit
All vanish in the light of the sword.
Entanglements cut off, rumination dies down,
And the web of feelings is rent asunder.
Where the spiritual edge is aimed, mountains crumble;
The demon kings of mundane planes are all routed.

This precious sword fundamentally has no form;
The name is set up because it has spiritual effect.
Learning the Tao and practicing reality
Depend on this sword;
Without this sword,
The Tao cannot be achieved.

Opening up the vast darkness,
Distinguishing heaven and earth,
Dissolving obstructions, transmuting objects—
All is included.
If you ask me to show it to you,
I bring it out before you—
Do you understand or not?

Drawing Back from Error to Truth

The Tao produces one energy
From open nonreification;
Who affixes labels,
Distinguishing phases of formation?

The one energy dichotomizes,
Producing two modes;
The clear rises, the opaque sinks,
Forming sky and earth.

The warp and woof of yin and yang
Is like a working shuttle;
The opening and closing of HEAVEN and EARTH
Is like a pumping bellows.

With the subtle combining of the two modes
There are the three components;
Seven apertures open,
Producing myriad species.

The infinite reality is a single whole,
Always present in daily activities;
Creation after creation,
Transformation after transformation,
Hundreds and thousands of workings—
None of them are beyond
This present mortal being.

If you can truly plumb
The root source by yourself,
The four signs and five forces
Are inherently complete within you.

Introspecting thrice day and night,
The will is undivided;
In the single source of eliminating materialism,
Accomplishment is multiplied a hundredfold.

Getting through the pass of vitality
And then the pass of energy,
One gains occult communication
With the pipes of heaven and earth.

In the groove everywhere,
One has guidance;
Every opening illumined,
There is no suffocating obstruction.

If you can perceive this,
You then make two faces into one die:
Raising your head,
You knock over the polar mountain;
Taking a step, you overturn
The blockade of the mystic wonder.

The unique design, simply evoked,
Expresses the true source;
It harmoniously combines myriad differences,
Resolving them in correct alignment.

Having refined the luminous spirit,
Emanate this spirit of light;
Transcend from the realm of form
Into the formless realm.

I see many practitioners today concocting wonders;
Arrogant and presumptuous, they show off and boast,
Claiming to have understanding.

A sharp wit and glib tongue
Are artificial brilliance;
Domineering talk of voidness
Is useless intellection.

Beginners are subject to deception;
Learned mystics are not liked.

Those who just show off strength for now
Are heedless of their final destruction;
Those who talk a lot in front of others
Are like selling water by a riverside.
Producing smoke and fire,
Their thoughts are off;
Pursuing objects, following fashions,
Their minds are narrow.

Toiling frantically at religious exercises,
They struggle madly to circulate vitality and energy;
Counting their breaths and massaging themselves,
They vainly aim for pleasant sensations.

Sinking into torpor,
Or rising in excitement,
They cannot extend attention;
Now torpid, now distracted,
What can be done?

When the spirit wanes away
And the energy dissipates,
How can this be cured?
When the body is exhausted,
Regret is useless.

If you see the straight path
Out of confusion,
To escape the burden of payment
Of the debt of harmful practices,
Then collect your scattered mind
And overturn your arrogant attitude.

Extend familial duty to serving teachers;
To get the teaching, first maintain discipline.
Extend sympathy for yourself to sympathy for all;
Not attacking or blaming others is based on generosity.

Without illuminating yourself,
You make your illumination complete;

Without aggrandizing yourself,
You make your greatness complete.

With no problems,
No cravings, no concerns,
Get rid of extremes,
Get rid of both arrogance and fawning.

To work on setting up the foundation
Requires strict discipline;
Carry out further refinement
In encounter with situations.

Use the sense of real knowledge
And the essence of conscious knowledge
To make the elixir pill;
Don't take mud for jewels.

Don't get mired in solipsism,
And don't think it's a matter
Of intellectual knowledge
Or learned understanding.

Raising a child within ultimate nonreification,
When the heaven of meditation
Is completely purified,
There's not the slightest wisp.

The mechanism of nine-restoration and seven-reversion
Is not inside and not outside:
The original nature of reality is ultimately formless;
The eternal open awareness is never obscured.

Embrace the basic, keep to the One, store it in openness;
Practice this seriously and diligently, don't be lazy.
Combine the four signs, unite the three bases;
Assemble the five forces, join the eight trigrams.

Cooking in the beginning
Of movement of positive energy,
Refining at the culmination,
There's extraction and addition;
Know when to proceed actively,
And when to withdraw into passivity.

Profoundly calm in open nonreification,
Operate the mechanism;
Deeply absorbed in ecstasy,
Spin the process of creation.

When the two medicinal ingredients
Enter the central chamber,
One stream of golden light
Illumines the four quarters.

The essence of consciousness
And the sense of reality
Are united by the go-between
Of the true and steady will.

Yin and yang join together,
Wife and husband in blissful union;
Like rain and clouds,
They forget day and night.
Energy stabilizes, vitality congeals,
Forming the spiritual embryo.

On producing the mystic pearl,
There is great amazement;
The four directions all at once
Are pervaded with great light.

Crystal clear everywhere,
Without seams or gaps,
All is one round sphere
Which no amount of money can buy.

I bow my head to students of Complete Reality;
Remember what I say—
If you will take this up directly,
It is the bridle to take hold of.

When the bridle of speech
Is put into practice, what then?
The true human without fixation
Rides upon a crane.

Poems

> Sense must be recovered, essence is always there.

Verses on Meditation Work

Opening Up Darkness

To restore the primal wholeness of the mind,
One must know how to remain unmoved and innocent
In spite of personal desires.
Stabilization of consciousness
Depends on a calm and steady will,
While enhancing awareness
Requires receptivity and docility.
Through attraction to truth
Combined with appropriate action,
Extraordinary consciousness
And ordinary consciousness are joined.
When inner sense of the essence of mind
Is kept in the center of attention,
With psychophysical vitality
And spiritual awareness
Yoked by unified concentration,
Then one is able to proceed by oneself
In the process of development.

Gathering Medicine

The timing involved in purifying consciousness
In order to clarify real knowledge
Is not a matter of terrestrial time;
It is to be discovered in oneself by concentration.

When the mind is not fixated
On external objects or internal impulses,
There is an access of energy,
Registered in inner awareness.
When emotions are inactive,
One can sense the essence of mind;
When generative energy is not dissipated,
Desire becomes a fuel for awareness,
And consciousness is stabilized by objectivity.
After combining intuitive and rational awareness,
And joining visceral and intellectual consciousness,
When mundane conditioning loses its command
And primal conscious energy is freed from adulteration,
Then it is possible to realize objective reality.

Promoting the Fire

Having gone through the time
Of the first arising of natural energy,
You naturally have true positivity
Returning according to the time.
The fire of concentration
Emerges from the heart;
A peal of thunder along with movement
Comes from within stillness.
Energy and spirit combining
Produce spiritual substance;
Mind and breath resting on each other
Form the spiritual embryo.
When you have passed through
The experience herein,
The nine apertures
Of the three passes all open.

Daily Activity

The sense of real knowledge
And the essence of conscious knowledge
Constitute the great elixir;

These are to be gathered in formlessness.
With doing and contrivance,
After all there's cogitation;
With no seeking or grasping,
There is no worry.
Ever clear, ever calm.
The mind pearl appears;
Forgetting objects, forgetting impulses,
The jewel of life's complete.
The two roads of movement and stillness
Free from obstruction,
The isle of immortals
Is right where you are.

Stabilizing the Body

The sublime principle of Complete Reality
Is not hard to practice;
Just avoid pursuing things,
Chasing sound and form.
When illusions do not invade you,
Feelings naturally end;
When the unified mind is unaffected,
How can thoughts arise?
Get rid of discrimination of others and self,
Preserve the celestial design;
Take yin and yang in hand,
Join tranquility and development.
I tell the eminent people
Who cultivate the elixir,
When you don't indulge in the senses,
The essence is complete and clear.

Combining Yin and Yang

To reach the Tao is basically not hard;
The work lies in concentration.
When yin and yang, above and below,
Always rise and descend,

The ubiquitous flow of vital sense
Naturally returns of itself.
At the peak of awareness,
Reality becomes accessible to consciousness;
In recondite abstraction,
Nondoing joins with doing.
When the clouds recede and the rain disperses,
The spiritual embryo is complete;
The creative principle comes into play,
Producing a new birth.

Passing Through the Barrier

After all, what's the difficulty
In the real eternal Tao?
It is simply in the daily activities
Of the present time.
Once you join action and calmness
And know how to open and close,
The twin orbs of creativity and receptivity
Revolve on their own.
There is an opening
For return to the root;
There is a pass
For restoration of Life:
Having gone through these two experiences,
One transcends the ordinary,
Goes beyond the holy,
And is as if set free.

Going Out and In

The valley spirit not dying
Is the mysterious female;
This is the opening and closing
Mechanism of activity and passivity.
Coming and going over and over, never ceasing,
They alternate successively, without deviation.
A white-headed ancient

Rides off on a dragon,
A blue-eyed foreigner
Comes back on a tiger.
What is realized
As a result of the work?
Throughout sky and earth
The moonlight shines.

A Warning

Mere talk of Zen
Is vain boasting;
Extensive discourse and lofty talk
Take matters further afield.
It is like seeking reality
Through empty forms,
Like producing visual distortions
By rubbing the eyes.
Though you pursue things,
They're after all illusory;
Snap your head around,
And you arrive at home.
Don't blame me for talking so harshly—
Opening up the heart,
There should be no blockage.

Drawing Back from Error

Thirty-six hundred side-door methods—
Fixated people are befuddled by them;
Daily wasting attention
On reifying views,
When will they ever understand Life
And return to the root?
Why speak of exceptional attainment
Of intellectual brilliance?
Expertise in intellectual knowledge
Is not worth discussing.
All forms and names,

All external characterizations,
Ultimately amount to no more
Than so much mental gymnastics.

Countering Demons

How can torpor and drowsiness
Be prevented in meditation?
Do you see the ghost faces and spirit heads?
Torpor and distraction both
Stem from turbidity in energy;
Thoughts of objects continue
Because of such conditioning.
When the tide comes in,
The water comes up to the banks;
When the wind is still,
There are no waves on the river.
When essentially serene,
Feelings empty, mind unstirring,
There's no torpor or distraction
In meditation,
No demons in sleep.

Revealing the Correct

Active and passive practice are easy,
The medicine is not far away;
The arising of natural energy
Is like the ocean tide.
When you know how to gather
Both mercury and lead,
All material cravings
Then will pass away.
Overturn myriad existents
And the three bases join;
Refine away mundanities
And the five energies arrive.
Freeing the embryo in ten months,
The alchemy is complete;

The infant's form appears
And visits the spiritual firmament.

HARMONIZATION

The three basic great medicines
Are will, mind, and body;
But if you fixate on will, mind, or body,
You are entangled in objects.
Tuning the breath requires tuning
The breath of the true breath;
Refining spirit calls for refining
The nonpsychological spirit.
On suddenly forgetting things and self,
The three flowers assemble;
On powerfully discarding impulses and objects,
The five energies arrive.
With thoroughly pervasive attainment,
There is no obstruction;
At all times, in all places,
One expresses Complete Reality.

CLARIFYING THE BASIS

Since the body is nonabsolute,
Labels are arbitrary;
Once there are labels,
The mind gets tangled up.
The waxing and waning of yin and yang
Polish present and past;
The rising and setting of sun and moon
Convey birth and death.
If you can maintain
Unified stability through time,
Then you'll know the stroke
Of midnight at noon.
Though dealing with the world
Is something that needs teaching,

The work of leaving the world
Must be clarified on your own.

Forging the Sword

An enlightened teacher taught me
To forge the blade of spirit;
What it all depends upon
Is the creative work of yin and yang.
Tempering the firmness of HEAVEN,
EARTH does the forging;
Fanning the fire of awareness
Is the wind of docility.
Having achieved unfailing concentration,
The mind-director is skilled;
Wiping out pernicious influences,
The will-general is valiant.
When eminent learners of Tao
Know the meaning of this,
It is easy for them
To shatter cosmic space.

The Moon Cave

The Moon Cave is clear and deep,
The environment most beautiful;
The one who dwells there
Makes a living upside down,
Refining the gold potion
In the jade furnace,
Cooking white snow sprouts
In the gold cauldron.
Operating the cosmic cycle,
Turning the handle of the Big Dipper,
Alternately passive and active,
Conveying the flow of energy,
Having passed through all the barriers
He freely sails the silver river in peace.

The Hut of Clarity

My hut is not an abode of idleness;
Ordinary people are not allowed
To see it on a whim.
A wife and husband make a living,
Three sons and three daughters
Form a group.
The world therein has always been vast;
The space outside is not really large.
If you ask the master what he does,
I reply that he faces south
To gaze at the north star.

Poems Extolling True Happiness

[1]
Buddhas and immortals are all products
Of people of the world;
Nevertheless, those astray
Simply do not know.
Either they compete
Out of greed for fame,
Or else they rush around
In a struggle for profit.
Groaning and sweating
Under the burden of business,
Laboring busily
To support wives and children,
Even if you're prosperous
And have a beautiful wife,
None of it will accompany you
When you pass away.

[2]
How can this compare
To Complete Reality, marvelous, unique?
Here is true happiness,
Known within one's heart.

The elixir comes from nonrefinement,
Refined in refinement;
The Tao goes to nondoing,
Done in doing.
Stopping thoughts, stopping entanglements,
Tune the generative energy;
Forget hearing, forget seeing,
Nurture the spiritual infant.
After the alchemical foundation
Is securely set up,
Five-colored light
Penetrates the curtains.

[3]
Use EARTH for the furnace,
HEAVEN for the cauldron;
Penetrate the subtleties,
Comprehend inner design,
And you'll attain immortality.
It's all a matter of controlling sense
And returning it to essence—
This is cooking mercury
And mixing it with lead.
Stop compulsive involvements
And the pill of elixir glows;
Keep correct concentration complete,
And the jewel crystallizes.
This is the method
Of extraction and addition;
No need to worry anymore
Asking about the mystery.

[4]
Active and passive practice are easy,
The medicines are not remote;
Creative evolution is just
Like the ocean tide.
The medicinal ingredients
Are just culled in nonbeing;
The fiery elixir is cooked

Wholly in concentration.
When the primordial and temporal conjoin,
All entanglements cease;
When the celestial and earthly commingle,
The five energies return to the source.
When obscurity is gone
And illumination is pure,
Then the work is done;
The true human emerges
And visits the spiritual sky.

[5]
To refine the elixir,
First harmonize energy and spirit;
The water of reality
Is repeatedly poured on,
The fire of wisdom heats it.
Focus the spirit on energy,
Purify energy by stillness,
Preserve purity by attention;
Then sense, essence, and will
Join into one:
The primal celestial comes back,
Conditioned mundanity dissolves.
The golden furnace upright,
A thousand spirits meet;
The work in the cauldron complete,
Myriad forms pay court.
The medicine made, the elixir complete,
The spirit goes free;
The whole body emerges,
Now completely bared.

[6]
The primordial ultimate spirit
Is subtle, hard to fathom;
Sense must be recovered,
Essence is always there.
Vitality and consciousness
Are divided into upper and lower;

The opening of the mysterious pass
Is right in the center.
When you know being is not being,
Then that is really being;
Understand voidness has no void,
And that is real voidness.
Nonbeing being, being nonbeing—
This is the very point;
The Great Sun glows scarlet
At the bottom of the billowing ocean.

[7]
Serene, unstirring,
One merges with true eternity;
Dissolving all obscurities
Spontaneously restores light.
In stillness the will
Fosters the spiritual being;
In concentration consciousness
Weds unconditioned knowing.
Inwardly stable in the midst of peril, energy grows;
Action coming from calmness, vitality's ebullient.
In the silver river
There's not the slightest shadow;
The gold moon appears alone,
Shining with spiritual light.

[8]
The marriage of the beautiful maid
To the metal man
Depends entirely on the work
Of the yellow woman to join them.
When husband and wife come together,
The clouds and rain of their feelings combine.
At leisure, they drink
In the mansion on the crimson hill;
Intoxicated, they sleep together
In the chamber of the purple climax.
Bliss in the evenings,
Happiness in the mornings,

Their sympathy is profound;
In a year they give birth to a baby.

[9]
There are husband and wife
In everyone's body,
But the ignorant are too fixed on delusions—
Instead of seeking creative evolution within,
They set up alchemical foundations outside.
They mistakenly take arts of sexual intercourse
To be the "nine-cauldron" of the ancient sages.
It's hard for such animals to repent;
Before long death will come after them.

[10]
I will tell you about
The husband and wife inside the body,
The blue-robed girl
And the white-haired old man:
When "metal" sense and "wood" essence combine,
Black mercury and red lead
Spontaneously commune sensitively.
Facing the moon and the breeze,
The spirit is free and blissful,
Producing endless clouds and rain.
If you can truly understand
This ultimate principle,
Crystallizing the embryo of reality
Is then a simple affair.

[11]
The nine-restored, seven-reverted great elixir
Should be sought by learners in concentration.
When you truly understand the spiritual mechanism,
The two medicinal ingredients then combine:
Three years' development
Is completed in an instant,
The work of nine transformations
Is done in a trice.
Now you take the cauldron and furnace

And turn them over;
Then the light of the elixir
Shines through the spiritual isles.

[12]
The unwritten transmission outside of doctrine
Is inherently complete in everyone.
The mystic breeze subtly clears the world,
The moon of wisdom beautifully stamps the hundred rivers.
Zen conundrums are all artificial metaphors;
Even direct pointing is still not the truth.
Conveying the experience which is before history
Is not in the Confucian circle of the absolute.

Alerting the World About the Four Conditions

Body, mind, society, events—
Four empty names:
How many confused people
Have been entangled by them!
Calamity and trouble come
From worldly power and materialism;
Vicious circles come
From obsession with objects.
In trackless serenity,
One may act at will;
Forgetting impulses when dealing with the world,
Let events change as they may.
When always letting go
In the midst of situations,
The foundation of life is secure,
Essence is complete and clear.

The Gourd

The seed of spiritual illumination
Is produced primordially;
Stem firm, roots deep,
The principle is naturally so.

Daily add the soil
Of the state of EARTH;
Irrigate at proper times
With the spring in WATER.
When the flower opens, white jade,
It shines with light;
When the fruit forms, yellow gold,
It is round and firm.
On completion, the top of the head opens up;
Here there is another universe.

The Mind Mirror

Take the ore of HEAVEN
And put it in the furnace of EARTH;
The totality of space
Becomes a single pattern.
When the manifestation of reality is perfected,
It is round and radiant;
Where consciousness is polished,
It shines with being as is.
Emanating light, it pervades the universe;
Put into storage, it is a tiny pearl.
Raising it up clearly,
The Whole Body appears;
It's still necessary to break through
To merge with the essential axis.

The Mysterious Female

The door of the female of the mystic school
Is not hard to know;
Collect body and mind
And contemplate within.
When you understand the principle
Of alternation of the two modes,
Then you know the timing
Of coming and going of the one energy.
HEAVEN and EARTH, movement and stillness,

Open and close without cease;
FIRE and WATER, awareness and vitality,
Rise and descend, mixing and separating.
Set up the alchemical foundation
At the point where thought returns.

Learning

Chan Buddhism, Confucian Noumenalism,
The Taoism of Complete Reality—
Three schools of teaching were set up
To contact later people.
For Buddhists, elements are nonabsolute,
It's necessary to see the essence;
As Confucians investigate phenomena,
They must maintain sincerity.
On the Taoist's alchemical stand
Are kept points of fire;
All kinds of atoms are melted down
In the spiritual mansion.
When you understand all differences
Are resolved in one goal,
Then on the bright terrace
All is spring, inside and out.

Verses on Freedom

[1]
On breaking through the opening of Chaos,
There are no Buddhas or Immortals.
This is no marvel outside mind,
And not mere verbal Zen.
I pass the days lightheartedly roaming,
And spend the nights freely sleeping.
Letting my body sink into the realm of the absolute,
I entrust all things to Heaven.

[2]
All created phenomena
Are dust, without exception.

Comprehending the principles of things,
I let go of mind and body.
Wherever I am I rest in meditation,
At all times I delight in reality.
To waken the people of the world,
I always use the marrow of the *I Ching*.

[3]
Reaching the subtlety of nondoing,
I don't go outside all day.
Impulsive involvements ended,
The celestial design remains.
In daily affairs,
The action of heaven is strong;
In everyday life,
The force of earth is calm.
I remind and suggest to my students—
Return to Life, go back to the root.

[4]
Passing through all barriers,
One merges with the Great Sameness.
Tortoise hair is naturally always green,
The crane's crest is originally scarlet.
What can be verbalized is not the eternal Tao;
Work that is "done" is external work:
The true creative evolution
Is in profound abstraction.

[5]
Having attained steadiness of body and mind,
I still the spirit and stabilize energy.
Body at ease, I transcend attachments;
Mind serene, I realize the uncreated.
Sun and moon come and go as they may,
HEAVEN and EARTH change freely.
Openness without obstruction
Reveals a unique great light.

[6]
There is nothing special in my daily activities
But to maintain unified central truthfulness.

In stillness I tune my breathing;
In action I follow common sense.
Hiding my powers to assimilate to society,
I contain my light and do not show illumination.
In true freedom and bliss,
I'm ever calm and ever clear.

[7]
As I serenely embrace nameless innocence,
Feelings about objects cannot invade.
As I fuse mercury and lead into powder,
Rubble turns to gold.
Seeing the ancient sages,
I reconcile Buddhism and Taoism.
Immediately opening, I transcend to reality,
Where there is no past and no present.

The Lamp in the Mirror

[1]
The precious mirror is basically formless;
The lamp of communication emanates wisdom's light.
Being-as-such is fundamentally brilliantly clear;
The body of reality is originally radiant.
The gold cauldron burns with true fire,
The flower pond bathes the great light.
The true meaning herein
Is not apart from the center.

[2]
In the quiet room I open the mirror of mind;
In the vacant hall I light the lamp of wisdom.
Outside is clear and bright,
Inside is effulgent light.
A tiny grain appears in the glow,
The silver moon is clear in the water.
In the gold crucible, suspended in space,
A grain of great elixir crystallizes.

Extolling the Lotus

[1]
One seed's spiritual sprout is different;
Others are not like it at all.
The spiritual body is fundamentally immaculate,
The true essence is basically pure.
The outward form is everywhere curved,
The holes within go all the way through.
Mud and mire cannot bog it down—
When it appears, the whole pond is red.

[2]
Our original pure immaterial seed
Is crystal clear throughout all time.
Because it dislikes mental and material greed,
It bides for a time deep in the mud.
It always intends to help people out,
Ever determined to overcome selfishness.
Of the many who try to take it,
How many really know what it is?

Building a Hut

[1]
Choosing from the whole land of open nonreification,
I find suitable conditions in the jade capital.
In building the foundation,
It must be steady and stable;
In setting up the cauldron,
It must be thoroughly level.
Standing up the polar mountain as a pillar,
I set across it the absolute as the main beam.
The blue sky is the roof,
The occupant enjoys the uncreated.

[2]
Leveling off the ground,
I finish the foundation the same day.

The mountains come in from the south,
The water flows out to the west.
The door is completely open,
The windows thoroughly clear.
Who are the companions in the hut?
The light of the moon,
The clarity of the breeze.

[20]
Veiled Words

> Those who do not clearly understand are externally fixated on body, mind, society, and events; and they inwardly dwell on sensations, conceptions, actions, and consciousness. Therefore they change along with the world, are born and perish along with forms.

Buddhist literature says if people want to know all the Buddhas of past, present, and future, they should see that the natures of the world of phenomena are all created by mind. This means that when there is creation, then there is change; creation and change both derive from mind.

People all think that what creates and changes myriad beings is the fashioner of creation and change, but I do not agree. There is basically no fashioner of creation and change; beings create and change themselves. How is this so? All beings have mind, and it is because they have mind that there is creation and change. This is what I call self-creation and self-change.

The forms of all in the world that has form are originally nonexistent. Producing existence where there was none is called creation. When there is production, then there is destruction; when there is destruction, there is reversion to nonexistence. This is called change. Repeated creation and change is the norm for beings.

The essence of the unique reality is fundamentally existent; it exists but has no form, so it has no creation or change. This is the norm of the Tao. People only know it has no creation or change, and think it does not create or change—they do not know there is great creation and change existing therein.

Who can know this without clear understanding? Those with clear understanding, those whose knowledge and wisdom are perfected, are able to see all phenomena as empty of absoluteness. Then the unified mind returns to tranquility, and lives independently in a transcendent state. Therefore there is no creation or change for them.

Those who do not clearly understand are externally fixated on body, mind, society, and events; and they inwardly dwell on sensations, conceptions, actions, and consciousness. Therefore they change along with the world, are born and perish along with forms.

What the eye sees is called form; received in the mind, it is called sensation. Once taken into the mind in the form of a mental picture, it is called conception. When conception continues, it leads to doing; this is called action. The result of action, conforming to the good or bad nature of the action, is called conditioned consciousness. The flurry of conditioned consciousness is the root of routine existence. Thus it is impossible to get out of creation and change.

Anyone who is not bound by illusory objects, not defiled by the impact of phenomena, not obstructed by wandering feelings, and not afflicted by craving, will then be able to see forms, sensations, conceptions, actions, and conditioned consciousness as empty of ultimate reality. Since these are empty, how can there be creation and change? This is what the Buddhists call the ineffable mind of nirvana.

, , ,

Taoist literature says being and nonbeing produce one another. That is, nonbeing produces being—this is creation; being produces nonbeing—this is change.

Taoist literature also says, "Effecting ultimate openness, keeping utterly quiet, as myriad things act in concert, I thereby watch the return." That is, watching return is knowing change; if you know change, you do not change, and if you do not change, how can there be creation?

Who can reach this but those who see clearly, without obstruction? Those of clear perception, pure and illumined, can see that body, mind, society, and events exist in insubstantial illusion. Existence makes things and beings, which revert to insubstantial illusions once they have reached their culmination.

Those who see in this way know the formless form is the true form. Because they nurture the formless form, they always preserve the bodyless body, and so they keep reality complete. When one is unadulterated, pure, completely whole, there is a merging with the infinite; in undifferentiated vastness, there is a merging with the unparalleled. Transcending even beyond open nothingness, this is called freedom from creation and change.

People with fixations are physically and mentally unsettled; assailed by thoughts and worries, they therefore lose the formless and the bodyless, and so they flow in the waves of birth and death, always sunk in the sea of suffering.

If you can collect body and mind, set aside thoughts and worries, not let inner states out, not let external objects in, and be inwardly and outwardly clear and serene, this is called clarification. When you get to the point where you inwardly forget the mind and outwardly forget the body, so that the unique reality is clear and you are like cosmic space, open and unobstructed, how can there be any creation or change therein?

, , ,

Confucian literature says, "Not envying, not seeking, no blame, no complicity." Not envying and not seeking means not being subject to creation; no blame and no complicity means not being subject to change.

The Connected Sayings commentary in the *I Ching* says, "At a distance, find it in things; nearby, find it in yourself." I say that "at a distance, find it in things" means you know all objects are insubstantial and temporary; "nearby, find it in yourself" means you know the physical and mental elements are all empty of ultimate reality.

By outwardly being aloof of all objects and inwardly detached from the physical and mental elements, you can accord with the celestial workings, be pleased with heaven, know the beginning and end of things, know the reason of the hidden and the obvious, know the explanation of life and death, find out truth, fulfill human nature, and arrive at the purpose of life. Because of being pleased with heaven, you do not worry; because of fulfilling nature, you do not doubt.

Who can reach this but those who achieve knowledge? Those who accomplish knowledge are sincere, lucid, calm, and stable; so they know that illusory forms continually arise and pass away, that the deluded mind is discriminatory and partial, that society and the times shift and change uncertainly, and that works perish and do not last.

When the refinement brought about through observation is thoroughly mature, this is called the accomplishment of sages. Because it is permeated by unity, there is no creation or change.

If you do not accomplish knowledge, you cannot determine the character of things; if you cannot determine things, you change and shift along with things—then where are essence and life?

, , ,

If there is fluid movement, not fixated, circulating throughout space, heaven and earth then meet in oneself, myriad things are complete in oneself. When you return to vision of the heart of heaven, myriad existents return to open nonreification; then creation and change cease.

Metaphorically speaking, if HEAVEN and EARTH do not move fluidly, sun and moon do not travel—then where are the combinations of yin and yang? If yin and yang do not interact, they do not ascend and descend—then how can myriad beings exist? The bodies of HEAVEN and EARTH are pure and unified; because they do not mix the aberrant with the true, and do not change, therefore there is no creation and no change.

The creation of creationless creation is great creation, the change of changeless change is great change. Those who see this thereby know that all things and beings in the world are temporary compounds, and that the operations of yin and yang are all illusions. Who but the most fluid in the world can keep up with this?

, , ,

Viewing the matter in this way, we can see that the three teachings—Buddhism, Taoism, and Confucianism—are just a matter of mind: creation and change depend on mind, and transcendence of creation and change also depends on mind.

In learning Buddhism, it is essential to see essence. To see essence, it is first necessary to remove habit-conditioned energy by means of certainly stabilized will, and to preserve clear lucidity by the power of strict observation. After that, see through all kinds of vain illusory mental states, and do not fixate on things, so that thoughts do not follow feelings.

Thoughts are the root of affliction, mental states are the seeds of reification. When thoughts arise, all afflictions arise; when thoughts cease, all afflictions cease. When mental states are produced, all sorts of reifications are produced; when mental states pass away, all sorts of reifications pass away. When thoughts arise, stop them—all come from mind. When you reach the point where "arising and passing away itself passes away, and quiescence is bliss," this is seeing essence.

Students today who cannot see essence are hindered by two obstructions, abstract and concrete. Abstract obstructions cannot be dissolved but by great perception; concrete obstructions cannot be dissolved but by great cessation. Great perception means cutting through by knowledge; great cessation means controlling by power.

When cutting through by knowledge is perfected, all abstractions are empty of absoluteness; when controlling by power is perfected, all concretizations are empty of absoluteness. When you realize the great emptiness of emptiness and the ultimate reality of reality, this is the consummation of great perception. Then thoughts and emotional consciousness of body, mind, society, and events all stop at once; this is the consummation of great cessation.

Learning Taoism is a matter of preserving essence. To preserve essence, it is first necessary to cut through delusions with the sword of wisdom, dissolve attachment to sense experience by maximizing the transcendent primordial consciousness and minimizing the temporally conditioned consciousness, and to use the power of concentration to forget feelings, cut off rumination, remove psychological burdens, and clarify the mind.

When the mind is clear, burdens removed, rumination ended, and feelings forgotten, this is called preserving essence. When the true essence is present, there is no creation or change.

Students today get carried away by emotional consciousness. If you want to get rid of emotional consciousness, first get rid of the fluctuating mind. When the mind does not fluctuate, then the body does not fluctuate.

Getting rid of the fluctuating mind begins with having no thoughts. When you have fully developed the habit of freedom from thought, you can reach a state of serene concentration free from dreams and thoughts. When this is fully developed, you can reach a state free from conception.

Freedom from dreams is important for the present; freedom from conception is important at the end of life. Free from conception, you do not create; free from dreams, you do not change. Not creating, not changing, you are not born and do not die.

The essence of the study of Confucianism lies in fulfilling human nature. Fulfilling human nature is a matter of clarifying enlightened qualities and resting in ultimate good. After you know where to rest, then you have stability; when you have stability, you can forget things and self.

The statement on the hexagram MOUNTAIN in the *I Ching* says, "Stopping at the back, you don't find the body; walking in the garden, you don't see the person. No blame." Stopping at the back means forgetting oneself; walking in the garden not seeing the person means forgetting things. Knowing how and where to stop—therefore being able to forget things and self and so to keep the celestial design intact—is called fulfilling human nature.

When people today cannot fulfill human nature, it is because of burdens of body and mind. Once there are burdens, there is blockage. It is necessary to apply firm decisiveness and effective resolution. By being firm and decisive you can forget things; by being effectively resolute you can forget self. When things and self are forgotten, you will surely fulfill human nature and arrive at the meaning of life.

, , ,

I observe that most people in the world think this body has a self in it. This reveals a serious lack of reflection. As this body exists due to creation, did it have a form before it was created, did it have a name, did it have a self? After it has changed, does it have a form, does it have a name, does it have a name, does it have a self? Since none of these exist either before or after, how can we cling to reification of self only in the interval between?

People do not realize that body, mind, the world, and events are fundamentally unreal in an ultimate sense; when we try to find past, present, and future, ultimately we cannot grasp them. The past has disappeared, the present changes from moment to moment, the future is uncertain.

Throughout the ages people have fixated on unreal objects in the midst of dreamlike illusion, forming the seeds of repetitious life cycles. Therefore they are born and die without hope of release.

If, on the other hand, people in the midst of these dreamlike illusory objects can experientially know them for what they are, and thus can dissolve fixations, they can reach enlightenment.

, , ,

One day I brought up this issue for my students to look into. Two or three of them understood to some extent, so I composed this essay for them, to convey mind by mind.

If you can realize directly, inwardly understand and tacitly comprehend, then you know how and where to stop, not recounting the past, not worrying about the future, not being attached to the present. When these three are combined, you attain great independence, you roam freely in the ocean of tranquility, wander in the homeland of nothing whatsoever, float in the realm of contentment.

When you get to this point, you will know that creation and change have no power over you. But there is still something yet higher. Tell me, what do you call that which is higher? Turn over the legs of nothingness, smash cosmic space to smithereens, and only then will you be done.

PRACTICAL TAOISM

TRANSLATOR'S PREFACE

Taoism, the original wisdom tradition of ancient China, may be rendered in English as "Wayfaring." In this manner of usage, the Way is classically defined in these terms: "Humanity follows earth, earth follows heaven, heaven follows the Way, the Way follows Nature." In the final sense, therefore, Taoism, or Wayfaring, refers to the pursuit of natural laws.

These natural laws are reflected in the body (earth), the mind (heaven), and in the order of the universe (the Way of Nature). The practice of Taoism, therefore, takes place in the cultivation and refinement of the natural capacities of the human body-mind continuum and its relationship with the social milieu and the natural world.

Taoist pursuit of natural laws extends beyond those recognized within a limited cultural context, seeking to uncover and activate latent sensitivities that enable the individual to enter into an increasingly intimate, vitalizing, inspiring relationship with Life in all of its manifestations.

According to classical tradition, Taoism cannot be encompassed within just one framework of expression. As a result of this particular quality, many diverse modes of Taoist activity emerged over the centuries. One of the most popular of these is the science of inner alchemy, which energizes the body and purifies the mind, thus producing a transmutation in consciousness enhancing the individual experience of life.

There are two main sourcebooks of internal alchemy, known as the Ancestors of Alchemical Treatises: *Triplex Unity*, by the second century CE adept Wei Boyang, and *Understanding Reality*, by the eleventh century CE adept Zhang Ziyang. Couched in cryptic symbolic language, these two texts spawned a great deal of commentary and not a little controversy. Eventually the opacity of alchemical terminology led some Taoist writers to adopt more explicit manners of expression in order to enable seekers to put the teachings into practice.

The present text is one such work, a collection of quotations from alchemical classics along with practical explanations by expert Taoists. It is attributed to a seventh-generation master of the Northern Branch of the Complete Reality School of Taoism, known as the Preserver of Truth. It contains sayings of many famous adepts, devoted specifically to elucidating the modes and manners of practical Wayfaring represented by the mysteries of spiritual alchemy.

INTRODUCTION

There are two ways of cultivating refinement. The *Classic of Wenshi* says, "If you can see the vital spirit, you gain lasting life; if you can forget the vital spirit, you gain transcendent life."

Forgetting the vital spirit means emptiness climaxes, quietude is attained, and vitality naturally transmutes into energy, energy naturally transmutes into spirit, and spirit naturally returns to emptiness. This is the study of the Great Way of absolute nonresistance.

Seeing the vital spirit means taking emptiness and quietude for substance, the firing process for function, refining vitality into energy, refining energy into spirit, and refining spirit back into emptiness. This is the study of driving energy by spirit.

Although the study of the Great Way of absolute nonresistance does not touch on vitality and energy, still one merges in reality with the Way, physically and mentally sublimated, appearing and disappearing in being and nonbeing, changing unfathomably, with a life span that is measureless. This is comprehending essence and then spontaneously comprehending life. This is including the lower in the higher.

Using spirit to drive energy involves vitality and energy, but one preserves their original harmony, working unceasingly. The ultimate harmony permeates and sublimates, producing liquid fluidity that can also make the physical unite with the spiritual to live without dying. This is comprehending life, with essence thereby abiding. This is progressing to the higher from the lower.

The Great Way of absolute nonresistance applies to the metaphysical body; driving energy by means of spirit applies to the physical body. Although these two are different in magnitude, nevertheless they are the realities of spiritual alchemy, the true source of the Great Way; there is benefit in realizing them, and they can be accomplished by practice. They are not like the minor arts of auxiliary methods, at which one may labor without accomplishing anything.

When I first met my teacher long ago, I asked for instruction on learning immortality. My teacher said that learning immortality may be artificial or real: the artificial is the way of the methodologists, while the real is the way of the wayfarers. Subsequently receiving instruction, fortunately I was able to transcend the ordinary. Now then, the arts of methodologists are such as consumption of the seeds of plants and trees and the essences of metals and minerals, and methods of culling yin to augment yang. The way of wayfarers consists of two points: forgetting the vital spirit and seeing the vital spirit.

Those who seek eternal life by techniques will inevitably ruin their own lives. Going by the Way, however, one will not only live long but also directly experience birthlessness. There is a great difference between the real and the artificial, the Way and techniques; those with perception will be able to distinguish them on their own.

Since olden times, however, there have been many Taoist books in which ancient teachers set up all sorts of similes, using objects to stand for terms, using terms to lodge meanings. This is because the true Way is hard to express, so they wanted to present clues without speaking clearly. That is all there is to it, but later students nevertheless got mired in words and clung to abstract metaphors.

If you let go of things, your body is not stressed; if you contrive no artificiality, your mind is naturally at peace. Serenity and lightness develop day by day, while involvement in objects grows thinner day by day. Your actions become further and further from mundanity, while your mind becomes closer and closer to the Way.

Some people display virtue and show ability in order to get others to support them. Some call on people for celebrations and funerals, in effect making business trips. Some affect seclusion as hermits but are actually seeking social advancement. Some offer people food and drink in hopes of later favors. All of these are clever operations of the crafty mind for gaining temporal profit. These prevent right action and so should all be abandoned.

As long as you do not start anything, others will not join in; even if others do start something, you do not join in. Gradually cutting off old entanglements, do not form new entanglements.

Foods include wine and meat; clothing includes fine silks; social status includes reputation and position; material wealth includes gold and jade; but these luxuries are all excesses of emotional desires, not good medicines that enhance life. People who pursue them bring about their own destruction. How confused can you get!

The second thing is to govern the mind. The mind is the ruler of the whole body, the commander of all the mental powers. When it is quiet, it produces insight; when agitated, it becomes unclear. Therefore, in the beginning of study of the Way, it is necessary to sit calmly, collect the mind, and detach from objects, so the mind does not possess anything. By dwelling in nonpossession, one does not cling to anything, spontaneously entering into absolute nonresistance. The mind then merges with the Way.

As for the source of the substance of mind, its root is the Way; but because the mind gets stained and obscured, it gradually becomes vagrant, eventually becoming estranged from the Way. If you clean the pollution from the mind and open up consciousness of the root of the spirit, that is called practicing the Way.

When the mind no longer wanders vagrant but merges with the Way and rests calmly in the Way, that is called return to the root. Keeping to the root without straying is called serene stabilization. Over a long time at this, diseases vanish, life returns, returns and continues, so you naturally come to know the eternal. Knowing means nothing is obscure; eternal means there is no change. Emancipation from birth and death really comes from here.

If you want to cultivate reality, first get rid of warped behaviors. With external affairs cut off, there is nothing to concern the mind; after that, you gaze inwardly with precise awareness. When you notice a thought arising, eliminate it. Eliminate thoughts as they arise, in order to bring about peaceful calmness.

Next, even if you don't actually have any obsessive fixations, floating random thoughts should also be eliminated. Practicing diligently day and night, not deviating for a moment, just extinguish the stirring mind, do not extinguish the shining mind; just accord with the open mind, not with the possessive mind. Then the mind does not depend on anything but always abides in truth.

To pacify and stabilize the mind, it is important to have no obsessions. If you dwell on openness, emptiness, or nonresistance with a clinging mind, this is still possessiveness, not nonpossessiveness. To abide in possessiveness causes the mind to toil; it is out of harmony with truth, and also produces sickness. As long as the mind does not dwell on anything and is imperturbable, this is authentic stability and accurate awareness. Use this for stabilization, and mind and mood will be in tune, becoming lighter and airier as time goes on. When you use this as a test, right and wrong become obvious.

Above the stabilized mind is vast openness, with no covering; beneath the stabilized mind is open vastness, with no dependency.

Eliminate confusion without extinguishing perception; maintain calmness without sticking to emptiness. Practice this consistently, and you will naturally attain true vision.

Whether the mind is ordinarily hyperactive or calm is a matter of long-term habit; it is very hard to have the discipline to stop the mind. One may try to stop it and yet be unable, or one may manage to do so temporarily and then lose it. The whole body flows with sweat under the duress of the struggle between losing and keeping; only after a long, long process of softening does one finally attain mature attunement. Do not give up your regular practice because of temporary failure to collect the mind.

Once you have attained some calmness, then you should consciously stabilize it at all times, whether working or still, sitting or reclining—even when dealing with things in the midst of clamor. Whether there is something to attend to or nothing to attend to, always be as if unminding; whether in quietude or in clamor, let your will remain unified.

The mind has been resting on objects all along, and so it is not used to independence; suddenly without resort, it is hard for it to remain at rest spontaneously. Even if you can pacify it for a while, it scatters in confusion again. Govern it as it arises, so that it does not become agitated. Eventually, after a long time, it will become tuned and tamed, able to be at peace naturally and spontaneously. Day or night, whatever you may be doing, always consciously stabilize it; if your mind attains stability, then you must nurture it calmly not allowing any annoyance. When you have attained some peace, then you can enjoy yourself, gradually becoming accustomed to it, becoming increasingly pure and aloof.

If things sometimes give rise to doubts, then for the time being do all the thinking you need to solve the matter, and you will also come to understand what you have wondered about. This is also an authentic root of wisdom. Once you have understood, stop and don't think anymore; if you keep on thinking, your intellect will damage your essence, ruining the principal for the sake of the interest. Even if you develop outstanding cleverness for a time, ultimately that will compromise long-term work.

If you are afflicted by false and random thoughts, abandon them as you become aware of them; if you hear criticism or praise, good or bad, ignore it all and don't take it into your mind. If you take it in, your mind will be filled; if your mind is filled, there's no room for the Way. Whatever you see or hear, be as if you hadn't seen or heard it, and judgmental evaluations won't enter your mind. When the mind does not take in externals, it is called the empty mind; when the mind does not pursue externals, it is called the peaceful mind. When the mind is peaceful and empty, the Way will naturally come to abide in it.

Once the inner mind has no attachment, external action has no artificialities. Since you are neither puritanical nor profane, praise and blame have no way to arise. Since you are neither an intellectual nor an ignoramus, profit and loss have no way to disturb you. In actual reality, you go along centered as your norm; strategically, you vary according to the times. If you can avoid getting dragged down, then you are wise in this way. If you try to control the mind too intensely, that will even cause sickness, resulting in psychological derangement.

If the mind is not agitated, then let it be; with relaxation and intensity in balance, you will always be spontaneously in tune.

If you employ thought and contrivance at the wrong time or for the wrong thing, and yet you consider yourself unattached, after all this is not genuine study. Why? The mind is like the eye: if even the finest hair gets into your eye, it is uncomfortable; if even a small matter concerns the mind, the mind will be disturbed. Once there is the affliction of disturbance, it is hard to concentrate. Therefore to practice the Way it is essential to get rid of affliction, for unless affliction is removed it is hard to attain concentration. It is like a fertile field, in which seed will not produce good crops unless the weeds are removed. Craving and cogitation are weeds of the mind; unless they are removed, concentration and wisdom will not grow.

If you extinguish all mental activity without choosing between the right and the wrong, you will cut off conscious knowing and enter into a trance of oblivion. If you let your mind act up without collecting it or governing it at all, then you'll never be different from an ordinary person. If you only cut off the sense of good and bad, so your mind has no refuge, letting ideas roam, expecting natural settling in this way, you are merely fooling yourself. If you carry out all sorts of projects claiming your mind is not influenced, this is fine talk but quite wrong in practice. Real students should especially beware of this.

Those who have the aspiration to reach the Way should conceive profound faith and devotion and cultivate practice in accord with the precepts. If you are consistent from start to finish, you will attain the true Way.

The third thing is true observation. This true observation is the way the wise attain prior awareness, the way the able practice skillful examination. Even a meal or a nap is a source of loss or gain; even a single act or a single word can be the root of disaster or fortune. Even clever maintenance of the branches is not as good as clumsy preservation of the root. Observing the root and knowing the branch is not a sense of haste either. So stop the mind, minimize concerns, and reduce contrivance. Body tranquil, mind free, you can then observe the subtle.

To cultivate the Way, the body needs food and clothing. There are some factors that cannot be neglected, some things that cannot be abandoned; accept them with an open heart, manage them with clear eyes, and do not let them impede or vex you. If you are annoyed or excited on account of things, sickness is already stirring in your mind—so what is "peace of mind"?

When there is something to strive for, don't give rise to ideas of gain and loss. Whether there is something to do or nothing to do, let the mind always be at rest. Seek as others do, but do not be covetous as others are; earn as others do, but do not hoard as others do. By not being covetous, you will be free of anxiety; by not hoarding, you will be immune to loss. Let your outward traces be like others, while your mind is always different from the vulgar. This is the model of real practice; it is essential to work on it diligently.

Even if you have severed entanglements and simplified affairs but still have afflictions that are hard to get rid of, just contemplate them methodically. For example, those most seriously afflicted by materialism or sensuality should realize that being influenced by materialism and sensuality comes from thoughts; if thoughts do not arise, there is, after all, nothing the matter. Know that thoughts of matter and sense are externally void, so the materialistic sensual mind is inwardly forgotten. When you forget thoughts, the mind is empty; who hosts matter? Scripture says, "Material forms are only ideas, and ideas are all empty—what have they to do with matter?"

If you give rise to hatred on seeing someone do wrong, that is like seeing someone try to cut his head off and then taking his knife to cut your own neck. When others do wrong on their own account, that is not your responsibility; why take on their evil and make it your own affliction? Thus when you see wrongdoers, do not hate them, and when you see people doing good, do not admire them. Why? Because both obstruct the Way.

Action is your own doing; destiny is given by Heaven. Action and destiny are to each other like echoes and shadows following sounds and forms; since they cannot be avoided, neither should they be resented. Only the wise really attain this; pleased with Heaven, knowing destiny, they therefore do not worry. How can they be made miserable by poverty or illness? Zhuangzi said, "Action enters in inescapably." Scripture says, "Heaven and earth cannot change their discipline; yin and yang cannot alter their action." This refers to true destiny—what is there to resent?

Suppose a courageous warrior encounters brigands; fearlessly he brandishes his sword and advances so that the brigands all scatter. Once the warrior's achievement is established, his honor and his pension continue to the end of his life. Now if poverty or illness trouble you, then they are brigands. If you have an upright mind, that is the courageous warrior. Intelligent contemplation is brandishing a sword. When troubles dissolve and disappear, then the battle is won. Profound calm and eternal happiness are the honor and the pension.

Whenever painful things happen to press on your mind, if you don't use this contemplation but instead develop an anxious feeling of being burdened, this is like one who encounters brigands but does nothing about them, abandoning his armor, turning his back on his troops, and running away. Incurring blame, abandoning happiness for misery—how can such a person even be pitied?

If poverty and illness pain you, contemplate this pain as deriving from having a physical self. Were there no physical self, afflictions would have nowhere to lodge.

Fourth is stable concentration. When there is no intention to concentrate and yet one is never unconcentrated, that is called stable concentration.

Control without obsession, relaxation without indulgence, no aversion in the midst of clamor, no vexation in the midst of events—this is true concentration. But one does not seek involvement in many concerns just because one is not troubled by things, and one does not take to clamor just because one is not spoiled by clamor. Freedom from obsession is the true norm; taking on tasks is for responding for happenings.

Fifth is awakening insight. Zhuangzi said, "Those who lodge in serene concentration radiate the light of Heaven." The mind is the house of the Way; when emptiness and quietude reach their climax, the Way lodges there, and insight is born. Insight comes from your basic essence; it is not something you have just now acquired. Because of confusion by greed and emotional attachment, however, it gets obscured and lost. By purification and softening, returning to purity and tranquillity, the original real spiritual consciousness gradually becomes clear of itself; that does not mean the insight has only now been specially produced.

Once insight has emerged, treasure it and keep it in your heart; do not allow excessive intellectualism to damage your concentration. It is not that engendering insight is hard; having insight but not exploiting it is what is hard. Since ancient times, those who forgot the concrete have been many, while those who forgot the abstract have been few. To be insightful but not exploit it is forgetting the abstract.

To be insightful but not exploit it makes for freedom from excesses on the Way, so one attains profound realization of true eternity. To be insightful but not exploit it, furthermore, is an artful means of enhancing stability and insight. Just enter into concentration to awaken insight; whether it happens sooner or later is not up to the individual, so do not hastily seek insight in concentration. If you seek insight, that will compromise concentration; if concentration is compromised, then there is no insight. When insight occurs without your seeking insight, this is genuine insight.

Insight enables you to know the Way; it is not attainment of the Way. Zhuangzi said, "In ancient times those who knew the Way nurtured intelligence by means of serenity; their intelligence developed, but they did not exploit it." This is called using intelligence to nurture serenity. Intelligence and serenity nurture each other, and harmony and reason emerge. Serenity and intelligence are stability and insight; harmony and reason are the Way and virtue. Intelligence without exploitation, resting in that serenity, when accumulated over a long time naturally turns into the Way and its virtue.

Sixth is attaining the Way. When there are precious minerals in a mountain, the plants and trees do not wither; when someone embosoms the Way, the physical body is permanently stabilized. By long-term cultivation, you transform the physical to be like the spiritual; refining the spirit to enter into the subtle, you unite with the Way. Then your intelligence shines boundlessly while your body is transcendent, without limit; you use the totality of matter and emptiness to function; you embody creativity to accomplish your work. True responsiveness has no set convention; your heart is on the Way and its virtues. The Way has profound power that gradually changes the body and the spirit. When the body conforms to the Way and thus merges with the spiritual, then one is called a spiritual person. With the spiritual nature open and fluid, the body does not deteriorate; because the physical being has assimilated to the Way, there is no birth or death. In concealment, the physical is assimilated to the spiritual; in manifestation, spirit is the same as energy. This is how you walk over water and fire without harm, cast no shadow in sunlight or moonlight, remain unruffled even if thunder shatters a mountain, feel unafraid even if bare swords clash right before you, view fame and profit as a flash in the pan, recognize birth and death as morbid. It is up to you whether you remain or pass away; you go in and out where there is no room. Even though your body is polluted matter, you still reach emptiness and sublimity; is not spiritual intelligence even deeper and vaster? The *Scripture on Quickening the Spirit* says, "When body and spirit are unified, that is the real body." The *Scripture on the Western Ascent* says, "By uniting body and spirit, one can last long."

The Way of absolute nonresistance has power that may be shallow or deep. When it is deep, its effect includes the physical body; when shallow, it only extends to the mind. Those whose bodies are affected are spiritual people. Those whose minds are affected only attain insight and awakening; their bodies do not escape perishing. Why? Because insight is a function of mind: use it too much and the mind is wearied. When you first attain a little insight, you get excited and talk a lot, so spiritual energy leaks out, and there is no spiritual light to bathe and nourish the body. This eventually brings about an early end; that is what scripture calls "liberation from the corpse." Therefore great people keep their illumination hidden, concealing their brilliance for the purpose of completeness; stabilizing the spirit and treasuring energy, they learn the Way and lose their willfulness. When spirit merges with the Way, that is called attaining the Way.

The body and mind of a person who has attained the Way have five times and seven signs. The five times of mind are: (1) more movement than stillness; (2) equal movement and stillness; (3) more stillness than movement; (4) stillness when there is nothing to do, returning to movement when things impinge; (5) the mind merging with the Way and no longer stirring even when impinged upon. Only when the mind reaches this last point is one at ease; the filth of wrongdoing disappears, and there are no more afflictions.

The seven bodily signs are: (1) actions are timely and the countenance is mild and pleasant; (2) chronic ailments disappear, and body and mind are light and fresh; (3) unnatural deterioration is remedied, restoring life to its original state; (4) life is extended thousands of years—such are called immortals; (5) the physical body is refined into energy—such are called real people; (6) energy is refined into a physical form—such are called spiritual people; (7) the spirit is refined to merge with the Way—such are called people who have arrived.

Even if you have studied concentration for a long time, if your mind and body do not have these five times and seven signs, you are shortening your years and polluting your constitution; when matter disintegrates, you return to the void. Under these conditions, it is not true to say of yourself that you have insight and awakening and have attained the Way. This can be declared mistaken.

Panshan's record of sayings notes, "Practitioners should establish a determined resolve and diligently refine the mind hour to hour, moment to moment, without anticipating the future. Do not harbor ambition to prevail and hope to attain transcendent freedom in that state."

Practitioners should view this body as like an ox being led to slaughter, every step bringing it closer to death. Thus death is what is on your mind; everything is cast off. Even when the things in your environment surround you with confusion, your eyes do not see any thing, your ears do not hear any thing. Forgetting every thing moment to moment, relinquishing even the body to say nothing of the rest, by refining the mind in this way, you will see results rapidly.

Practitioners keep their minds on the Way in the midst of activity as well as in quietude, in all situations, whether walking, standing still, sitting, or reclining. Unchanged by encounters with demons, unmoved when beleaguered, you are just so when at ease and just so when in peril too. Relinquishing this body without reservation, diligently progressing straight ahead, unafraid of life and death, you are then an individual with determination.

When you start to practice refining your mind ground, you must take your previous subjectivity, attachments, schemes, evaluations, hopes, calculations, antagonisms, and rivalries and cut right through them. Also take your previous obsessions with alcohol, sex, money, power, competition, judgment, clinging, craving, selfishness, perversity, ambition, and greed and stop each one of them. When you have no entanglements outside, then your body is light and exuberant; when you have no obsessions within, then your mind is light and exuberant. Inner and outer lightness and exuberance eventually become unadulterated and thoroughly familiar; then you must still be vigilant in keeping this intact at all times, careful of what you say, moderating food and drink, and minimizing slumber. With outside and inside assisting each other, mundane defilements are cleared away with nothing left at all; at that time your own original life, your basic spirit, spontaneously appears, able to act with autonomy. Then you are an unsurpassed Wayfarer.

Practitioners must do something about the ingrained habits and biased thoughts in their minds. Energetically refine your mind to relinquish them. Even the body must be relinquished when its limit arrives—how much more so all that is in the thoughts, which is all unreal! You must clear all that away, and then you will then have no psychological afflictions obstructing you.

Things outside the body, abstract or concrete, are not worth keeping in mind or keeping the mind on them. They come and go before our eyes like mosquitoes; when we brush them away, they speed up. If we make fierce attempts to dismiss those things that are hard to get out of our minds, that in itself is a seed of futile routine!

Twenty-four hours a day, understand your own mind ground: when thoughts arise, see if they are false or true. If they are false thoughts, then immediately extinguish them. If they are true thoughts, then apply them. Day or night, at all times, at every moment, when active or when still, shatter mental inflexibility.

When you fall into error, chase it away; chase it and chase it until not a trace remains. Then the original source will be clear and clean.

Even the slightest error should be eliminated. Even the smallest virtue should be developed.

One cut severs all. When the one thought of true eternity continues unbroken forever, then there is no decay.

If you are coming and going all wrapped up in myriad things and myriad situations, even if you want to respond harmoniously, you must be able to be in charge of yourself and not just pursue things. It is like protecting your eyes: whenever there is any dust, you close your eyes and do not let it in. Keep yourself protected like this, and eventually you will see the effect. As long as the mind lets anything in, it is drawn by that, and you cannot be in charge of yourself.

When practitioners refine the mind and respond to events, they must first have inner autonomy and inner peace; then they will hit the mark every time when they respond to external events. Even if you are broken and crushed, just let the mind not move. As for which is first and which comes after, both are conditional—what definite substance do they have? The mind should be "dead," while the potential should be alive. Just go on responding to what is most immediately urgent, peacefully and calmly, without agitation or ignorance. This is what is called always being responsive while always being serene.

When things come up, you must see through them; when situations occur, you must respond to them.

Even though external objects are conditional, practitioners have to respond to them. If you respond without ego, your mind is essentially empty, and there is no obstruction when events come up. So emptiness does not interfere with myriad things, and myriad things do not interfere with emptiness. It is just as the myriad forms and myriad beings in the universe have their individual activities but do not interfere with each other. If you keep a self-image in mind, it will inevitably be brought to bear on anything that comes up, so there will be a reaction that cannot be gotten over in a hurry, resulting in collisions that agitate your mind. Once your mind is agitated, you cannot be at peace; even if you work hard all day, you'll just toil without accomplishing anything.

When you are in the midst of a lot of people, or when you have a job to do, be sure to guard your mind so that it cannot be influenced; always look for your own mistakes, and do not be concerned with the errors of others.

As it is said, "Firm and decisive, fiercely determined, cut right in two with a single stroke." People who would be greatly cultivated should work on the mind in this way. If you do not arouse a determined will and sharpen a resolute, decisive attitude but merely pass the days at leisure just as you are, even if you say you are practicing the Way, you cannot wake up and cannot get free. Ultimately you are wrapped up in arbitrary entanglements, drifting into emotional opinions. The wheel of birth and death continues to revolve, and the Way cannot be realized.

Scripture says, "Inwardly gazing on the mind, the mind has no such mind; outwardly viewing the physical body, the form has no such form. Observing things at large, things have no such thingness. Once these three are understood, you only see emptiness." This is the practice of dismissing being and returning to nonbeing. Usually people's minds are inwardly involved with preoccupations and random imagination, while their bodies are outwardly involved in honor and disgrace, profit and loss; and for things at large they have so much craving and attachment. These are three conditions, but in sum if you are fixated on a single one of them, this is why the ancient wizards taught people that practice requires that one first depart from being; if you do not cling to being, it is empty of itself.

As for the saying that mind has no such mind, all random ideas, fixations on objects, and calculating scheming are illusory and unreal. They arise from illusory objectifications and disappear as illusory objectifications; when you look for any reality, none can be found. Therefore it is said that the mind has no such mind.

As for "the physical form has no such form," and "things have no such thingness," physical form and things disintegrate before long, ultimately returning to nothing. This is observant insight, or understanding; once you can understand, you will naturally be detached from illusions, so delusions and random imaginations spontaneously disappear without having to be eliminated. Because thoughts in the mind are all empty, therefore it is said one "only sees emptiness." This is a matter of transcendental knowledge, not run-of-the-mill quietism.

"Contemplating emptiness, it is also empty; there is nothing for emptiness to empty." This is said to get rid of the word *emptiness*. When you are fixated on being, you need to attain the power of emptiness; when you are able to be empty, there is just this "emptiness" in your heart. Thus this "emptiness" becomes an obstruction to your mind. How so? This is called getting addicted to the medicine, thus producing disease.

If practitioners cling fixedly to emptiness, they are the same as people who stick to existence. That is why ancient wizards also taught students to remove this "emptiness." So scripture says that when you contemplate emptiness, it is also empty, as there is nothing for emptiness to empty.

"Since what is emptied is nothing, nothingness that is naught is also nonexistent." This now has us dismiss nothingness too. Once emptiness is gone and becomes one nothingness, there is still awareness of this nothing; this cognition of nothing is also an ailment, so it must also be forgotten.

Generally speaking, those who work on the great practice should not have any fixation at all. As soon as there is the slightest fixation, it doesn't matter whether the object of attachment is existence, emptiness, or nothingness—all become binding fetters. Therefore it is imperative to get rid of them; after that is sublime.

"Since nonexistent nothingness does not exist, there is profound calm and eternal peace." When you get to this point, there is nothing to get rid of anymore; the manifestation of pure, whole, uniform, natural reality is clear and calm, not coming out or going in. Thus it is called profound calm and eternal peace.

These sayings discourse on the work of emptiness; first penetrating by insight into the highest and most profound mystery, then bringing out the word *understanding*, which is utterly essential. The next two sections are redundant, so I make no notes.

The foregoing passages—some complex, some simple, some shallow, some deep, some analytic, some general, some proceeding from start to finish, some opening up in the middle—are all about the work of purifying and refining the mind in order to merge with the wonder of the Great Way of absolute nonresistance. If those who wish to learn will combine all this in practice, they will, I hope, not be far from the Way.

ESSENTIAL SAYINGS TO ASSIST POTENTIAL

The *Classic of the Beginning of Culture* by the Keeper of the Pass says, "In those who skillfully detach from consciousness, consciousness turns into knowledge."

Zhang Ziyang's *Alchemical Directions* says, "To use things to refine the mind, there is nothing else to do but not keep things on your mind; then complete serenity is possible."

The *Discourse on Mind* by the Celestial Teacher of Emptiness and Tranquillity says, "Do not fear the arising of thoughts; just beware of tardiness in noticing. The arising of thoughts is sickness; not continuing them is medicine."

The *Secret Discourse on the Mysterious Pass* by the Master of the White Jade Moon says, "Have no mind on things and no things in mind."

Calling the Way, a collection by the Master of Eternal Spring, says, "When not a single thought leaves the heart, this is true emptiness."

The Master of the Cloudy Portals said, "At the first stage of meditation, thought becomes still. At the second stage of meditation, breath becomes still. At the third stage of meditation, the energy channels become still. At the fourth stage of meditation, there is total extinction and entry into great concentration."

Hao the Ancient said, "In quietude, refine energy; in the midst of clamor, refine the spirit."

In his record of sayings on resolving confusion, Barefoot Liu said, "You must conquer your mind on a single needle, a single blade of grass."

It is essential to forget feelings and conscious perceptions to gradually return to the Way. Perceptions are seeds of birth and death; if you keep consciousness of perceptions in mind, then you will conceive feelings about objects. If there are no objects inside you, then how can outward objects occur? If outward objects do not occur, inner objects do not emerge; so inside and outside are peaceful and quiet.

When mind kills objects, you are a wizard. When objects kill mind, you are a mortal.

The *Water and Cloud Collection* by Master Tan of Eternal Reality says, "When people revolve ceaselessly in routine birth and death, it is just because they are mindful." The Master of the Mountain of Virtue said, "When minding occurs, all kinds of things occur; when minding disappears, all kinds of things disappear." If not a single thought occurs, then you shed birth and death. Therefore enlightened people cultivate their behavior, detaching from emotion, breaking down obstinacy and blunting sharpness, working to overcome and eliminate unwholesome states of mind in order to see the original face before birth.

Master Liu of Eternal Life said, "When you mentally penetrate something, you get out of its shell; when you penetrate myriad things, you get out of the shell of myriad things. Only then do you witness the Great Way of absolute nonresistance. If you cannot penetrate, and so remain in a state of inaction, that is called rigid voidness."

The commentary on the *Scripture of Purity and Serenity* by the Master of the Undefiled says, "Superior people of brilliant intelligence with intense insight let go of their whole beings, as if they had never even been born; they have no fixations at all. Then the mind source is spontaneously clear and calm, and true nature becomes manifest of itself."

Wang Chongyang's *Collection on Complete Reality* says: "There is a way to conquer the mind. If the mind is always calm and still, dark and silent, not seeing anything, neither inside nor outside, free of all thoughts and mental images, this is the settled mind, which is not to be conquered. If the mind gets excited at objects, falling all over itself looking for beginnings and ends, this is the confused mind, which ruins the virtues of the Way and undermines essence and life—it should not be indulged. Whatever you are doing, always strive to conquer perception, feeling, and cognition, realizing these are afflictions. Putting your nature in order is like tuning a stringed instrument. If the strings are too tight they will snap, while if they are too loose they will not be responsive. When tautness and relaxation are balanced, then the instrument is ready. It is also like making a sword; too much iron and it will snap, too much tin and it will bend. When iron and tin are balanced, then the sword is useful. Tuning and refining your true nature is a matter of embodying these two principles."

The *Mount Pan Record* of Wang the Cloud Dweller says, "Beware of gossiping about people and personalities, trends and fashions."

When some accomplishment gives you some sense of superiority, more accomplishment gives you more of a sense of superiority. Once you have a sense of superiority, then you have a self-image, which creates a massive obstacle. How can you attain the state of emptiness of mind? You have to increase your resolve and break yourself under all things, always taking a back seat to other people, thinking you are not as good as others in any way; then you can get rid of pride and a sense of superiority.

The experiences that may occur in stillness are of very many sorts, but all of them are productions of one's own consciousness which appear because of stillness. An ancient said, "Whatever has form is unreal." If you want to eliminate consciousness, the conscious spirit still remains, metamorphosing into apparitions that confuse the mind host. If the mind host is not disturbed, seeing is like not seeing; like space, there is nowhere to grasp. Then any apparitions spontaneously disappear, as there are no objects that can bewilder the mind, and no things that can disrupt it.

If you are tranquil and unagitated, how can bedevilment occur? These manifestations appear because mental wandering has not ended; remain essentially calm, and they will disappear of themselves.

When beginners polish and refine their minds, as they attain a state of stillness, extraordinary experiences or visions may occur. If they take these experiences seriously, they will become attached to falsehoods; if this is not eliminated, it will develop into incurable mental illness.

Some ask, "Those who study illustrative stories and read scriptures and classics say they are illumining the mind in the ancient teachings; is this true?"

People who practice cultivation basically refine themselves to enter from ordinariness into sagehood. If people who are not willing to make this their task just make a living on the sayings and writings of others, using up all their time pursuing literalist studies, what does this ultimately accomplish? When death comes calling, not a single phrase, not a single letter will prove useful.

This sole point of effective luminosity that animates the body has always been pure; what lack do you complain of? If you can understand it clearly yourself, it is a basis for transcending the ordinary and entering into sagehood. If you really believe this, work on it, and understand your own story, then why count the treasures of others anymore?

The *Assembled Essentials* says, "Always examine yourself: have false ideas and thoughts stopped? Are involvements with external objects at a minimum? Am I unmoved in contact with things? Are black and white undifferentiated? Are mental images in dreams accurate and unconfused? Is my heart at peace? In this manner you can measure the depth of your entry into the Way."

The above teachings all are methods of empty quietude, approaches to the Way. The essential mechanisms are all mentioned, without any concealment; if you practice in accord with them, you may be sure of attainment. The only thing to worry about is failure of will.

Some people complain that there is nothing to grasp, nothing to hold on to. What they don't realize is that the Way is basically without attachment, so to seek it with a grasping mind is inherently self-defeating. To enter the Way, the mind of a practitioner should be like space; if there is any clinging, that becomes an affliction. Then when you get sick of this affliction and want to get rid of it, you draw on yourself an extra burden on account of contrived effort. Therefore nothing compares to being careful of the beginning; if there is no clinging to start with, you will end up without affliction. So don't seek isolated skills or disciplines that are easy to perform just because this nonattachment is hard to manage, for if you do you will ruin yourself.

Some ask if the Great Way of absolute nonresistance can prolong life. Lao-tzu said, "What gives us life is the Way; what enlivens us is the spirit." If you can keep mindful of the spirit, even if locked in death energy, you can cause the dry bones of seven generations of ancestors to have living energy. Wen-tzu said, "The highest masters nurture the spirit; lesser ones nurture the body. When the spirit is clear and the mood equanimous, then the physical body is at peace. This is the basis of hygiene." Wen-tzu also said, "When the spirit is not focused externally, that is called spirituality; to keep the spirit intact is called integrity." Speaking on this basis, absolute nonresistance is truly the foremost principle of long life. However, while it may be that long life comes about spontaneously if you keep the spirit intact, nevertheless if you seek long life you are fixated on long life. Lao-tzu said, "Even I am gray; who can keep intact forever?" Long Life Liu said, "How can you seek eternal life by means of a temporal body?" How fine these words are—practitioners of mysticism can thereby be free of confusion.

With the decline of the Way of wizardry, the true teaching is not flourishing, while false teachings are popular. Beginners don't know how to orient their efforts, and true guides in this quest are hard to find; the blind are leading the blind, into a pit of fire. If you withdraw and seek it in books, you find complicated ramifications, so your questions grow more and more; the true vehicle is easily obscured, while tangential methods are so abundant that they block you, ultimately leaving you with no basis for progress or detachment. At a loss, you may simply stop, or you may slight faith and act arbitrarily, destroying your body and losing your essential nature. This is very lamentable.

Now in order to sweep away worn-out cliches I open up what has not yet been opened, enabling people of later generations to realize what is mistaken and what is accurate, to understand how to get started and how to arrive at the goal. In this way I hope to revive religion somewhat and block the waves of madness.

THE WAY OF ETERNAL LIFE THROUGH PERCEPTION OF VITAL SPIRIT · *The bases of alchemy: The absolute, yin and yang, substance and function*

Zhang Ziyang said, "The way of restorative alchemy is most simple and easy; it is like a circle." Yu Yuwu said, "What is the circle? It is the Absolute of the *Book of Changes*. When the Absolute goes into motion, it produces yin and yang. When motion culminates, it reverts to stillness and in stillness produces yin. When stillness culminates, it returns to movement. Movement and stillness in alternation constitute bases for each other. This is the wonder of Creation, the natural course of the Way."

Zhang Sanfeng said, "The absolute is the Way of nonresistance and spontaneity. The two modalities are yin and yang. The absolute is the basic spirit; the two modalities are vitality and energy. The absolute is the matrix of the alchemical elixir; the two modalities are true lead and true mercury. Symbolized by a circle, the absolute is itself infinite. This is also called the Great Transmutation, which is none other than the countenance before birth. 'Absolute unity containing true energy' is a reference to the state of the universal inception, prior to the division of the two polar energies."

Yi Zhenzi said, "The physical cannot produce the physical; what produces the physical is not physical, it is energy. What produces energy is not energy, it is the Way." He also said, "The myriad differences in the physical form change and do not remain; only the unity of energy does not change. But the unchanging energy perishes, while the cause of its unchanging remains."

Although the way of wizardry is not beyond yin and yang and the five elements, nevertheless yin and yang and the five elements cannot operate themselves without the absolute. The absolute is the unifying law of yin and yang and the five elements. If you want to operate yin and yang and the five elements in your own body, do not by any means focus your effort on yin and yang and the five elements. You must concentrate on the absolute, practicing being unborn; then yin and yang and the five elements will operate spontaneously and naturally without your having to seek to operate them. This is an unknown truth that brings out the whole matter by getting to the gist of it. If you are confused about this and work on operating yin and yang and the five elements, well, yin and yang and the five elements are not things that can be operated by human knowledge or technique. The slightest deviation in your practice can lead to a hundred bizarre changes; you may go to your death without turning back, ultimately unable to operate yin and yang and the five elements.

ALCHEMY TAKES ITS RULES FROM CREATION

The *Classic of Invisible Correspondences* says, "Observe the course of Nature; hold to the conduct of Nature." Spiritual alchemy certainly takes its laws from Creation, but not by practicing imitation of each individual particular. The ancients were mentally meshed with Nature and acted in concert with its course, the Way. Thus does the energetic operation of the body spontaneously conform to Nature. If you seek the elixir by obsessively trying to imitate the traces of Nature with the secular attitude so commonplace today, that's not it!

FOUNDATIONS OF ALCHEMY · *Furnace and cauldron*

Some ask what the furnace and cauldron are. Li Qing-an said, "Body and mind are the cauldron and furnace." An alchemical text says, "First take Heaven and Earth for the cauldron; then make a ball of yin and yang and cook it." Heaven is mind, Earth is body. People today who set up an external furnace and cauldron are mistaken.

The furnace and cauldron are the body and mind. To cultivate refinement, there has to be the body; then spirit and energy have a base and do not disperse, and the work has a basis on which to be carried out. This is what is called borrowing the temporal to cultivate the real. Since the furnace and cauldron are the means by which substances can be cooked and transmuted, the Master of the Pass used the term *pot*, which was later changed to furnace and cauldron. Using this symbolism for the body can be considered clever and apropos. There are many different terms, such as the inner furnace and outer furnace mentioned in the *Triplex Unity*, but their essential meaning does not go beyond this. Yu Yuwu said, "In spiritual alchemy, the cosmic void is the furnace and cauldron; in the cosmic void there is a natural subtle function, spontaneously occurring." This cosmic void has no self, no person, no inside, no outside: how can furnace and cauldron express it? Yuwu is just using a simile to make his point; that is not his underlying meaning.

A POINT FALLS INTO THE YELLOW COURT

The *Book of Balance and Harmony* says, "After mating in the chamber of Heaven, a point falls into the Yellow Court."

When the point falls into the Yellow Court, where does it wind up? What people don't realize is that practitioners should just mate spirit and energy. There is no need to ask where the result winds up, because it settles in its place naturally. Medical texts describe the processes of digestion, absorption, and elimination as occurring naturally, without people having to arrange them. Similarly, the true energy in the body rises and descends, starting from the source and returning to the source, naturally having its own place of abode; what need is there for people to visualize it in order to arrange it?

ALCHEMICAL INGREDIENTS · *Basic energy is where the body is born*

The *Triplex Unity* says, "The body a human receives is originally a nothingness; basic vitality circulates, getting a start from energy."

While it is true that human birth comes from the combination of sperm and ovum, nevertheless what makes birth possible is the energy of the basic harmony of heaven and earth. Without this energy, even if there are sperm and ovum they cannot make a being. So evidently the true energy of basic harmony is the root of the physical, the place where the body is born. As people receive this energy while yet unborn, it can produce being out of nonbeing, causing the body to grow and develop. So if you cultivate this basic energy today, why couldn't you prolong life, see eternity, escape constriction, and become spiritually transformed?

Basic Vitality

The Master Embracing Unity said, "The firing and harmonizing of absolute unity cultivating gold alchemical elixir refines just two things: vitality and soul."

The Master of Silent Sunlight said, "Why must cultivation need yellow sprouts for roots? The basic energy in the human body arises daily; it is just because of not knowing how to preserve and nurture it that it is invaded and stripped away by two distortions. What two distortions? Environmental extremes are distorters of energy; emotional extremes are distorters of sense. These two distortions are robbers of basic energy, attacking it day and night; thus basic energy is thinned and weakened, even to the point of morbidity. Ancient wizards knew that preservation of life is a matter of keeping basic energy stable. Nevertheless, it fluctuates easily. Why? Only basic vitality can keep it stable. That is why it is an established method of cultivation to teach people to make basic vitality rise to preserve basic energy, combining them in one place, completely stable and steadfast, not worn out or scattered. If you can ward off the attacks of the two distortions, only then can you prolong life, see forever, and not die!

Zhang Ziyang said, "When vitality fills you within and energy melts it, it rises with energy to constitute true lead."

The statements by the first two wizards indicate the reason practical alchemy uses basic vitality; the last statement indicates the function of basic vitality.

Basic Vitality is Sexual Vitality

Zhang Ziyang said, "Using vitality, use basic vitality; this is not sexual vitality."

Basic vitality and sexual vitality are fundamentally not two things. When someone is not feeling sexuality, there is no location in the body where vitality is. Medical literature says that the genitals are the seat of vitality; it also says that each of the internal organs has stored vitality. In reality, there is no vitality abiding in specific places. Vitality merges into basic energy, without taking on form or substantiality; only practitioners of the Way can concentrate the basic energy and distill the vitality. Because this vitality arises spontaneously with sexual feeling, it is called basic vitality. Ordinary people do not know how to distill it and cannot extract the vitality for practical use, so the basic vitality cannot develop. In sexual intercourse, basic energy changes into vitality, which descends from the brain down the spine and out the urethra; this semen is a material substance, representing the vitality of sexuality. When it arises in true unity, it is basic vitality; when it leaks out during sexual intercourse, it is sexual vitality. As transmutations of basic energy, basic vitality and sexual vitality are one; it is a mistake to split them into two.

Basic Energy Produces Basic Vitality

Master Ziyang said, "When basic energy is born, basic vitality is produced."

Hu Huncheng said, "Collect primal generative energy for medicine." This primal energy of true unity is undifferentiated within abstract ecstasy; wizards take this energy and refine it into an elixir, calling this the seed of realization. The energy of absolute unity containing reality is the undifferentiated energy prior to the division of heaven and earth. It is the communion of basic energy in the body. After basic energy is born, basic vitality is produced; this is the arising of initial positive energy in the body. Vitality and energy are one thing; when we speak of energy, vitality is included. This is why it is said that energy is life-increasing medicine.

Detachment from Emotional Consciousness to Nurture Basic Harmony

Yu Yuwu said, "The science of spiritual alchemy is all a matter of the uniform energy of basic harmony, from which a wealth of transformations evolve."

Master Ziyang said, "To preserve basic harmony, nothing takes precedence over detachment from emotional consciousness."

The reason things sprout in spring and not in summer, fall, or winter is because of harmony. When people are free from emotional consciousness, then their energy is harmonious. When energy is harmonious, it mellows and expands, and the harmony of heaven and earth also responds to it. Would it not then be possible to extend life?

Nowadays people's desires and emotions get excited in the midst of daily activities, so the action of their energy is flighty, unstable, suffocated, and depressed. It is as if the weather were suddenly cold and then suddenly hot, scorching in winter and frosty in summer—is this basic harmony? Since it is inharmonious, there is the possibility of aberration and illness, destructive to life—how then could one hope for longevity, eternal vision, and attainment of the Way? So it is said that to preserve basic harmony, nothing takes precedence over detachment from emotional consciousness.

Alchemy Requires Interruption of Craving

The *Mystic Mirror of the Great Leader* says, "Pure yang rising is called energy; pure yin descending is called fluid. Energy and fluid combined in the bones and vessels is called marrow. Energy and marrow combined in the prostate is called semen. When heart energy is in the liver but the vitality of the liver is infirm, then the eyes are dim. When heart energy is in the lungs but the vitality of the lungs is not full, the flesh is thin and weak. When heart energy is in the kidneys and genitals but the vitality of the kidneys and genitals is infirm, the energy of the spirit is diminished. When heart energy is in the spleen but the vitality of the spleen is infirm, the teeth and hair loosen and fall out. Among the vital organs, the genitals are the pivot of vitality, while the heart is the office of energy. When true vitality is in the genitals, the other vitalities spontaneously return to the lower field; when true energy is in the heart, the other energies naturally return to the capital."

The *Simpleton* says, "When water has a source, the flow will be long; when a tree has a root, its foliage will be luxuriant. When a house has a foundation, its pillars will be upright; when people have vitality, their lives will be long."

The *Classic of the Yellow Court* says, "To prolong life, beware of haste in the bedroom; excessive intensity inevitably makes the spirit weep." It also says, "Give up debauched lust, and focus on preserving vitality; then you can live with but little land and a modest house."

Master Ziyang said, "When vitality is lost and basic energy does not arise, then original positivity does not appear."

Practical wizardry is a matter of stabilizing vitality; then the root is strong and living energy flourishes daily. If a lustful attitude is not stopped, spiritual roots will not be firm; then the accumulation of vitality thins daily, and the production of basic energy lessens daily. Gradually you reach exhaustion and even death. Chan Buddhists say in this regard, "If you study meditation and contemplation without interrupting craving, that is like steaming sand to make rice—no matter how long you may steam it, you'll never get anything but hot sand, not rice." So if you want to build up basic energy, first you should stop debauchery and lustfulness; this work must be done with a clean mind free from thoughts. Worldly people ignorant of this use physical pressure to stop the emission of semen in sexual intercourse, thinking that to be prevention of leakage. They do not know that vitality is to be stabilized before it has created a concrete substance. If you wait till it has made substance and then try to stop it, the semen may not be emitted but the spiritual energy is long gone. How ignorant it is to keep deteriorating, stagnant matter accumulating in the pelvic region, thus producing bizarre ailments! Even more in error are blind teachers who go on to fool people by saying they should draw their semen up their spine, calling this "restoration of vitality to repair the brain."

Basic spirit using medicine

Some ask which is most important—vitality, energy, or spirit. Master Ziyang said, "Spirit is most important."

The basic spirit is the true mind, which is the true essence. The medicine used therefore is not material medicine; the subtle action of the work of wizardry is all in this essence. Ancient custom listed it as a medicine, but later Taoists ignorant of the root source of the Great Way often disregarded this. So basic spirit wound up as a "medicine," with an extra "intent" outside the basic spirit to employ it. Nothing could be more incoherent than this. It is no wonder people don't attain wizardry!

The Basic Spirit Is the Thinking Spirit

Master Ziyang said, "Using spirit, use the basic spirit, not the thinking spirit."

He also said, "What is the basic spirit? Once the absolute has divided, we are imbued with this point of living light, which is basic essence. Basic essence is nothing other than energy that is congealed and alive." And, "When the basic spirit appears, the basic energy arises; when basic essence is restored, basic energy is born."

Some ask if the basic spirit and the thinking spirit are one or two. Mind, essence, and spirit are one: it is called basic spirit by virtue of being imbued with the point of living luminescence from Heaven. When this basic spirit is later moved by emotional consciousness, the basic spirit sinks into emotional consciousness and turns into the thinking spirit. In reality, even though thought has emotional consciousness, the basic spirit is always complete and whole, neither defective nor lacking. If people can turn their attention back to this and detach from their emotional consciousness, then the thinking is none other than a subtle function of the basic spirit!

The Opening of the Mysterious Pass

Li Qing-an said, "As for the opening of the mysterious pass, wherever material elements or physical forces adhere is not it, and yet it cannot be sought outside the body."

He also said, "Just seek inwardly twenty-four hours a day, in the midst of all activities: what is it that speaks and keeps silent, that sees and hears?"

He also said, "The ancients just wrote the word *center* as an indication for people. This word *center* is the opening of the mysterious pass. The center does not mean inside as opposed to outside, nor does it mean the center as opposed to the four directions, nor does it mean the center as the middle. Buddhists say that when you don't think good or bad this is your original face. Taoists say this is where thoughts do not arise."

Chen the Blank said, "It takes no more than the method of turning the light around and looking inward, cleaning up thoughts."

The Master of the Jade Valley Stream said, "The central issue is having an upright mind and sincere intention."

This indicates that the basic spirit is the opening of the mysterious pass.

Chen the Nirvanic said, "Just sit quietly in stable concentration with no thoughts in thoughts. When this work is pure, you become unified, silent all day, like a hen sitting on her eggs. Then you naturally see the opening of the mysterious pass, so vast there is no outside, yet so minute there is no inside. From this you cull primal whole energy, which constitutes the matrix of the alchemical elixir. Practice diligently, and you will be able to ride with the wizards of old."

Master Ziyang said, "This opening has no borders or edges, no inside or outside; it is the root of spiritual energy, the valley of absolute nonresistance."

This indicates that absolute nonresistance is the opening of the mysterious pass. When you are absolutely empty and utterly still, there is no more self; you only feel a mystic merging with the universe, with spiritual energy fermenting therein. This is the finest state of cultivation, so it is called the opening of the mysterious pass.

The handle of alchemy

The *Classic of Hidden Correspondences* says, "The North Star is the mainspring of the sky; the mind is the mainspring of the human being."

The *Treatise on Gold Liquid Restorative Elixir* says, "The river source where the medicine is produced, the subtle directions for extraction and addition in the firing process, and even the incubation and completion of the elixir are not apart from the function of the mind."

Master Ziyang's *Alchemical Directions* says, "The reason mind is considered wondrous is that energy comes from its opening, while vitality follows its call. Since energy comes from its opening, when the mind is harmonious the energy is harmonious, and when the energy is harmonious the body is harmonious. When the body is harmonious, the harmony of heaven and earth responds. So when emotions are strong and thus energy is inharmonious, it is because emotions arise in the mind. As for vitality following its call, when men and women have sexual intercourse and their vitality flows, it is also the mind that causes it. When the mind is pure, thoughts are pure; when thoughts are pure, vitality is born."

Master Tan of the Purple Corona said, "Spirit is like the mother; energy is like the child. Summoning energy by spirit is like a mother calling her child, who is sure to come."

Mind is certainly the handle of wizardry. Even though everyone has mind, however, not everyone attains wizardry. This is not the fault of mind itself but the fault of the mind lingering on desires and thus being unable to be quiet and empty.

Barefoot Liu said, "Spirit and energy have a natural affinity, like child and mother, but as long as they are separated by mundane feelings, they cannot meet. If you lessen mundane feelings a bit, to that extent circulation will take place."

Yu Yuwu said, "When mind is steady, spirit is stable and energy is harmonious; there is natural circulation up and down through the three chambers, and the hundred channels naturally flow freely."

Li Qing-an said, "Mind returns to empty silence, the body enters nondoing, and inside and outside are forgotten; at this point, vitality naturally changes into energy, energy naturally changes into spirit, and spirit naturally returns to emptiness."

Li Qing-an also said, "When body and mind are both quiet, Heaven and Earth merge; in real potential's subtle response, naturally occurring, an extraordinary movement takes place. In this movement is where the 'heart of heaven' is seen: the medicine, furnace, and cauldron are herein; the various functions of the three bases, eight trigrams, four forms, and five elements are all in this."

Speaking from this point of view, if the mind is not quiet and empty, then it fails to do its job; even with vitality and energy there, it cannot make use of them. Why do people today speak only of refining lead and mercury and not of mastering mind?

Alchemical operations · *The mysterious female*

Li Qing-an said, "The mysterious female is the mechanism of the closing and opening of Heaven and Earth. The *I Ching* says, 'Closing the door is called Earth, opening the door is called Heaven.' Cyclic closing and opening represent cyclic movement and quiescence. This is what Lao-tzu meant by 'using it without force.' "

Li Qing-an also said, "Master Ziyang said that the mysterious female is the place where thoughts arise. This is correct. I say that the place where thoughts arise is the root of birth and death—is this not the mysterious female?"

Lao-tzu said, "The open spirit not stagnating is called the mysterious female." *Open* means empty; the open spirit refers to taking care of the spirit so that it is empty, unoccupied, and open. *Mysterious* means subtle. *Female* refers to the fact that emptiness is where things are born. The open spirit is the mysterious female. Limitless subtle functions are born from within the open spirit; this is the opening of the mysterious female. This is the orthodox explanation; next is Li Qing-an's twofold explanation. Later generations singled out a specific place in the body as the mysterious female and claimed that the open spirit is based on the mysterious female. But if the open spirit were based on the mysterious female, that would mean it would have adherence; then it could not be open spirit. There are also later expositors of the mysterious female who explain it in dozens of ways, adding more and more confusion and error!

THE BELLOWS

The *Tao Te Ching* says, "The space between Heaven and Earth is like a bellows, empty and uninhibited, producing more and more with movement."

The *Treatise on the Rise and Descent of Yin and Yang* says, "If people can emulate the rising and falling bellows action of heaven and earth, breath going out when opening, breath going in when closing, the going out like the energy of earth rising, the going in like the energy of heaven descending, rising and descending alternately, then you can equal the perpetuity of heaven and earth."

The *Tao Te Ching* speaks of the bellows simply as a simile for subtle function in emptiness; when later generations borrowed it to express the mechanism of rising and descending, this was a good idea too.

Nowadays when Taoists speak of pumping the bellows, they do not mean pumping a bellows; they mean tuning true breathing. If you know the furnace and cauldron but not the bellows, then yin and yang are separated; even though furnace and cauldron be set up, they are useless. If you know how to pump a bellows but not how to tune true breathing, then you're missing the essential subtlety whereby the pumping is done. How will you snatch the wholesome energy of heaven and earth to crystallize the elixir?

Sixty hexagrams symbolizing the alchemical firing process

The *Triplex Unity* says, "In the mornings, [the *I Ching* hexagram] Difficulty deals with things; in the evenings [the hexagram] Darkness should be accepted. Use a hexagram for each day and night, according to the order, up to Settled and Unsettled, reaching the dawn twilight; when you come to the end, you start again."

Originally the lines of the *I Ching* hexagrams were just used in opposite pairs to correspond to the rise and descent of the alchemical process. The two hexagrams Difficulty and Darkness, for example, are opposites. In terms of the structure of the Difficulty hexagram, from the first line up to the top line is like yang fire, the "fire" of positive energy, rising from below up to the crown. Seen upside down, as if starting from the top line of Difficulty, it becomes the hexagram Darkness; this is like the yin convergence, or passive union, descending from above to the Yellow Court in the center. The pair is just one hexagram, seen upright and upside down. This is like the alchemical firing process; it is basically only one "fire" or energy, but there is rise and descent.

The other hexagrams are also like this, consisting of eight complements that can also be seen oppositely. If you comprehend this, then the mechanism of the firing process is in yourself, and you can do without the hexagram lines.

Symbolizing the firing process by the year, month, and day, humanity and duty, joy and anger, reward and punishment

The *Triplex Unity* says, "Spring and summer, rest on inner substance, from the Rat to the Dragon and Snake; fall and winter are appropriate for external action, from the Horse to the Dog and Boar. Reward and punishment correspond to spring and autumn; darkness and light conform to cold and heat. The words of the *I Ching* lines contain humanity and duty; anger and joy occur according to the time."

Ancient wizards used the opposite pairs in the sixty hexagrams of the *I Ching* to symbolize the rise and descent of one energy; this can be considered brilliant, but it did not cover the matter of waxing and waning, so they talked about this in terms of the seasons of a year and the waxing and waning of the moon in a lunar cycle. Everyone can see the waxing and waning of the moon in the sky, so using this to observe the functions of waxing and waning of yin and yang in our bodies is indeed clear and easy to understand. Nevertheless, the mechanisms of movement and stillness are still not thoroughly comprehended in this manner, so people use the time of day to express them. Generally speaking, the times from the hour of the Tiger (3:00–5:00 A.M.) to the hour of the Dog (7:00–9:00 P.M.) are active, while the hours of the Boar (9:00–11:00 P.M.), the Rat (11:00 P.M.–1:00 A.M.), and the Ox (1:00–3:00 A.M.) are still. This is all there is to it, but it is imperative to know measure, to avoid excess and insufficiency, so there are also expressions using the terms humanity and duty, joy and anger, and reward and punishment. Ancient wizards drew on symbols and exemplifications, so layers upon layers of perception emerge, but in the final analysis there is not a single excessive word. These should be understood by practitioners—why overlook them just because they are symbolic?

INTENT AS THE GO-BETWEEN

Master Ziyang said, "Is intent only the go-between? The science of spiritual alchemy can never be apart from it, from beginning to end."

The Master of Round Unity said, "The reason practical wizardry needs intent is essentially just to assess the operation and keep it in balance. Intent is associated with the spleen; that is why wizards call it true earth. True earth means harmony. Now in medical practice, a pulse may be floating or sinking, slow or rapid, empty or full, but as long as there is stomach energy, one does not die. So the stomach energy is also harmony.

"In spiritual alchemy, active and quiet exercises must not be off balance in the slightest; if there is any imbalance, it usually results in illness. Throughout it is essential to assess relative gravity, relative buoyancy, relative strength, and relative freshness and to adjust them, causing yin and yang to match each other, so water and fire are evenly balanced, not allowing excess, which would cause other troubles. If not for intent operating this assessment, how could you guarantee you won't make a mistake and go wrong?"

Zhang Sanfeng said, "What is intent? It is the outward function of the basic spirit; it is not that there is also intent in addition to the basic spirit."

Master Ziyang said, "Mind is the natural leader: when it is used without artificiality, then what activates it is the basic spirit. This is the alchemical use of mind."

So you should not overactivate intent. Once you overactivate intent, you are trying to force progress and not being natural. The problems caused by the toil of forced exercises are not trivial; even if you use them skillfully, you still do not escape attachment, contrarily increasing the ailment of intention. This is why votaries of the Sect of Life do not reach the Great Way of absolute nonresistance.

The location of the awareness of the basic spirit is intent; awareness without an effort to be conscious is skillful use of intent. If you have even a single thought of deliberate arrangement, then you are overactivating intent.

THE WAY OF SEEING VITAL SPIRIT AND PERPETUATING LIFE · *Alchemical tasks · Stabilizing the furnace and setting up the cauldron*

In *Precious Writings of the Nine Realized Ones*, the Master of Pure Sunlight said, "Those who would cultivate alchemy first make the furnace upright. The furnace surrounds the cauldron; it is the body. The furnace is divided into eight faces, namely the ears, eyes, mouth, nose, form, color, nourishment, and taste. These are the openings of the bellows: one should always guard them, not letting the eight influences of wind and cold, heat and humidity, hunger and fullness, and fatigue and ease damage them externally and not letting the six brigands of hatred, craving, ebullience, anger, sorrow, and indulgence damage them internally."

The True Lord of the Undifferentiated Origin said, "If those who cultivate their bodies always have their basic energy broken, then their vital spirit cannot be whole. It is necessary for the vital spirit to be complete and the energy whole before it is possible to develop life to become an immortal."

Beginning learners should first understand the stabilization of the furnace and setting up of the cauldron: be careful of your activities, moderate consumption, regulate temperature, minimize slumber, collect body and mind, be sparing of vitality, be sparing of energy, be sparing of spirit; make the body peaceful, the spirit complete, and the energy strong, and then this body and mind can be the furnace and cauldron into which medicine can be put. Without this preparatory work, the furnace and cauldron will break and leak and will not be suitable for use; if you try to put medicine in there, you will have trouble. Yu Yuwu had a saying, "If you have medicine and carry out the firing process, then metal will be pressured by fire to leap up to the heart chamber, where it turns to water and then subdues the fire so that there is no problematic overheating. If you carry out the firing process without medicine, then empty yang will rise aggressively; you will only burn your body."

First, prepare a quiet room.

The quiet room does not have to be in the mountains or the woods. It may be in the city or in the provinces. As long as you have a place that's useful for the purpose, it doesn't matter where it is. The room should not be too bright, for that would hurt the yang soul, and it should not be too dark, for that would hurt the yin soul. There should be no objects in the room but an incense burner and a bench.

Second, develop will.

In this endeavor, unless you concentrate on developing your will on account of birth and death, you are highly likely to give up along the way. Therefore you must have unbending determination, persistent thought, and unflagging energy; first let go of yourself, then let go of your holdings, and be unfazed by sickness or even death. Only then have you any hope of success.

Alchemy doesn't work if you are inconsistent. If you work on it when you are in the mood, but then get distracted by things and slack off when this mood wanes, then your spirit is influenced and your energy taken away when you are not practicing, just like someone with no accomplishment at all. Even if you get into the mood to work again, it will be like lacing with too many missing strings—it won't be effective at all.

What you must do is bury your past: cut off the time that has already gone by and don't ask about it. Just rouse your vigor from this moment on, working consistently with all your effort whether or not there is anything to deal with, whether the situation is pleasing or displeasing: a day like an hour, a year like a day, a millennium like a year. Then there is no day or night, no noon or midnight, no dawn or dusk, no end or beginning of the lunar cycle, no partiality or completeness, no opening or closing; you do not hope to ascend to wizardhood and do not set up a limit, except for this whole lifetime. Only thus do you gain a little bit of accord.

Third, set aside involvements.

Taoist study cannot have any externals burdening the mind. If you are preoccupied with family affairs, political or professional affairs, social intercourse, charms and spells, curing and divining, literature, riding, music, martial arts, gambling, or handicrafts, all of this will inhibit your mind and confuse your essential nature, so you should be very wary of it.

Fourth, practice sitting.

When you sit, spread sitting mats thickly to prevent physical discomfort and pain. Loosen your clothing and belt to prevent stagnation of energy.

To sit in the lotus posture, first put the left foot on the right thigh, then put the right foot on the left thigh. In the half lotus posture, the left foot is on the right foot. Either way will do. Next, put the left hand in the right palm, such that the thumb tips are propped up against each other. Slowly lift your body up and move from side to side to achieve a proper balance of relaxation and tension. Then sit up straight, such that your waist, spine, and neckbones support each other, ears aligned with shoulders, nose aligned with navel, the tongue against the upper palate, lips and teeth touching. The eyes should be slightly open; they should not be completely shut, for this is the "ghost cave in the mountain of darkness," where it is extremely easy to become oblivious and unseeing, and it is also possible to become possessed.

The body should be straight, like Buddha, not leaning to the left or right, not tilting forward or backward. Don't lean against a support, lest you become lazy. Sitting should be relaxed and natural. The shoulders should not be too erect, for if they are too erect it is hard to persevere. Practice should not be too intense, for if too intense it will be easily interrupted. The essential thing is to find the mean.

The breath should pass through the nose. Respiration should not be coarse, should not be forced, should not be suppressed, and should not be stopped. Inhalation and exhalation should be smooth and gentle, but you should not fix your attention on this.

Once your physical posture is steady and your breathing is tuned, relax your abdomen and do not think of good or bad at all. When a thought arises, notice it; once you become aware of it, it is not there. Eventually you forget mental objects and spontaneously become unified. If you get this, you will naturally feel light and fresh; this is what is called the method of comfort.

For those who have already awakened, this is like a dragon finding water; for those who have not, just develop your will, and you will not be cheated.

When you come out of concentration, move your body slowly and get up calmly and carefully. Preserve the power of concentration at all times, like taking care of a baby, and the power of concentration will be easy to perfect. As it is said, to search for a pearl it's better if the water is calm; if the water is agitated, it will be hard to find. When the water of concentration is calm and clear, the pearl of mind appears of itself.

THE RIVER SOURCE WHERE MEDICINE IS PRODUCED

The *Triplex Unity* says, "Metal is the mother of water; the mother conceals the fetus of the child. Mercury is the child of metal; the child is hidden in the womb of the mother."

Yu Yuwu said, "Water is the root source of the great elixir. Heaven produces water, its place in the north, represented by the water trigram; this is where the medicine in our bodies is produced. Alchemy is based on water; metal vitality is produced in water."

This refers to basic vitality being produced in the genitals. Yuan the Absolutist said, "Wizards borrow the genital region for the ground of production; this is not using the genitals, but though one does not use the genitals, nevertheless practical exercise is done within the genitals." That is why the genitals are considered the "river source where the medicine is produced."

Some people, not knowing the meaning of this, simply hear that wizardry does not use the heart and genitals and then seek outside the genitals. They say the central aperture between the genitals and kidneys is where true yang lies hidden, and that alchemical praxis simply uses fire to press this true yang out to function. But if true yang is hidden in an aperture, how is that different from being hidden in the genitals? And how does using an aperture differ from using the genitals? The major teaching of wizardry regards everything in the ordinary body as temporal residue and does not use it. If there were actually basic energy lying concealed inside an aperture, it too would be a temporal residue. These are biased views unworthy of discussion.

The receptive is the abode of the way

The *Triplex Unity* says, "The Receptive is calm and collected; it is the abode of the Way."

This refers to how basic vitality is produced. Although basic vitality is produced in the genitals, nevertheless it is impossible to produce it without being calm and collected. The yang energy of a year is born in Return, based on The Receptive. The moonlight of a month is reborn at the beginning of the lunar cycle, based on the end of the lunar cycle. The yang energy of a day is born in the midnight hour, based on the late night hour. These are the same as our basic vitality being produced in collected calmness. All these energies arise from collection, so the great elixir has its abode in The Receptive.

Yang disburses, yin receives

The *Triplex Unity* says, "Male yang disburses, disseminating mystery; female yin transmutes, encircling the center."

It also says, "Yang endows, yin receives; female and male need each other."

These are general expressions of the principle of disbursing and receptivity of yin and yang in heaven and earth and all things.

It also says, "Constancy and accord are patterns of earth, accepting the disbursement of heaven."

This refers to The Creative disbursing energy to The Receptive and The Receptive accepting it accordingly.

It also says, "The sun gives power; the moon thereby gives light."

This refers to the sun giving light to the moon.

It also says, "The mother takes in rich liquid, which the father gives."

This refers to the father giving energy to the mother.

aperture really existed, it would be more important than the internal organs—so why is it not listed in medical classics and anatomical charts? Why don't people lacking in basic energy take medicine to treat this aperture?

The fact is that those on a small path, a sidetrack, mistakenly indicate a particular place in the body and have people concentrate mentally on this place, calling that congealing the spirit in the energy aperture. Among people who follow this without understanding, there are always those who make themselves ill. This is how "congealing the spirit in the energy aperture" causes people to go wrong.

So what is the energy aperture? It is the flower pond. What is the flower pond? The Master of True Sunlight said, "The flower pond is in the ocean of energy." If you cling to the word *aperture* or *opening*, you will try to find a corresponding opening inside the body; then if we call it the flower pond, you will seek a pond inside the body, and if we call it an ocean, you will seek an ocean in the body. Will that do?

Essentially, alchemy borrows the genitals as the ground of production. This is metaphorically called the ocean of energy because it is a pool of energy; it is metaphorically called the energy aperture because it is deep and located below. It is metaphorically called the flower pond because it is where the golden efflorescence arises. That's all there is to these terms. To make the elixir, all that is required is that energy sink into this place. That is why it is called congealing spirit in the energy aperture; it does not mean deliberate focus of concentration there! The Master of Eternal Spring said, "When it is present somewhere, then it is absent somewhere; when it is not in a particular place, then there is nowhere it is not."

Alchemy produces being from nothingness. If you fail to seek the mechanism in nothingness and instead create ramifications of being, is that not a mistake?

Turning the Light Around to Illumine Inwardly

Master Yuan of the Cosmic Void said, "The method of congealing the spirit in the energy aperture is simply a matter of gathering in your seeing, reversing your listening, and turning around the light to illumine the inward."

This is precisely where basic energy is produced. Basic vitality arises from being calm and collected, to be sure, but if the heart energy does not descend to mix with the genitals, and the genitals receive nothing, how can it collect productively?

Filling cosmic space is one basic energy alone: this energy is heaven, while the great mass formed of the residue in this energy is earth. The waning and waxing of this energy are yin and yang.

Every year in autumn and winter this energy withdraws into the earth. Then at the solstice it starts to rise again. As it keeps on being produced and developing, it accumulates and gradually rises. When it reaches its peak, then it gradually wanes again. This is the way it has been throughout time.

This energy is what causes plants to sprout from the earth; without this energy, the earth cannot produce anything. So that which produces things is earth, while that whereby things are produced is the energy of heaven. It is just a matter of being able to collect and disburse it. Similarly, in alchemy, it is necessary for the heart energy to descend and mix with the genitals and the genitals to receive and collect it before it is possible to produce transformation.

Congealing spirit in the energy aperture

Verses on Restoring Life says, "The sun moves into the moonlight."

The Master of the White Jade Moon said, "All you need to do is congeal spirit in the energy aperture."

These sayings refer to the descent of heart energy into intercourse. This is called chasing the dragon to the tiger or putting mercury into lead. Congealment does not mean solidification: spirit is most ethereal, most subtle, able to fly into the heavens and plunge into the earth—how could it be solidified? So-called congealing of spirit means stopping thoughts and returning spirit to the heart so that it does not run outside; then energy also returns to the body, gradually sinking into the energy aperture.

Some ask if the energy aperture really has an opening or not and just where this aperture is. Hu the Whole said it is between the kidneys and the genitals. The Preserver of Truth said, "Once people are born, the true energy of basic positivity is dispersed throughout the body, potentiating perception, speech, and activity; how could there by any logic to considering it confined within one aperture?" If this

Master Cai's *Alchemical Guide* says, "Spirit in a human being is like fire in wood: if the fire does not come out, the wood remains; if the spirit does not go out, the body survives. When fire gives off light outwardly, the fuel is being used up; when the spirit's intellect is racing outwardly, wholeness is disintegrating."

Yu Yuwu said, "Spiritual wizards' method of cultivation has people turn their light around to illumine the inward, breathing universal harmony. This is all about return to the root source, going back to the beginning where energy is received at birth."

Turning the light around to illumine inwardly is not a matter of fixating on a special locus and deliberately focusing attention there. It is nothing more than using emptiness and stillness to return the spirit to the inside.

Generally speaking, the mind of an ordinary person just races around outside day in and day out. All of its external devices and skills are only visible reflections of the light of spirit. If your spirit is wholly directed to attention on externals, then you are not aware of your own self.

Right now, you needn't search elsewhere or seek afar. Just take the externally focused spirit and collect it back in, letting go of all mechanical cleverness, single-mindedly storing it inside, eliminating mixed-up thoughts. This is reversing the gaze to illumine inwardly. In reality, the gaze gazes on nothing; the illumination illumines nothing; and yet there is never lack of insight and perception.

Throughout the whole human body, there is only one basic energy, without distinction of heart, liver, spleen, lung, kidney, or genital energies. Ordinary people, however, are subject to compulsions of senses and objects, so this energy drifts and disperses externally. Alchemy involves no other skill but turning the light around to reverse the gaze and collecting this energy into the most recondite depths; after a long time, creativity will take place spontaneously therein.

Beginning Work on Turning the Light Around to Illumine Inwardly

The *Tao Te Ching* says, "Concentrating your energy, making it supple, can you be like an infant?"

The Master of Eternal Spring said, "It is just a single spiritual efficacy, without any mixed thoughts, like an infant with no conception of externals."

The Preserver of Truth said, "Concentrating energy and making is supple is a matter of forgetting emotional consciousness. The shortcut to forget emotional consciousness is in mind and breathing resting on each other. If the mind and the breathing are always resting on each other, then emotional consciousness is naturally forgotten without trying to forget."

Immortal Sister Ho said, "The stem of life is in the true breath."

The "Womb Breath" section of the *Jade Classic of Supreme Purity* says, "When you are in your mother's belly before being born, you breathe along with your mother without seeing or hearing; there is just breath there. Then when you are born and the umbilical cord is cut, the point of real basic energy masses under the navel. Day after day the spirit goes out, energy shifts, and eventually you no longer preserve the breath that was there in the womb."

The *Collection of Transmissions of the Way* says, "What you exhale is your own basic energy, emerging from within; what you inhale is the wholesome energy of heaven and earth, coming in from outside. If the root source is stable and the basic energy is not diminished, then the wholesome energy of heaven and earth can be absorbed in the interval of a breath. If, however, the root source is not stable, vitality is exhausted and energy weak, your basic energy leaks and your chamber of the fundamental goes unrepaired. The wholesome energy of heaven and earth you breathe in leaves with exhalation, while the basic energy in your body does not remain your own but is taken away by heaven and earth."

The *Treatise on the Womb Breath* says, "If you breathe out without having spiritual mastery, then the one breath is incomplete; if you breathe in without mastering spirit, the one breath is incomplete then too."

Yu Yuwu said, "Throughout the twenty-four hours of the day, just cause the mind to drive the energy at all times, so that energy and spirit combine; then the physical body will survive."

He also said, "The essential thing is to keep the spirit and the breathing resting on each other, with energy and spirit keeping each other at all times."

He also said, "The method of alchemy is to have creative active energy descend to mix with receptive passive energy, cause the out-breath and inbreath to unite, and make firmness and flexibility match and mate as husband and wife, making them a unity. Then spirit and energy return to the root, essence and life join as one, and the ultimate elixir is conceived therein."

He also said, "After all, it is no more than a matter of mind and breath resting on each other, such that there is inner sensing of yin and yang and the combining of spirit and energy."

The *Four Hundred Words on Alchemy* says, "When spiritualized energy enters the root, if closure is extreme you err on the side of intensity, while if relaxation is extreme you err on the side of carelessness. Just bring about a fine continuity, not allowing interruption. After that the spirit will eventually congeal on its own, and the breath will eventually settle on its own."

Su Dongpo said, "The method of following the breath is to go out with the breath and in with the breath; follow it continuously, and one breath abides. You may feel this breath coming from the pores; clouds evaporate, fog disperses, illnesses disappear, obstructions vanish, and you spontaneously realize clear understanding."

Zhu Huai's *Guide to Tuning the Breathing* says, "When quiescence reaches a climax and you are empty, this is like a spring pond in which the fish become still after movement, like insects in hibernation; with living energy opening and closing, the wonder is inexhaustible."

Chao Wen said, "When mind and breath rest on each other, the mind becomes calm and the breathing regular; eventually this can produce superior concentration. When spirit and energy combine, spirit is harmonious and energy is clear; harmony and clarity eventually can bring about prolongation of life."

Point to the Mystery says, "Just manage to be aware, breath after breath; this will exchange the physical body, a flow of liquid jade."

Chen the Blank said, "Breath after breath returning to the root is the matrix of the pill of gold."

The Preserver of Truth said, "When the breath makes a sound as it goes in and out, that is called carelessness; when exhalation and inhalation are not thorough, this is called stagnation. When there is repeated shortness of breath, this is called panting. Not careless, not stagnating, not panting, continuously present, working without strain—this is called breathing. Carelessness results in scattering; stagnation results in binding; panting results in laboring; maintaining 'breathing' results in stabilization. So-called tuning the breathing simply means seeing to it that you are not careless, not stagnating, and not panting."

Tuning the breath is beginner's work. Ordinarily people's minds and thoughts have rested on things, both abstract and concrete, and have been stuck to them so long that if they were to detach from objects, they would be unable to stand on their own; and even if they can stand on their own temporarily, before long they revert to a state of distraction and scatteredness. That is why the method of mind and breath resting on each other is used: to control the mind in order to refine away its coarseness. Once you get the mind detached from objects, then just be empty; you don't need to tune the breathing anymore.

If you manage to reach the state where there is no sky and no earth, no self and no other, then what breath is there to tune? This method is the most rapid shortcut, the easiest and most benign, unlike methods such as keeping the mind on the "elixir field" in the lower abdomen or the "central yellow" in the thorax. It is a reliable basis of practice. The Meditation Master of Essential Emptiness said, "In people of the highest potential, if thoughts do not arise, it is not even necessary to pay attention to the breath. But if you notice a thought arising, just tune the breath once, paying attention to it for the moment and stopping when there is no thought. Don't focus attention too intensely!"

Autumn Cicada Liu's *Secrets of Realization* says, "Gradually concentrate energy to make it unresisting. As soon as you sense your breathing unresistant and gentle, this is return to the root. I call this return to the ocean of the fundamental. When you sense return to the ocean of the fundamental with certitude, then forget it. Forget without oblivion, perceiving it mentally."

The Master of Complete Unity said, "If you use attention, that's not forgetting; if you forget, you cannot perceive mentally. So it seems that these two cannot be combined, doesn't it?" The Meditation Master of the Peak of the Center said, "Total presence of mind is called 'perceiving'; utter disappearance of whims is called 'forgetting.' Forgetting and perceiving are one yet two, two yet one. When you forget, your mind is profoundly calm and ever perceptive; when you perceive, nothing stands on its own, and all is ever forgotten. This is true forgetfulness and true perception. Many have constrained perception by speaking only of mentally perceiving!"

Secrets of Realization says, "If you become oblivious or distracted by going along with perception, this is the extreme of emptiness. This is serious, this is dangerous—you need to be guarded and calm, as everything acts up at once."

The Master of Complete Unity said, "The extreme of emptiness means that people are ordinarily so scattered in a thousand thoughts and myriad cogitations that the home has no master; it is as if deserted. If you suddenly try to collect it, you cannot hold it steady, and you are unable to be serene; that is why you become confused along with perception. This is not merely a matter of oblivion and distraction: once this thought is let loose, there is nowhere it won't go—that is why it says 'everything acts up at once.' "

"The way to cure this is to melt falsehood the moment you sense random movement, and return to reality. The way to return is simply to forget deliberate attention to perception.

"This exercise is the mainspring of movement and stillness, the teaching of gathering in the spirit as soon as it goes out. When you come to this, just beware of not maintaining alertness."

Secrets of Realization says, "If you are unable to overcome something by perception, then dismiss it by adaptive response. Once the adaptive response is done, then forget it."

The Master of Complete Unity said, "When, as it says, 'everything acts up at once,' then whether you are active or at rest, you perceive this consciously. If you are too scattered, the power of conscious perception is incapable of calm independence. If you then attempt forced repression, that will lead to greater excitement and unease. Therefore you should employ other means, adapting responsively until things gradually settle down on their own.

"In Chan Buddhism, for example, besides sitting meditation there is prostration, scripture recitation, and walking meditation; all of them are for overcoming obstructions, and they should not be done with excessive intensity. One should ease up a bit, to gradually get a balance between relaxation and hurry. When dealing with things adaptively, if you do not flow along with the movement, you overcome obstacles. When you have attained some peace and equilibrium, then forget it while yet being aware of it."

Secrets of Realization says, "Just remain on the brink of existence in all activities, a fine continuity, spirit and energy resting on each other in the primordial state before the absolute, uninterrupted."

The Master of Complete Unity said, "All activities means walking, standing, sitting, and reclining. Remaining on the brink of existence means that consciousness is centered. Spirit and energy resting on each other in the primordial state before the absolute depicts the state in the womb before birth, where there is neither emotion nor knowledge, but only pure unadulterated wholeness. Only when you reach this point can you recognize it."

Secrets of Realization says, "Remain centered, thus bringing about harmony, and desires will not be able to move you. If desires cannot move you, then energy embraces spirit. When spirit and energy follow each other, spirit is clear, energy peaceful, and you enter into the Vastness."

The Master of Complete Unity said, "This 'center' is most difficult to describe; it's not that there is a central location. In reality it just requires this state not to be shaken or stirred, profoundly calm and serene, naturally bringing about harmony and not being moved. This exercise is called embracing the basic and maintaining unity."

THE WOMB BREATH

The *Triplex Unity* says, "Exhalation and inhalation nurture each other; stilling the breath, they become husband and wife."

The *Treatise on the Womb Breath* says, "Spirit and energy join and preserve the internal breath."

Yu Yuwu said, "The universe breathes within; that is why it endures. If people can breathe internally like the universe, they too can endure as long as the universe."

The *Collection of Great Works on Alchemy* says, "Breathing out, heart and lungs; breathing in, liver, kidneys, and genitals. Breathing out, you contact the root of heaven; breathing in, you contact the root of earth. Breathing out, the dragon howls and clouds rise; breathing in, the tiger roars and wind rises."

The *Southern Flower Classic* says, "Complete people breathe from their heels."

The *Classic of the Yellow Court* says, "Behind, there is a secret door; in front, the gate of life. Exhaling the sun, inhaling the moon, respiration remains."

Some ask where the place of respiration of real people is. Liao Zhanhui said, "Opposite the navel in front and the kidneys in back, in the center there is the true gold crucible; this is the place of real breathing."

Fan Dezhao the Illumined said, "When inner energy does not go out and external energy does not come in, that does not refer to holding your breath"

Nowadays many speak of tuning the breath, and some teach people to hold their breath. Is this correct? No! *The Secret of the Sacred Embryo* says, "One energy masses in the ocean of energy, and the genital energy does not rise; then the breath stabilizes."

Generally speaking, when you tune your breathing for a long time, the longer you do it, the more solidified your spirit and the more subtle your breathing. Eventually there is no breathing in the nose, just a subtle breath coming and going over the navel, like a fetus in the womb. That is why it is called womb breathing.

This is great stabilization of spiritualized energy; it occurs naturally, not by deliberate holding and forced stopping or any other contrived means. As long as people congeal the spirit without thought, they will not fail to accord.

If emotionalized perception is not forgotten, thoughts go on and on, and the spirit is neither stable nor calm; then there are countless difficulties, and no one can attain the marvel. So it was said by Master Yuan of the Cosmic Void, "What is essential is to work on forgetting machinations and cutting off thoughts." Master Siao the Realized said, "Maintain oneness, and breath does not come and go." *The Secret of the Sacred Embryo* says, "A single thought does not arise; a single idea does not stir; there is not the slightest miss at all." How could this refer to control and suppression?

Practical refinement must reach womb breathing before energy returns to the ocean of the fundamental; this is the process of "gestation." If you close your eyes and keep silent, yet you breathe through your mouth and nose as ever, then your spiritual energy is still leaking; when the period of gestation is done, there will be no emerging and flourishing of energy and growth. The Master of Eternal Spring said, "The slightest lack of stability in the breath, and your life is not your own."

THE PRIMAL

The *Triplex Unity* says, "Wholeness goes right into nonresistance."

It also says, "A primal whole, female and male go along with each other."

Yu Yuwu said, "There is no other act to cultivating refinement than culling primal unified energy for the matrix of the elixir."

He also said, "Spirit concentrates, energy collects, and they merge into one: inwardly you do not sense your body; outwardly you are not conscious of the universe. As you merge with the Way, myriad cogitations disappear, leaving an undefinable, indescribable state, which might be called 'absolute unity.'"

When practical cultivation reaches the womb breath, then the eight energy channels all become still, and you enter into undifferentiated wholeness. This is precisely the time of "intercourse." The energies of the five elements of the body meet in the elixir field. This is called gathering the five elements and combining the four forms. This is called absolute unity containing true energy; this is called the primal unified energy. Cultivation must reach this stage before you can penetrate heaven and earth and take over creative evolution.

It is impossible, however, to reach the marvels of heaven and earth without utter emptiness and quietude. That is why ancient wizards said, "Do not seek Creation in the loins; seek the Primal in the heart."

THE ARISING OF POSITIVE ENERGY

The *Triplex Unity* says, "Imbued with the original, empty and unattached, plant vitality in the offspring."

Yu Yuwu said, "The marvel of the gold elixir is conceived in the primal and born in the temporal. What is the primal? Tranquil and unstirring, profound abstraction prior to the differentiation of the absolute. What is the temporal? Sensitive efficacy, ecstatic buoyancy, after the differentiation of the absolute. The primal is just one energy; in the temporal it subsequently turns into true vitality."

The Master of Silent Sunlight said, "The primal is the reality of pure creativity, pure positive energy. The temporal is the product of basic original vitality, so it is called *water*. Primal basic energy is the true energy of the sacred father and sacred mother: what is produced is basic original vitality, not basic original energy."

The Master of True Sunlight said, "The true energy latent in the genitals is called lead. In the energy is the water of true unity, referred to as the tiger, which is the silver in lead. Genital energy is transmitted to liver energy; liver energy is transmitted to heart energy; heart energy, by way of the absolute, becomes liquid. This is called cinnabar. The presence of true positive energy in the liquid is called the dragon, which is the mercury in cinnabar."

In these terms, the primal basic energy in the genitals is true lead yang, while the basic vitality is silver tiger yin. The liquid in the heart is cinnabar yin; the wholesome positive energy in the liquid is mercury dragon yang. Once the basic original vitality has risen, then it can keep the wholesome positive energy stable. This is what Master Zhongli referred to as beginning by using yin to keep yang. Old wizards used to generally call this true lead controlling mercury; this deserves careful thought.

Culling

The Master of True Sunlight said, "When transmission is carried out, govern it methodically. Cause genital energy not to run out, and cull the water of true unity; see to it that the heart liquid isn't wasted away, and cull from the liquid wholesome positive energy."

Master Ziyang said, "Culling means gathering true lead from the genital region and taking true mercury from the heart field."

Verses on Restoring Life says, "Culling requires intimate communion and truthful discernment. It is most difficult to find the channel of intent; it is easy to lose the cold spring."

Ziyang's *Alchemical Directions* says, "The method of culling is born in the mind; you need to forget it before you seek." It also says, "Seek in forgetting, forget in seeking; cull in forgetting, forget in culling."

Chen the Blank said, "When body and mind are unmoving, that is culling medicine."

Originally there was no "culling" in the science of wizardry, but there is a resemblance to culling in the use of true lead in the genitals and the use of true mercury in the heart. That is the only reason for the use of the term *culling*. In general, it is a matter of "gathering" without deliberate gathering, "gathering" without gathering anything; "taking" without deliberate taking, "taking" without taking anything. Don't get stuck on the imagery of these two words!

People in later times confused others even more than they had been by incoherent explanations. The ancient wizards' use of the name and image of culling was not intended to have people apply this literally. What they taught people was to be careful about function, because when positive energy first arises, it is very easily lost—if the body stirs, the energy disperses; if attention relaxes, the energy is also dispersed; if random thoughts occur, the energy is also dispersed; if you are startled or upset, the energy is also dispersed. Therefore at the time of culling it is imperative that body, mind, and attention be quiet and unstirring in order to regulate energy. Only then does primal energy come under control and does not wind up getting scattered and escaping at random. The energy then rises naturally in an orderly way, descending into the elixir field to become a supreme treasure. This is evidently what Chen the Blank meant when he said, "Body and mind unmoving is culling medicine." It does not refer to toilsome exercises in imagination and visualization!

Keeping the Attention on Heaven

Yu Yuwu said, "In the primal, congeal the spirit in the Earth umbilicus to produce medicine; in the temporal, shift the spirit into the Heaven cauldron to make the elixir."

He also said, "From morning to evening, the basic spirit resides in Nirvana."

The Master of Complete Unity said, "This is called the key at the crown; this is how energy is caused to rise."

The Master of the Cosmic Void said, "From ancient times to now, who does not know that the mind is the house of the spirit—so how can people talk about the spirit residing in Nirvana? This is a mistake resulting from misunderstanding of pictorial images of wizardry."

Actually, Nirvana is the seat of purity and emptiness; the spirit residing in Nirvana means the original spirit in its immaculate purity rising above and beyond vitality and energy; it does not mean dwelling in the brain.

In wizardry, Heaven is the mind and Earth is the body. Congealing the spirit in the Earth umbilicus is the beginning of alchemy: it is just a matter of congealing the spirit, whereupon energy spontaneously returns to the body and eventually flows naturally into the genital region.

It is like turbid water wherein the sediment eventually sinks on its own; it is not a matter of fixed concentration. At this time there is just a spiritual brilliance: when you sense this energy returning to the ocean of the fundamental, this is perceiving it without ever having used any deliberate effort to do so. As long as you keep aware of it this way, the energy will stay below, unable to rise, so at this time it is imperative to forget and no longer watch it. Then the true fire emerges spontaneously, and true yin rises naturally.

When the spirit returns to the crimson chamber of the heart, it is effortless and natural, so it is called shifting the spirit into the Heaven crown. Again, this does not mean that the spirit dwells in the Nirvana chamber in the brain. During the process of incubation, the spirit is always effortless; energy rises and descends naturally, without dwelling on the Nirvana chamber morning and night.

The various metaphors and pictorial representations used in wizardry became the objects of fixations. People eventually clung to the Nirvana chamber to the point where they confusedly got involved in deliberate intentional attempts to produce inner movements of energy, not realizing themselves what they were doing.

The Preserver of Truth said that the issue of whether mind can drive energy is a matter of whether or not it can manage the job, not a matter of where it abides. When an emperor rules a whole continent, does he have to preside personally over each and every locality to maintain order? The path of refining the spirit values having no fixations: to rest the spirit in the Nirvana chamber is to cling to the Nirvana chamber. This might be called a technique of moving energy, but as refinement of the spirit, I don't know—it actually disturbs the spirit!

The rising and descending through the three chambers spoken of by the ancients is spontaneous rising and descending, not rise and descent caused by the person. What they called the operation of the cycle is spontaneous operation, not an operation carried out by the person.

The central path

The *Triplex Unity* says, "Transformative action circulates everywhere; contraction and expansion repeat over and over."

It also says, "If you practice this unremittingly, clouds and rain of abundant energy will overflow like a pond in spring, liquid as melting ice. From the head it flows to the feet, then ultimately rises again, coming and going, penetrating limitlessly, passing through the center of the valley."

Yu Yuwu said, "The essential task of alchemy is to open the passive and active energy channels. That is because these two channels, the passive and the active, are the body's oceans of yin and yang. If people can open these, then all channels will open, resulting in unobstructed circulation through the body. The central path in the body is the proper route of rise and descent of yin and yang through the body; opening it up is not an exercise of energy, not a visualization, not metallic vitality, and not exercising the mind, respiration, and spine. It is the Way of breathing universal harmony and preserving the truly basic."

Opening the passive and active energy channels is the greatest marvel of the Sect of Life. Because the energy of Heaven operates unceasingly, Earth does not collapse; by virtue of unceasing operation of energy in the human being, the physical body does not decay. That operation is natural, spontaneous operation, not the operation of breathing exercises with all that squeezing and stretching, huffing and puffing. This seems to be what is meant by the saying, "A hinge pivot does not rot; flowing water does not go stale."

Jiang of the Green Mist said, "The human body is major yang in the left foot and major yin in the right foot, while in the soles of the feet is the Welling Spring, which gives forth two energies, watery and fiery, which go from the feet into the coccyx and rise to join the twofold kidney: the left to the hall of the kidneys, the right to the seat of vitality. One is watery, one fiery; one is a tortoise, one a snake. Together they foster each other and thus rise up the spine, through twenty-four vertebrae, combining in the seat of wind and rising to the Nirvana chamber, descending from Nirvana to the Hall of Brightness, then dispersing to irrigate the five faculties, then descending the windpipe into the Crimson Chamber, and then flowing again into the original seat. Day and night the circulation flows unceasingly, all natural and spontaneous, not something done by movements of the hands and feet."

Nowadays people all drift into sidetracks; unaware of the subtle principle of spontaneous silent operation in absolute nonresistance, they misapply energy induction exercises, meditations, and visualizations to the point where they become delusional. Their aberrant practices have the negative effect of producing sickness. The jaundice found among followers of the White Lotus Path and the bloating seen among followers of energetics are both evidences of this.

The firing process

Hu the Whole said, "This fire erupts in the ecstasy of true vitality, perfuming and steaming the whole body. Since it basically has no form, how can there be a process?"

Chen the Blank said, "The true fire basically has no process; the great medicine is not measured in weight."

The Master of the White Jade Moon said, "Mind is spirit; spirit is the fire. Energy is the medicine. To refine the medicine into elixir means to drive energy by spirit so as to attain the Way."

The words of these three old wizards can indeed be considered of critical importance. But driving energy by spirit requires precise clarification of the way of driving. There may be excess or insufficiency in practice: to adjust and correct this is what is called driving. This is also what is referred to as the process.

There is "no process" in the sense of no process delineated by measurements of time. There is a process in the sense of watchfulness and wariness. Only with such an understanding can we talk about the firing.

The *Triple Unity* says, "Watch with diligent care; check for cold and warmth."

Chen the Blank said, "The essential key of the firing process is to be sought in the true breath." He also said, "Positive energy arises in the ocean of the origin; fire erupts within water. The circulation of the universe and the repetition of creation are not apart from one breath."

Master Ziyang said, "Leisurely guard the medicine furnace, watching the firing process. Just settle spirit and breath, and let naturalness be so."

The firing process is all in applying effort to thought. Chen the Blank said, "Thoughts should not be aroused; if thoughts arise, the breathing is rough. Attention should not be scattered; if attention scatters, the fire goes cold."

The Old Teacher of the Open Channel to Reality said, "When thoughts arise, the breathing is rough; when breathing is rough, it blows too hard on the fire. Just tune the true breathing, causing it to be peaceful and even, avoiding agitation and excitement."

The firing process basically stands for the phases of advance and withdrawal of one energy, nothing else. When it is said that the firing has not been transmitted, that means it cannot be transmitted, not that it is kept secret. The provenience of the true fire cannot be reached by words; it is all in the human being. Generally speaking, when application of attention is too intense, this is called overheating and dryness; if too lax, this is called wetness and coldness. What you must do is find a balance of relaxation and intensity, neither forgetting nor fostering. This is the true firing process. It is said to be untransmittable because there is not a fixed rule.

When the firing process starts, human power cannot work with it; all you can do is be empty and calm and hold the rudder firmly, not letting miscellaneous thoughts disturb it. Allow it to happen naturally and spontaneously; when it has "perfumed and steamed" once, it naturally produces yin, turning into liquid that descends and irrigates the inner organs. When you have a feeling of sweet juice in your throat, that is a sign it is happening. At this point, just keep empty and calm, not disturbing it at all, and it will naturally congeal. Remain silent and still for a long time; then you may get up very, very slowly. Jiang of the Green Mist said, "When it comes, greet it with attention; when it goes, send it off with the eyes. Greeting it with attention is called the go-between; sending it off with the eyes is called the green maiden." This is mixed up in artificialities, a big mistake!

The subtlety in promoting the fire is in closing all openings tightly: if you give rise to any miscellaneous thought at all, then you are not sealed tight, and the medicine will run off.

INCUBATION

The *Triplex Unity* says, "The three lights submerged, incubate the seed pearl."

It also says, "Close the three treasures—ears, eyes, and mouth; do not let them act up. Real people plunge into the abyss; floating buoyantly, they keep to the compass center."

It also says, "When the fire energy works protectively within, then water needs no brilliance. Openings closed, you do not talk; speaking seldom, accord with wholeness. Once the three are locked, stay in an empty room, body relaxed, letting willfulness go, and return to absolute nonresistance. Freedom from thought is the normal experience; this is immovable. When the mind is single, it does not go wild. Sleep in the embrace of spirit; when awake, be watchful of presence and absence."

The Master of Complete Unity said, "Incubation just requires constant preservation of the true breath, causing spirit and energy to be in constant intercourse. At no time is there no true breath, so at no time is energy inoperative. Since there is no time that energy is not operating, there is no time when you are not carrying out the firing process."

Yu Yuwu said, "In quiet concentration, embrace nonresistant, harmonious energy, exhaling very subtly, inhaling very finely, up to Nirvana, down to the Gate of Life, circulating unceasingly, spirit and energy never for a moment failing to cluster together."

PUNISHMENT AND REWARD

The *Triplex Unity* says, "Dragon east, tiger west, warp and woof, hare and cock, punishment and reward meet, joyful on seeing each other. Punishment establishes execution and restraint; reward is in charge of productivity. In the second month, the elms drop their leaves and the second Dipper star faces east; in the eighth month, wheat grows and the Dipper bowl rests in the west."

The firing process in intervals requires the concepts of the time of the hare and the time of the cock. Why do punishment and reward depend on each other? Reward is in charge of promotion and inspiration, associated with the second lunar month; punishment is in charge of execution and restraint, associated with the eighth lunar month. Punishment in the second month means descent within ascent; reward in the eighth month means ascent within descent. These images are used to symbolize potential danger. The times of the hare and the cock, dawn and dusk, refer to when ascent and descent have reached halfway, where it is easy for attention to scatter, so that ascent does not proceed upward and descent does not proceed downward. This results in stagnation that creates a lot of trouble. Therefore it is said that there is punishment in reward and reward in punishment, so that people will guard their attention as they would a citadel, not letting it scatter.

Refining the spirit

The *Book of Balance and Harmony* says, "Followers of Taoism seek lead in the seat of water; followers of Buddhism cultivate concentration in the chamber of fire."

It also says, "The upper pass is refining spirit back into emptiness. When the work reaches this point, not a single word applies."

Qing-an said, "The unique transcendental experience is to be sought outside of words. If you encounter it everywhere, realizing it and penetrating it, then returning to the perfect light of the absolute, the radiance of awareness pierces without resistance, penetrating effectively. Essence and life are both cultivated; body and spirit are both sublimated. When you are one with cosmic space, it is not hard to stand shoulder to shoulder with Wizards and Buddhas."

This passage shows the one great continuity of practical cultivation. Previous statements referred to refinement of vitality into energy; without the work of refining spirit, it will never be possible to attain transcendence. At most you might preserve your life, lengthen its span, and remedy deterioration and illness. The *Four Hundred Words on Alchemy* says, "Lead and mercury returned to the earth pot; body and mind are silent and immobile." When body and mind are unmoving, there must be that which is unmoved; unfortunately, devotees of life science do not explain it clearly. If you keep previous views, seek with greed, and become obsessively fixated, you bind yourself without rope. I'm afraid you'll be unable to see where your birth star is.

The Master of Complete Unity said, "When incubation reaches the stage of the infant manifesting form, it is still young and immature in its comings and goings, easily disturbed, still needing defense against leakage on impact. One is not yet able to 'enter the marketplace with hands extended.'"

Crystallizing the Elixir

Some ask what crystallization of the elixir is. Qing-an said, "When body and mind are united, spirit and energy merged, essence and sense as one, this is called crystallization of the elixir, symbolized by the sacred embryo."

A master wizard said, "The original real essential nature is called the gold elixir pill."

Ding-an asked, "When the elixir crystallizes, is it visible?" Qing-an replied, "Yes." "Does it have form?" "No." "If it has no form, how can it be visible?" Qing-an said, "Gold elixir is just a name—how could it have form? That it is visible does not mean it can be seen with the eyes. The *Tao Te Ching* says, 'When you look at it you cannot see it; when you listen for it you cannot hear it—this is called the Way.' But even though you cannot see it when you look, never are you not seeing it; even though you cannot hear it when you listen for it, never are you not hearing it. It is not within reach of ears and eyes. It is like the wind shaking trees and raising waves—you can hardly call it nonexistent, but when you look at it you cannot see it, and when you grasp for it you cannot apprehend it, so you can hardly call it existent. The substance of the gold elixir is also like this."

Wang the Cloud Dweller said, "The substance of the gold elixir is like space, without resistance inside or out. Nothing hangs on it, nothing stains it; brilliantly luminous, it illumines infinity."

Devotees of life science all talk of cultivating vitality, cultivating energy, producing being from nothingness, forming an infant that, born of the energy of sacred father and spiritual mother, is empty and effective, unlike a living human being. This doctrine is false.

Zhang Huangju said, "Creation gives life to people; its coming is subtle and simple, its ultimate extension vast and stable. If the infant actually had physical solidity, it would shortly be as solid as a living person—how could it be a spiritual subtlety?"

The Master of Eternal Spring said, "The 'infant' is our individual soul, our true essence, pure positive energy without adulteration. It is not that there is actually an 'infant' in the belly." He also said, "If there is the slightest confusion of thought, the spirit is not purely positive."

The Master of the White Jade Moon said, "As long as people have no mind in mind and no thought, this unadulterated clarity, immaculate, is called pure positivity."

Wizards originally just taught people to nurture the spirit, but people get lost and drown in desires and are unable to cut right through, so the notion of eternal life was set up to induce people to cultivate refinement. When worldly people crave immortality, only then are they willing to put down habitual desires and single-mindedly refine vitality and energy; so they have inner focus and think less of externals. When they have cultivated refinement to the point where energy rises and descends through the three chambers in the torso and head, the bliss felt in the body is indescribable; then they develop such a huge craving for this that they disregard everything. Here the mind has focus and gradually attains peace and quiet, so the original basic spirit gradually becomes manifest. This is the "appearance of the infant." From there, you enter into absolute nonresistance, where your mind has no attachments, myriad cogitations melt, and the basic spirit appears, coming and going freely, unobstructed by the physical body. This is transcendent liberation. In reality, this is just a matter of temporarily using refinement of vitality and refinement of energy to focus the mind and nurture the basic spirit so that it is effective.

Release from the Matrix

Li Qing-an said, "Embodiment beyond the body is called release from the matrix." He also said, "When the positive spirit leaves the shell, this is called release from the matrix."

Some ask about transcendent release. The Master of the White Jade Moon said, "Transcendence means the emergence of the spirit; release means liberating change of the ordinary body."

These sayings all talk about leaving aside the ordinary body, just refining the basic spirit back into emptiness, not about maintaining a physical presence in the world. So obviously the advanced wizards did not concern themselves with immortality. Why are people today so eager for eternal life?

The following question has been posed: those who attained the Way in ancient times made even this ordinary body nonresistant, so they could enter water and fire, penetrate metal and stone, walk in space without falling, and not be blocked by contact with solidity.

This is what is called the preservation of pure energy. As it is said, in disperson it is energy; in concentration it is form. This is called sublimation of body and mind, uniting with the Way. Now if one would have to relinquish the ordinary body to attain the constitution of wizardry, how could this not mean one had failed to reach sublimation of body and mind?

Master Gan of the Pure Wind said, "Before you have reached true emptiness, the yang spirit is hard to free." The Master of Eternal Spring said, "Before you have reached true emptiness, the yin spirit is also hard to free."

The ancients' liberation from the matrix and spiritualization was in every case based on the climax of emptiness and stillness, the attainment of selflessness. When people today go anywhere in dreams, it is because they are not stayed by the physical body; when they wake up, they are stuck here and cannot remove themselves to great distances because the physical body stops them. Therefore liberation from the matrix and spiritualization are possible only after true emptiness and selflessness.

It may be asked why refinement of vitality into energy does not result in transcendent liberation. Fan Dezhao's work *Accord with Reality* says, "Those who cultivate energy to take on form are yogis; even after a thousand years they still have the same old bodies and never attain the Way." Thus our Celestial Teacher said, "Even if you are long-lived as a tortoise or a crane, you are not a spiritual wizard."

In ancient times, master Qingjing, who lived for three thousand years, questioned Pengzu about sexual energetics. Asked if Qingjing were a wizard, Pengzu said, "No. A celestial dragon can form a pearl; when the pearl is done, the body spontaneously withdraws, so it is called a celestial dragon. What that adept practices is like the dragon. If you refine your body, then your spirit and energy may change to manifest the unfathomable, but this is still limited to transformation of energy. On Royal House Mountain there are accomplished Taoists of the Bone Removing Cavern who leave behind their physical bodies, because whatever has physical form cannot ascend."

Now if even a body produced by cultivation is still limited in its energy transformations, what about the physical body inherited from your parents? Even if you have cultivated refinement to the point where you ascend to the highest heavens and live for countless years, you are still within the domain of transmutations of yin and yang and have not been able to enter into formlessness. As long as you have not entered into formlessness, you are still enslaved by the polar energies of the universe; how can there be any transcendent liberation?

Meng Yin said, "What can compare to the uncontrived entry into reality? With one leap you enter directly into the realm of the enlightened."

Returning to the origin

Is there still creative evolution after liberation from the matrix? Qing-an said, "There is still creative evolution. An ancient said, 'Embodiment beyond the body is not yet wonderful; when cosmic space itself is shattered, only then is complete reality revealed.' So after liberation from the matrix, it is essential to tread solidly on real ground; when you are one with cosmic space, that is perfect attainment."

This subject is something wizards had long left unspoken until Qing-an gave this unexpected explanation. His vision may be said to have gone beyond that of other masters. In overall terms, when you reach this stage, you have to take everything you've realized, everything you've attained, and banish it all at once to the land of birthlessness. Only then will you be in accord. If you retain any personal view of transcendent liberation, then as before you will drift into emotional consciousness, far estranged from the Way—how can you attain union with cosmic space?

Twin cultivation of essence and life

Master Zhang Ziyang said, "If you start with essence, it's hard to apply it in practice; if you start with life, there's a concrete way of approach. Even if the achievement is one, nevertheless there is something better about starting with essence."

Li Qing-an said, "The best people have already planted roots of virtue and have inborn knowledge; once they directly comprehend essence, they naturally comprehend life."

Essence and life are one matter. The reason people die is that the body and spirit separate. The reason the sense organs are useless after death even though they are still there is that there is no spirit to manage them. Obviously the spirit is the manager of the body; when the spirit departs, energy dissipates, so how could life exist outside of essence? If you divide them into two for twin cultivation, differentiating them into prior and latter, that is not quite right. Why? When you cultivate essence, life is therein. As the Celestial Master of Open Serenity said, "When spirit is restored to the body, energy returns of itself." No one has ever been able to accomplish intercourse to produce the elixir without being outwardly nonresistant and serene. Indeed, first refining vitality into energy—thus cultivating stabilization and liberation from the matrix—is roundabout and difficult to achieve fully. If you can realize the body of reality, why worry that the physical body will not be sublimated?

The three passes from effort to effortlessness constitute the gradual method; cultivating the upper pass so as to include the lower two passes is the sudden method. Now you should directly practice refinement of spirit back into emptiness: when you reach the state of utter emptiness and silence, vitality spontaneously evolves into energy, and energy spontaneously evolves into spirit. The handle is in your grip; your destiny is up to you. This is penetrating the three barriers with one shot. This is simplest and easiest, most direct and quick; those on the Way should thoroughly appreciate this.